Commissars, Commanders, and Civilian Authority

Russian Research Center Studies, 79

Commissars, Commanders, and Civilian Authority

The Structure of Soviet Military Politics

Timothy J. Colton

Harvard University Press
Cambridge, Massachusetts
and London, England
1979

Library of Congress Cataloging in Publication Data

Colton, Timothy J   1947-
    Commissars, commanders, and civilian authority.

    (Russian Research Center studies; 79)
    Includes bibliographical references and index.
    1. Civil supremacy over the military—Russia.
2. Russia—Armed Forces—Political activity.
3. Kommunisticheskaia partiia Sovetskogo Soiuza
I. Title. II. Series: Harvard University. Russian
Research Center. Studies; 79.
JN6520.C58C64   322'.5'0947   78-23342
ISBN 0-674-14535-6

To My Parents

Acknowledgments

In the course of preparing the several versions of this study, I have drawn liberally on the knowledge and advice of others. The improvements in the book are the best measure of these individuals' wisdom, but I wish also to acknowledge here a number of specific contributions.

This book evolved initially under the balanced direction of Samuel P. Huntington and Adam B. Ulam. To Professor Huntington I owe a particular debt of gratitude. He helped spawn my interest in civil-military relations, urged me to fashion my work on the Soviet Union with an eye to comparative insights, and patiently saw several of my attempts at comparative analysis move in the direction of intelligibility. Professor Ulam, always with great kindness, reminded me of the need to acquire the direct knowledge of the Soviet experience without which serious comparisons could not be made. In particular, he directed my attention to the rich military memoir literature. The late Merle Fainsod guided my first efforts to analyze the military party organs and provided encouragement out of all proportion to my performance.

Over the last decade, Jerry Hough, as teacher and critic, has contributed enormously to this study and to my general understanding of Soviet politics. His prodding was especially important in leading me to question preconceptions of how the Communist party functions and also in spurring my interest in the concrete details of institutional machinery and career patterns. All too often in the Soviet field, particularly in recent years, these matters have been slighted, to the detriment of both our immediate understanding of Soviet reality and our contribution to social science theory. I hope this book begins to measure up to the standards Professor Hough has set.

My colleague, Gordon Skilling, has likewise assisted me immeasurably in general terms. He was also a thorough reader of the manuscript, pointing out many shortcomings in logic and execution. I am greatly obliged to Dale R. Herspring for many hours of stimulating conversation on generals and commissars. His attentiveness to some of the more abstruse lines of argument pursued in Part Three helped me avoid some serious pitfalls. William E. Odom also read the manuscript in its entirety at a busy juncture and provided incisive comments on it. Roman Kolkowicz and John Erickson have at several points conveyed detailed and very useful reactions to my findings and ideas, and Matitiahu Mayzel has shared with me his exceptional knowledge of Soviet military history. Donald Forbes kindly facilitated the preparation of the tables in Chapter 2. The following individuals read part or all of one version or another of the manuscript and assisted in its development: Paul Cocks, Helen Desfosses, Herbert Dinerstein, Mary Ellen Fischer, Richard Gregor, Franklyn Griffiths, Thane Gustafson, Grey Hodnett, Christopher Jones, Sanford Lieberman, Donald Schwartz, and Peter Solomon, Jr.

The Russian Research Center provided a congenial and rich setting for much of the research embodied in these pages. I am especially grateful for the diligent efforts on my behalf of the Center's librarian, Susan Jo Gardos. I have also benefited at various stages from the generous support of the Canada Council, the Government Department of Harvard University, and the Centre for Russian and East European Studies, Scarborough College, and the Department of Political Economy in the University of Toronto. Aida D. Donald and Joan Ryan have been skilled and considerate editors of the final version.

Much of the material in Chapter 8 appeared in my article in *Soviet Studies*, 29 (April 1977), 185-213. I wish to thank the journal for permission to use it here.

To my wife, Patricia, goes my heartfelt gratitude for many hours of inspiration, many hours of reading, and many more of waiting. To small Patricia, who has grown up with the clatter of the typewriter and the clutter of piles of Soviet newspapers, go my assurances that it was, indeed, all worthwhile.

Contents

Tables

Figures

Commissars, Commanders, and Civilian Authority

Introduction

In comparative perspective, no political phenomenon in recent decades has been more striking than that of military intervention. Particularly in modernizing societies, where army rule is now "the most common form of government," the soldier in politics has become a commonplace figure.[1] Clemenceau's dictum about war being too important to be left to generals has been stood on its head: politics, it is now often said, is too important for generals to leave to politicians.

This behavior has confounded many familiar ideas about political change. Not least of all has it challenged notions about the unique susceptibility of nations undergoing rapid modernization to Communist revolution and development along Leninist lines. If there is a characteristic regime of the transition to modernity, it seems today more likely to be rule by soldiers than government by a Marxist-Leninist political party.

Yet, whatever the status of the general as a historical alternative to the party secretary, on the secretary's own stage the general has unmistakably been cast in a supporting role. The student of comparative politics cannot help being impressed, as was Samuel Huntington, by the fact that "no communist government in a modernizing country has been overthrown by a military coup d'etat."[2] This observation holds true above all in the first Communist state, which in its seventh decade sustains the largest peacetime army in history. Although the Soviet Union's experience of "building socialism" has been immune from few of the social and political traumas usually associated with modernization, the regime certainly has been spared disruptive challenge from its military instrument.

The record has been flawed by occasional cases of real or imputed disloyalty. Hundreds of Soviet officers deserted in the early stages of the Civil War. In World War II a captured general, Andrei A. Vlasov, led a futile resistance from enemy territory. One group of former officers is said to have formed a "democratic movement" in the Vorkuta camps in the late 1940s, and in the last decade a small number of active and retired soldiers, the best known of them the former general Petr A. Grigorenko, have participated in dissent activity.[3]

But clearly these have been acts of unfocused discontent and individual conscience, not of collective will. They stand out sharply against a history of sustained acceptance of civilian authority. The military establishment and the officers who command it have consistently upheld and obeyed the civilian party leadership. "Soviet officers," as Defense Minister Andrei A. Grechko noted in 1974, "are a reliable bulwark of the party and government."[4] There has been no Soviet Nasser or Suharto—not even a Lin Piao.

This political quiescence is the basic fact with which this study begins and toward the understanding of which it proposes to make a contribution. How does one explain it? Soviet and Western theorists have approached the question in very different ways.

Soviet authorities have made no serious attempt to work out a systematic theory of civil-military relations. They have rejected several of the prerequisites of theory, including the notions of clear definition of terms and comparability of like experiences.

Soviet spokesmen have refused, for example, to acknowledge that their army (frequently in this study "army" is used as shorthand for "military establishment") has political preferences that can be discussed separately from the interests of the Communist party or of society as a whole. They often insist in quite simplistic terms that the army is "an inalienable part of the people" and that its development "has never been and will never be something set apart or isolated from other spheres of party and state activity."[5] It follows that the army's acceptance of civilian authority does not require specific explanation.

The master theme in Soviet discourse has been the description, not the explanation, of civilian supremacy. The main motif is the so-called "principle of party leadership of the armed forces," which amounts to an enunciation of the party's right to enjoy in military affairs the same sovereignty it holds in other areas of national life. This theme is often enunciated in sweeping fashion. In the leading text on military strategy, for instance, we read of the influence of the party "on all sides of the life and activity" of the military.[6] A favorite formula is of the party as "collective organizer, leader, and educator" of the forces. There are frequent and vague references to the fact that its leading role is increasing or intensifying.

At times, however, Soviet discussions are rather more precise in distinguishing three specific modes or channels of party leadership. The first and most important is the civilian party executive's determination of fundamental military policy. The party leadership is hierarchically superior to the military establishment, and it alone "directs and coordinates the activity of all state and public organs for the strengthening of the country's defense capability."[7] Its decisions are subject to challenge, as an often cited Central Committee decision of December 1918 stated flatly, neither by "individual comrades nor by any particular group." "The policy of the military department, as of all other departments and establishments, is conducted on the precise basis of the general directives issued by the party, in the person of its Central Committee, and under its direct control."[8]

If the first channel of direction is from above, the second is from within, through individual military officers. The overwhelming majority are members of the party or Komsomol and as such are said to embody the party's spirit and convey its priorities and decisions. Thus one sees mention of "the community of the Communist worldview among the entire staff," and of the commander as "the representative of the party in the armed forces."[9]

There is also a third mode of party leadership, known in Soviet parlance as party work or party-political work in the army. It is the responsibility of a specialized organization inbedded within the military but reporting ultimately to the civilian party executive. This organization—its current title is Main Political Administration (*Glavnoe Politicheskoe Upravlenie*) of the Soviet Army and Navy—comprises an elaborate matrix of agencies. I will usually refer to them in the aggregate as the military party organs, but official discourse uses several names—party organs, political organs, party or political apparatus. The organs' full-time officials have specific titles and ranks; normally they are known collectively as political workers or officers (*politrabotniki*), party workers, or party-political workers. The first political officers were called commissars.

Clearly the military party organs occupy a strategic position on the civil-military boundary. They are acknowledged in Soviet thinking as a major form of party leadership, one which "exerts party influence on every aspect of the life and activity of the forces."[10] But the organs are, to repeat, only one of several such modes. They have not been central to any coherent Soviet explanation of the army's political quiescence. Western scholarship, on the other hand, has endowed them with far-reaching importance.

Most Western analysis of Soviet military affairs has been directed more at the content of military policy than at the process of military politics.[11] Powerfully reinforced by the dependence of much of the research on government initiative and funding, this preoccupation with policy has often produced an overconcentration on actors at the highest echelons, a short-term time perspective, and an indifference toward comparative analysis. Thus, in generalizing about Western approaches to army-party relations and other aspects of military politics, I am speaking of work in which such matters normally have been of secondary concern. Nonetheless, the reader should be aware of its central assumptions and findings.

Specialists on the military have tended to accept the major understandings that underlie most scholarship on the Soviet Union. They have been especially inclined to assume that the main dynamic of Soviet politics is the process whereby the party controls society. While the Soviet perception has been of monolithic unity of army and party, Western scholars have seen precisely the opposite—a basic dichotomy between two institutions with incompatible objectives and styles. Fearing challenges to its monopoly of power, the party "inevitably has a primary concern for control over the military."[12] This anxious pursuit of hegemony clashes with the military's concern for efficient performance of its professional function, and as a result, as Roman Kolkowicz has said, the relationship between party and army is "essentially conflict-prone and thus presents a perennial threat to the political stability of the Soviet state."[13]

Scholars who subscribed to the totalitarian image of Soviet society argued that the army-party conflict, profound though it was, had been thoroughly suppressed by multiple party controls. In recent years analysts have continued to profess the chronic nature of the antagonism but have maintained that, especially since Stalin's death, it has been manifest rather than latent. The regime persists in applying controls, which are still essential to stability, but it no longer can succeed in "concealing the many strains and disagreements" between the two institutions.[14]

Some notes of discontent with this approach have been sounded, particularly in the work of William E. Odom, but these have been provocative and prefatory remarks, not detailed empirical treatments.[15] The image of interinstitutional conflict resolved by party penetration and control remains the dominant model in the field.

It is against this background that the third mode of party leadership—through its organs within the army—has acquired such importance in Western analysis. The relationship between the command hierarchy and the military party organs is thought to be fraught with intense and direct conflict. From the days of the earliest commissars, the organs have been primarily a "watchdog" mechanism for controlling command officers. To quote from Kolkowicz's description:

> Their essential functions may be summed up as (a) to observe activities in the units and to pass the information to higher levels of the apparatus; (b) to "politicize" military personnel through intensive indoctrination and political education; (c) to regulate the advancement of officers so that only those who are desirable from the Party's point of view are promoted to positions of authority; (d) to supervise and control military as well as political activities within the unit; and (e) to prompt desired action or conduct through intimidation, threats of dismissal, public humiliation, or outright coercion . . . The result . . . is the anomaly of an up-to-date military machine that is forced to wear a horse collar of ideological and political controls.[16]

The conflict between the political organs and the military command (unless otherwise specified, "military command" refers to all commissioned officers other than political officers) is said to be related in two ways to the overall adversary relationship between party and army. First, it is representative of the general struggle for influence, expressing it in day-to-day frictions and disagreements. "The history of tension between these two groups [reflects] the perennial problem of reconciling political control with professional military efficiency." Political officers are "little else than a mixture of bully and toady," "not really soldiers at all and in constant conflict [with professional commanders]."[17]

But second, and more important, the conflict between command and party organs is perceived as having largely determined the outcome of the broader relationship. Party supremacy rests primarily on institutional controls, and the military party organs are, in Kolkowicz's words, *the Party's crucial instrument of control.* It is principally their "relentless effort at politicization and control [which] keep[s] the military politically and ideologically docile and administratively manageable."[18] Commanders have accepted civilian authority primarily because commissars have kept them from doing otherwise.

This book will both analyze certain important features of the structure of Soviet military politics and offer a new explanation for the stability of army-party relations. Its first concern is with *how* army and party have interacted; its second is with *why* their relationship has persisted without essential change.

The greater portion of the book provides the first detailed Western examination of the military party organs. Emphasis will be placed on the roles of the organs in military life and politics and on the clues their members' behavior holds for the study of civil-military relations. But attention to other actors will be required to make this behavior intelligible and to illuminate more general issues of institutional development and interaction.

The basic rationale for this detailed study of the military party organs is to generate evidence about the question of persistence in army-party relations. Can the organs be considered the crucial instrument of civilian control, as is commonly asserted? The answer, in my opinion, must be emphatically negative. A revised understanding of the military party apparatus raises the possibility that Soviet soldiers have been capable of assuming more assertive political roles than they have hitherto done. The root question about their acceptance of civilian authority must be reformulated and addressed in the light of the experience of military participation in politics in other societies.

Part One
The Military Party Organs

The Structure of the Military Party Organs

1

The military party organs make up the principal interface between the Communist party and most aspects of military life. They are the party's main administrative extension into the army, their officials the only sizable cadre of party employees dealing with military matters. It is within the voluntary party organizations attached to them that most military men join the party and perform the duties of membership. In myriad ways their operations affect every soldier from the General Staff executive in his Moscow office to the platoon commander and raw recruit on the drill field.

The organs constitute a large and complex organization whose structure must be laid out clearly before its behavior can be examined. The military party apparatus shares some characteristics with other arms of the party, but some are uniquely its own.

The Organizational Hierarchy

The basic structural principle of the military party organs is hierarchy. All constituent parts are accountable to a single central agency, the name of which has usually been synonomous with the entire organization. The first party agency for military work preceded the revolution—the so-called Military Organization of the Central Committee, which was formed in April 1917. Since 1918 the name has changed eight times. For convenience I will mainly use the most recent designation, Main Political Administration or MPA.[1]

The MPA has had no serious rival to speak as the party's military voice for five decades. Since the mid-1920s its pre-eminence has been formally acknowledged in the party rules. The original All-Russian Bureau of Military Commissars at first lacked clear status as an arm of the party, but by late 1918 it was said to be "acting in the very closest contact and upon the directives of the Central Committee."[2] Subsequent directives, beginning at the Eighth Party Congress in March 1919, specified that the MPA bore exclusive responsibility for military party work. Strictly speaking, the Secretariat of the Central Committee has never contained a department for supervision of the military corresponding to its departments (currently about twenty in number) that parallel most areas of state administration. The MPA is the closest thing to such an agency: under the rules it "works with the rights (na pravakh) of a Central Committee department."

This mandate was not acquired without a bureaucratic struggle. The Bureau of Military Commissars had to fight in 1918 to displace no fewer than four competitors attached to various military departments.[3] A major challenge was mounted several years later by a civilian organization, the Main Political Enlightenment Committee (Glavpolitprosvet), which was ceded control of general political education in the army in early 1921. After aroused MPA officials complained openly about the arrangement, and in many cases actually held on to the prized function, political enlightenment in the military was returned to MPA jurisdiction in late 1922.[4]

The MPA's central organization has changed somewhat over time. It has always been headed by a chief (nachal'nik), usually with several deputies. Since August 1960 the chief has been supplemented by a bureau, which is entitled to arrive at decisions on all matters by majority vote but must implement them through his directives.[5]

Central MPA management was first organized along functional lines, with departments for major activities such as agitation, publishing, and personnel assignment. By the late 1920s branch departments were added for work in naval, air, and armored units. After the war there was a complete shift to branch organization, with the MPA reduced to a supervisory organ for separate administrations directly in the ground, naval, and air forces. Functional organization was reintroduced in 1950, replaced by the branch model in 1955, then revived in 1958. Since that time the MPA has had functional administrations for organizational-party work, cadres, and propaganda and agitation, and smaller departments within and separate from the administrations for (currently) finance, culture, Komsomol and youth affairs, the press, social sciences instruction, and "military sociological research." Since 1967 there has also been a political administration (polituprav-lenie) subordinate to the MPA in each of the five major services—ground forces, strategic rocket forces, air force, air defense forces, and navy—and in the mid-1970s administrations were also established in the railroad troops and the military construction apparatus.[6] (The two militarized police forces—the border troops of the Committee on State Security [KGB] and internal troops of the Ministry of Internal Affairs [MVD]—are located outside the regular system of military command and have political administrations which are not subordinate to the MPA.)

Extending downward from these central offices is the backbone of the military party organs, a hierarchy of full-time political officers appointed from above and paralleling the command line. At each level of operation there is a single political officer in charge of all political work. His relationship to the commanding officer at his level is a complex one. Table 1 shows how the formal relationship has changed, using the administrative categories of the dominant service, the ground forces.

There have been two basic patterns of formal relationship. In the first, the political officer at the given level is officially independent of the commander. This was the model generally adopted when political workers were introduced in 1918. At the regiment and division levels the political officer was called a military commissar (*voennyi komissar*, commonly contracted to *voenkom*). He was not subject to the commander's orders, and his assent and cosignature were required on all orders to subordinate personnel. At higher levels the party worker's formal office was membership in a collegial decision-making organ, called a revolutionary military council, on which he sat with the commander and several other officers.

As Table 1 indicates, this collegial arrangement has generally persisted at senior levels of command, higher than division. The collegial organ has been termed a military council (*voennyi sovet*) since 1937. Fully empowered councils have existed in the headquarters of the major services since 1958, and more recently at the head of the railroad and airborne troops. Little is known about the precise powers of these bodies; the only members publicly identified are the commanders, chief political officers, first deputy commanders, and chiefs of staff. Military councils also operate at the head of each of the major territorial commands—currently sixteen military districts (roughly equivalent to fronts in wartime) in the ground forces, two air defense districts, four groups of forces in Eastern Europe, and the four naval fleets. (Commands and political organs do not exist at this level in either the air force or the strategic rocket forces; rocket formations are directed from Moscow, and air units are either centrally directed or subordinate to regular military or air defense districts.) There is provision as well for military councils at a third level, the step intermediate between territorial command and combat formations—army in ground and air forces terminology, flotilla in the navy. These are

Table 1. Structure of the military party organs

Level of organization (ground forces terminology)	Party organ	Responsible political officer
Ministry of Defense	Main Political Administration or equivalent	Chief of Main Political Administration or equivalent
Service (vid) headquarters	Political administration (politupravlenie) in major services since October 1967 (in strategic rocket forces since April 1963); also February 1946-March 1953, April 1955-April 1958. At most other times branch administration or department existed in MPA headquarters. Navy had separate MPA December 1937-February 1946, February 1950-March 1953.	Member of military council since April 1958. Member of military council (advisory only) January 1947-April 1958. If separate political administration in existence, this officer usually simultaneously its chief; from April 1958 to October 1967, officer simultaneously deputy chief of MPA. Before 1947 senior officer variously commissar, deputy commander for political affairs (zampolit), assistant commander for political affairs (pompolit).
Military district (group of forces, front)	Political administration. In most cases entitled political department (politotdel) June 1918-September 1925.	Member of military council (except June 1934-May 1937) and chief of political administration or department. Two posts combined except in wartime, May-June 1937, July 1950-November 1957. In June 1934-May 1937 and January 1947-July 1950, officer also zampolit.

Army	Political department	Member of military council (with same exceptions as at district level) and chief of political department. Posts combined.
Formation (*soedinenie*) (usually division)	Political department	Zampolit and chief of political department. Two posts combined since May 1943. Was commissar March 1918-March 1925, May 1937-August 1940, July 1941-October 1942.
Unit (*chast'*) (usually regiment)	None	Zampolit. Was commissar March 1918-March 1925, May 1937-August 1940, July 1941-October 1942. Was pompolit March 1925-May 1937.
Major subunit (*podrazdelenie*) (usually battalion)	None	Zampolit since August 1955. Was political instructor (*politruk*) December 1941-October 1942. No officer at other times.
Minor subunit (*podrazdelenie*) (usually company)	None	Zampolit since January 1967 and also October 1942-May 1943, January 1950-August 1955. Was politruk October 1919-March 1925, May 1937-July 1940, July 1941-October 1942. Was pompolit March 1925-May 1937. No officer at other times.

essentially wartime commands; they exist in peacetime only in key border areas and groups of forces abroad and currently number no more than fifteen.

Membership in the military councils at the crucial district and front level has varied. The commander and his chief political colleague have always belonged. Civil War councils could include as many as five or six other men, among them chiefs of staff, logistics officers, and representatives of civilian agencies such as the railways. A major change came in 1925 with the uniform addition of the most important civilian in the locality, the first secretary of the principal local party organ. This membership was evidently allowed to lapse, but it was renewed in 1937 (when the councils were restored following a three-year interval) and has persisted in peacetime ever since (with the exception of the period from January 1947 to July 1950). Numerically, the military command has predominated in the councils since early in World War II. The councils of wartime fronts and combined forces armies consisted of the commander, the political member of the military council (*chlen voennogo soveta*), a second member responsible for logistics, and (later in the war) the commanders of aviation and artillery and, in some cases, the chief of staff. Since 1958 district and army level military councils have included the commander, the senior political officer, at least one local party secretary, the first deputy commander, the chief of staff, and several other leading officers, usually the commanders of specialized force elements.[7]

At lower levels a second and quite different model has come to prevail, one in which the political officer is unequivocally subordinated to the commander. In this system of unitary or one-man command (*edinonachalie*), the commanding officer can issue orders on all matters without the concurrence of his political colleague. The system was introduced in a few exceptional cases during the Civil War and early 1920s (usually with commanders who were long-time party members), but in March 1925 it was ordered put into gradual effect at all command grades below army. The transition was virtually complete by 1930. Depending on the level, the political officer was either a deputy or an assistant commander for political affairs (commonly contracted to *zampolit* or *pompolit*). Almost two decades were to pass before this pattern gained permanent acceptance. A period of great instability was inaugurated on May 8, 1937, when commissars were abruptly reintroduced. The commissar model was then revoked on August 12, 1940, reinstated in the first month of the war on July 16, 1941, and replaced for the final time by one-man command on October 9, 1941. (Timing varied by several days in the navy.) Edinonachalie has remained in effect ever since 1942. Of the two interwar designations, zampolit—deputy commander for political affairs—has been retained. The levels at which zampolits have been assigned have changed considerably over time, as can be seen from Table 1. They now work at all basic levels of troop organization from company (containing about a hundred men) to division (normally about ten thousand).

At junior levels, the responsible political officer has little full-time staff help. Each regiment does have a club whose head is a cadre political officer, and since 1967 regiment and battalion zampolits have had full-time propagandists as assistants.

At the levels of division and above, however, there are sizable administrative staffs, which normally are referred to as the party or political organs proper. At the district level this organ bears the same name as its counterpart at the service level—political administration. Each administration has a chief (concurrently member of the military council), two deputy chiefs, functional departments paralleling the MPA's administrations, and a number of instructors and inspectors who are the main contact with lower links in the apparatus. Far more visible and more revered in MPA tradition is the political department (politotdel). Such departments are found in all armies and divisions (using ground forces terminology) and in some smaller detached units not subordinate to division commands. They exist also at a number of points not in the normal line of command, among them central administrations of the Ministry of Defense, district-level staffs, academies and research institutes, some construction agencies, large naval bases and munitions depots, and military commissariats (recruitment offices) at the oblast and republic levels. The head of the politotdel serves simultaneously as deputy commander (or deputy chief) for political affairs. He is assisted by a deputy department head, several instructors (for youth affairs, organizational work, culture, and records), a propagandist, and sometimes a director for the formation's party school. Each political organ also has appended to it a party commission of five to ten members empowered to ratify lower decisions on party admissions and penalties. Its secretary is a permanent member of the party organ's staff.[8]

This is indeed a formidable machine. The last reliable estimate of overall size, of 30,000 full-time political officers, is for 1963. Numbers have almost certainly increased since then. The addition of propagandists and company zampolits in 1967 would account for almost 10,000 new officers in the ground forces alone. Some slots may have been filled by internal transfer, but it seems reasonable to put current MPA strength at about 40,000. This number is especially impressive when it is realized that this is a quarter to a third the size of the entire civilian party apparatus.[9]

Party Membership Base

Like the hierarchy of appointed political officers, membership in the party by individual military men also predates the revolution. There were 26,000 Bolsheviks in the old army in June 1917 and 76,000 by the time of the October Revolution.[10] Table 2 summarizes the data on membership since 1918. The major trends are clear: rapid growth during the Civil War, from 1924 to 1933, and before and during World War II, sharp decline during both postwar demobilizations and the Great Purge and its prelude, and little change absolutely or relative to army size at other times. Membership has stabilized at about one fifth of military personnel. In relation to the membership of the party as a whole, the military contingent has in wartime been as high as 50 percent (March 1920) and 55 percent (January 1944). In peacetime it has been much less, currently less than 5 percent of all members and about 6 percent of male members.

This membership has come partly from incidental recruitment and deliberate "mobilization" of civilian party members, mainly in wartime. This brought in 260,000 members during the Civil War and about 1.6 million in World War II. The second source has been party admission within the army, usually by way of a candidate stage of at least one year. This also peaked during World War II, when the 2.7 million members and 4.1 million candidates recruited under relaxed requirements were three quarters of all party admissions.[11] In peacetime this second channel has been the principal one (since 1945 almost the exclusive one), and it has accounted for a substantial (but decreasing) proportion of admissions into the party as a whole. Between the wars party admissions in the army averaged 10 percent of the national total. In 1962 they totalled 161,600, amounting to 25 percent of all new members across the country (32 percent of all new male members). Admissions in the military were curtailed somewhat in 1965. They averaged only 50,000 a year from 1971 to 1976, about 10 percent of all party recruits (14 percent of all new male members).[12]

As Table 3 shows, party membership has not been a cross-section of military ranks. Rank-and-file soldiers and sailors have been underrepresented, usually drastically so, in keeping with MPA chief Andrei S. Bubnov's observation in 1925 that in military party life "the command element plays a dominant role."[13] Besides the clear bias in favor of officials (which is visible throughout the party), the fact that the average age of admission is the late twenties militates strongly against membership for the rank and file, particularly short-term conscripts (most of whom now are eighteen or nineteen years old).[14] Preferential admission for lower ranks was put into effect several times, on the basis of class origin in the mid-1920s (when the party as a whole was

Table 2. Party membership in the military establishment

Date	Number of primary party organizations	Number of party members and candidates	Party members and candidates as percentage of personnel
January 1919	2,900	50,000	-
August 1920	7,000	300,000	8
January 1922	5,690	73,000	4.6
March 1923	-	63,000	10.5
September 1924	-	45,000	8.0
October 1925	4,318	63,416	11.3
January 1927	5,800	78,250	13.8
January 1928	6,001	82,018	13.8
January 1930	6,760	102,749	15.9
May 1930	-	160,000	-
July 1932	-	300,000	-
January 1934	-	231,200	25.6
January 1937	-	150,000	9.6
January 1938	-	147,500	-
January 1939	5,000	226,000	-
January 1940	10,968	669,854	-
June 1941	13,799	654,000	12.7
January 1942	23,614	1,234,000	-
January 1943	-	1,939,227	-
January 1944	-	2,702,500	-
January 1945	-	3,030,715	25 (est.)
July 1945	61,870	2,984,750	26.2
January 1946	-	2,041,000	-
October 1967	-	710,600 (est.)	22
February 1974	-	705,000 (est.)	20

Sources: Iu. P. Petrov, *Partiinoe stroitel'stvo v Sovetskoi Armii i Flote (1918-1961)* (Moscow, Voenizdat, 1964), pp. 30, 33, 107-108, 150, 153, 224-226, 281, 283, 312, 328-329, 393, 396-397; I. B. Berkhin, *Voennaia reforma v SSSR (1924-1925 gg.)* (Moscow, Voenizdat, 1958), pp. 40, 412; K. E. Voroshilov, *Stat'i i rechi* (Moscow, Partizdat, 1937), p. 611; Iu. P. Petrov, *Stroitel'stvo politorganov, partiinykh i komsomol'skikh organizatsii Armii i Flota (1918-1968)* (Moscow, Voenizdat, 1968), pp. 237, 247, 329; *Istoriia Velikoi Otechestvennoi voiny 1941-1945*, 6 vols. (Moscow, Voenizdat, 1960-65), VI, 332-333, 342, 369; *Pravda*, October 13, 1967, p. 5; *Kommunist vooruzhennykh sil*, 1974, no. 4, p. 73. Slightly different figures for the 1920s and 1930s are reported in A. A. Epishev et al., *Partiino-politicheskaia rabota v Vooruzhennykh Silakh SSSR 1918-1973 gg.: Istoricheskii ocherk* (Moscow, Voenizdat, 1974), pp. 118, 154.

Table 3. Composition of party membership in the military establishment (by percent)

Date	Rank and file	NCO's	Total rank and file and NCO's	Civilian employees	Officers and officer candidates
January 1920 (field forces only)	-	-	Almost 75	-	About 25
January 1924	-	-	20	-	-
January 1925	16.5	13.5	30	-	-
January 1927	-	-	40	-	-
January 1928	-	-	42	-	-
January 1937	-	-	1	-	-
January 1939	-	-	25.1	-	-
July 1940	-	-	40.8	-	-
June 1941	-	-	34	-	-
July 1942	24	18	42	-	-
January 1944	-	-	57	2	41
July 1946	10	-	-	-	-
July 1947	5.7	-	-	-	-
January 1949	3.3	-	-	-	-
July 1950	1.7	10	11.7	-	-
January 1957	0.9	6.3	7.2	-	-
January 1959	1.8	8	9.8	14.7	75.5
July 1960	4.3	10.5	14.8	-	-
January 1962	7.1	13.6	20.7	-	-

Sources: Petrov, *Partiinoe stroitel'stvo*, pp. 224-225, 304, 329, 388, 394; Petrov, *Stroitel'stvo politorganov*, pp. 93, 408, 449, 490; Aleksandr Geronimus, *Partiia i Krasnaia Armiia* (Moscow and Leningrad, Gosizdat, 1928), p. 169; N. M. Kiriaev et al., *KPSS i stroitel'stvo Sovetskikh Vooruzhennykh Sil* (Moscow, Voenizdat, 1967), pp. 232, 433.

vigorously recruiting members from working class backgrounds) and in the late 1930s, and on the basis of battlefield distinction during the war with Germany. But each time the trend was reversed, through either implicit indifference to principle (after 1928) or explicit change of principle (after 1945). A drive for increased rank-and-file and NCO representation was launched in the late 1950s (during a period of rapid party growth) and brought the two groups' share to a fifth by 1962. Yet this still left the party organizations as essentially a preserve of the officer corps.

As of 1973, 40 percent of all party members in the military were officers in staff organizations.[15] Stable distribution of party membership over the previous decade would mean that officers would outnumber all others in party organizations in the military units by about two to one. Yet such an assumption would understate officer dominance. Clearly the rank and file has suffered more from the post-1965 decline in admissions, particularly since the new military service law of 1967 decreased service for most conscripts by one year (thereby reducing their exposure to MPA recruitment efforts).[16]

The organization of individual party membership has been fixed by a series of eleven Central Committee instructions, the first issued on January 5, 1919, for the uniform party cells to be created in all regiments. Directives have recorded five changes in organizational base for the primary party organization, as the cell came to be called in March 1934. The main engine of change has been the fluctuating density of party membership. Increasing density in 1920 prompted a shift of the primary organization down to the company level. It was moved up to the regiment in 1934 during declining membership, down to the battalion in May 1943 at the height of wartime recruitment, and back to the regiment in January 1950 after demobilization. Since September 1960 primary party organizations have been allowed at the battalion level in cases where the regiment contains at least seventy-five party members; in other cases the primary organization remains at the regiment level. Within the primary party organizations, subsidiary organizations and groups have been sanctioned, usually at the company level. Most of these were dissolved after 1965, but there is some trend toward reinstating them.[17]

Unlike the cadre political organs, the mass party organizations are in theory democratic. Membership is voluntary, and admission can be granted only by vote of a general party meeting (subject to confirmation by the party commission). Organizations must meet at least once a month. Every year they elect by secret ballot executive officers to "conduct current work": a committee of nine to thirteen in large organizations, which in turn chooses a secretary and one or two deputies; a five-to-nine-man bureau and a secretary in organizations of fifteen to seventy-four members; a secretary only in smaller organizations. In party groups, the sole executive bears the title party group organizer (partgruporg); he is either elected or appointed, depending on the size of the group. Democratic form was generally suspended only during World War II, when all committees and bureaus were coopted and elected secretaries were replaced by appointed organizers.

It should come as little suprise to the student of Soviet politics that the reality is far from democratic. Freely elected party committees did exist at army and division levels in 1918, but they soon proved incompatible with the appointed politotdels and were abolished in October of that year. The basis for the subjection of the remaining elective bodies to the cadre political organs is usually stated as the principle of "direct leadership" from above. For all practical purposes, party secretaries and committees are appointed assistants to the full-time cadre of political officers. Their elections are subject to confirmation (*utverzhdenie*) by higher party organs, which are also obliged to lead and direct (*vozglavliat' i napravliat'*) all electoral meetings.[18] There is no question that initiation and prior approval from above are standard practice.

Numerous cases of disregard for electoral formalities and members' preferences can be drawn from the press of the Stalin era. We read from 1935, for instance, that a regiment party bureau, hearing of the decision of the division politotdel to replace its secretary, "did not even find it necessary to coopt [him] as a member of the bureau, obviously considering this an empty formality." This was depicted as a normal occurrence.[19]

Concern for form has been greater since the death of Stalin. There are even occasional reports of candidates nominated by higher-level agencies being rejected by party organizations and of new nominations being made.[20] But on the whole there can be no doubt that superior party organs still dominate the process of selection. The relationship is unmistakable in such vignettes as this exchange between an officer and his wife:

"Love [the officer tells his wife], you can be happy. I'm going on party work." . . .
"Where?"
"To another garrison far from here, as secretary of the party bureau of a unit."
"That is good, Vania. But you are supposed to be elected, as I understand it."
"Everything will be all right," he answered calmly. "The political organ is recommending me."[21]

Within the party organization, the bulk of the administrative work is handled by the secretary, whatever the official acclaim for collective leadership. It is he who collects membership dues, maintains records, carries on routine correspondence, attends the multitude of conferences organized by higher organs, and distributes most of the party assignments (*partiinye porucheniia*) which members are expected to carry out. The secretary "often carries on his shoulders almost all practical business. He is, in the words of the proverb, the tailor, the reaper, and the pipe player."[22]

Auxiliary Organizations

The most important auxiliary to the military party organs is the Komsomol (Young Communist League) network. Table 4 displays its growth since its inception on a regular basis in 1924. As with the party, Komsomol membership has experienced spurts and lags in growth and climbed to over half of total Soviet membership in wartime. Komsomol membership has outnumbered that in the party since 1925, except for the last three years of World War II. It now includes 60 percent of military personnel and amounts to about 6 percent of USSR-wide membership.

Unlike the party, the military Komsomol is primarily an organization for the rank and file and NCO's. Officers and officer candidates have always been a decided minority—8 percent in 1966.[23] Eighty-three percent of all soldiers and sailors were Komsomol members in 1977, and naturally this membership is heavily concentrated in the

Table 4. Komsomol membership in the military establishment

Date	Number of primary Komsomol organizations	Number of Komsomol members	Komsomol members as percentage of personnel
July 1924	-	30,000	5.3
July 1926	5,300	84,312	14.7
January 1927	-	120,000	20.5
July 1930	6,000	177,000	-
January 1934	-	-	23.9
January 1937	-	405,600	28.3
January 1939	5,100	798,500	-
July 1941	10,000 (est.)	1,931,000	44 (est.)
January 1942	20,000 (est.)	1,742,500	-
January 1944	69,000	2,379,500	-
January 1945	62,790	2,369,600	-
June 1945	-	2,393,345	21.1
January 1949	26,780	1,272,000	44.3
January 1951	-	-	40
October 1967	-	1,938,000 (est.)	60
July 1972	-	2,025,000 (est.)	60

Sources: Petrov, *Partiinoe stroitel'stvo*, pp. 248, 252, 254, 307, 321, 323-325, 423-428; Voroshilov, p. 611; Petrov, *Stroitel'stvo politorganov*, pp. 260, 422-423; *Pravda*, October 13, 1967, p. 5; *Kommunist vooruzhennykh sil*, 1972, no. 13, p. 13.

combat units. Most conscripts—over 70 percent of the 1973 call-up—
arrive as Komsomol members, so organizational recruitment is much
less important than for party ranks.[24]

Like the party organizations, Komsomol organizations have been
regulated by formal Central Committee instructions, the most recent
issued in 1974. Primary Komsomol organizations with elected committees and secretaries (called groups for the assistance of the party
until November 1930, cells from then until March 1934) existed at the
same administrative level as primary party organizations until June
1954, when they were moved to the battalion level six years before the
party. They are clearly designated as ancillary agencies, "active assistants" of the party organizations, and are supervised by junior political officers, by special political organ departments and branches, and
by a core of party members (including half of all Komsomol secretaries).[25]

Another important auxiliary is the military press. Publication of
newspapers, magazines, other periodicals, and books is "carried out
under direct leadership" of the MPA and its subsidiaries, and political
organs "check the content and ideological direction" of all such publications.[26] The MPA also trains military journalists and part-time cor-
respondents. The press network stretches from *Krasnaia zvezda*, the
daily organ of the Ministry of Defense (whose editor is a member of
the MPA bureau), through daily district newspapers, to the wall
newspapers and ad hoc "lightning bulletins" (*molnii*) put out directly
in the units.

Finally, the military party organs attempt to tap mass energies
through a variety of volunteer efforts. All cultural establishments, including military clubs and libraries (these are a direct responsibility of
the MPA), have councils (*sovety*) to assist with program development
and management. Wives' councils (*zhensovety*) function in most
units, providing political study, civil defense preparation, and even
job training. Individuals are encouraged to work as nonstaff (*vnesh-
tatnye*) agitators, propagandists, and instructors—without pay and,
usually, in their spare time. Party and people's "control" bodies have
functioned in the military under various titles since the 1920s. In 1963,
at the height of the campaign for "popular initiatives" sponsored by
Khrushchev, there were established "groups of party-state control"
(voluntary bodies, although usually headed by a cadre political officer, charged with exposing "bureaucratism" in administration) as
well as "ideological commissions" with even vaguer mandates. In
1965, as happened throughout the Soviet Union, these were replaced
by a "people's control" network with more sharply defined inspectoral
duties. The people's control committees, groups, and "posts" are su-

pervised by both the MPA and the department of military and administrative organs of the USSR Committee of People's Control.[27]

While the political organs' ability to enlist volunteer support is considerable, one should also note that they have placed informal limitations on the scope and autonomy of such activities. Even at the height of the post-1963 drive there were complaints about the tendency of party officials to view it as "some kind of a campaign [which] will pass" and to "continue to work with the old methods." Others were said to adopt the new forms "for appearance's sake, in order to escape rebuke for ignoring the demands of the times," and to "remember about [them] only when it is time to put together a report on their work for superior establishments."[28] By the late 1960s the curtain had been drawn on "attempts to artificially force the development of social initiatives."[29]

Structural Integration with the Military Command

The military party organs have been a conspicuous exception to the general Soviet rule of strict structural separation of party agencies from the more numerous and larger state bodies (particularly the government ministries) that do the bulk of the routine governing of Soviet society and have formal "administrative rights" (the authority to issue commands and instructions binding with full force of law).[30] The MPA has always been distinctive. "In distinction from the civilian party organizations," one early authority wrote, the military party organs are "a form which . . . appropriately combines party and state functions."[31] The current head of the MPA, Aleksei A. Epishev, restated the principle in 1970: "The political administrations and departments are, in terms of the content and character of their work, party organs. But at the same time they carry out the functions of a military-political apparatus, and in connection with this they are provided with defined administrative rights. This is dictated by the particular features of the development and tasks of the armed forces."[32]

At the highest levels, the formal terms of integration have changed somewhat over the years. One constant has been the MPA's representation along with the high command on a series of collegial bodies charged with discussing the broad lines of national military policy. (The current title of this collegium is the Main Military Council; it appears that several political officers sit on it.)[33] There has been more variation in the MPA's legal relationship to the government agency which administers the military forces, the Ministry of Defense (or People's Commissariat, as it was called prior to 1946). From 1930 to 1945 the MPA chief was concurrently one of several Deputy People's Commissars of Defense.[34] Since then, however, this man has not held formal office within the ministry. Between 1953 and 1958 the MPA was officially referred to as the MPA of the Ministry of Defense, but at no time since the war has its chief been said to be a subordinate or deputy of the Defense Minister. The MPA has its own lines of accountability to higher party authorities. It "accounts for its work to the Central Committee," although it does "report to the Minister of Defense on the political and moral condition of the personnel and on political work in the forces."[35]

Whatever this lack of clarity, substantial forms of high-level integration with the military command do exist. The MPA has always been defined as the political organ of the military establishment, regardless of the official designation. Even though its headquarters are not now formally part of the ministry, it is clearly portrayed as a vital component of the overall defense establishment. Epishev, notwithstanding his lack of statutory Defense Ministry office, is routinely listed among the men in "leading posts in the armed forces," and has a set niche in such lists (currently fourth, behind the Minister of Defense and two of his first deputies). He helps receive foreign military delegations, takes tours abroad with other officers, and assists at most ceremonial occasions.

Several forms of shared responsibility also bind the MPA and the ministry. New political organs are "created by the Ministry of Defense and the MPA." MPA duties include "checking the implementation . . . of orders and directives" of the minister, and orders on "the most important questions" in the MPA's activity are issued jointly by the minister and the MPA chief.[36] The MPA "participates in drawing up regulations, manuals, and other leading documents" of the ministry, all of which contain major prescriptions for political work.[37] It also "takes part in the selection, assignment, and rating of leading military cadres," and in turn many senior MPA appointments must be cleared by Ministry of Defense officials.[38] Personnel decisions at lower levels are also interconnected.

Below the peak, structural integration is rather more clear. There is a formal order of superordination and division of labor. Responsible political officers are either deputies of commanders or fellow members of military councils. The political organs are superior agencies for all personnel in military units below them, entitled to issue binding orders and directives. Conversely, they "are subordinate (*podchinennye*) to the military command" as well as "to the respective superior political organs."[39] Even commissars were subject to orders by commanders at higher levels, and this pattern still applies to all political officers. All political workers also take direct orders from commanders at equivalent levels (except for members of military councils, who formally at least must abide only by decisions of the council as a whole). Individual political officers have defined spheres of competence and lines of subordination linking them both with command and with other political officers. Illustrative of this dual subordination is the position of the regiment zampolit. He is required by internal service regulations "to report in appropriate time" to the division political department, but he is also "subordinate to the regiment commander" and is "the direct superior of all personnel in the regiment." The regulations specify his precise duties in eleven categories.[40]

There are two other elements of structural integration with the military command. The first is the system of military rank. When personal ranks were introduced in the army in September 1935, political officers had a separate hierarchy (from junior politruk to army commissar first class). Since October 1942, however, all political workers have held ranks in precisely the same order as other commissioned officers (from lieutenant to marshal, with variations for the navy and other specialized services). So Epishev, the senior political officer, is a general of the army (the same rank as, say, the current chief of military logistics), his deputies are usually colonel-generals, and so on down the line to the company zampolit, who normally is a senior lieutenant. Political officers enjoy all the prerogatives and are subject to all the obligations of rank. They wear uniforms and insignia which are indistinguishable from those of other officers.

A final mode of structural integration with the military command is the strong representation of commanders (all nonpolitical officers) among the nominally elected executives of party organizations. As of the early 1960s, 60 to 75 percent of regiment and ship commanders were reported to be sitting on party committees and bureaus in different localities.[41] In 1970 more than 70 percent of regiment commanders were bureau or committee members in many districts, and in 1976 the figure for the Group of Soviet Forces in Germany was 85 percent.[42] This high incidence of membership (one gains the sense that it is even higher among subunit commanders) means that officers predominate numerically in most elective organs. In one military district in 1962, line command, staff, and engineering officers made up about 70 percent of the members of these bodies.[43] It would appear from press descriptions that at least half of the members unaccounted for in such a figure are cadre political officers and that most of the rest are NCO's. Representation for short-term conscripts is extremely rare; it is somewhat less uncommon for voluntarily re-enlisted soldiers and sailors, particularly if they hold the ranks of ensign and warrant officer instituted in 1972.

The same holds true for the secretaries who do most of the routine work within the party organizations. In 1969 only 15 percent of these men worked full-time as secretaries; the rest were part-time or unreleased (*neosvobozhdennyi*), holding official posts (as subunit commanders, staff officers, and so on) in addition to their party positions.[44] (This double load of duties leads to frequent complaints of overwork.) Of all secretaries chosen in 1971, 45 percent were staff officers or commanders of companies or larger units, 20 percent were cadre political officers, and most of the rest seem to have been officers at the platoon commander grade.[45] Most of the nonofficers identified in the press as party secretaries are NCO's. A few are ensigns or warrant officers, and in some specialized organizations (usually with construction, commercial, or manufacturing missions) the party secretary may be a civilian employee of the Ministry of Defense without military rank.

Integration with the Civilian Party Organs

Like all Soviet institutions—including the Ministry of Defense—the MPA treats the party's sovereign body between congresses, the Central Committee, as the ultimate authority whose dictates it must obey. As is common for major Soviet organizations, the MPA is represented on the same Central Committee that guides its work. Far from monopolizing military representation on the committee, the MPA has had a status greatly inferior to the military command, especially since the late 1930s (see Table 5).

In practice, the MPA and the military command alike take instructions from the party Politburo, the executive of the Central Committee. At this level, MPA and military representation has been much less substantial. Only one MPA official—its chief from June 1942 to May 1945, Aleksandr S. Shcherbakov—has sat (as a candidate member) on the Politburo, and he had earned his seat before taking over the MPA. Most Politburos prior to 1955 contained one nonprofessional defense administrator (Leon Trotsky, Mikhail V. Frunze, Kliment E. Voroshilov, Nikolai Bulganin). Since then there have been two experiments with a seat for a professional soldier heading the Defense Ministry (Georgii K. Zhukov in 1956-57, Andrei Grechko for the three years before his death in April 1976). Grechko's succession as minister by Dmitrii F. Ustinov—a civilian Politburo member who has spent his entire career dealing with defense production, most recently as Central Committee secretary—marks at least a temporary reversion to the pre-1955 pattern.

If the line of vertical integration is clear, the horizontal integration between the military party organs and the Central Committee's administrative apparatus, the departments in its Secretariat, seems to be

Table 5. Military representation on party Central Committee (members and candidates)[a]

Party congress and year	Military command	Political officers	Total military representation	Military percentage of total
Fourteenth, 1925	1	2	3	2.8
Fifteenth, 1928	2	2	4	3.3
Sixteenth, 1930	4	2	6	4.3
Seventeenth, 1934	7	2	9	6.5
Eighteenth, 1939	13	4	17	12.2
Nineteenth, 1952	26	2	28	11.9
Twentieth, 1956	18	0	18	7.1
Twenty-second, 1961	30	1	31	9.4
Twenty-third, 1966	28	3	31	8.6
Twenty-fourth, 1971	29	3	32	8.1
Twenty-fifth, 1976	27	3	30	7.0

Sources: Stenographic reports of congresses and author's biographical files.

a. These figures do not reflect the several cases of formal cooptation or removal of members by resolution of the Central Committee, nor the more numerous cases of informal elimination through arrest or execution (affecting 12 men, all between 1937 and 1941). There are minor discrepancies between some of these figures and those cited in other Western works.

far less extensive. The technical distinction between the departments and the MPA (which only "works with the rights" of a department) is rigorously maintained and is reinforced by other elements of segregation. The MPA is assigned exclusive responsibility for party work in the military forces by the party rules. It is the MPA that maintains the register (*uchet*) of all party and Komsomol members in the army, gathers statistics on them, and supplies political organs with blank forms of party documents.[46] MPA headquarters are located, not in the Central Committee building near the Kremlin, but among Ministry of Defense installations elsewhere in Moscow (on Frunze Street, a stone's throw from the General Staff offices). Unlike the departments proper, the MPA has its own periodical (*Kommunist vooruzhennykh sil*, Communist of the Armed Forces, published twice a month), and there is almost no detailed coverage of its work in the Central Committee's daily newspaper (*Pravda*) and journals.

Still, it would be going too far to suggest that there are no links whatever between the MPA and other parts of the central party apparatus. These ties have certainly been affected by the personal relationship between the MPA chief and the General or First Secretary of the party. On at least two occasions (with Lev Z. Mekhlis in 1937 and Epishev in 1962), an MPA head was appointed who had a long and close association with the party leader. Ties were also no doubt closer than now during the two brief periods when the MPA chief was simultaneously a Central Committee secretary with broad supervisory concerns (under Bubnov from 1925 to 1929 and under Shcherbakov during the war).[47]

Even within the bounds of general MPA autonomy, there is still room for some interaction with the civilian party apparatus. The Secretariat as a whole apparently discusses some major questions concerning military party life at its sessions.[48] Much more common, however, is contact between the MPA and army and several of the Secretariat's specialized departments.

The main responsibility here lies with the Secretariat's monitor of key appointments in the state bureaucracy, currently called the administrative organs department. This department has no policy initiation responsibilities, but it oversees personnel matters in the courts, procuracy, militia, secret police, and civil defense and civil aviation networks along with the military establishment. In the mid-1920s its predecessor's work is said to have been closely tied with the MPA's cadres administration, but it is not clear how much this link was due to the fact that Bubnov was on the Secretariat.[49] The department has certainly never had direct responsibility for assigning personnel in the MPA or elsewhere in the military sphere. The MPA and its subsidiaries "take care of the selection, assignment, and training of cadre political staff," and the Ministry of Defense does the same for commanders through its cadres organs.[50] Where the administrative organs department does play a role is evidently in the review and confirmation of major appointments.

Top MPA officials—the chief and his deputies, the heads of MPA administrations and departments, the heads of all political administrations and departments—fall within the *nomenklatura* (confirmation list) of the Central Committee.[51] These men would seem to number about one thousand. All commanders on military councils are also said to be "confirmed by the Central Committee," and party leaders presumably make periodic reviews to well below this level—probably, as in the MPA, to the division level.[52] This would put the total military contingent on the Central Committee nomenklatura at somewhat over two thousand men.[53] (If confirmation extended to the next grade, regiment commander and equivalent, the number would be over twice as large.)

The administrative organs department can be expected to maintain files on these officers compiled from a number of sources (including, one can assume, the secret police, who are supervised by this same department). The department may have the formal authority to confirm some appointments on its own. More likely it acts mainly to collate and supplement information about senior personnel flowing to party leaders through the regular communication channels of the MPA and Ministry of Defense. It appears to funnel such information through a single Central Committee secretary (Ustinov for most of the period since Khrushchev's fall, Iakov P. Riabov since Ustinov's appointment as minister in 1976). The head of the department (currently Nikolai I. Savinkin) frequently appears at important military functions, attends party conferences in the forces, and signs some military obituaries. In recent years Savinkin's first deputy (V. I. Drugov) and several department officials, including two men (now I. P. Potapov and A. E. Volkov) identified as heads of sectors, have also been reported at military gatherings.[54] The department's competence has no doubt been enhanced by the fact that all four of its heads since the mid-1950s— Valentin V. Zolotukhin, Aleksei S. Zheltov, Nikolai R. Mironov, and Savinkin—have had prior experience in the MPA, ranging from four years for Mironov to twenty in the case of Zheltov.[55]

Careful note should be taken of the modesty of the administrative organs department's capabilities and status. With a staff of probably no more than fifty men, of whom perhaps twenty are in its military sectors, it does not seem to have the personnel to deal in detail with the hundreds of thousands of commissioned officers beyond the Central Committee nomenklatura.[56] Even here, it is unlikely that its wishes alone could decide major appointments. The department (not to mention its military sectors) is clearly outranked by the professional military in stature within the party itself. Only since 1971 has a single department official (Savinkin) had candidate status on the Central Committee. When Savinkin signs obituaries he does so only after ten or more military names.

Given its responsibilities for the security forces and civil defense, the administrative organs department seems to play some role in coordinating party work in these areas with that in the army. It is also, along with the department for organizational-party work, an occasional conduit to the MPA and the military for information about strictly intraparty matters such as the exchange of party documents of 1973-75. The only military questions in which the organizational-party work department seems to participate regularly are those relating to Komsomol affairs, concerning which national Komsomol officials are also consulted from time to time. Representatives of two other Central Committee departments, those for propaganda and culture, sometimes attend MPA meetings on ideological questions, presumably to help integrate civilian and military propaganda. They do not, however, make major speeches or policy pronouncements in the military sphere. There is also a specialized Central Committee department which supervises the defense production ministries, but it has no writ whatever within the armed forces.

At the local level we find the same general principle of MPA autonomy prevailing, a fact not appreciated by Western analysis which refers in broad terms to control of the military by local party leaders.[57] MPA extraterritoriality (*ekstraterritorial 'nost'*) was firmly established by the end of the Civil War. The 1919 Central Committee instruction prescribed vertical subordination to the MPA for all party cells and agencies in the field forces, although it put cells in rear areas under the jurisdiction of local party committees (which had helped found some of them and, in some cases, "led them day by day").[58] In June 1921 the party leadership extended the vertical pattern to the entire military establishment, ruling that local party agencies "cannot change the resolutions or instructions of [the MPA] or political departments."[59] This decision was strongly challenged in 1924 by a number of local party organs, particularly the Moscow committee, which formed "party centers" for military work and claimed the right to override MPA decisions. After MPA chief Bubnov led a vigorous campaign for autonomy, the leadership reaffirmed the 1921 edict, recorded in the party rules the MPA's immunity to lateral control, and also placed party work in the new territorial militia (which was to be disbanded in the 1930s) under MPA direction. Political organs were required to maintain close communication with local party authorities, but political work in the army was firmly concentrated in MPA hands.[60]

There has been no recurrence of the 1924 crisis. In statutory terms, the military party organs and the military as a whole are exempt from routine supervision on the part of the local party organs. It is clearly specified as illegal (*nezakonno*) for local party bodies to attempt decisions that in any way bind or obligate (*obiazut*) military personnel.[61] Even the most sweeping assertions of the responsibilities of local party agencies make no mention of day-to-day jurisdiction in military life.

The prime reason for this is usually said to be the army's mobility and hence unsuitability for management by territorially fixed authorities.[62] This rationale has assuredly been reinforced since 1945 by the stationing of large forces abroad and the growth of the high seas fleet, and probably by the introduction of weapons (particularly strategic missiles) which the regime is particularly anxious to control directly from Moscow. But other considerations have weighed as well. The MPA's greater cohesion and centralization after the mid-1920s made it much less vulnerable to local pressure. MPA leaders themselves have fought hard for their autonomy. Bubnov's defense of MPA rights was presaged by resistance to local "pretensions" and "local officials . . . concerned with [extending] the limits of their powers" even during the Civil War.[63] In more recent years, the occasional local attempts to infringe upon the arrangement have been condemned by political officers as useless and harmful.[64]

The MPA's wish to be left alone has been congruent with the evident reluctance of many local officials to become involved in yet another taxing sphere of work. Faced with even the minimal demands of communication with military organizations, the typical response for local leaders has been to "confine themselves to saying this work is important while in practice giving it secondary status."[65] Furthermore, unlike some Communist regimes, the Soviet leaders have always been concerned with insulating the military against currents in local politics which might draw it into larger policy debates in which its participation is not desired. (The important consequences of this choice are discussed in Chapter 11.)

Again, the impression should not be left that there are no ties at all at the local level. When senior commanders speak of "constant support and attention" to military needs on the part of local party officials,[66] they are not merely mouthing slogans. There is, in the first place, an arena of informal contact and collaboration necessitated by the sheer exigency of performing related functions on a common territory. These encounters occur between military and civilian organizations as autonomous units, and the MPA plays no special role in them. Negotiations occur, for example, on the use of rail and other transport facilities, employment of military labor in disaster relief and harvest campaigns, civil defense and paramilitary training, conscription management, and the provision of servicemen with housing, local services, and consumer goods. In any of these areas, a bottleneck or disagreement may mean that military officers will have to "turn for a decision to the corresponding party and soviet organs."[67] During World War II there was much more extensive cooperation than at other times, particularly concerning supply of the army and military mobilization of the population.

But Soviet spokesmen attribute greater theoretical significance to more formalized avenues of contact, and in these the MPA is sometimes more intimately involved. One such link is reciprocal representation on decision-making bodies. Of these the least consequential are the local and regional soviets, on which 14,000 servicemen now sit.[68] In World War II, "city defense committees" (usually headed by the local first secretary and containing several military officials) were formed in about sixty centers threatened with German occupation and granted "the full plenitude of party and state powers." They were not, however, authorized to interfere in military operations or organization, and they were dissolved at the end of the war.[69] In both wartime and peacetime, local party leaders' main access to military decisions has been through the military councils of districts, fleets, fronts, and armies, on which several dozen local party secretaries now sit along with political officers and commanders.[70] In turn, thousands of military men—6,000 in 1973—are members of local party committees. As of 1976 military officers (all of them, it should be noted, commanders rather than political officers) were full members of the bureaus of six of the fourteen republican central committees, and these committees contain an average of eight officers as full members. There is somewhat less substantial military representation at lower levels.[71]

The party rules also continue to require military party organs to communicate with local party authorities and systematically inform them about their work. The several hundred military delegates to national party congresses are selected at region-wide conferences (except for forces stationed abroad), and several local party officials are usually reported as attending military party gatherings at the district level. A special channel of interaction is the large system of patronage (shefstvo) between military units and civilian establishments, including party and Komsomol organizations. Initiated in the 1920s to provide short-term economic assistance to the army, the system now has as its purpose "mutual enrichment" through social visits, joint cultural and educational projects, and voluntary work on amenities. Shefstvo on cultural matters is formally supervised by MPA headquarters and by a commission attached to the central committee of the cultural workers' trade union, but most working contacts are on a local basis.

Impressive though these formal ties may seem on paper, the content of behavior is usually very different (at least in peacetime). The operations of the shefstvo system, which are well documented in the press, are illustrative of this disparity between performance and official prescription. The system's quantitative scope is vast—600,000 projects in 1969 alone—but political officers are frequently berated for "not assign[ing] it sufficiently serious significance."[72] Virtually every discussion of shefstvo criticizes it for shallowness and perfunctoriness. Participants are reported as valuing it only "from the point of view of narrow departmental interests, . . . naked utilitarianism." Projects are "timed purely for holiday and jubilee dates" and have a "formal, paradelike character" and even "the attributes of amusements." Mutual reserve is said to permeate even festive gatherings, with each side seeing the other only "across the table of the presidium," as one officer put it.[73]

The same point applies to the involvement of local party secretaries in military councils. Merle Fainsod's search of the protocols of the Smolensk party bureau from the interwar period unearthed no evidence that it concerned itself with military affairs except for conscription and planning for wartime mobilization.[74] Nothing suggests any fundamental change since. Quite aside from the questionable coherence and effectiveness of the military councils (see Chapter 3), serious doubts can be raised about the quality of local participation in them in peacetime. Local party executives are bound to be limited by the almost invariable failure of their jurisdictions to correspond to military districts. They are also without administrative support for their ostensible military roles, making it quite likely that, like one Leningrad party secretary in the late 1930s, they will be "unable to find the time needed to work in the military council."[75]

Given these liabilities, local participation in military affairs and in the operations of the military party apparatus seems sporadic at best. In particular, there is no sign of a routinized local role in the sensitive process of personnel selection in either the army command or the MPA. Nothing indicates that any military officer has ever been on the nomenklatura of a local party organ, or that there is systematic local review of cadre changes. Of greater potential significance is informal patronage arising out of personal contact and friendship. Some local party leaders seem to develop such relations with senior officers stationed in their areas (there are a number of indicators of this, including remarks in military memoirs and the order in which civilians sign military obituaries). Probably some local first secretaries are also capable of influencing specific military assignments. Yet this does not appear to be a common occurrence. The only case I have located in the memoirs concerns intercession in favor of a senior aviation officer in 1942 by Andrei A. Zhdanov, the head of the Leningrad party apparatus but also a very important national politician (as Central Committee secretary and full member of the Politburo).[76] Nikita Khrushchev's memoirs describe his familiarity with a number of officers during his service in Moscow and the Ukraine, but he does not claim to have influenced their careers.[77] I have been able to detect no correlation between senior military appointments since the war and the holders of major civilian party offices at the regional or national level.

Much the same image applies to participation by the MPA and military command in local party activity. Fainsod found that the district commander rarely attended sessions of the Smolensk party bureau.[78] Soviet sources have long commented upon imperfect military attendance at local committee sessions as well as the tendency for delegates (including political officers) to "act merely as representatives and shun practical work."[79] The officially sanctioned exchange of information seems to have made little impact on the general pattern. Prewar investigations discovered "no mutual exchange of current information" and that local committees "rarely discuss reports by the political organs."[80] It is a tribute to the stability of this relationship that in the late 1950s, during the last extensive public discussion of it, descriptions were almost identical. Several observers could write of communication only in the future tense, and the head of the MPA characterized contacts as episodic and fleeting. According to another report, "Military representatives have rarely been invited to visit city party activists and representatives of city party committees have rarely been in the military units."[81]

Official disapproval of segregation carried to extremes is genuine, but it has never progressed so far as to call into question the basic model of military and MPA autonomy. Clearly the situation is not seen as intolerable by any of the major actors, and none of the periodic campaigns to "consolidate ties" has seriously attempted to restructure the relationship. The Brezhnev leadership has not even felt it necessary to mount such a campaign, seemingly accepting a pattern they could alter only with great effort and likely undesirable side effects. One factor which undoubtedly would raise the cost would be MPA resistance. To comprehend this concern for boundaries we must now turn to the evolution of the MPA's organizational role.

The Roles of
the Military Party Organs

2

Soviet statements about the tasks of the military party organs are sometimes quite sweeping. It is said, to give one example, that the organs have an "all-round responsibility," that they "can never say, 'This is not our business,' or, 'This does not concern us.' "[1] Yet the political organs' operations are far more ordered than such declarations would suggest. Their roles have been shaped by formal prescription, limited by the capacities of their officials and by informal understandings, and institutionalized by the passage of time.

The party organs have played three definite roles: political insurrection, political control, and military administration. The nature and mix of these have changed over time, and one mission—military administration—has come to predominate. At first subverters of the old Russian Army, then controllers of the leading personnel of the new Red Army, the military party organs have become comanagers of the modern Soviet Army.

Political Insurrection
Bolshevik military organizations before 1917 were dedicated to turning to the party's advantage what Lenin perceived as early as 1902 as a "quickening of the democratic spirit" in the old army.[2] After a decade of stagnation, the party network moved toward this goal in 1916-17 as the armed forces and the old regime disintegrated in war and revolution.

Soviet spokesmen have been inclined to overstate the party's military accomplishments in the insurrectionary period. True, efforts at recruitment (especially of common soldiers and sailors) were impressive, and the party's Military Organization was able to distribute fifteen newspapers and several million pamphlets, organize a rudimentary secretarial service, and dispatch hundreds of agitators. But none of this justifies the subsequent claim by the organization's nominal head, Nikolai I. Podvoiskii, that it was the instrument by which the party "captured the army."[3] The army was in fact so shattered by its own rank and file that in the end virtually nothing remained to capture. The only effective force in the demolition was the essentially anarchic soldiers' committees, and these remained beyond Bolshevik control (except for brief primacy in one army-level committee).[4]

Even in strictly organizational terms the party network was flawed. The editors of its main newspaper quarreled several times with the Central Committee. It exercised only partial authority over military Bolsheviks (jointly with territorial organizations), and its tiny staff essentially merged in October with the Military Revolutionary Committee (MRC) of the Petrograd Soviet, the civilian body which led the decisive rebellion.[5] The party's presence in the army paled before that of its two main socialist rivals, the Social Revolutionaries (SR's) and Mensheviks, whose newspapers reached twenty times as many military readers. The SR's greatly outnumbered the Bolsheviks everywhere except near Petrograd, as was confirmed by their 43.2 percent share of the military vote in the Constituent Assembly elections in November (as compared to the Bolsheviks' 38.3) and their decisive victory on every front but the Western and Northern. Lenin was embellishing the truth when he said that the results showed the army to be "halfway Bolshevik."[6]

One positive legacy of the revolution was the experience of the earliest party commissars, men whose title, inherited from the French Revolution, bore widely recognized connotations of exceptional and far-reaching authority.[7] (It was used by the delegation that arrested the tsar in March 1917 and by members of the Soviet government—people's commissars—until 1946.) Commissars were introduced into the army by the Provisional Government in April 1917, mainly to preclude "wrong steps" by the command but also to supervise relations with civilians and propagandize the troops.[8] The first Bolshevik commissars were appointed by the Petrograd MRC specifically as plenipotentiaries to incite insurrection. In the five days before November 7, about 300 commissars were sent to military units and at least that many to civilian locations in the area of the capital. Many played important parts in the actual seizure of power by distributing weapons, rallying sympathizers, and leading the takeover of government strongholds.[9]

The new Soviet regime sought to universalize this pattern the day after its founding by decreeing that commissars were to operate in all military units in order to "suppress any attempt at counterrevolution" and reorganize the army "on the basis of spontaneity and democratization."[10] The commissars fared well in central agencies, where they supplanted most officials by late November, but they were thwarted elsewhere by soldiers, officers, Provisional Government commissars, and the numerous elected and self-appointed spokesmen for local interests (some of whom called themselves commissars). By the end of 1917 the fronts had various forms of leadership, but the only important difference among them was in the degree to which each was without influence over the men and immune to instructions from the capital.

On balance, the first commissars were far from an unqualified success. According to Podvoiskii, they actually slowed down the progess of the revolution and were much less useful than the regime's informal agents and sympathizers.[11] Ultimately it was not party organization but the disorganized actions of the soldiers and sailors that saved the day. The old army "melted . . . like snow in spring," and the government demobilization decree was mere recognition of this inchoate force.[12] The army was not won for the party, but it was denied to the party's enemies by the party's allies of the moment.

Political Control

Western scholars have readily identified the role with which the party organs in the new Red Army were invested in 1918—political surveillance of a military command whose values and interests were considered alien to the regime. The backdrop was the decision to use as the core of the new command the same officers of the tsarist army whose authority the party had helped undermine only months before. In the two years after the determination was made in March 1918, almost 50,000 former officers—"military specialists" (*voenspetsy*), as they were called—including several hundred generals, were fitted into posts at every level from courier to commander-in-chief. When this painful concession to necessity sparked a vigorous "military opposition" within the party, Lenin was quick to accuse it of amateurism and nostalgia for "underground printing presses [and] discussion circles."[13] Yet there was no denying that many ex-officers had "bourgeois" origins, that few seemed enthusiastic about the party, and that sizable numbers (perhaps 40,000) were to fight for the Whites in the Civil War.[14] Most distressing were the commanders who fled Soviet lines or led their units over to the enemy. During the first major battles of the war in the summer of 1918, desertion claimed almost every officer in the relocated General Staff Academy in Ekaterinburg, many commanders in Ufa, Iaroslavl, and Cheliabinsk, and the head of the entire

Eastern Front (an ultraradical SR who declared "revolutionary war" on Germany before being killed).[15] Other defections followed for at least a year.

Commissars with nebulous duties and lines of accountability had been present in some of the first volunteer units in early 1918, where some even took direct command of the men.[16] The mass induction of the military specialists brought both the creation of a central agency for political officers (the predecessor of the MPA, founded April 6, 1918) and the clear designation of the role of controllers and watchers. "We must assign [the military specialists] work," Lenin declared, "but along with this we must keep vigilant watch over them, putting commissars around them and counteracting their counterrevolutionary plans."[17]

The commissar's basic resource was his right to cosign all military orders. But, as Trotsky emphasized, he was empowered to use whatever means were necessary to prevent treason. The commissar "stands over each military leader, follows his actions, controls his every step . . . If the commissar notices that the military leader is threatening an action that endangers the revolution, he has the right to deal mercilessly with the counterrevolutionary all the way to the point of shooting him."[18] There were perhaps times when commissars exercised this prerogative, although I have been unable to find accounts in the available sources. Coercion could also be applied short of violence. When one officer refused to carry out his duties, his commissar and party committee "had to surround him with a convoy and force him to work."[19] In such circumstances, the political department of the Eastern Front was probably depicting a common pattern in late 1918 when it reported that "our commanders . . . are extremely frightened and humbled by the power of the commissars and military revolutionary councils."[20]

It is tempting to see in the simple picture of the stern revolutionary standing watch over the "humbled" commander an image of enduring applicability. However, this would be misleading in the case of many political officers even during the Civil War. To the extent that the political control role was prescribed, many failed to live up to it fully. Party leaders were soon railing at "commissar-grumblers" and commissars "who have not been the last to leave" besieged posts.[21] Weakness of even a directly ideological nature was visible. One of the two illustrations in the essay on betrayals in the official war history of the 1920s was a joint defection by a commander and his commissar; likewise Trotsky gives a vivid account of a commissar and commander taking over a ship and steaming up the Volga after their regiment was shelled.[22] As early as the autumn of 1918 there were rumblings about politically unreliable students in the first training courses for political officers, and by the end of the year "a significant number of . . . bandits, drunkards, traitors, and so on among the commissars" had been shot.[23]

Yet there is a more telling reason for the inadequacy of the simple image of political control. Whether or not the military party organs played the role of guardian of the military command imperfectly, they were already becoming involved with new tasks. MPA chief Sergei I. Gusev noted shortly after the Civil War how "the work of the commissars soon came to encompass a field incomparably wider than keeping watch over the military specialists," a point that is echoed by modern Soviet historians.[24]

Military Administration

The Civil War saw the inception of a trend that Western analysts have been slow to recognize—what Mikhail Frunze, Trotsky's successor, characterized in 1924 as "the transformation of our commissar staff *from controllers into administrators* and organizers of the Red Army."[25] This does not mean that the military party organs relinquished (or have since then relinquished) their interest in controlling behavior. After all, the word "control" (in its broadest meaning, as modification or limitation of behavior) is often used interchangeably with "administration" or "management" in Western literature on organizations. Any administrator must be concerned with controlling at least some of the members of his organization or organizational subunit. What distinguishes administrative control from political control is that the former is modification of behavior in pursuit of an organization's or enterprise's own ends rather than those of an extraneous organization or cause. The question to pose about the military party organs, then, is not whether they have exercised control over others' behavior but whose behavior they have controlled and to what end. On both dimensions, major change occurred early in the organs' development. The prime target group became enlisted men rather than commanders, and the ends evolved from exclusively political goals to primarily military ones.

Some attention to ordinary soldiers was entailed in the original role of political control of commanders. Even with pistols drawn, commissars could not unilaterally keep officers loyal. The only sure way, as Trotsky attested, was to "direct our attention to the lower strata" and there to "create a base that will render futile . . . attempts at counterrevolution."[26]

But this adjustment of focus was prompted by other considerations as well. One was a relaxation in the urgency attached to surveillance of the command as the Civil War proceeded. Most of the mobilized ex-officers seem to have accepted the new order with genuine grace, a tendency encouraged by the fact that four fifths of them were not former cadre officers at all but men whose only military training came in World War I and who lacked clear ties to the old regime.[27] Most attempts at flight involved highly disorganized units early in the war, often ones cut off from supply lines or surrounded by hostile troops; under these conditions by no means all commissars acquitted themselves more favorably than commanders. The numbers of officers involved were small (Lenin put them in the hundreds), and by 1920 there were barely any tries at defection.[28]

The dependability and expertise of most military specialists assuaged many of their antagonists well before the subdual of the military opposition at the Eighth Party Congress. "Life itself is defeating the opponents of the 'specialists,' " one previous doubter wrote in January 1919. "From the front we are hearing cries of 'Give us specialists!' "[29] Among the early converts were a number of commissars. What is more, the ex-tsarist officers were a fast-declining segment of the command. By the end of 1920 Soviet schools had turned out 40,000 "Red commanders," many of them already members of the party and later to be termed "links in the great Communist organization surrounding the former officers."[30] Men trained before the Revolution made up 75 percent of all commanders at the end of 1918 but only 15.5 percent two years later (albeit disproportionately represented in senior posts). This was the same ratio as Red commanders; the rest were former soldiers and NCO's without formal military education but whose officer careers had been entirely in the Soviet era.[31]

If commanders were becoming less worrisome, the opposite was true of the enlisted men. As the war progressed it became more and more clear that the greatest obstacle to victory was the uncertain commitment and resistance to organization of the mass of conscripted soldiers. By mid-1919 *partizanshchina*—"the partisan spirit," most often used to mean refusal by the rank and file and junior officers to accept discipline and routine—was being described as the paramount military problem. To Lenin it was responsible for "immeasurably more calamities . . . than all the betrayals of the military specialists."[32] Its most vivid manifestation was large-scale desertion. In 1919 and 1920, 200,000 soldiers fled front-line units and 2.8 million refused to report for duty—this in a total force of only 5.5 million.[33] It was peasant conscripts, appalled by the war and eager to return to the land, who formed the mass of the deserters, and it was they who, according to the official war history, came to be "the main concern of the work of the political organs."[34] There was little choice in the mat-

ter. If political officers had concerned themselves entirely with scruti-
nizing commanders, there would soon have been no one left to command.

Thus by as early as May 1918 one finds the head of the political
apparatus, Konstantin K. Iurenev, insisting that commissars be *the
unifying link between the generals and the masses,* as well as the
guardians of the military leaders."[35] Official pronouncements at this
time begin to stress the necessity for cooperation with commanders in
the name of mobilizing the rank and file for victory. Commissars were
required to "ensure the immediate and unconditional execution of
commanders' operational and combat directives." They were to "inculcate in soldiers . . . the necessity for revolutionary order and
discipline."[36] By the end of the Civil War a national conference of
political officers could describe their work as "part and parcel of the
command and administration of the forces."[37]

Such duties were especially pressing in units commanded by military
specialists, but they were assumed to some extent virtually everywhere. They were, in fact, voluminous even in cases where commissars with control powers had been removed, as happened in a number
of units commanded by party members as early as 1919. In these instances it was found that assistants for political affairs had to be
appointed because commanders were "not physically capable" of
combining political duties with their own.[38]

A vital concomitant of the administrative role was the appearance
of clear commonalities of interest between political and command officers. This kind of affinity was to surface in the administrative politics of the military establishment to the point that in May 1919
Trotsky, wearied by prolonged bickering with a group of commanders
and commissars on the Eastern Front, complained to Lenin: "These
front-line attachments (*frontovye priviazannosti*) are our general misfortune."[39] They were to be a recurrent feature of military politics ever
after.

A more general convergence of interest was evident as against the
common soldiers, in whose eyes the commissars increasingly were
seen as instruments of higher authority who were no less exacting than
the commanders. Trotsky remarked in 1919 that in units where soldiers engaged in "inane mockery" of the military specialists, "relations
with the Communist commissars, with these political 'specialists,' are
no less hostile than with the military specialists."[40] An equally direct
correlation was drawn by the leaders of the Kronstadt rebellion of
March 1921, the last gasp of rank-and-file anarchism. Considering
political officers the incarnation of the hated "commissar state"
(*komissaroderzhavie*), they put dismantlement of the MPA among

their leading demands. One of the sailors' first acts was to arrest the commissar of the Baltic Fleet, Nikolai N. Kuz'min, who was later put on display at meetings and derided as a pampered "general" for the other side.[41] In an ironic testimony to change, this rebellion against commissars was put down by a Soviet force commanded by four former tsarist officers.

Changing Roles: Political Control and Military Administration

There is little controversy about the eclipse of the insurrectionary role, but the same cannot be said about the military party organs' development from controllers into administrators. Western research remains grounded on the supposition that the shift in roles has not taken place at all. Yet evidence from the Civil War suggests that even at the outset the administrative role coexisted with the control mission and that the forces moving this role into primacy were well under way. For most subsequent periods military administration has clearly outweighed political monitoring as an element in the party organs' behavior. The military party apparatus has lacked the attributes expected of an effective control organization (see the discussion in Chapter 4). Its officially assigned role and standards of success also point to administration rather than political control.

Assigned Role. The regime has explicitly substituted military administration for external political surveillance of the command hierarchy as the principal purpose of the military party organs. Although it is difficult to accept some Soviet claims that this came about by prior design, it should be clearly understood that the choice was in fact made.

Even during the Civil War, some were beginning to predict the displacement of the monitoring function: "The growth of Red officers from the proletariat . . . will render superfluous any special political guardianship over the army in the person of the commissars." Such forecasts took pains to observe that this shift "would not bear upon the necessity of . . . political work," which actually would gain in importance.[42]

This prediction materialized in the mid-1920s with the introduction of one-man command and the replacement of most commissars by political deputies and assistants, without the right to cosign military orders. Official spokesmen were categorical in stating that "the role of guardian and 'nursemaid' . . . is now retreating into the past," and that such a role "has become, . . . to put it frankly, unnecesary." The commissar as watchdog was now to yield to what Frunze depicted as the commander's "collaborator, fellow worker, and [fellow] organizer," whose efforts would be concentrated on "political work as such . . . work at the political and military preparation of the Red Army."[43]

Some political officers disagreed with this policy—although their main objection was not to the principle of freeing commanders from routine surveillance but to the practical possibility that commissars would "soon join the ranks of the unemployed."[44] But the emergence of the administrative role had already made such a prospect quite remote, as defenders of the new policy pointed out in acid tones:

To argue that political work "is coming to naught" now that one-man command is being introduced is to misinterpret not only the meaning of political work but the very spirit of our military development. The shortsightedness of comrades who think this way can be explained only by their subjective and abnormal understanding of commissars, the senior political workers, as above all political "controllers." [This] has prevented them from seeing the fundamental and growing significance of the commissars as leaders of political work. And the leadership of political work is far more important than political control. It is precisely one-man command in its developed form which will fully confirm the role of political work. It is precisely one-man command which will lead to a full coordination of political work with all other dimensions of the structure and leadership of the Red Army, will allow the saturation of every side of it (organization, administration, and tactics) with political work.[45]

In 1929 the administrative role was recorded in the army's first field regulations, which stated succinctly: "The basic task of political work in the Red Army is the attainment and consolidation of the Red Army's readiness to do battle."[46] By this time the theoretical basis for full integration of political work with overall military administration was also well developed. A seminal book by Fridrikh L. Blumental', an instructor at the MPA's main training establishment, the Tolmachev Military-Political Academy (later the Lenin Academy), was the most explicit. "It is incorrect," he declared, "to say that the political organs have some sort of 'independent' tasks, separate from military ones." Their distinctive methods and concerns "can in no way mean that the political organs have the right to cut themselves off from routine operational tasks, which [they] are obligated to facilitate and serve . . . and to put at the head of all their work."[47] Similar conclusions were reached in the basic interwar text on strategy, by the deputy chief of the Red Army Staff (and a former tsarist officer), Vladimir K. Triandafillov. Since future warfare would make far heavier demands of troops than before, he saw that "political steadfastness and moral attitudes" would be central to victory. Political work was indispensable, and its main purpose was inculcation of the will to victory—seeing to it that "whatever the difficulties, the army knows what it is fighting for."[48]

Official pronouncements about the military party organs' explicit goals over the last several decades have not differed in any important way from the declarations of the 1920s (except perhaps in the turgidness of style). Such pronouncements invariably refer to the organs as being implementers or conductors (*provodniki*) of party policy in a general sense, but statements of this sort are just as commonly made about the command hierarchy and indeed are frequently uttered with reference to virtually every administrative organization in the Soviet Union. When declarations of the political organs' objectives indicate *how* they are to pursue the party's overall goals, they do so by emphasizing the organs' contribution to the effective functioning of the army as a military organization and insist that the organs should be judged essentially by the degree of that contribution: "Raising the combat readiness of the forces is the main goal of party work." "Questions relating to the attainment of the forces' constant and reliable military preparedness have been, are, and will remain the chief and vital ones in all our party-political work."[49]

The primacy of the administrative role makes some of the structural characteristics of the military party organs more understandable. The granting to the MPA of administrative rights makes good sense if it is intimately involved in military management. The same can be said of its close structural integration with the military command and, with equal emphasis, of the weak integration with most civilian party agencies.

The proposition that military administration rather than external surveillance of the officer corps has been the political organs' principal goal needs to be qualified in several ways. A major reservation should be recorded about a particular period—1937 to 1942—during which the MPA's appointed role was far less clear than at any other time. The reintroduction of commissars with full cosigning powers in 1937 and again in 1941 gave political officers the access to commanders' routine actions which had been considered necessary to exercising the role of external political control until the mid-1920s. On both occasions Soviet leaders undoubtedly chose to give the party organs the opportunity to intervene more directly in military decision making. Nor is there any doubt that this was somehow related to the acute crises—the Great Purge and the war—into which the regime and the army were moving. But beyond this we can say very little about motivation. Neither the 1937 nor the 1941 decree resurrected monitoring of commanders as an explicit organizational goal (indeed, retrospective Soviet analyses insist that a control function such as existed during the Civil War was entirely excluded under the new arrangements).[50] And at neither time did the regime's actions indicate that it saw the political organs as a more dependable instrument than the military command. Within days of the 1937 decree the MPA itself was assaulted by the purge, and the section of the 1941 order instructing commissars to signal about officers "unworthy of the name" said expressly that both commanders and political officers were to be attended to in such fashion. Nonetheless, whatever the complexities, generalizations about the political organs' prescribed role in the half decade ending with the final adoption of unitary command in 1942 must be made with great care.

One should also be cautioned against imagining that the Soviet leadership has at any time decided that it is undesirable or unnecessary for military officers to be politically loyal. The renunciation of surveillance of the command hierarchy as the central objective of the military party organs meant that party leaders now judged that basic loyalty was already assured and that military officers' individual decisions no longer had to be—or no longer could be—scrutinized by party plenipotentiaries in terms of their implications for political stability.[51] The military party organs do continue to make one deliberate contribution to political stability—through their large program of political education of both officers and enlisted men. This effort is well integrated with military training and often receives rather low priority from the MPA (especially as it affects officers). Yet it does have distinctive features and warrants separate analysis (see Chapter 3).

A final qualification has to do with the chances that the publicly prescribed role is not important—either because it does not embody the regime's actual intentions or because it is not reflected in the military party organs' actual behavior. Perhaps the leadership has all along wanted political officers to act as guardians of commanders and has for some reason disguised this aim. Or perhaps the MPA pays lip service to the administrative role but actually functions as an apparatus of political control and manipulation. Obviously this possibility cannot be disproved without looking in depth at the behavior of the party organs. But a preliminary question can be posed about the criteria that would be used to evaluate the success of efforts directed at maximizing political control.

Standards of Success. The problem of devising standards for measuring progress toward stated goals is inherent in all large organizations, particularly public agencies. As Herbert Simon has argued, the

overall goals public organizations seek to realize rarely "provide sufficiently concrete criteria to be applied to specific decisional problems."[52] This point pertains especially well to the MPA's original
mission of external political control, the role most scholars have
assumed it continues to play. It is natural to ask—how would the military party organs judge that political control of officials was being
achieved? By what standard would they judge a person's beliefs or
actions to be consistent with the value of political control?

In the *revolutionary politics* of 1917 and the first months of the
regime, success standards were reasonably plain. Success could initially be construed as interference with the operations of the old army,
then as keeping units of the new army from being used for counterrevolutionary ends. In both cases "political" questions involved
fundamental choices about values that implied actions (supporting or
opposing the Bolsheviks) that were highly visible and easily distin-
guishable from one another. The military party organs were strug-
gling to implant a new political order in hostile soil, and the line between friends and enemies was tolerably easy to draw.

In the *factional politics* that intruded briefly upon party life in the
military in the 1920s (and not examined in detail in this book), there
were also fairly evident yardsticks for gauging political control. Success could be equated with adoption of resolutions condemning opposition factions within the party leadership, denial of elective and
appointed office to opposition sympathizers, and ultimately disgrace
and elimination of these men altogether. Thus when MPA chief Vladimir A. Antonov-Ovseenko (in his famous Circular no. 200 of December 24, 1923) authorized free discussion of Trotsky's platform,
he was promptly removed on instruction of the Politburo in favor of
Bubnov, by then an adherent of the majority Stalin faction. Communists supporting Trotsky (particularly in Moscow and Kiev) were
censured. The MPA itself was "purged of Trotskyites and a check was
made of staff and school cells where they had attempted to hide."[53]
The MPA's Tolmachev Academy was torn by "a number of battles
and misunderstandings" during which almost two thirds of its students were expelled.[54]

A similar but less protracted conflict attended the campaign against
the united anti-Stalin opposition in 1926-27 (composed of supporters
of Trotsky and Zinoviev); most of the opposition's few military supporters were found in Leningrad. The last of the intraparty oppositions, the so-called "right deviation" led by Bukharin, does not seem
to have attracted significant military or MPA support, and in December 1928 a Central Committee resolution could properly refer to the
army's steadiness on programmatic questions.[55] Throughout these
several years clear disagreement on grand issues of political objectives

and leadership was quite widespread in the Soviet system as a whole. This made some conflict inevitable, but it also made the evaluation of the military party organs' performance a manageable task for MPA officials and the civilian party leadership alike.

A decade after the end of open debate over ideological issues by groups committed to leadership factions, the army was subjected like most of Soviet society to the *terroristic politics* of the Great Purge. This was factional politics without mercy—and without factions. The mechanisms of earlier struggles were now harnessed to the violent exegesis of Stalin's power, with little or no reference to the actual political convictions of the victims. The military party organs were to suffer as much as the command hierarchy from the violence and from the absence of intelligible criteria for political acceptability. Political control and uniformity may have been an implied goal of every Soviet organization in 1937 or 1938, but there were virtually no standards for judging behavior in light of that goal.

For most of Soviet history (including much of Stalin's lifetime), military politics has been essentially *bureaucratic politics*—a process quite unlike the revolutionary, factional, and terroristic variants. It has had much in common with bureaucratic politics elsewhere. The major participants are appointed administrative officials. There is general acceptance of the basic values of the political system's leaders, and those who do not share these beliefs have little opportunity to make their preferences known. Most conflicts concern how to perform or evaluate highly specialized and routinized tasks, integrate the contributions of individuals in the interest of some larger organizational purpose, or allocate resources among bureaucratic sectors or subunits.

In such a context, standards for judging that the value of political control has been satisfied in any particular decision are far from self-evident. This is not to deny that the military party organs take political considerations into account in making decisions. If one defines a political act in Harold Lasswell's broad terms as one "performed in power perspectives" and involving "control over others on the basis of lesser or greater sanctions," then surely many MPA actions are political to some extent.[56] Indeed, this statement can be made with equal accuracy for the command hierarchy. All officers exercise power (involving quite drastic sanctions) over rank-and-file soldiers and subordinate officers. Most officers come into political conflict with other officers over issues of varying moment arising from their official duties. And all are subject to the political authority of the leaders of the Soviet state and party. The key question about the military party organs is not whether they make decisions on a political basis but whether they possess a clear rule or standard for making such decisions which compels or permits them to decide in agreement with the preferences of party leaders. To this second question the answer should be a tentative no.

The original targets of MPA surveillance and control, the military specialists from the old army, have long since given way to commanders whose exposure and commitment to the regime are not essentially different from those of full-time party officials themselves. Even the military specialists had lost much of their tainted status by the mid-1920s, when Kliment Voroshilov, the head of the army and a one-time member of the military opposition, could see "virtually no difference" between them and other officers.[57] The ranks of the former cadre officers were greatly thinned by the retirement of all commanders older than forty-four in late 1921. By 1930 ex-tsarist officers (most of them with only World War I experience) comprised only 10.6 percent of officer personnel (6.7 percent at company and battalion levels), and a majority were members of the party.[58] Many of those who remained served with distinction at the highest levels until well after World War II—among them seventeen marshals or equivalents, one War Minister (Aleksandr M. Vasilevskii), seven post-Civil War chiefs of the General Staff, and seven full or candidate members of the party Central Committee.[59]

Another standard for gauging political commitment and control might be membership in the party. The restriction of membership to a minority of commanders might indicate that party officials felt confident that military officers could and should be sharply distinguished from one another in terms of their attachment to party values, and that the right to participate in the affairs of the ruling party could be conferred or withheld on the basis of an individual officer's actions. Yet this distinction, too, has been drained of most of its discriminatory power. As Table 6 shows, the tiny Communist minority among officers grew quickly into a sizable majority. By the mid-1930s the proportion of party and Komsomol members was more than two thirds, and since 1945 it has hovered around 90 percent.

Such aggregate figures actually understate the party's saturation of senior echelons. In 1933 some 67.8 percent of officers were Communists, but among them were the commanders of all military districts, 93 to 95 percent of divisions, and 88 percent of regiments.[60] A similar gradation occurs, at a higher absolute level, in the modern army. The 75 percent who are now party members includes virtually all officers with ranks of major or higher and apparently most commanders down to the company level.[61] A compilation of biographies of men who have reached the rank of marshal or equivalent shows that every single one has been a member of the party. At the next rank grades, of the more than one thousand generals and colonels

Table 6. Party and Komsomol membership among military officers (by percent)

Date[a]	Party members and candidates	Komsomol members	Total party and Komsomol
1920	10.5	-	-
1921	20.0	0.0	20.0
1922	22.5	-	-
1923	29.5	-	-
1924	31.8	-	-
April 1925	-	-	49.8
1927	54.0	-	-
January 1930	52.5	4.1	56.6
July 1933	67.8	4.0	71.8
1936	64.7	5.9	70.6
July 1940	54.6	22.1	77.7
January 1941	-	-	79.9
October 1952	-	-	86.4
February 1958	-	-	86
October 1961	-	-	90
March 1966	-	-	93
March 1972	71	17	88
February 1974	75	15	90
June 1976	-	-	about 90
October 1977	-	-	over 90

Sources: K. E. Voroshilov, *Stat'i i rechi* (Moscow, Partizdat, 1937), pp. 153, 230, 445; N. M. Kiriaev et al., *KPSS i stroitel'stvo Sovetskikh Vooruzhennykh Sil* (Moscow, Voenizdat, 1967), pp. 147, 199; *Istoriia Velikoi Otechestvennoi voiny 1941-1945*, 6 vols. (Moscow, Voenizdat, 1960-65), I, 464; S. S. Lototskii et al., *Armiia Sovetskaia* (Moscow, Voenizdat, 1969), p. 149; *Pravda*, October 10, 1952, p. 5, and February 23, 1958, p. 3; *XXII s"ezd Kommunisticheskoi Partii Sovetskogo Soiuza: Stenograficheskii otchet*, 3 vols. (Moscow, Gospolitizdat, 1962), II, 119; *XXIII s"ezd Kommunisticheskoi Partii Sovetskogo Soiuza: Stenograficheskii otchet*, 2 vols. (Moscow, Politizdat, 1966), I, 415; *Krasnaia zvezda*, March 24, 1972, p. 1; June 3, 1976, p. 2; October 27, 1977, p. 2; *Kommunist vooruzhennykh sil*, 1974, no. 4, p. 73.

a. Post-1945 figures are inclusive of political officers.

(and equivalents) whose deaths were announced between 1956 and 1975 an overwhelming 96.2 percent can be positively identified as party members; omissions in the biographical data may mean that the actual percentage is even higher.

Table 7 provides useful information on the distribution of party

Table 7. Incidence of party membership among generals, colonels, and equivalents (by percent)

Category	N	All periods	1918 and 1919	1920 to 1924	1925 to 1929	1930 to 1934	1935 to 1939	1940 and later
				Period when officer joined military				
All officers	1,062	96.2* (N=1,062) (Sig=13%)	95.0 (N=519)	98.4 (N=128)	98.8 (N=81)	97.0 (N=101)	98.7 (N=79)	98.7 (N=75)
Career specialization								
Troop command	644	99.4*	99.1*	100.0*	100.0*	100.0*	97.4	100.0*
Engineering	215	98.6*	97.2*	100.0*	100.0*	100.0*	100.0	100.0*
Academic	93	77.4*	72.9*	80.0*	80.0*	70.0*	100.0	100.0*
Logistics	59	96.6*	97.6*	100.0*	100.0*	100.0*	100.0	100.0*
Medicine	35	71.4*	58.8*	50.0*	100.0*	100.0*	100.0	66.7*
Procuracy	16	100.0*	100.0*	-	-	100.0*	100.0	100.0*
		(N=1,062) (Sig=0%)	(N=519) (Sig=0%)	(N=128) (Sig=0%)	(N=81) (Sig=0%)	(N=101) (Sig=0%)	(N=79)	(N=75) (Sig=0%)

Age at joining military

Under 20	280	98.9*	97.7*	100.0*	100.0	100.0*	100.0	100.0
20-24	326	98.2*	97.8*	96.0*	100.0	100.0*	95.8	100.0
25-29	90	96.7*	95.6*	100.0*	100.0	92.9*	100.0	100.0
30 and over	48	72.9*	55.0*	50.0*	100.0	71.4*	100.0	91.7
		(N=744)	(N=376)	(N=95)	(N=60)	(N=85)	(N=64)	(N=63)
		(Sig=0%)	(Sig=0%)	(Sig=0%)		(Sig=0%)		

Highest rank reached (ground forces terminology)

Colonel-general	116	99.1*	98.6*	100.0	100.0*	100.0	100.0	–
Lieutenant-general	379	96.3*	95.4*	98.1	100.0*	100.0	100.0	90.0*
Major-general	476	96.4*	94.2*	98.0	100.0*	96.7	100.0	100.0*
Colonel	91	91.2*	85.0*	100.0	75.0*	88.9	95.0	100.0*
		(N=1,062)	(N=519)	(N=128)	(N=81)	(N=101)	(N=79)	(N=75)
		(Sig=3%)	(Sig=0%)		(Sig=0%)			(Sig=3%)

Social origin[a]

Worker	217	99.1*	98.9	100.0*	100.0	97.4	100.0	100.0
Peasant	224	98.2*	86.8	100.0*	100.0	100.0	100.0	100.0
Employee or other	51	96.1*	96.6	85.7*	100.0	95.5	100.0	100.0
Unknown	216	95.8*	94.1	97.1*	100.0	100.0	94.7	100.0
		(N=708)	(N=344)	(N=96)	(N=55)	(N=75)	(N=60)	(N=59)
		(Sig=12%)		(Sig=9%)				

Table 7.

Category	N	All periods	1918 and 1919	1920 to 1924	1925 to 1929	1930 to 1934	1935 to 1939	1940 and later
				Period when officer joined military				
Branch of service[b]								
Ground forces	790	95.6*	94.8	97.7	97.4	95.1	98.4	98.4
Navy	68	95.6*	88.2	100.0	100.0	100.0	100.0	100.0
Air and rocket	204	99.0*	97.3	100.0	100.0	100.0	100.0	100.0
		(N=1,062) (Sig=7%)	(N=519)	(N=128)	(N=81)	(N=101)	(N=79)	(N=75)

Sources: Calculated from obituaries printed in *Krasnaia zvezda* from 1956 to 1975 of generals (ranked to colonel-general), colonels, and their equivalents. Chi-square was obtained for all subpopulations. Subpopulations marked with asterisk (*) are ones for which probability of obtained chi-square occurring with random distribution is less than 15 percent. Probability of randomness is noted under subpopulations in parentheses (Sig=).

a. Officers for whom no information on date of birth was available were not used in breakdown by social origin.

b. Air and rocket officers include artillery specialists.

membership among the generals and colonels. The first column shows how frequency of membership varies according to time of military recruitment, career specialization, age at entering military service, eventual rank, social origin, and branch of service. However, when the sample is broken down by period of military recruitment, much of the systematic variation either disappears or diminishes greatly over time. When one controls for time of recruitment, variation by branch of service is not statistically significant, social origin is a significant predictor for only those officers recruited in 1920-24, and eventual rank is significant for only the 1918-19 and 1920-24 cohorts. Age of military recruitment is inversely related to party membership until the mid-1930s, clearly because older men were more likely to have been cadre officers before 1917. And career specialty is strongly related to party membership in most periods, with troop commanders almost sure to join the party and men not in charge of combat soldiers less apt to do so (particularly medical officers and academic personnel, who were also more frequent carry-overs from the old army).

These figures surely demonstrate that the party and the military party organs have been successful in insisting that most officers—and men in basic command posts almost without exception—make a public display of overall faith in the Soviet system by joining the party. But the low level of selectivity also indicates that belonging to the party has ceased to function as a political standard in the sense in which it did at an earlier time. If the party has been open to virtually every successful military professional (with certain exceptions), then Jerry Hough's observation about industrial managers applies equally well to the military: "A demand that a Soviet administrator be a member of the Communist Party is 'political' in much the same sense as the demand that the American administrator swear that he is *not* a member of the Communist Party. In both cases the basic question is one of loyalty to the system as a whole, and in both cases that loyalty —and the formal demonstrations of it—usually comes to be taken for granted as the stability of the political system itself is no longer seriously challenged."[62] Such a broadly conceived demand is hardly likely to provide Simon's concrete criteria for specific decisions.

Certainly the meaning of party membership—and consequently the ability of the military party organs to make political decisions on a distinctive basis—would be very different if joining the party, or entering it early in one's career, gave an officer a decisive professional advantage. Western scholars seem to take such an advantage for granted when they write that one of the MPA's key functions is "to regulate the advancement of officers so that only those politically desirable are promoted" (without offering concrete evidence of how this function is performed).[63] All major appointments in the Soviet military are undoubtedly political in the broadest sense, and one can easily demonstrate that the military party organs participate in making decisions about career advancement and promotion. But does this necessarily mean that they bring to the process radically different criteria for decision, or a clear standard for judging political desirability? While more detailed discussion of the MPA's role in personnel selection must wait until Chapter 5, it should be noted at this point that aggregate data about career patterns suggest that the analyst should be skeptical about the military party organs' possession of distinctive standards for making such choices.

In fact, Table 7 points to no evident relationship for most periods between eventual rank (which can be taken as an index of professional success) and the probability of an officer's being a party member (presumably a good indicator of political merit as the party organs would define it). Similar lack of correspondence occurs if the rank of party members is matched with the time elapsing between army recruitment and entry into the party.

To be sure, Table 7 does indicate a positive association between the likelihood of party membership and ultimate career success for those generals and colonels who entered military service in 1918-19 and 1925-29. Setting aside the 1925-29 group (where only the small number of colonels accounts for the variation), it is possible to time in detail the entry into the party of the members of the large generation of 1918-19 (a cohort which dominated the high command until the 1960s). Such an exercise is quite revealing. As Table 8 shows, commanders who eventually reached the two highest ranks (colonel-general and lieutenant-general) were slightly less likely to have joined the party at an early date than those whose careers were less successful (the major-generals and colonels). Party membership among the more successful officers overtakes that among the less successful only between the sixth and tenth years of military service, then falls behind again slightly until the middle of the third decade (which coincides for this cohort with the middle of World War II). Judging from these data, it seems much more plausible to say that career advancement qualified a man for party membership—even early in the Soviet period—than that party membership guaranteed career advancement.

The meaning of party membership would also be different if the decision to apply were a personal choice among alternative values. In the early years, entering the party was such an undertaking for many military men (as it was throughout the Soviet system). It was not unheard of for important officers recruited in the Civil War still to be outside the party two decades later (as occurred with nine men of

Table 8. Incidence of party membership among generals, colonels, and
equivalents specializing in command work and recruited in 1918-19
(by percent)

Years of military service	Highest rank achieved (ground forces terminology)	
	Colonel-general or lieutenant-general (N=191)[a]	Major-general or colonel (N=106)[b]
0	23.0	29.2
5	61.8	65.1
10	81.2	78.3
15	84.8	89.6
20	88.5	92.5
25	99.5	98.1

Source: Constructed from obituaries in *Krasnaia zvezda*, 1956-75. Column
1 omits 26 officers for whom date of joining party could not be ascertained;
column 2 omits 15.
  a. Average age at joining party 26.6.
  b. Average age at joining party 26.3.

eventual marshal's rank), whereas others had joined the party well
before the revolution.[64] But this diversity has dwindled greatly. Party
membership has become a predictable mark on an aspiring officer's
record rather than an individual and variable decision. Table 9 displays this clearly. The mean lag of party recruitment behind military recruitment has diminished markedly (although the figure for
post-1939 officers is probably deflated by one or two years by the
overrepresentation of wartime recruits, who amount to fifteen of
seventeen men in this group). Of more significance is that the variability of that time lag has contracted sharply, as is evident from the
decreasing standard deviations in the fourth column. While conclusive
statistics are lacking, there is nothing to suggest that this decline in
variability has been reversed in recent years. Most officers (particularly troop commanders) now seem to join the party in predictable
fashion within several years of the midpoint of the first decade of their
careers, often shortly before or after graduation from military school
(presumably the juncture at which professional prospects are becoming clear). Of a thousand lieutenants studied by military sociologists
in 1969 (most aged twenty-two to twenty-six), 59.4 percent were
already party members, 6.8 percent were party candidates, and 28.8
percent belonged to the Komsomol. Only 5.0 percent were not in

Table 9. Timing of entry into party among generals, colonels, and equivalents specializing in command work

Period when officer joined military	Average age		Time lag	
	Joined military	Joined party	Average	Standard deviation
All periods	20.5	25.9	5.3	6.6
1918-19	20.9	26.5	5.4	7.4
1920-24	18.5	25.6	6.7	6.6
1925-29	20.2	25.7	5.4	5.0
1930-34	20.8	24.6	3.9	4.5
1935-39	21.3	25.2	3.1	3.5
1940 and later	19.7	23.3	3.4	2.1
	(N=459)	(N=395)	(N=520)	(N=520)

Source: Constructed from obituaries in *Krasnaia zvezda*, 1956-75. It will be noted that more observations were available for calculating columns 3 and 4 than for columns 1 and 2 (which require a date of birth). Thus column 3 is not exactly equal to column 2 minus column 1. Of the 17 officers who joined the military in 1940 or later, 15 did so between 1940 and 1944. For these 15, average time lag before party recruitment is 3.1 years (standard deviation 2.0). For the 2 officers who joined the military later, average time lag before party admission is 5.5 years.

either organization.[65] (That this 5 percent is half the proportion of the entire officer corps which is outside the party and Komsomol—see Table 6—suggests that many officers in this category are either students or civilian specialists called up from the reserve for temporary service.)

The impression of routine-bound party admission is strongly reinforced by the frequent Soviet acknowledgment of entry standards for officers that are lenient to the point of indifference. There are persistent reports of "efforts to bring into the party every officer without exception" and "to draw into the party every platoon and company commander, every engineer, technician, and other specialist regardless of their political preparation, consciousness, or wish to be active party fighters." A typical account of haste in admissions describes how an officer "has only to write an application and immediately the party bureau convenes. Within a day or two there is a party meeting and immediately after this a party commission session. All in all three days pass and the applicant has his party card."[66]

How, then, do the political organs draw the line between friends and enemies? Whence do they derive standards for appraising a man and his performance? There are no alien specialists from an earlier regime to ring with guards. There are no opposition factions proclaiming heterodox programs. Everyone who matters is a party member by matter of course.

The official Soviet answer—which must be measured against reality in subsequent discussion—is that standards of success are derived essentially from the success criteria of the army itself. These criteria apply to the concrete activity of the organization in which the MPA is imbedded, not to ideological questions or issues of ultimate political loyalty. They are accepted as bearing upon an objective (maintaining Soviet security) that the regime has repeatedly declared to be vital to its survival. A recent Soviet text draws the connection clearly: "The basic criterion in evaluating the effectiveness of all measures undertaken by the political apparatus is the state of the combat efficiency and battle readiness of the unit or subunit."[67] Party work is evaluated essentially by the extent to which it contributes to the success of the military establishment in which it occurs.

The success criteria of the army are not without their ambiguities. There is no simple formula for combat efficiency or battle readiness, particularly in peacetime when the all-important test of arms is anticipated rather than experienced. There is room for personal and principled disagreements about means of proceeding toward military effectiveness and ways of judging that it has been attained. Yet there is little about the military party apparatus's role and composition that makes it likely that such disagreements will find its officials consistently on one side and military commanders consistently on the other. The "general and common line of work of commanders, staffs, and political organs" that one MPA official described in 1967 implies common dilemmas and, often, similar and interrelated responses.[68]

The Military Party Organs
in Military Administration

3

Having identified military administration as the political organs principal role, one might now ask what this role entails. What part do political officers actually play in making military decisions? How do they carry out their tasks, and how do these relate to the work of other officials? How effective has their performance been?

One-Man Command and the Division of Labor

Soviet spokesmen discuss administrative authority in the army, and thus the relationship between commanders' and political officers' powers, in two substantially different senses. One one level, the discussion concerns overall responsibility (*otvetstvennost'*) for the administrative unit, meaning literally the capacity to answer for the unit's members. Here the distinction is quite sharp between one-man command (edinonachalie), which has been in effect at the division level and below since October 1942 and during several interludes prior to that, and the original commissar system. Under edinonachalie, only the commander, according to the decree in effect since 1942, has "full . . . responsibility for all aspects of the military and political life" of his men.[1] He can overrule all other members of the unit and is entitled to speak on their behalf with external agencies. In contrast, in the commissar pattern this formal responsibility was shared equally by two persons. "The military commissar," to quote a 1937 statement, "answers together with the commander for all spheres of the military, political, and economic life of the unit."[2] It was this global responsibility which was unified with the introduction of edinonachalie in the mid-1920s, then reallotted again on four separate occasions between 1937 and 1942.

Apart from overall responsibility, Soviet theory also discusses the particular function (*funktsiia*) or direct responsibility (*neposredstven-naia otvetstvennost'*) of specific military officers, and normally it treats the distribution of these functions as something quite distinct from the assignment of overall responsibility. Specific functions were not explicitly reallocated in the decrees of 1925 to 1942. For instance, it was stipulated in the 1920s that even under full edinonachalie the political officer would continue to provide "direct leadership and practical attainment" of political work.[3] The same distinction holds in the modern army. The regiment commander, for example, "bears complete responsibility for [all] combat and political preparation," but he also has specific duties (mainly concerning combat training, personnel records, and finances). It is the regiment's deputy com-mander for political affairs (one of five deputy commanders) who "bears direct responsibility for the organization and condition of party-political work."[4] None of the decrees of 1937-42 expressly re-structured this division of labor. Commanders remained charged mainly with combat preparation and leadership, and political officers (whether commissars or deputy or assistant commanders) primarily with political work itself.[5]

There is no reason in theory why the equal sharing of overall re-sponsibility between commander and commissar should be incom-patible with a reasonably clear division of specific functions. In prac-tice such an arrangement was perhaps feasible in the Civil War, when militarily illiterate commissars used their cosigning powers strictly to verify that commanders' orders were not counterrevolutionary. How-ever, this kind of solution did not prove workable after 1937, and for two main reasons.

In the first place, the reinstatement of commissars brought with it the informal anticipation that the division of specific tasks would somehow be affected. The very title connoted extraordinary authority without sharp boundaries, the kind of mandate that had led early commissars to complain of the burden of having to serve as "judge, in-vestigator, agitator, organizer, and dictator."[6] The commissar of 1937 and 1941 was no longer the bearer of a distinctive revolutionary morality, but he did have a set of particular concerns whose status relative to those of the commander was now elevated. Although of-ficial pronouncements never specified how far commissars were to in-trude on the commanders' specialized realm, some degree of instrusion was implied in both the cosigning power and the vehement denuncia-tion of *pompolitstvo* (the habit of thinking like a pompolit or assistant commander for political affairs). The uncertainty virtually guaranteed that "some commissars . . . would substitute for commanders, and sometimes even try to place themselves above the commanders" and that some commanding officers would in turn "react toward their military commissars with prejudice." It may be that these quarrels were rare and that most officers "found the way to normal and businesslike relations,"[7] but this was more in spite of than because of official prescription.

The second factor that confounded the later experiments with commissars was the resistance of many political officers to the changes in behavior demanded by official edict. If uncertainty tempted some commissars to substitute for commanders, it motivated others to revert to the pattern of deference to commanders established after 1925 while paying lip service to the new form—satisfied, as MPA chief Aleksandr I. Zaporozhets put it in 1940, "simply to change masks."[8] Many commissars were said to make no effort to find out the contents of the papers given them to cosign. "Why should the commissar worry about the plans for combat training?" one commissar inquired in 1938. "This is the unit commander's business. The commissar has enough work without it."[9] This halfhearted performance was due in part to the ambiguity of the regime's own intentions, but to the extent that it departed from them it also reflected the subduing effect of precedent. Regardless of their new responsibility on paper, many political officers acted as they had before. "Many commissars are not taking and do not want to take upon themselves their full load of responsibility and continue to play the role of pompolit, passive observers . . . simple appendages to the unit commanders."[10] This makes quite believable one commander's recollection in his memoirs that his relations with his political officer underwent "no special change" in this period.[11]

The commissar, with his indeterminate mandate, was thus the child of uncertainty, the cause of further uncertainty, and the victim of it. Given the expectations that accomplished his reinstatement, a clear definition of specific duties was neither greatly desirable nor practicable. It was the vagueness of task definition that made the commissar system "a brake on the improvement of the administration of the forces" (in the words of the October 1942 decree) once the perception of emergency had passed, and that brought about the arrangement's apparently irrevocable demise.

Under edinonachalie, the assignment of both responsibility and functions has been much clearer than during the commissar era. This is particularly true of overall responsibility, which now is bestowed exclusively upon the commanding officer. His orders are "law for his subordinates,"[12] including his political deputy (zampolit), and political officers are constantly urged to impress this fact upon others.

The commander's statutory superiority is reinforced by a pre-dominance in personal rank. Most zampolits have a military rank one grade lower than their commanders, and some are two grades lower. (Most elected party secretaries are one rank lower still.) The zampolit never outranks the commander, and it is unusual for him even to have identical rank.

Formal lines of subordination and rank are mirrored in more subtle signs. The commander is acknowledged to be the main figure (*glav-naia figura*) in his organizational unit.[13] Invariably he is given the place of honor at formal gatherings. He is always listed first in press and historical accounts, military orders, and government announce-ments. A military unit is often referred to as the unit of the com-mander ("the regiment of Colonel Petrov"), but never as that of the zampolit or party secretary (merely "the regiment where Major Ivanov is zampolit").

The commanding officer clearly has a wide array of prerogatives and powers for asserting his primacy, and most commanders utilize them fully. He is entitled, for instance, to reassign his political deputy to "any sort of administrative or technical task quite unrelated to his duties as zampolit" as the need arises.[14] He is also capable of im-posing his own priorities on his political subordinate's specialized work. One often reads of commanders unilaterally rescheduling po-litical activities or withdrawing soldiers from them for other duties, with full acceptance by political officers. In 1946, for instance, one sees a politotdel instructor routinely reminding political officers to clear lecture plans in advance with the commander, lest "it turns out that he cancels the lectures due to lack of time or for other reasons."[15] In 1961 a submarine zampolit could tell a civilian journalist matter-of-factly that he could observe the sailors watching a political film only "if conditions permit." The film, it turned out, was postponed for two days because the commander declared a training alert, a fact not con-sidered worthy of special comment. The zampolit's broadcasts over the ship's radio system were brief and at the pleasure of the commander: "I cannot use the radio for long. It is needed for command use."[16]

The primary source of the commander's power is of course his formal pre-eminence, granted him by the regime "to make possible the flexible (*gibkoe*) and efficient leadership of the troops under any con-ditions."[17] But he derives a further advantage over the political officer from the near certainty that he will surpass him in technical training and competence (although the political officer, at least in recent years, will not be ignorant in this respect). The commander can also be ex-pected to be senior to his political deputy in age, military service, and even party experience—all this a consequence of the fact that, because the cadre political apparatus has normally not extended to the lowest level of troop organization (platoon, and in many periods even company), the political officer at a particular age is likely to be found at a higher administrative level than a career commander.[18]

The commander's position is also buttressed by two conventions concerning his relations with the voluntary party organization in his unit. First, party organizations in the military (except in construction, manufacturing, commercial, and cultural organizations) have been specifically denied the formal right of checking (pravo kontrolia) of managerial activity which was granted to most civilian party organizations in 1939. Unlike a factory director or collective farm chairman, a military commander cannot be called upon to account for his actions at a party meeting or before the elected party executive in his unit. Although any party member can be criticized, the official actions of the commander are categorically exempt from criticism: "Criticism of the orders and instructions of commanders and chiefs is not permitted at party meetings."[19]

Second, the great majority of commanders who are party members have the right and indeed the duty to direct the work of their party organizations. This right, frequently cited in the press from the early 1940s onward, was incorporated in Central Committee instructions beginning in 1958. In the language of the 1973 instruction, the commander "depends (opiraetsia) upon the party organization and directs (napravliaet) its activity toward the successful carrying out of combat tasks, the implementation of military and political training, and the strengthening of military discipline."[20] Soviet spokesmen are quick to point out that the officer cannot issue commands (komandovat', a word which has overtones of peremptoriness) to the party organization as such. But he possesses specified powers of inducement which he is urged to use. He is to "participate in the entire life of [the party organization] and in the discussion of pressing problems, speak systematically at meetings and committee or bureau sessions, orient (orientorivat') the Communists, and prompt (podskazyvat') them on how best to mobilize the soldiers for the implementation of plans . . . and the consolidation of order and organization."[21]

How, then, does the political officer deal with a commander possessing such a formidable array of powers? Unquestionably his principal resource is that it is he who is charged with routine administration of political work. Since the mid-1920s it has been recognized that the commander need concern himself with only the basic questions in the political field and "cannot . . . be a specialist in all the details" of party work.[22] The specialist is the political officer himself, for whom political work is a full-time concern. His specialty is seen as a legitimate enterprise contributing to overall military goals, and thus Soviet officials see no inconsistency in calling simultaneously for "further strengthening of edinonachalie and the improvement of party-political work."[23]

The division of labor and the political officer's stature as a specialist give him ample powers of persuasion even on quite basic questions touching on his area of competence. He is entitled by military regulations to participate in planning and decision making that affect his duties. The regiment zampolit, for instance, is obliged to take part in working out the regiment's monthly work plan.[24] Most commanders seem to take their zampolits' opinions into account on important questions, and to defer to them on matters of political training just as they normally follow the advice of other specialized deputies and colleagues. Most would probably find, like the naval commander who wrote of his political officer in his memoirs, that it was "useless to argue" with him on specialized subjects: "On such a matter he knew how to insist on his own opinion and convince me that this was exactly how I should act."[25]

Apart from his prerogatives, the political officer normally possesses detailed information about subordinates and their behavior which is of value to the commander in making decisions. The political officer is not the only source of such information, but, because of the networks of communication in the party and Komsomol organizations which converge on him, he is not one whom many commanders can afford to ignore.

The commander's propensity to consult and defer to his political colleague is greatly encouraged by limitations on his time and energy. "The commander, burdened with a great many official tasks and duties, is simply incapable of personal participation in every aspect of political work, in regulating everyone and everything."[26] Indeed, the most common criticism of commanders' approach to political work is not that they interfere excessively in it but that they are too ready to delegate responsibility for it entirely to political officers. "Surely it is no secret that we have commanders who are little interested in the content of political work and who sometimes simply brush it off, [saying] 'I have enough to worry about, party-political work is my zampolit's business.' "[27]

If cooperation breaks down and the commander refuses to defer to his political deputy, the latter is bound to obey the commander's order. Once this is done, however, the political officer has always had the right of appeal to superior officials, including senior political officers (to whom he reports regularly at any rate). The difficulty here is that he cannot count upon automatic support, or even a fair hearing, from above. There is no evidence that senior party organs welcome disputes involving subordinates or that they are disposed to look favorably upon political officers who bring such altercations to their attention. Even during the Civil War their first inclination was to "patch up conflicts by peaceful means,"[28] and this seems still to be the rule. If a conflict persists, it is quite possible that the superior political organ will side with the commander involved, particularly if this officer has been discharging his duties efficiently and can argue that his differences with the political officer came because he was "ardently carrying out his duties."[29]

Thus far the discussion has touched on only the administrative levels of division and below, where one-man command has been in effect for decades. Attention must now be turned to higher levels of operation where military councils, collegial bodies containing both commanders and party officials, have been in charge for all but two brief periods.

Several practices have been stable throughout the military councils' history: collective discussion of all major questions, chairmanship of the council by the commander, and the right of dissidents to appeal to higher authority. (Matters were radically different only between June 1934 and May 1937, when no councils existed, and between January 1947 and July 1950, when councils were consultative [soveshchatel'-nye] organs and political officers were direct deputies of commanders.) During World War II council procedures were fluid, and there seems to have been no formal mechanism for arriving at a decision. Some memoir accounts mention votes being taken, but others describe only discussions or exchanges of views. The main formal constraint on the commander was the requirement that all orders and reports be cosigned by the first (political) member of the council.[30] For most of the time since the war the military councils have had the authority to "decide on all the most important questions" by majority vote. Members disagreeing with a decision "have the right to report their opinions to the Central Committee, government, and Ministry of Defense." Cosignatures on orders and reports are evidently not required.[31]

It is obvious that the military council does not conform to a Weberian standard of plainly drawn spheres of competence and lines of authority. Soviet spokesmen do not even agree on how to define the council. (Most refer to it as a "collegial form of leadership," but some say it merely "helps the district commander avoid mistakes and take the correct decision."[32]) Certainly a personally difficult military council member can be a burden upon any commander, particularly if he has independent political influence with the party leadership (which was the case on some wartime fronts).[33]

However, it is far from obvious that the military council is always, as Western specialists have tended to see it, a "despised control organ and bottleneck in the military chain of command."[34] Most Soviet discussions suggest that the councils usually lack the coherence and sense of purpose to act as a serious encumbrance to a firm commander. Their sessions are said to be irregular, their agendas imprecise, and their decisions diffuse. "The fact is," MPA chief Filipp I. Golikov remonstrated in 1958, "that certain military councils have not worked actively enough and have not met in full session for a long time. Sessions of military councils have often been replaced by broad conferences, and the decisions taken have suffered from lack of concreteness."[35] Despite vague reports of improvement, almost a decade later the head of the political administration of the navy, Admiral Vasilii M. Grishanov, could report on naval military councils in even less flattering terms: "The questions to be discussed at sessions are not always thought out, especially as regards their concreteness. Their agendas are too broad. Preliminary work by responsible officials on the problems that the military councils discuss is often superficial. The decisions taken are often grandiose and abstract. It is hard to understand at first just what they mean."[36]

Within the council, the commander's formal position is distinctly paramount. As chairman of the council, he presides at all meetings. He and his staff draft all orders and plans, which are issued in his name. He is normally the line superior of most other members and could presumably win majority votes on that basis alone. He draws further strength from his informal stature, particularly the acknowledged technical competence and organizational ability which his appointment to such a major post implies. We read in memoirs of wartime front commanders being referred to by subordinates as *khoziain* (boss or master), not a likely term for a man at the mercy of his colleagues.[37] As at lower levels, the commander is afforded symbolic primacy at meetings and in written communications. He is also almost certain to outrank all other members of the council, usually outstripping the cadre political worker by at least one grade. (The political officer normally has the same rank as the first deputy commander and chief of staff.) In April 1978 political officers had ranks equal to commanders in only two of the thirty-three military councils at the district and service levels (in one of which a relatively young officer had recently assumed command). In sixteen cases the commanding officer was one rank higher, and in fifteen instances two ranks higher. In a number of cases since the war the disparity has been three grades, and indeed prior to the late 1950s disparities of three or even four ranks were quite common. On only one brief occasion has the head of the political administration outranked the commander.[38]

Information about wartime decision making indicates that com-

manders have taken full advantage of their formal and informal status
in most military councils. Some accounts show commanders curtly
terminating meetings after being displeased by the course of discussion.[39] One political officer was so frustrated at being "unable to correct the commander" that he was reduced to wandering aimlessly
around front lines until killed by a German shell.[40] A memoir description of one council session presided over in 1942 by the commander of
the Forty-seventh Army (and future Defense Minister), Andrei Grechko, is certainly not a picture of a gathering of equals:

> The military council session began at exactly the designated time
> and continued for an hour and a half. The commander gave the floor
> to the chief of staff, who summed up the situation briefly . . . The
> commander gave the chiefs of the reconnaissance and operations de-
> partments of the staff and the member of the military council for lo-
> gistics a chance to express their opinions. [Evdokim E.] Mal'tsev [the
> first member of the military council] discussed political work in com-
> bat. After reviewing the results of the exchange of opinions, General
> Grechko announced (ob'iavil) the decision . . . "And now, comrades,
> to work," he added. "Every minute is precious."[41]

To be sure, the plurality of decision makers and the option of appeal have made conflict possible. To a degree, this has been encouraged by the regime, which obviously has felt that political officers can
contribute to decisions and that safeguarding their role is worth the
cost of some discord. The possibility of disagreement should also
augment the flow of information upward to superior military agencies
and ultimately to the civilian party leadership itself. War Minister
Vasilevskii acknowledged this consideration in 1950 when he argued
for replacement of zampolits in senior commands by unsubordinated
military council members (who had not been appointed since 1947):
"Practice has shown that the deputies of commanders-in-chief and
commanders, finding themselves in a position subordinate to commanders, . . . have completely ceased to supply information to the
party Central Committee."[42] (Vasilevskii mentioned only the Central
Committee—to which he was to be selected in 1952—but clearly he
was also concerned about the information reaching him as the country's top military official.)

But to say that some disagreements will occur and that superior
agencies will have the opportunity to resolve them is not to say how
superiors will decide. Here evidence indicates that the most likely outcome will be to uphold the commander, not the political officer. In the
most famous dispute within a military council during the Civil War—

involving Stalin as a member of the council of the Southern Front fighting around Tsaritsyn in the autumn of 1918—central party and military leaders decisively supported the commander.[43] The general pattern was the same in World War II, with the irony that Stalin as boss was now upholding the commanders. For instance, when word reached Stalin in 1943 about dissension between the commander of the Sixtieth Army, Ivan D. Cherniakhovskii, and his military council member, Zaporozhets (a former head of the MPA), it was Zaporozhets rather than Cherniakhovskii who was within two days recalled to Moscow and replaced.[44] Testimony to the commander's advantage is the fear of Khrushchev in 1942 (while a political member of the military council of the Stalingrad Front) that "Stalin wouldn't support me" if the commander of an army (a full level below Khrushchev) "went over my head."[45] The misgivings of an ordinary MPA official (Khrushchev was already a member of the Politburo) about challenging the commander in his own military council must have been still greater.

There is unfortunately no direct evidence about appeals to superior authority since the war. But nothing intimates that political officers would have better prospects of success than before. Probably the most widely accepted mark of influence in Soviet politics is membership on the party Central Committee. Even on this intraparty scale, it is the military command rather than the MPA that has dominated since the 1930s (see Table 5). It is only reasonable to infer that on most issues the party leadership would resolve conflicts in favor of the more prestigious group, the commanders. Only two political officers (MPA chiefs Golikov and Epishev) have been full Central Committee members during the last two decades. Since 1966 two others have had candidate status—the chief political officer in the Moscow Military District, Konstantin S. Grushevoi, whose membership probably reflects his long personal ties with General Secretary Leonid Brezhnev; and the head of the political administration of the strategic rocket forces (currently Petr A. Gorchakov), whose addition may well say more about the status of the rocket forces than about the MPA.[46] The 1976 Central Committee, by way of comparison, had nineteen commanders as full members and eight as candidates. Commanders also have higher status than political officers on local party committees.

One should not be misled by the emphasis here on conflict. Certainly the military councils have not been without internal disagreement. Colonel-General Konstantin V. Krainiukov, an MPA chief after the war, was describing a common pattern when he wrote in his memoirs of "heated, businesslike discussions" in the council of the First Ukrainian Front, of which he was a member in 1944-45.[47] But it is also

true that few of the known intracouncil disagreements have pitted
political officers against commanders in any systematic way. It is not
unusual for reports of disputes over wartime operations to show a
political officer supported by one or several command officers, and
even for his judgment to be opposed by other political officers from
his own or another level.[48]

It is also of crucial importance not to overemphasize the frequency
and intensity of conflict within the councils. It is quite safe to say that
they have on the whole been cooperative bodies. Krainiukov is typical
in recounting that his front's council, whatever the occasional disagreements, generally "worked amicably, actively, and cohesively,
[without] contradictions, failures to agree, or chronic frictions." The
forces pushing commanders and political officers toward agreement
and cooperation have far outweighed the forces inducing conflict.

Political Education in the Army

In looking at the specific duties performed by the political organs, it
is natural to begin with the system of political education which they
operate. This effort has always been considered by Soviet theorists to
be vital to the army's efficacy as a fighting organization. For this reason it is planned in conjunction with combat training and its success is
measured (in theory, at least) by military competence. "The effectiveness of ideological work in the army and navy is measured by the
concrete results of military training."[49] Nevertheless, this "link with
life," as it is called, is far from perfect, and much of the program's
content is starkly ideological. Its several components merit separate, if
brief, consideration.

Preparation of Activists. The military party organs have always
been in charge of preparing servicemen willing to be distinguished as
political activists either in or following military service. In times of
crisis, especially in wartime, there have been special campaigns to
train the needed personnel, but for the most part the task has been
entrusted to a permanent network of party study (*partiinaia ucheba*).

The system has had two tiers—a broad one mainly for the rank and
file, with Komsomol as well as party members admitted, and a more
selective one principally for officers and full members of the party. In
1932 the broad layer, of circles of party study, embraced 400,000 servicemen, a third of them not party members; only 6,000, mostly officers, attended the more advanced Communist universities. Since the
war the two forms have been called evening party schools and evening
universities of Marxism-Leninism. Each meets four hours a week for
most of the year, thus representing a substantial commitment of leisure time for students. The previous disparity in size has narrowed,

but the distinction in clientele remains sharp. The evening schools graduated about 70,000 men a year in the 1960s, from one-year courses for enlisted men and NCO's and two-year programs for officers in garrisons without evening universities. The universities still cater mainly to officers (90 percent of their clientele in 1971), particularly those involved in political instruction, discussion groups, and agitation work. They are much larger than before the war (enrollment was 40,000 in 1963, the last year for which a firm figure is available, but it was said in 1973 to have "increased by almost one and a half times in recent years").[50] Over the last decade emphasis in the curriculum has shifted from relatively abstract ideological issues to subjects with more immediate application to political work.[51] Political seminars and circles (*kruzhki*) also operate in some units, apparently with little standardization of curriculum, and the political organs manage a round of political conferences and seminars similar to that found in most Soviet institutions.

Political Work with Civilians and Adversaries. Political education of audiences outside the army—Soviet citizens and the civilians and troops of foreign countries—has been sharply restricted in both time and scope.

Work with Soviet civilians in peacetime has generally been confined either to the ambit of the shefstvo system or to the indirect means of preparing soldiers to assume politically valued tasks after discharge (such as helping to organize collective farms during the First Five-Year Plan, working in the virgin lands in the 1950s, or volunteering for remote construction or resource extraction sites in the 1970s). Other projects—excursions by agitators to factories and farms, participation in campaigns for elections to local soviets, contacts with youth groups —do take place. But the basic principle remains, as in the 1930s, that these "can be carried out only without the slightest detriment to military training."[52]

The political organs have embarked upon large-scale education of external groups only in wartime. During the Civil War the MPA created "revolutionary committees" as the first arm of the regime in liberated areas, requisitioned food and transport, distributed literature at "agitation points" in railroad stations and other places, propagandized foreign prisoners of war, and encouraged White troops to desert.[53] In World War II it printed newspapers in German, Finnish, and Rumanian for prisoners, sent agitators into prison camps, dropped millions of pamphlets behind enemy lines, and helped re-establish Soviet institutions in the wake of the line of advance. In September 1944 the military party organs were given initial responsibility for relations with the local populace in non-Soviet areas, and their duties included "assisting democratic [pro-Soviet] parties," helping form local admin- istrations, and "studying the political attitudes" of the population. Over the next several years the MPA organized political lectures, con- certs, and films and distributed newspapers and literature to millions of inhabitants of Soviet-occupied countries.[54]

Since the war the MPA has operated a relatively inconsequential program to promote friendly relations with the populations of allied countries where Soviet troops are stationed. It has also cooperated with the political organs of Warsaw Pact armies during joint exercises (particularly in propaganda efforts), and it exchanges delegations, lecture groups, and information with them on a regular basis. The MPA's Lenin Academy provides training to political officers from a number of allied countries, like most senior Soviet academies. The MPA is charged as well with briefing and supervising servicemen (usu- ally sailors) who come into extended contact with foreigners in non- allied countries.

Political Education of the Troops. The principal focus of the MPA's political education program has been the rank-and-file servicemen and NCO's, particularly the great majority who do not plan to re-enlist. These temporary soldiers are to be endowed with political attitudes that will both make them better fighters and serve them in good stead in civilian life.

In terms of general socialization goals, the army's attractiveness as a "school of communism" stems from the youth and malleability of its members, their intimate and prolonged contact, and the availability of experienced instructors. So evident was this superiority during the early decades of Soviet rule that the army was often referred to as the country's single most important arena for political education ("the sole . . . point of assembly," Stalin called it, "where people from vari- ous provinces and regions come together, study, and are schooled in political life").[55] Thousands of servicemen, especially from rural areas, received their first exposure to the party's ideas (and often to modern values of any kind) in the interwar Red Army.

The growth of the regime's systems of education, mass communica- tion, and political organization has invalidated this claim to pre-emi- nence, but political training in the military does remain an important thread in the overall network, "continuing the process of Communist education . . . begun in the family, school, and productive process."[56] Because conscripts have already been familiarized with the regime's basic values, the emphasis is now on reinforcing and maintaining the desired attitudes and beliefs. The most potent enemies are perceived as indifference and skepticism rather than outright ignorance of ideology. There is a growing conviction in MPA policy statements—evidently a consequence of foreign policy detente, and a perception not confined to the MPA or the army—that without a deliberate "intensification of our work on the ideological front" such attitudes will worsen and will be played upon by Western psychological warfare to the detriment of both political and military goals.[57]

Recently the positive role of such training, and of the citizenship-building qualities of military service in general, has attracted increasing attention from Soviet leaders. At the Twenty-fifth Party Congress in 1976, Leonid Brezhnev drew the connection clearly: "In speaking about educational work, comrades, it is impossible not to dwell on the enormous role which the Soviet Army plays in this matter. Young men arrive in the soldierly family with no experience in the school of life. But they return from the army already people who have gone through the school of tenacity and discipline, who have acquired technical and professional knowledge and political training."[58]

Although there is a certain amount of rendering necessity into virtue here, program objectives are complex and intertwined. The army is seen as a school of life, inculcating politically desirable attitudes in a general sense, but also as exposing soldiers to specific points of party ideology. What is more, the internalization of civic virtue is seen ultimately as indispensable to *military* success. It has been a central point of Soviet military theory since the Civil War that in the modern world it is moral and political superiority which ultimately determine the outcome of armed conflicts. Since the "revolution in military affairs" accompanying the introduction of nuclear weapons in the 1950s, Soviet theorists have taken the line that the necessity of "moral-political and psychological preparation of personnel" has actually increased. "Our party has always been occupied with these problems . . . but under contemporary conditions their significance has increased immeasureably. This is explained by the features of future war, by the appearance of weapons of massive striking power, by the . . . widespread use of means of psychological influence on the part of the likely enemy."[59]

Of the various instruments for making enlisted men better citizens and better soldiers, by far the most colorful was the agitation train (*agitpoezd*) of the Civil War, which brought party literature and ideas directly to the front lines complete with visual aids, mobile theaters, and even orchestras. Most peacetime forms have been less stirring. Since 1923 every company barracks has had a "Lenin room" for exhibiting political materials and holding meetings. The military press, which is supervised by the MPA, is of course laden with political information and exhortation, and the political organs are also responsible for producing textbooks and other political materials and for distributing and displaying civilian political publications. In recent years there has been a trend toward the use of television, with the junior political officer acting as commentator and adviser.

The basic mode of instruction, however, has since the mid-1920s been the political class (*politicheskoe zaniatie*). These compulsory sessions have taken up a considerable portion of the training week— five hours in most units since 1958 (including an hour of political information on current events), and as many as ten hours a week in the 1930s. Despite recent experiments with seminar methods and invocations to use a "complex approach," the political class is still essentially a lecture delivered from a prepared text. Groups are led by officers, usually platoon commanders, and normally consist of several dozen men. Their aim is to deliver, simply and repetitively, official party doctrines and positions on current policy. Special emphases can be added as needed. These can focus on events of general significance— the hundredth anniversary of Lenin's birth, an upcoming party congress, the 1977 discussion of the draft Soviet constitution—but they also can be related directly to military mission. In 1968, for example, troops about to be assigned to Czechoslovakia were steeled to meet "face to face with every imaginable intrigue by counterrevolutionary forces"; the following year, political classes on ships in the Mediterranean were imparted "great emotional effect" by the proximity of American vessels.[60]

Political classes fall far short of the ideal. They continue to be plagued by organizational problems such as poor scheduling and even irregular attendance.[61] More serious are the inadequacies of substance and spirit that have defied repeated ameliorative campaigns. One reads in the 1930s about "abstractness, schematism, dryness, and bookishness," or of classes characterized by "empty talk full of great discoveries and pat answers."[62] Recent discussions are forced to strike a similar note, in spite of the formal repudiation of the rote learning common under Stalin. "There is still not always a firm struggle for high quality in every political class." Some classes "are carried out on a low level and in divorce from reality," and bored listeners "often lose track of the contents."[63] Clearly the classes' deficiencies are often more grating than in earlier times to increasingly literate servicemen. (Eighty percent of current conscripts have at least ten years of school, as compared to 12 percent in 1941.)[64]

Political Instruction of Officers. The military command has been included in the system of political education, and with many of the same problems. Senior officers attend meetings of party activists two or three times a year, usually following Central Committee plenums, and are briefed on current policy developments. More important for most officers have been the obligatory political meetings during the work week which have been in effect for most of the army's history. These amounted to fifty hours a year when first systematized in 1925 (although "experienced party members" could be exempted) and the total was increased to ninety hours in several stages in the late 1930s. The mandatory program yielded to flexible measures during the war. In 1946 "independent study" under general supervision of the political organs was approved, but the next year the obligatory lectures and seminars were reinstituted, totaling twenty-four to forty hours a year. Independent study was again sanctioned for most commanders in 1953 (see Chapter 8 for the relation to Defense Minister Zhukov's dismissal in 1957), only to be replaced in December 1957 by the program still in effect. This compels all officers except those in several exempt categories to spend fifty hours a year (about a fifth of the total expected for soldiers) in "groups of Marxist-Leninist preparation."[65] The exempted, including officers involved in party study, political instruction, and courses at higher military or civilian schools, are quite numerous; in one fleet they comprised 37 percent of all commanders in 1969.[66]

The curriculum in the officers' groups has been subject to some change. In the last two decades of Stalin's lifetime it was limited to simple (in fact simple-minded) texts such as Stalin's famous *Short Course* on party history. It now is arranged in a more ambitious two-year cycle with five basic subjects: Marxist-Leninist philosophy, political economy, party history, scientific communism, and Leninist military doctrine. Those who have mastered this material go on to study "philosophical problems of military theory and practice," and civilian-educated officers called up from the reserve follow a somewhat altered program. Political education in military academies and schools is carried out by social science faculties under MPA supervision.[67]

This program is in theory superior to the classes for ordinary soldiers, but in fact it is often as dreary and repetitive. Part of the problem lies in the dryness of the subject matter, lack of preparation of the instructors, and limitations of a basic lecture format devised in an age when there were few textbooks. These sometimes result in spotty attendance and inattention to political study "for years on end."[68] More commonly, officers act as expected but do so in a highly ritualized manner. "Some comrades study the same themes year after year, essentially stamping around in one place." "Officers sit [at group meetings] and repeat what most of them already know. There are no sharp questions, no polemics, no clashes of principle. The material slides by so easily you cannot get a toehold in it. People sit down, chat, and leave."[69]

These problems of content and delivery are assuredly not unique. What is peculiar to the instruction of commanders is the low priority which the military party organs themselves assign to the task. Clearly many political workers have been lax in enforcing even the minimal standards set by the regime.

This secondary priority is evident from the remarkably consistent criticisms of political officers for failing to apply pressure to commanders who shirk their study duties. Even during the Great Purge, commissars were accused of condoning low attendance of commanders at ideological classes and of "not really knowing the state of the political study of commanders."[70] A report in 1940 lamented that the political organs' interest in ideological study often "amounts to the casual posing to students of party history of questions such as, 'How many chapters [of the *Short Course*] have you studied?' or, 'What chapter are you working on?' "[71] Precisely the same sort of comment appears in the modern military press. The political education of commanders is said to be outside the field of view of some political organs, and political officers often see "no need . . . to bother officers" with it. There have been repeated complaints about commanders assigned to lead ideological discussions who "take the podium and 'sound out' in a monotone a text prepared by someone else," but "the occasions are still rare" when even a verbal reprimand is administered for such conduct.[72]

This low priority is evident also from the reluctance of political organs to spare human and material resources for the task. Men delegated to prepare political lectures for officers have sometimes been given "every kind of auxiliary assignment," and one political administration went so far as to refuse them working space.[73] Moreover, there is no evidence that the MPA provides career incentives that would discourage this kind of behavior. One outstanding case illustrates the point. In early 1958 the political administration of the Baltic Fleet was severely criticized for acquiescing in senior officers' virtual ignoring of political study in 1957. Had this been of central concern, the careers of the fleet's leading political personnel would presumably have suffered. Yet only several months later the member of the fleet's military council for the previous two years (Grishanov) was made chief political officer of the entire navy, a post he has held ever since.[74]

Mobilizing Military Personnel
Much of what the military party organs do has only the remotest connection with what a Western social scientist would call political

considerations (having to do with the distribution of values and power in society). The most highly valued role of political officers is to serve as direct elicitors of military performance. They focus some of their attention on other officers (command and political) at lower levels of military organization, a fact which enmeshes them thoroughly in administrative politics. But their day-to-day efforts are aimed primarily at rank-and-file servicemen, whom they induce to contribute to organizational success by means that can best be called persuasive or mobilizing. They do this in four main ways.

Providing Heroic Inspiration. Political officers are expected to stimulate their subordinates to greater effort, especially in combat, by using a mix of ideological, nationalistic, and personal appeals. They are supposed to explicate war and battle aims, show example under fire, and give recognition to individual courage. Ideal performance is typified in a soldier's description of Reznikov, commissar of a cavalry regiment in 1941-42:

The soldiers came to love him like a father. In our first battle the commissar showed us with direct personal example how to act. During the attack he was out ahead of us, fighting like three men and all the time shouting, "Come on, boys! Beat the fascist swine so not a single one escapes with his life." When the battle was over, we relaxed in a wood. The commissar went from one group to another. His conversation made us forget our weariness, troubles, and losses. With me the commissar talked about my family, with Teplov about his bravery. Teplov was glad to hear the commissar's praise for saving two of our vehicles. Then we had a general discussion around the fire. We listened in fascination to what a marvellous life our land would have when the fascist occupiers were destroyed. Afterwards, on the commissar's suggestion we sang our favorite heroic song.[75]

Many commissars such as this must have been among the more than 100,000 political officers killed in the war.[76]

Ability to live up to such a standard is partly a function of personality. Some political officers have borne less resemblance to Reznikov than to Galin, the ineffectual agitator in Babel's *Cavalry Army*, with his twitching eyelid, flat voice, and unrequited love for the regiment washerwoman. But performance has also depended on context. Heroic inspiration is difficult to generate during the monotonous rhythm of peacetime training, whatever the personal qualities of the inspirers. One often reads of political officers looking and feeling superfluous during simulated combat exercises. "Some political workers are not always able to find their place during the course of an exercise . . . They often confine their activity to the preparatory phase and become helpless on the march, in the flux of battle." Thus political officers who might in genuine hostilities be paragons of valor are said on maneuvers to "drive around in the club vehicle," "take charge of the field kitchen," or act as "orderlies at pass control points."[77]

Off the training field, the political organs provide indirect inspiration by inculcating martial and patriotic virtues. Museums and "rooms of military glory" are maintained in the units, containing portraits and busts of regiment or ship heroes, descriptions and photographs of the feats of the unit, mounted decorations, and the like. Many subunits have "military corners" serving the same purpose on a smaller scale. Political officers also organize veterans' reunions, expeditions to battlefields and monuments, and films and literary exhibits on war themes.

Maintaining Morale. One of the party organs' main tasks is to maintain servicemen's general sense of satisfaction with military life. They do this first of all by operating the network of social and cultural services in the forces. They are responsible for all military clubs: the company Lenin rooms, which contain (along with political materials) space for lounging, bulletin boards, light reading, television sets, and chess and other games; the regiment clubs; and the officers' clubs and larger "Houses of the Soviet Army and Navy" at the division level and above. Political officers and party organizations are urged to help establish special-purpose clubs (for film viewing, stamp collecting, and the like), and Komsomol organizations and military clubs take a major responsiblility for promoting sport activity. Also under MPA jurisdiction is the system of military libraries, mostly at the regiment level, which contained 115 million books in 1977.[78] A large film distribution system developed between the wars continues to operate, as do other professional forms of entertainment and a large number of subsidized amateur organizations. The MPA currently supervises all 7 professional theaters, 47 song-and-dance ensembles (including the world-famous Aleksandrov Ensemble), 200 literary organizations, 500 amateur film studios, and more than 1,000 cultural centers in the military.[79] Civilian performers are also imported on contract and through the shefstvo system.

The second way the political organs strive to maintain morale is by dealing with dissatisfaction arising out of poor living conditions, group tensions, and individual frustration and boredom. "Political workers must be concerned . . . with the creation in each collective of correct human relations, of a receptive, creative, and truly comradely atmosphere."[80] MPA statements (including those in the several recent MPA works on military psychology) frequently argue that this kind of atmosphere is even more necessary in peacetime than when soldiers are engaged in actual combat, particularly when training and watch duty involve long periods of tedium punctuated by brief episodes demanding quick reaction and a high degree of teamwork. Such conditions are most commonly found in naval, air defense, and missile units, and it is in these branches that the political organs' morale-building efforts have been most assiduous over the last several decades.[81]

One practical manifestation of this policy is the monitoring of food and housing conditions. Political officers "check the work of supply services, dining rooms, storerooms, warehouses, garden plots, and military trade enterprises." They also participate in the selection of logistics and services personnel.[82] Particularly since its department for military sociological research was established in 1967, the MPA has collected information on living conditions on a systematic basis, sometimes by means of survey research.

Political officers are also expected to perform many of the functions which would be carried out by chaplains in most Western armies. The party worker must be a man to whom "the soldiers will come with open heart," one who "knows how to listen to people."[83] He provides comfort in times of personal distress and is expected to intervene with superiors when official action is justified on compassionate or other grounds. Occasionally he will intercede with officials outside the army entirely, as in this example of the sensitivity (chutkost') of one politotdel chief, Vadim Shornikov:

The family of a young officer had temporarily rented a [civilian] apartment and everything was going normally. But suddenly due to complex circumstances the officer was told to vacate the apartment. Yet he had two small children—how were they going to manage? Naturally the family was thrown into confusion. And it turned to the chief of the politotdel for help. The simplest thing to do would have been to tell them that the unit had no free housing space and they would have to wait. But Shornikov met with the chairman of the gorispolkom [municipal executive], explained the situation, and resolved the problem. The officer now fulfills his duties peacefully and with redoubled energy.[84]

The MPA-operated press acts as a more open safety valve for minor tensions and is a frequent source of redress for servicemen feeling ignored by superiors or otherwise unhappy. Most complaints aired in the press are routinely referred to political officers for investigation. The military party organs are thus both the first avenue of appeal for disgruntled personnel and the first line of defense for the administrative system.

Of equal importance is the heavy involvement of political officers in assuaging personal, generational, and even ethnic frictions. This last question drew considerable attention throughout the interwar period, but particularly after the dissolution of autonomous military organizations for non-Russians in the 1930s, when circles for "union education" were formed in all units. During World War II the MPA mounted an especially vigorous effort to cement Soviet patriotism, hastily recruiting cadres from republican party organs, launching special propaganda appeals, organizing Russian-language classes of up to two hours a day, and publishing fifty newspapers in non-Russian languages. Ethnic issues have received renewed emphasis in the last decade, from an organization that is as thoroughly Russified as any part of the military establishment. (Like the applicants to any military school, candidates for MPA schools must pass tests on Russian language and literature; every head of the MPA since 1942 has been of Russian nationality.) The political organs "attempt to reinforce in every soldier the awareness of belonging to a single socialist Motherland, to a great international army."[85] Political workers supervise "circles for the study of the Russian language" in some units, and make efforts to combat "elements of national conceit and harmful habits of seeing a national basis for every disagreement or personal insult."[86] This role will presumably gain in importance in the 1980s as demographic trends force conscription of larger numbers of non-Russians and non-Slavs.

Reinforcing Discipline. The maintenance of order and discipline was probably the paramount task facing the Civil War commissar, and it has remained a vital duty ever since. The military party organs are required to "work for the consolidation of edinonachalie and military discipline, . . . for the unconditional implementation of military duty and of the orders and instructions of commanders and chiefs."[87]

In wartime, political officers have reinforced discipline in drastic ways. The 1941 decree on commissars ordered them to wage "merciless struggle" against cowards and deserters and report any betrayal to the security organs. In the opening weeks of the war some political workers summarily shot men fleeing combat or preaching defeatism.[88] Even a year later commissars were being told not to "waste propaganda or persuasion" on obvious cowards.[89]

In peacetime, the party apparatus has used less extreme methods. In the first place, it propagandizes military regulations, the oath of service, and the requirements of official duty. Special talks are used to condemn disrespect for superiors, carelessness with equipment, tardiness, drunkenness, and the influence of "unofficial leaders . . . of negative characteristics."[90] Political officers teach soldiers "love and respect for their military uniforms" and are even expected to check that headgear and ribbons are worn properly and shirts tucked in neatly.[91] A special object of concern in propaganda and instruction is the maintenance of "military and state secrecy." Political workers routinely warn servicemen against "carelessness in correspondence and excessive chattiness in radio or telephone conversations."[92]

In addition to propaganda, the political organs impose specific party or Komsomol penalties that reinforce other sanctions against offenders. Thus a soldier who damages a tank or shows up intoxicated for a parade may well find himself expelled or suspended from the Komsomol (a penalty which is bound to have implications after discharge) as well as subject to punishment by his commander. (This pattern also applies to officers; see Chapter 5.)

Finally, political officers strive to mobilize peer pressure against actual and potential offenders. Ill-behaved soldiers are liable to have their affairs discussed before general meetings or open Komsomol sessions, and may have to criticize themselves and pledge improvement. This method was especially popular in the late Khrushchev years but was amply used earlier. Recently, political workers have also been encouraged to apply further pressure by corresponding with the parents of unruly servicemen. This seems to be a particularly common tactic when the soldier has behaved improperly (as likely as not, under the influence of alcohol) in the presence of civilians.[93]

It should be noted that measures such as these are usually carried out in close concert with the commanding officer concerned, and often at his initiative. It is standard to read that a commander faced with a recalcitrant soldier "took the necessary measures on his part and at the same time advised the party committee to discuss this question at its session," or that a commander "had decided to punish" a seaman but "decided to wait a little with stern measures and to submit his transgression for public discussion" at a Komsomol meeting.[94] If junior political officers are criticized for their handling of discipline questions, it is not for leniency or intervention in cases where no wrong has been committed, but usually for overreacting to violations and neglecting persuasion in favor of coercion.

Encouraging Technical Competence. A final contribution to military performance has been the military party organs' encouragement of technical competence. In part, they have acted directly to provide soldiers with the skills needed to use complex weapons and fight modern war. During the early years a major effort was directed at abolishing illiteracy, mainly among peasant soldiers. Between 1919 and 1928 the MPA's "schools for the liquidation of illiteracy" and other courses are said to have taught 550,000 illiterates to read and write.[95] The program was briefly revived during the demobilization of the late 1940s in some areas.

Around 1930 the political organs began to impart more complex information related directly to military tasks. MPA chief Ian B. Gamarnik told a 1931 conference that party workers must do their part so that soldiers "completely master battle equipment and the complicated forms of modern combat."[96] In 1933 the MPA established a special department for propagandizing technology. Technical themes surfaced in MPA literature, and evening lectures and "technical circles" were made a regular responsibility.

This activity has been intensified since the war. The party organs sponsor "rationalizing" campaigns in which soldiers are exhorted to make suggestions about how equipment can be used and maintained. Technical circles, lectures, seminars, and displays are organized regularly and political officers are instructed to lead "the organization of military technical propaganda, the popularization of the experience of advanced soldiers who skillfully use their weapons, and the campaign for the literate use and maintenance of military equipment."[97] The Komsomol organization in a tank company sponsors evening circles for the study of armored equipment; the zampolit of a model aviation unit lectures flyers on safety themes; political officers in air defense units discuss maintenance of antiaircraft batteries in low temperatures and the phasing of antenna feeder systems.[98]

Although this effort can only be supplementary to the regular program of technical instruction, it is a major concern of the political officers. There has even been a tendency for technical information to supplant more explicitly political themes. The best illustration is the twice-weekly political information sessions for enlisted men and NCO's, which are stated often to be concerned with narrowly technical questions or even to be "turned into routine reports or instruction periods on combat training."[99] Reports have shown them dealing with such topics as maneuvering tanks in water, ship watch duty, carbine shooting, and order in the mess hall.[100]

In addition to dispensing technical knowledge directly, the military party organs have employed indirect means to stimulate its acquisition. The most important has been "socialist competition" in the assimilation of technical knowledge and the mastery of equipment. Inaugurated in 1929, this program was soon strongly influenced by the civilian Stakhanovite movement (it was referred to as military Stakhanovism in 1935-36) and it concentrated on animating soldiers to exceed norms and set records in construction, preparation times, and marksmanship. After falling into disuse during the war, socialist competition was revived in 1957. The record-breaking approach has been replaced by competition among individuals and units for the meeting of prescribed norms of technical proficiency, in which obligations are agreed upon and achievement is periodically assessed against them. Winners can acquire pendants and badges, special red banners for their units, and preference in admission to officers' schools.

Organizational Successes and Shortcomings

The limited Western literature on the MPA has assumed that its activities are harmful in military terms. Evidence of this chapter suggests that such a pattern cannot be taken for granted and that Soviet claims as to the indispensability of the military party apparatus's contribution should not be dismissed out of hand. We should be prepared to take seriously Marshal Ustinov's declaration that "it is difficult to overestimate the role and significance of party-political work," and even Brezhnev's recent observation that without the political organs, "neither tanks nor shells nor airplanes would have brought victory" in the country's wars.[101]

It may be objected that the structure and behavior of the military party organs offend against major Western standards, notably those of the familiar monist model of organization developed by Max Weber. Yet it cannot be forgotten that Weber's ideal type, with its clearly defined hierarchy of offices and precise rules for action, has long been recognized by most administrative theorists as having serious inadequacies. If these more contemporary yardsticks are taken into account, Soviet military administration may not be nearly as disorganized as has usually been thought.

In strict Weberian terms, the crosscutting lines of authority and overlapping spheres of responsibility which the political organs superimpose on the military hierarchy are highly undesirable. But in the light of Herbert Simon's finding that dual supervision is quite common in large organizations, the Soviet military looks far more normal. Again, using a stringent Weberian criterion, it is reprehensible for a soldier to have to take orders from both a commander and a political officer. But if there is not, as Simon argues, "any reason why an individual cannot accept certain decisional premises from one superior and other nonconflicting premises from another," then again Soviet military administration seems much less of an anomaly.[102] If basic premises were in conflict—if the military party organs sought ends that were inconsistent with those of the command hierarchy—the situation would indeed be different. But, with exceptions early in Soviet history, the MPA and military command have pursued ends that are mutually consistent and interdependent. The Soviet Army seems to bear out the conclusion reached in a recent survey of studies of military organization—that "individuals and work units readily manage to coordinate their activities despite some ambiguity over formal authority, so long as both parties clearly acknowledge the existence of a work relationship."[103] The work relationship between the political organs and the Soviet military command is clearly an intense and resilient one and has in fact been insisted upon by the party leadership.

Many aspects of the MPA's actual program also compare favorably with Western practice. The round of political classes and exercises looks less abstract if one subscribes to Rensis Likert's view that for optimal organizational performance each member "must feel that the organization's objectives are of significance and that his own particular task contributes in an indispensable manner to the organization's achievement of its objectives."[104] Likewise the use of the political officer rather than a line commander as the first point of appeal to administrators may assist the military hierarchy in combining accessibility and social distance from subordinates in the way recommended by Peter Blau and Richard Scott.[105] And the whole preoccupation with communication and education may be seen as paralleling the change in the basis of authority and discipline that Morris Janowitz has discerned in the American military—the "shift from authoritarian domination to greater reliance on manipulation, persuasion, and group consensus."[106]

However, it is also true that the military party apparatus is, by frequent admission of its own officials and other Soviet observers, a flawed organization whose performance has consistently fallen short of promise. Some of the reasons for this are no doubt peculiar to the MPA or to public administration in the Soviet Union. Yet one can also usefully see in the apparatus the more general shortcomings of all large bureaucracies. No portrait would be complete without mention of these.

Perhaps the fundamental defect has been the MPA's susceptibility to what Robert Merton called the displacement of goals, the enshrining of bureaucratic procedures as ends in themselves.[107] "One frequently finds party-political measures being undertaken purely for the sake of form and not exerting real influence on personnel."[108] Projects are implemented " 'for the record,' so that 'carried out' can be marked on the graph," and political officers tend to rate their success "according to purely external, formal indicators—the numbers of meetings, decisions and resolutions adopted, reports received."[109]

The conversion of procedures into valued ends is directly reflected in the allotment of political officers' work time. For example, the preparation of written plans and reports—to which other officials must react in kind—takes on intimidating proportions. "We all write and write," a young political officer protested in 1936, saying he spent 70 percent of his time at paperwork. "We often have no time to work by ourselves, no time even to be in the subunits."[110] In 1947 the complaint emerges again: "The political organ is, to put it simply, buried in paper. From morning until evening all its officers write long memoranda and compose plans."[111] Dozens of additional examples could be culled from the recent press, many of them first-hand accounts written with a tinge of bitterness.

A similar continuity of criticism can be found in regard to another favorite bureaucratic procedure, the meeting or conference. One reads in the 1930s of "multihour speeches, innumerable meetings, instruction sessions, and conferences" which "often flourish in place of concrete, businesslike party work."[112] Little had changed three decades later when the chief political officer in the Pacific Fleet, Admiral Mikhail N. Zakharov, complained of political officials' "chronic 'illness' —a penchant for speechifying." He described one political department in which officers attended twenty-eight major meetings in a single month. "On some days party leaders had to attend several meetings. 'All we do is attend meetings,' several of them complained. 'We have no time to work.' "[113]

The enshrinement of bureaucratic procedure has had several important effects on the MPA's procedures themselves. An obvious one is that the achievement of even normal results is time and energy consuming. If a communication "has to 'stroll' around the departments and administrations,"[114] then the outcome may take weeks or months to appear.

A second important consequence has been that the military party organs, concerned as they are with routine and precedent, sometimes react poorly to challenge and crisis. Problems that cannot be conceptualized in the familiar categories are either ignored or dealt with only when they become pressing enough to attract the attention of superiors. The organs are often likened to fire brigades, storming to and from outbreaks with little result. "A fire alarm rings somewhere and everyone rushes to the place of the incident. Then smoke arises from somewhere else and everyone hurries over there—a great deal of fuss but little benefit."[115]

The absorption in routine and regularity has a third result—hostility to change. Many of the attempts to introduce major new ideas or methods amount to little once the initial fanfare is over. "At conferences and meetings you often hear from political officers words such as, 'We have reformed,' 'We have turned our work around,' and so on. But in fact there are no visible accomplishments. Everything goes on as before."[116]

Finally, a system based on rules and routines has inevitable implications for the official himself. The party worker often seems the archetype of the impersonal bureaucrat Weber both heralded and feared. The political officer may be hailed in theory as the soldiers' amiable link to higher authority, but he is often admitted in practice to be "a stern official with whom they cannot share their thoughts."[117] Political workers are supposed to share the soldiers' concern over living and work conditions—and clearly many do have this concern— but others evince "literally olympian detachment" or stand aside impassively from such problems.[118] Political officers are intended to deliver stirring reports and lectures, but in reality they "often take the tribune with lectures written by others [and] read them despondently, with all the energy of melting ice," "run through lectures as if playing a gramophone record for the hundredth time."[119]

Trotsky's leather-jacketed commissar, with a gun in one hand and a fiery pamphlet in the other, is now a dim and receding image. He lives on only in the history books and in recollections like that of a staff officer who in 1968 mourned a dead Civil War colleague ("Now that was a political worker!") and contrasted him with the contemporary political officer, the creature of organization, "with neither spark nor fervor . . . like a train conductor, with only seriousness on his face."[120]

The Monitoring Capability
of the Military Party Organs

4

Enough basic information has been provided on the military party organs to allow entertainment of more explicitly political questions. Before examining the organs' political behavior in specific settings, we must deal with the issue raised in Chapter 2 of their capability for acting in politics as an instrument of external party control over military commanders.

A useful organizing concept is Anthony Downs' model of the monitoring organization—the "separate monitoring organization for inspecting and reporting on performance."[1] Western scholars have seen the military party apparatus as precisely such an agency. But is this the case? Does the MPA, whatever its announced objectives and role in troop management, have the attributes of an organization designed to play in military politics the role of watchdog over the command hierarchy? If so, can it be expected to be an effective monitor? Is it an organization through which central party leaders can be thought likely (in Downs' language) to "extend their power so that nearly everyone in [the] operating bureau [the military command] is under surveillance by persons [political officers] who are closely allied to the top level [the party leadership]"?

Discussion can fruitfully be addressed to Downs' point that a monitoring organization can function capably only if there is "a fundamental conflict of interest" between it and the operating bureau it surveys. Since "monitors are rewarded for finding and reporting 'evils' and operators are rewarded for preventing or concealing them," the effectiveness of monitoring agencies "can be maintained only if a definite tension exists between their members and the members of the operating bureaus they monitor."

This indispensable tension seems to depend upon the monitoring agency fulfilling four conditions. First and fundamental is that it see surveillance of operators as its clear and sole task. If it shares operational responsibilities, "excellent performance must take promotional precedence over zeal in reporting deviations," since the monitor will be under the same pressures to produce results and conceal shortcomings as the organization it was set up to watch.

Second, there must be no exchange of personnel between the monitoring and operating agencies. "If officials were constantly shifted back and forth between the inspectors and the inspected, monitors would be motivated to ignore many mistakes and deviations in hope of being treated similarly when they were being inspected." Other consequences would likely follow as well, particularly contagion of values between the two groups.

Third, the members of the monitoring agency ought to be furnished with only the knowledge suited to their surveillance task. They should not be steeped in the norms, values, and skills of the operating organization, except to the extent needed to comprehend and report on behavior.

Finally, there should be a minimum of personal contact between the two agencies. Downs suggests rules against social fraternization, rapid rotation of monitoring officials, employing monitors only in groups, and measures to create positive hostility between monitors and operators.

The Division of Labor as a Disunifying and Unifying Factor

Military administration rather than external control is the MPA's central role, and this role is carried out within the terms of a reasonably clear and stable division of labor with the military command. While this has at most times encouraged the development of similar broad outlooks, it would be misleading to imply that the work relationship has been entirely free of tension.

Differences arise among individual officials just as they surface in any bureaucratic setting. The adjudication of such disputes was no doubt more difficult in the commissar era, when the allocation of authority was unclear, than it is now. Friction has always been possible when officers from either side take actions that clearly exceed their prerogatives. There are occasional reports of this kind of dispute in the press. Typical is the outbreak in 1966 between a naval commander and his zampolit, coming when the commander overstepped his rights by ordering the rescheduling of a party meeting without consulting or even notifying the political officer.[2]

Much more substantial, however, were the conflicts stemming from uncertainty and dissatisfaction over the several changes in the official division of labor ending in October 1942. Friction was certain to accompany such major redefinitions of authority. In the 1920s some former commissars tended to "view their conversion to pompolits as a demotion,"[3] a reasonable reaction. Feelings erupted in March 1928 when the head of the Tolmachev Academy, Iakov L. Berman, publicly demanded reconsideration of the "forced implementation of edinonachalie" and resolutions to this effect were adopted in a number of garrisons, particularly in the Belorussian, Ukrainian, and Leningrad military districts. The military leadership condemned the group in June and a Central Committee resolution followed in October 1928. Most of the leading dissidents were demoted, and by January 1929 conferences of political workers had publicly renounced their views.[4]

Later revisions in formal authority occasioned similar, if less drastic, discontents. When commissars became zampolits in 1940, as one political general recollects in his memoirs, "new relations did not always evolve smoothly. Some political workers were unable to reconcile themselves to the loss of their rights as commissars. Some commanders' heads swam from the fullness of their 'unlimited' power."[5] The reintroduction of edinonachalie two years later also gave rise to many doubts, a deputy MPA chief wrote later. "We were accustomed to political workers enjoying rights equal to the commanders', but now all of a sudden they had become the commanders' deputies!"[6] It was evidently the fluidity of task definition that prompted Vasilii N. Gordov, the commander of the Thirty-third Army, to suggest to Stalin in June 1943 that he "liquidate the army military council as a superfluous and useless organ" and subordinate all political officers to corresponding staffs.[7]

While it would be incorrect to dismiss completely such disagreements, it would be even less useful to exaggerate their significance. Relations between the political organs and the military command have not been dominated by conflict on this issue for several reasons.

The first is that the division of labor has been fixed for more than three decades at most levels. Controversy over it was lively only during the late 1920s and in the half decade of experimentation after 1937. Moreover, underlying the formal changes before 1942 was a considerable continuity in basic functions.

Second, the regime has acted firmly to suppress the conflict that has occurred, judging such tension within the army "extremely damaging to its combat capacity," as the 1928 Central Committee resolution put it.[8] The leaders of the 1928 opposition were dealt with sternly, and most were to be liquidated in the Great Purge a decade later (see Chapter 6). It is difficult to imagine official tolerance of the 1928 tactics—

when supporters of Berman "went around to a number of garrisons, trying to draw new people into the struggle"[9]—at any later point. General Gordov had his career terminated for his bold suggestion about the military councils—although not until more than three years after his letter to Stalin and only five months before the temporary conversion of the councils into advisory bodies.[10] Defense Minister Zhukov's dismissal in 1957 was said to have been occasioned in part by his infringements on MPA rights, although the case for his having done so appears very doubtful in retrospect (see Chapter 8). On the whole it seems clear that the costs of questioning such a cornerstone of policy as the prescribed place of the political apparatus have deterred most potential Bermans and Gordovs, or at least convinced them to seek recourse within the prevailing institutional framework.

Third, we should note that cleavages of opinion on division-of-labor questions have by no means separated party workers and commanders into two neatly juxtaposed groups. It was the head of the MPA, Ivan T. Smilga, who was the most energetic exponent of an early transition to one-man command during the Civil War. He first recommended this in early 1919, and in December he and others at a national conference of political officers suggested that the office of political commissar be liquidated forthwith. A majority of delegates stopped short of this but did advocate removal of commissars from commanders who belonged to the party.[11] In the 1920s MPA chief Andrei Bubnov was coauthor of the key policy proposals on edinonachalie and fought tenaciously against the 1928 opposition.[12] At this time and later, MPA misgivings were mitigated by the measures taken to reduce the costs of the move to unitary command, most important the transfer of able commissars to command posts (see the following section) and the continuation of perquisites and material benefits for former commissars now subordinated to commanders.[13]

Nor were all commanders unhesitatingly certain of the benefits of one-man command. A substantial proportion seem genuinely to have appreciated the virtues of the commissar system and to have had reservations about its abolition. Some Civil War commanders were grateful for commissars' authority with the rank and file, as Trotsky several times remarked, and a similar perception was behind the welcome extended by at least some to the return of commissars in the midst of the 1941 military disaster.[14] The commissar system also lessened the commander's burden in the area of political training. "It was much easier with the commissar," a battalion commander confided to a colleague in 1942. "People mainly asked him about political work."[15] An indolent commander might even pass on to his com-

missar other tasks he would otherwise have had to take in hand—
as in the regiment in the mid-1920s where the commander abdicated
many of his drill and instruction duties and spent most of his time
"planning or writing articles for the newspaper."[16] Finally, the commissar could be a convenient crutch in making, defending, or avoiding painful decisions. MPA chief Sergei Gusev observed that in Civil
War military councils many commanders "gladly went for collegial-
ity because of their fear of responsibility."[17] Likewise Bubnov could
complain in 1925 of commanders' "reluctance to take upon themselves
full responsibility," and in 1942 some commanders "were afraid of
the great responsibility edinonachalie would place on them."[18]

If all three of these points suggest that conflict over the assignment
of authority between command and political organs has not been
nearly as significant as has usually been assumed, a fourth and crucial
point needs to be made. The central fact about this division of labor is
not how it apportions tasks but that it apportions them at all. Not
only has the division of labor not normally been a major disunifying
factor, it usually is a major integrating factor. It consigns to command
and political officers different tasks, to be sure, but tasks that
contribute to highly interrelated goals. The military party organs
share routine operational responsibilities with the command—and this
is in exactly the way Downs' model predicts a monitoring organization cannot be allowed to do. Rather than being a body apart, charged
only with observing military activity and reporting deviation from
the party leadership's standards, the MPA is enmeshed, intricately
and irrevocably, in that very activity.

One obvious consequence is the strong incentive for the political
officer, being invested with functions at which he cannot succeed in
isolation from the officials with whom he works, to develop a flexible
and cooperative working relationship with them. Few sensible officers
take long to discover the manifest truth that the first deputy chief of
the MPA voiced in 1972: "Success will be achieved only if the
commander, political worker, staff, and party organization work, not
every man for himself, but with coordinated efforts."[19] This is not a
guarantee of cooperation, but it surely is a powerful inducement for it.

A related point concerns attitudes toward the environment surrounding the organizational unit. The political officer's commitment
to the unit's success would have little meaning unless he had a corresponding interest in the resources and opportunities having to be
acquired from without in order to facilitate success. It was mainly
this kind of concern that propelled the military party organs into
bureaucratic politics from very early in their history. Even the Civil
War commissar often came, like the commander, to identify his im-

mediate political interest with that of the organizational unit over which the two presided. This was in no way inconsistent with a fervent commitment to the party and the revolution, for it could be precisely the passion for victory that led a party official to press a sectoral interest, particularly if the commander to whom he had been assigned was at a political disadvantage because of his background. As one division commissar explained in the Civil War, it was natural for the commissar, being "interested more than anyone else in the swiftest possible organization" of the Red Army and of his unit, to feel he must intervene with outside agencies in order "to increase appropriations [of] uniforms, equipment, weapons, and every kind of provisions," without which his unit could not fight for the revolution.[20]

Interchange of Personnel

The MPA and military command have never been distinct career lines. There has always been substantial interchange of personnel as a matter of deliberate policy. MPA chief Epishev reiterated the norm in 1970: "If a political worker wants to take up command, staff, or logistics work and has the disposition for it, he can always satisfy his wish. The doors of higher military education establishments of all specialties are open to him, as to any officer up to the defined age. At the same time every commander, engineer, technician, staff officer, or logistics officer with the desire and necessary characteristics can become a political worker."[21] At several junctures up to 1942, access to command positions was used as a safety valve for dissatisfied commissars. Mobility across the boundary has also helped alleviate acute cadres shortages and has been credited with more general benefits such as efficient distribution of personnel, gratification of career preferences, and improvement of mutual understanding.

Let us deal first with transfer from political to command ranks. This was common in the Civil War, when commissars were often appointed as commanders in the field and others were redirected by way of military schools (they made up 21 percent of the first enrollment at the General Staff Academy).[22] Subsequently a large number of the "best prepared" commissars were sent directly to command work or were enrolled in military academies or schools. Many more were switched during the reform of the mid-1920s, when Frunze insisted that "each commissar who has a taste for command work must have the full opportunity to become a commander."[23] Former political officers were 20 to 50 percent of the entrants to major academies in 1924-25, and by 1929 they accounted for a third of all full one-man commanders.[24]

Reassignment into the rapidly expanding military command continued throughout the 1930s. In 1931, for example, more than 1,000 transfers took place, mostly at junior levels.[25] Demand was greatly enhanced by the Great Purge and then by the rapid prewar expansion of the officer corps. It was not unusual in the late 1930s for a political officer to move directly into a senior command post. Petr A. Smirnov, for instance, went straight from chief of the MPA to head of the navy in December 1937, and Georgii K. Savchenko from commissar to commander of artillery troops in February 1939.[26]

World War II brought much larger emergency transfers. About 4,500 political officers were moved to command posts by October 1942, and the pace was greatly accelerated by the return of edinona-chalie and the elimination in 1943 of subunit zampolits, both of which released numerous party workers for reassignment. In the year after October 1942 more than 140,000 men—more than the MPA's total strength at its maximum—were sent to command positions, usually by way of six- or twelve-month retraining courses. All told, 150,000 political officers made the transition during the war; by May 1945 they were in command of 300 regiments and filled thousands of other posts.[27]

This movement has certainly persisted since the war. The bulk of the flow has been at subunit levels, although considerable effort was expended between 1958 and the mid-1960s in fostering it at the regiment plateau and higher. In the year ending in May 1960 about 1,500 political officers were sent to command posts, but little success (and some resistance) was reported above the battalion level.[28] Transfer has continued since 1965, but only at subunit grades and "within the limits of feasibility and voluntarism."[29] Eventual transfer is unexceptional enough for a story to ask about a young zampolit: "His current stage of officer's service is only the beginning. What will he be next—a political worker, a commander, a vehicle engineer? It is difficult to say."[30]

This sustained inflow has meant that the military command has always contained a substantial proportion of former political officers, with periods of service in the MPA ranging from several months to two decades or more. This presence was highly visible during the interwar period. Of the three men who served as overall head of the military between Trotsky's dismissal and the war, two (Frunze and Voroshilov, who between them held the post for all but one year) had previously worked as political officers. So had five of the seven heads of the navy, who occupied that position for every year except one (Viacheslav I. Zof, Romual'd A. Muklevich, Vladimir M. Orlov, Smirnov, and Nikolai G. Kuznetsov) as well as three of five heads of the air force, filling the post for all but three years (Petr I. Baranov,

Iakov I. Alksnis, and Iakov B. Smushkevich). A glance at the inter-mediate military leadership in the middle and late 1930s also shows ex-commissars in many major positions—First Deputy People's Com-missar of Defense (Mikhail N. Tukhachevskii, who was a Civil War commissar for only several weeks), commander of the Far Eastern Front (Vasilii K. Bliukher, Grigorii M. Shtern), chief of military in-telligence (Ian K. Berzin), head of air defense (Aleksandr K. Sediakin), district commander (Iona E. Iakir, Nikolai V. Kuibyshev), fleet com-mander (Grigorii P. Kireev), and head of a central military adminis-tration (Ernest F. Appoga, Anton S. Bulin, Dmitrii I. Kosich, Petr M. Oshlei, Fedor V. Rybin, Efim A. Shchadenko, and Iosif E. Slavin).[31]

Former political officers have also constituted an appreciable por-tion of the military elite in more recent years. Of the 138 commanders appointed (as of the end of 1975) to a marshal's or equivalent rank and for whom biographies are available, twenty-two officers (15.9 per-cent) have been former political workers. Average time spent in po-litical work (for the sixteen for whom this information is available) has been 6.4 years.[32]

The less detailed biographies of the much larger number of generals and colonels who died in the twenty years up to the end of 1975 show a considerably smaller proportion of former political officers (sixty-two men, or 5.8 percent). Complete data would almost certainly show ex-political officers making up more than 10 percent of the generals and colonels. Whatever the comparison with the marshals, this is still quite substantial representation. Even the sixty-two officers known to have made the transition are more than a third the size of the com-parable group who remained in the MPA (175 men). Information on the timing of transfer is available for thirty men, and it shows con-siderable continuity—one transfer in the Civil War, ten in the 1920s, six in the 1930s, two in World War II, and eleven after 1945. The 5.7 percent average includes 16.9 percent of logistics officers, 6.3 percent of procurators, 5.6 percent of engineers, 5.3 percent of troop com-mand and staff officers, 3.2 percent of academics, and 2.9 percent of medical officers.

As in the 1930s, the positions held by former political officers since 1945 have been formidable indeed. In the first decade after the war former party workers occupied posts including commander-in-chief of the ground forces (Ivan S. Konev), head of armored, artillery, and chemical troops (Pavel S. Rybalko, Mitrofan I. Nedelin, Ivan F. Chukhnov), chief of logistics (Andrei V. Khrulev), chief of communi-cations (Ivan T. Peresypkin), deputy minister in charge of construc-tion (Vasilii E. Belokoskov), commander of the navy (Nikolai Kuznet-sov), deputy commander of the navy (Nikolai E. Basistyi, Pavel S.

Aban'kin, Filipp S. Oktiabr'skii), deputy head of the air force (Fedor
Ia. Falaleev, Grigorii A. Vorozheikin, Filipp A. Agal'tsov), deputy
head of air defense (Daniil A. Zhuravlev), chief financial administrator (Iakov A. Khotenko), and head of the main cadres administration
(Fedor F. Kuznetsov, a former MPA chief, and future MPA heads
Golikov and Zheltov). Since the mid-1950s former political officers
have also filled a wide array of senior positions, among them commander of the strategic rocket forces (Nedelin), commander and chief
of staff of Warsaw Pact troops (Konev, Mikhail I. Kazakov), chief of
logistics (Semen K. Kurkotkin, who has been in that post since 1972),
deputy logistics chief and head of that function for the air defense
forces (Nikolai P. Anisimov, Vasilii M. Shevchuk), head of military
construction (Aleksandr I. Shebunin), head of the main cadres administration (Afanasii P. Beloborodov), deputy minister in charge of education (Kirill A. Meretskov), commander of long-range aviation
(Agal'tsov), head of the major paramilitary organization, DOSAAF
(Dmitrii D. Leliushenko), chief of railroad troops (Pavel A. Kabanov), head of the central vehicles administration (Ivan T. Korovnikov), chief of staff of the Moscow Military District (Mikhail I. Golovnin), director of a senior military academy (Stepan A. Krasovskii,
German K. Malandin), and even commander of a space vehicle (Pavel
I. Beliaev).[33]

If transfer of political officers into the military command has been
common, what can be said about movement in the opposite direction?
There was considerable mobility of commanders into MPA posts during the Civil War and early 1920s, although there was no conscious
planning for this. In one division surveyed in 1925, 34 percent of the
commissars and assistant commissars had held a command commission.[34] Between 1926 and 1931 there was systematic recruitment of
young commanders, usually platoon or company commanders (who
were the only approved candidates for the preparation courses which
provided the bulk of junior political officers), but transfer at more
senior levels was "extremely insignificant."[35]

Much more rapid mobility of command personnel into important
MPA posts occurred during the middle and late 1930s. In 1938, for
instance, a regiment commander, Nikolai N. Vashugin, was made
member of the military council of the Leningrad Military District.[36]
The press reported similar transfers at lower levels. Fifty members of
the 1938 class of the Stalin Mechanization and Motorization Academy
were sent directly to commissar posts.[37]

There were some transfers into junior and senior political posts in
World War II, but statistics are not available. A few prominent examples appear in biographical data—for instance, Ivan Z. Susaikov, a

career commander who was by 1942 chief political officer on the Briansk Front—but clearly the overwhelming movement was in the opposite direction.[38]

It is difficult to ascertain how common lateral mobility into major
MPA positions has been since 1945. The most obvious case is Marshal
Golikov, the chief of the MPA from 1958 to 1962, who began as a
political officer but had been a commander since 1931, serving as head
of military intelligence, commander of three wartime armies and two
fronts, chief of cadres, and most recently as director of the Tank
Troops Academy.[39] Golikov strongly promoted recruitment of commanders, and the press reported many successes around 1960. There
was the same resistance to disturbance of routine as with transfer in
the other direction, but Golikov's program was at least a qualified
success. In the year prior to May 1960, several thousand commanders
were appointed as political officers—a sizable proportion of the
roughly 30,000 political workers.[40] Transfer has persisted in the last
decade, although within the same constraints as apply to political
officers becoming commanders. A "large number" of commanders still
go directly into the Lenin Academy, the finishing school for senior
political workers, and the press often prints biographies of men making the transition.[41] Much more significant in quantitative terms has
been the continued recruitment of young commanders into junior
MPA posts for most of the postwar period. Indeed, from 1951 to 1967,
young officers (usually platoon commanders) were again the only
approved candidates for MPA training courses.[42]

Biographical information on the 175 political officers ranking as
generals or colonels who died in 1956-75 reflects this inflow at junior
levels poorly. Twenty-eight men (16.0 percent) are identified as having once occupied command posts. At least as many obituaries had
lacunae of up to two decades during which the man was very likely on
command work. A conservative estimate is that 25 percent were former commanders.

Clearly the proportion of ex-commanders has been much higher
among less senior MPA officials. In 1962 almost half of all political
officers—43.8 percent—were former commanders.[43] This proportion
probably exceeded half before the practice of moving junior commanders directly into political work was abandoned in 1967.

Thus interchange of personnel between the MPA and the military
command has been massive and sustained. Perhaps not every political
officer can say as one did in wartime, "I feel the commander within
myself," but, for many, service in the other hierarchy has not been an
unusual event.[44] The same applies to the army command, although to
a somewhat lesser extent. The likely consequences for the MPA's

monitoring capability are obvious. Interchange has reduced tension with the military command, created expectations by many members of each side of eventual service on the other, and helped form a pool of shared experience and values. This has been greatly reinforced by the trend toward professionalization.

The Professionalization of Careers in the Military Party Organs

The political organs of the Civil War were staffed by means of improvisation, and consequently the original commissars had little by way of common background except their claim to be revolutionaries. While major assignments in the organs were rarely given to members of the top party leadership (Stalin, who served on the military councils of several fronts, was an exception), large numbers of promising young party workers with experience in the Red Guard, propaganda activity, or the various facets of organizational work were sent into the MPA. Others came from every conceivable walk of life—soldiers and seamen, loggers and tool makers, university dropouts and poets. Some were foreigners (including Bela Kun, leader of the 1919 Hungarian revolution), some were non-Communists, and a few were women. Almost all arrived at the front without serious preparation.

The diversity in citizenship, party affiliation, and sex was eliminated by the mid-1920s. More important to comprehend fully is the positive career orientation with which political officers have been inculcated, one best summarized in the word "professional." Political work in the army is almost never discussed as a category of some broader kind of party administration that would include work in the economy and other civilian spheres. Rather, it is accepted as "a special world with its own complexities and problems." It is a profession (*professiia*), an art (*iskusstvo*), a calling (*prizvanie*) with its own professional skill or craft (*professional'noe masterstvo*).[45]

This specialization, moreover, is conceptualized in explicitly military terms. Between the wars political workers were categorized as belonging to the army's command and political staff (*kompolitsostav*) or leading staff (*nachsostav*). Since the readoption of the term "officer" during World War II, political workers have been recognized as part of the officer corps (*ofitserskii korpus*). They are routinely placed on lists such as Khrushchev's 1957 inventory of "commanders, military engineers, political workers, and other military specialists."[46]

Clearly the Soviet image of the political officer is as a professional soldier—fully consistent with Janowitz's definition of professional soldiers as "professionals in violence," "men who have committed themselves to a career in service, men who are recognized for their 'expertise' in the means of warfare."[47] Behind this image is a reality which can be analyzed in terms of the two components of Janowitz's definition. First, work in the MPA and in the army has become, for most members, a lifetime commitment. Second, political officers have been provided with specialized training.

Political Work as a Lifetime Career. The notion of service in the military party organs as a permanent commitment and career dates from the early 1920s, when the regime decided on indefinite main-tenance of a military establishment and denounced turnover (*teku-chest'*) of MPA and command cadres. Since then the great majority of political officers have been recruited as young men and have spent their entire working lives in the army. This has been the preference not only of most political workers but of MPA and civilian party leaders, who have seen it as the only way to train and assign personnel in orderly fashion.

There was, to be sure, a substantial lag in the arrival of career soldiers at the apex of the military party organs, a lag increased by a tendency to appoint some of the most senior officials (particularly the MPA chief) on the basis of overall ability or the personal confidence of the party leader. The five heads of the MPA up to 1929—Iurenev (1918-19), Smilga (1919-21), Gusev (1921-22), Antonov-Ovseenko (1922-24), and Bubnov (1924-29)—could all be described as profes-sional revolutionaries. All had joined the party before 1905, had been arrested for underground activity prior to the revolution, and had their first military experience in 1917 or the Civil War (except for Antonov-Ovseenko, a former military cadet).[48] For most of the following two decades, even as the MPA as a whole was being professionalized, the man at its head was a generalist administrator with considerable seasoning in civilian work but minor military qualifications. Ian Gamarnik (1929-37), a Civil War commissar, spent the 1920s in local party work, ending as first secretary of the Belorussian central committee. Lev Mekhlis (1937-40, 1941-42) had a decade of military experience (as a soldier and Civil War commissar), but his intervening career had been in the central party apparatus and as editor of *Pravda*. Aleksandr Shcherbakov (1942-45) was a Central Committee secretary with extensive experience in local party ad-ministration (and was simultaneously head of the Moscow party committee throughout his term in the MPA). Iosif V. Shikin (1945-49) was a former teacher and local party official who joined the army only in 1939.[49]

These men came from widely varying backgrounds and experienced work in the MPA as only an episode in a diverse career. Seven of the nine went on to nonmilitary posts (in diplomatic service, education, the Central Committee apparatus, and the organs of state or people's control).[50] The other two, Gamarnik and Shcherbakov, died in or immediately after leaving office.

In 1937 the MPA was first headed by a man who could be called a professional soldier. Anton Bulin, temporary chief in that year, had been a political worker since 1918 except for two years in the early 1920s (he had been commissar of the Peterhof garrison in October 1917). Petr Smirnov, his successor, had spent his entire career in the military. Cut from the same cloth was Aleksandr Zaporozhets, MPA chief between Mekhlis's two terms (1940-41), who had served as a company politruk in the Civil War and moved up as battalion and regiment commissar, secretary of a division party commission, head of the politotdel of a military research institute and an infantry division, then commissar of the General Staff. Mikhail R. Shaposhnikov and Ivan V. Rogov, heads of the naval MPA from 1937 to 1946, had followed a similar path. The two of these men who survived the Great Purge (Rogov and Zaporozhets) remained in the military until their deaths in 1949 and 1959.[51]

It was these officers, not the Mekhlis's and Shcherbakovs, who set the pattern for the future and were representative of most of their subordinates. The typical political officer of the prewar period had lived most of his adult life in military barracks. He had probably joined the party while in army uniform. And he had received at least rudimentary training in an MPA or military school or academy.

But career specialization was complicated by another factor—the need to import sizable numbers of civilians directly into MPA jobs during times of severe shortage of cadres. This happened mostly between 1931 and 1945, but it has continued to be reflected in the makeup of the MPA elite.

The first mobilizations of civilians were in 1931 and 1932, when 4,500 men were brought into minor positions, most of them young, unpaid activists or low-level party or Komsomol functionaries without military experience. A number of them—including Pavel I. Efimov, the first deputy chief of the MPA from 1958 to 1974, and Mikhail Kh. Kalashnik, a deputy chief from 1958 to 1972—were to survive in important posts for over four decades.[52]

The next inflow came during the Great Purge, when 200 civilians were sent to the Lenin Academy and 100 went directly to MPA jobs, some expressly to further the purging process. One prominent arrival, Fedor Kuznetsov, formerly the deputy director of an automotive plant, had as head of the party committee of Proletarsk raion in Moscow in 1937-38 distinguished himself by "unmercifully unmasking enemies of the people." In the spring of 1938 he became the head of the

MPA's cadres department (and, eleven years later, the head of the MPA itself).[53]

Another 9,200 civilian party workers were imported in three mobilizations between August 1939 and mid-June 1941, but by far the largest intake came as part of the war effort. The 13,850 civilian party officials mobilized included 270 Central Committee officials, 500 local party secretaries—among them the heads of the three most important regional party organs (Khrushchev, Shcherbakov, and Zhdanov) and Khrushchev's eventual successor as party leader (Brezhnev, then the secretary supervising defense industry in Dnepropetrovsk)—as well as 1,265 other local party officials within the Central Committee's nomenklatura and all 3,000 students in the central party schools.[54] Many of those with prior military service or training (and some with neither) moved directly into important posts.

Clearly these men were not, initially at least, military professionals in any meaningful sense of the term. When the Karelian first secretary, Gennadii N. Kupriianov, was named member of the military council of the Fourteenth Army in 1941, he had to be reminded by an assistant to put on military dress because he "had completely forgotten that now I was a military man."[55] Some were anxious to return to civilian life, giving to army service the limp commitment displayed by one former local party secretary, Kortylev, who was by 1943 head of a brigade politotdel: "Somehow he could not get involved in army life. He had a poor understanding of battle and a weak grasp of equipment. Armo [Babadzhanian, his commander] held his hard-working political deputy in high esteem, but good-naturedly called him his 'conscript' . . . Kortylev . . . could not distinguish an anti-aircraft shell from an antitank shell. He bore the sneers (*nasmeshki*) patiently, and sometimes joked about it, but it seemed to me that he was in no great hurry to acquire a grasp of military affairs. Evidently he was convinced that he could do without this in his work ('Once the war ends, it's back to the *raikom* [raion party committee]')."[56]

Not least of the transitions which the outside recruits had to make was to acquire the respect of the cadre political officers—the unflattering description of Kortylev comes from the memoirs of a career MPA official. Nonetheless, one is struck by the rapidity with which many of these men assimilated military values and style in the heat of an intensely nationalistic war. Arsenii V. Vorozheikin, eventually one of the leading fighter aces of the war, later recalled in his memoirs his transformation within several years from a young civilian party worker, with "no wish whatever" for military service, into the commissar of an air squadron, "imbued with the heroism" of the army and "dream[ing] of great feats."[57] It took less than a year for a former Central Committee and planning official, Semen I. Shabalin, to develop "incredible contempt" for the lack of military competence of civilian party executives in the vicinity of the Briansk Front, to which he had been assigned as military council member in 1941.[58]

At no point, even during the war, did these general administrators predominate numerically in the military party apparatus. The total number of civilians recruited between 1931 and 1945 was 27,850, and even without allowances for losses this represents only a quarter of MPA strength as of mid-1942. Even at the next to highest level, the front and fleet military councils, the generalists were overshadowed by career soldiers. Of the forty-six men who held such posts for at least three months, three were full Politburo members (Lazar Kaganovich, Khrushchev, and Zhdanov) and ten others were civilian members of the Central Committee, but thirty-two (69.6 percent) were cadre political officers with a higher military-political or military education. Most of the first members of military councils of armies (and all in tank armies) had both a higher military education and prior combat experience.[59] Most of the senior wartime recruits were demobilized by 1947—including thirty men who had served as members of military councils or heads of political administrations of fronts and fifty who had held corresponding positions in armies. Also leaving were 95,000 political officers from the subunit and unit levels, a number more than three times the total of civilian administrators mobilized since 1931 and presumably including the great majority of them.[60]

Since 1945 soldiers committed to the military for life have outweighed generalists in the MPA by a large and growing margin, although the latter group has not been insignificant (due mainly to earlier recruitment decisions). Fedor Kuznetsov, the head of the MPA for most of the four years before Stalin's death, had a diverse background but had been in the army for eleven years and was to remain until his retirement in 1969. Kuznetsov's tenure was briefly interrupted in 1951 by a man (Konstantin Krainiukov) who spent altogether half a century in the military party apparatus, and their counterpart in the navy (Semen E. Zakharov) was a product of the 1932 mobilization with no prior civilian administrative experience. From 1953 to 1957 the reunified MPA was headed by Aleksei Zheltov, a graduate of the Frunze Military Academy who had been a commander for more than a decade before entering the MPA. After a year's interlude in the Central Committee apparatus, Zheltov spent twelve years as director of the Lenin Academy and is now deputy head of the main veterans' organization. His successor, the professional soldier Golikov, has already been mentioned; he still works as an inspector in the Ministry of Defense.[61]

The chief of the MPA since May 1962, Aleksei Epishev, is best classified as a generalist with solid military credentials. He has been party organizer in a tank plant (1938-40), first secretary of three local party organs (1940-42, 1945-46, 1949-51, 1953-55), defense industry executive (briefly after the war), Ukrainian party secretary in charge of cadres (1946-49), Deputy Minister of State Security (1951-53), and ambassador to Romania and Yugoslavia (1955-62). Prior to 1953 his career ran in close parallel to Khrushchev's, and this presumably weighed heavily in his selection in 1962 (although it was not sufficient to prompt his replacement in 1964). Whatever his other attributes, Epishev has considerable military experience. Beginning in 1930 he served in the army in minor command posts, then attended the elite Mechanization and Motorization Academy, from which he graduated in 1938 with qualifications that would have entitled him to a major command appointment. He worked as a political officer throughout the war, as member of the military council of two armies.[62]

Although Epishev crisscrossed between civilian party posts and the MPA, this clearly has not been a common experience since the end of postwar demobilization. We know that in 1950 the Central Committee Secretariat did recruit some MPA personnel, including some students at the Lenin Academy—a development which was probably connected with the transfer to the Secretariat of the academy's director, Shikin, a former head of the MPA. But the number involved seems to have been small and there is no indication that this became common practice. Some of the 1950 recruits later returned to the MPA—I am aware of one case in 1953, one in 1955, and another in 1956.[63] The record shows only very selective movement since 1950. In 1952 the head of the political administration of the Moscow Military District (Valentin Zolotukhin, a local party official prior to the war) was transferred to the Central Committee apparatus, where he became head of the administrative organs department in 1955.[64] There was also some limited interchange immediately following Stalin's death, evidently connected with the struggle for his succession. Leonid Brezhnev was made first deputy MPA chief in March 1953 (he remained until February 1954), and in September 1953 a career political officer of Georgian nationality (Vasilii P. Mzhavanadze, the member of the military council of the Carpathian Military District) was named head of the Georgian party during the purge of clients of Lavrentii Beria. Since that time the number of known transfers has been minuscule. One naval political officer (Ivan S. Rudnev) is known to have been made first secretary of a raion committee in Sevastopol' in 1955, but he returned to the MPA several years later. Zheltov's brief posting to the administrative organs department came in 1958-59, and his predecessor and deputy, Zolotukhin, returned to the MPA (as chief political officer in the Leningrad Military District) in 1960.[65]

Except for these rare individual cases—none of which, judging from available information, has occurred since Epishev's appointment in 1962—there has been no reported interchange with the civilian party organs since the late 1940s. Virtually the only access to a career in the military party apparatus has been at the bottom.

Useful at this point are several pieces of information from the biographies of the 175 MPA generals and colonels who died between 1956 and 1975. As Table 10 shows, the political officers tended to join the party at quite an early age—2.1 years prior to entering the army for this sample (compare with Table 9, according to which commanders join the party 5.3 years after the army). The civilian recruits of the 1930s and 1940s are heavily overrepresented in this sample (they were older than others recruited at the same time and have tended to die sooner). It is mainly these men who bring the time lag below zero, and also who account for the increasing variability in the sequence of joining army and party (the opposite of the decreasing variability observed for commanders).

Table 10. Timing of entry into party among generals, colonels, and equivalents specializing in political work

Period when officer joined military	Average age		Time lag	
	Joined military	Joined party	Average	Standard deviation
All periods	23.8	21.5	-2.1	6.0
1918-19	18.3	19.5	1.5	2.3
1920-24	19.9	20.9	1.0	2.5
1925-29	22.0	21.8	-0.2	1.8
1930-34	24.9	21.8	-3.0	4.6
1935-39	24.0	23.6	-0.9	5.5
1940 and later	30.0	22.6	-8.5	7.8
	(N=137)	(N=119)	(N=140)	(N=140)

Source: Constructed from obituaries in *Krasnaia zvezda*, 1956-75. It will be noted that more observations were available for calculating columns 3 and 4 than for columns 1 and 2; thus column 3 is not exactly equal to column 2 minus column 1.

Even these data are not supportive of a view of political officers as a uniform group with life experiences radically different from those of other military men. After all, the two-year lag in joining the army occurred in the lives of very young men. While the typical political officer in the sample joined the party at age 21.5 (4.4 years younger than the average commander), he also entered military life at age 23.8 (only 3.3 years older than the commander), surely young enough to be susceptible to further attitude change. If one excludes the twenty political officers who had been in the party at least ten years before entering the army, the average age for joining the party becomes 21.6 and for joining the army 21.7—this second figure only 1.2 years older than the average for commanders.

Of the 175 political officers, 139 (79.4 percent) came into the army without civilian administrative or professional experience. All thirty-six with such experience were recruited between 1931 and 1942, twenty-six of them in 1940-42. Twenty-four (13.7 percent) had worked in civilian party administration, ten (5.7 percent) in science or education, and one each (0.6 percent) in economic administration and the secret police. Eight men (4.6 percent) acquired civilian experience after or between periods of military service (including four of those with prior civilian experience), six in party work and one each in economic planning and the secret police.

Table 11 compares political workers with other officers in terms of civilian experience. It shows their rate of prior experience to be higher than that of any group other than military procurators and much higher than the mean rate for all nonpolitical officers.[66] However, the picture is quite different for subsequent civilian work. Here political officers are significantly less apt to pursue a civilian career than other officers, ranking behind all categories except troop command specialists. A military engineer, for example, is three times more likely to follow his military service with a career in related civilian fields (economic administration, research, or education) than a political officer is to enter civilian party work after leaving the army. If one measures professionalism by a man's tendency not to pursue another career after entering military life, political officers may actually be more professional than most other military men. (This statement must be qualified for the former civilian officials who left the MPA immediately after the war; none was included in this sample.)

Another point about career patterns relates to service in the secret police. The MPA's capability as a monitoring organization would undoubtedly be enhanced if its officials frequently served in the security police—whose main function is certainly a monitoring one

Table 11. Civilian administrative and professional experience among generals, colonels, and equivalents (by percent)

Civilian experience	Political	All non-political	Troop command	Engineer-ing	Academic	Logistics	Medical	Procuracy
				Career specialization				
Prior experience								
None	79.4	94.4	98.3	90.2	84.9	94.9	88.6	62.5
Party administration	13.7	0.5	0.3	0.5	0.0	1.7	0.0	6.3
Economic administration[a]	0.6	1.2	0.2	4.7	1.1	1.7	0.0	0.0
Science and education[a]	5.7	2.3	0.6	3.3	10.8	0.0	8.6	0.0
Secret police	0.6	0.8	0.8	0.9	1.1	1.7	0.0	0.0
Other	0.0	0.8	0.0	0.5	2.2	0.0	2.9	31.3
Subsequent experience								
None	95.4	92.3	95.5	87.0	88.2	91.5	85.7	81.3
Party administration	3.4	0.5	0.2	0.0	0.0	1.7	0.0	18.8
Economic administration[a]	0.6	3.8	2.2	9.8	2.2	5.1	0.0	0.0
Science and education[a]	0.0	2.1	0.3	3.3	8.6	0.0	14.3	0.0
Secret police	0.6	0.9	1.6	0.0	0.0	0.0	0.0	0.0
Other	0.0	0.4	0.3	0.0	1.1	1.7	0.0	0.0
	(N=175)	(N=1,062)	(N=644)	(N=215)	(N=93)	(N=59)	(N=35)	(N=16)

Source: Constructed from obituaries in *Krasnaia zvezda*, 1956-75.
a. Economic administration category includes engineering positions in economic enterprises; science and education includes medical positions.

—before or after their work in the army. Notwithstanding Epishev's brief tenure in the Ministry of State Security, the equivalent of today's KGB (where he presumably was "Khrushchev's man"), political officers do not display any particular tendency to combine police and military careers.

There was some transfer of students in MPA schools to NKVD units shortly before the war, and at about this time there was also limited interchange of high-level personnel (for instance the appointment of the chief political officer in the NKVD border troops, Konstantin F. Telegin, as head of the political administration of the Moscow Military District in July 1941). This intertransfer came, significantly, at a time when a number of NKVD officers were moving into the army command (among them Pavel A. Artem'ev, who became Moscow district commander).[67] Epishev served in the Ministry of State Security when that agency was an object of intense concern to major party politicians, and at least two MPA officials (one a generalist with a background like Epishev's, the other a career political officer) are known to have been transferred into the ministry between 1951 and 1953.[68] Neither this experience nor that of a decade earlier points to any general pattern of interchange between the MPA and the secret police. There has been enough movement back and forth to make it easy to find senior KGB officials in the 1950s and later whose earlier careers had included at least a brief stint in the MPA—as well as other KGB executives who are former military commanders.[69] Likewise, one can identify officials in the MPA in the last several decades who have had brief or extensive experience in the KGB or its predecessors (the outstanding example being Semen P. Vasiagin, the chief political officer in the ground forces since 1967, who worked in the party organs of the NKVD border and internal troops from 1933 to 1941). [70] Yet it can be said with equal certainty that some senior commanders have had similar experience—among them the deputy head of the army's cadres administration from 1947 to 1969 and the commanders of three military districts between 1957 and 1973.[71]

The information of the 1956-75 obituary sample is useful on this score. It contains only one political officer (0.6 percent) with prior experience in the secret police and one with subsequent experience. This is obviously a low ratio, and as Table 11 demonstrates it is significantly lower than the rate of interchange reported for nonpolitical officers.

What does the future hold? Without question the trend is toward further professionalization and compartmentalization of careers. With no sizable input from civilian party agencies in three decades, generalist administrators are now a significant leavening in only the highest echelons of the MPA, and even there they will have virtually disappeared by the early 1980s. Over half of all politotdel chiefs are now less than forty years old and thus will have entered the MPA long after recruitment of civilian officials was common.[72] The average political officer has had no experience of party or administrative work in industry, agriculture, the arts, or any other civilian area, and he can count on remaining in the military until retirement.

A related development that has received increasing attention is the "continuity of generations" within the military party organs. Soviet discussions have pointed with warm approval to young political officers who have chosen military life in the footsteps of their fathers. One man is said to have entered political work because he wanted to be like his father, a commander, and many students in the new MPA schools are the sons of political officers. In 1972 *Krasnaia zvezda* could even profile "a family of political workers" in which both sons had followed their father into the MPA.[73]

This trend and the underlying specialization that it reinforces will reduce even further the area of concern common to military and civilian party work. When official spokesmen wrote in the 1920s of "a kind of one-sidedness (*odnobokost'*) among military party leaders, a noticeable detachment from general party work," they were speaking of a situation they believed should and could be remedied.[74] That complaints of this sort are no longer made is testimony, not to any curtailment of professionalization (which is far more advanced than in the 1920s) but to the regime's acceptance of its full consequences.

Specialized Education. The second aspect of the professionalization of the MPA, the provision of its personnel with specialized training which includes a firm grounding in military affairs, has had a long and not always smooth history. The commissars of the Civil War received minimal prior training. Several hundred were given eclectic preparation at the Sverdlov Communist University in Moscow, and a few more went through MPA courses for club and library officials. But most received their only instruction in primitive programs in the field lasting no more than several months. Given the pressures of the war, pausing to study "was for fully understandable reasons considered almost a crime."[75] This attitude changed radically and irreversibly in the 1920s, due partly to policy choice and partly to the insistence of political officers themselves (frustrated at being "universalists [who] know everything and nothing").[76] By 1923 it was taken for granted that there was "no place for political workers who will not study military affairs or have a careless attitude toward it," and the goal was proclaimed of making every political officer a specialist in his particular branch of arms.[77]

Schools for political officers were organized at the military district level in 1922, first for one year and then for three. By 1926 there were thirteen such schools, with 3,000 students working at a curriculum that was 40 percent military subjects, with the rest divided between general and political education. In 1926-27 the schools were replaced by ten-month courses which admitted almost exclusively platoon commanders. The need for cadres led to the re-establishment of military-political schools in 1931 and their rapid growth in following years. Special courses for political officers were also opened in many command schools and "technical minima" were fixed for political workers of all ranks. The network of schools was expanded again after the purge, then switched to an emergency footing during the war, eventually with three-month terms. Wartime students spent up to 93 percent of their time on outright military training. Some 240,000 men graduated from the schools by the end of the war, and technical minima were again set for all ranks.[78]

Since 1945 the system has changed twice. Military-political schools were retained until 1951, when the MPA reverted to the 1926-31 method of retraining junior commanders in ten-month courses. Finally, in 1967 a network of higher military-political schools was inaugurated, giving MPA recruits for the first time an education equal, at least in formal distinction, to that obtained in a higher command school or civilian university. (Previously, MPA schools were classified as secondary and were open to students with eight or even fewer years of prior education.) Most graduates from the four-year courses are assigned as company zampolits with the rank of lieutenant. Applicants can be civilians or military personnel aged seventeen to twenty-three; the early classes were divided equally between the two groups. Military subjects include tactics, weaponry, topography, and signals.[79]

The most salient theme in recent discussions of the preparation of political officers is the emphasis on specialization. It has become the rule, as the senior political officer in the strategic rocket forces said in 1977, "that the political officer must master to perfection the same military profession which the fellow soldiers in his unit or subunit have mastered. My comrades from the other services of the armed forces will confirm that, for example, the political worker in the motorized infantry must be perfectly capable of using infantry weapons and know the tactics of combined-forces battle; in the artillery troops he must be able to prepare the information needed for an artillery round and to direct it accurately; in tank units he must be adept at driving a tank; in the air force he must be able to fly a combat aircraft . . . In the rocket forces he must know the structure and basic functional principles of the major technical systems involved in contemporary rocket weaponry, and also the means of putting them into use. As we all know, this is not a simple matter . . . It includes much of what goes into the preparation of an engineer."[80] The new higher MPA schools are designed to reflect this concern. One school, in L'vov, prepares students for cultural and press work anywhere in the military. The other eight are highly specialized according to branch of service, training officers for infantry units in Novosibirsk and Rostov, for tank and artillery service in Sverdlovsk, for the navy in Kiev, for air and air defense units in Kurgan and Leningrad, for construction duty in Simferopol', and for engineering work in Donetsk. It is unclear whether the new schools will help produce "service mentalities." What is clear is that they will contribute further to the technical competence of political officers in all branches.

The basic establishment for retraining senior political officers has been the Lenin Military-Political Academy in Moscow, called the Tolmachev Academy prior to 1938. The academy, "an inseparable and vital part" of the armed forces, has generally prepared men for regiment-level positions and higher. Since the war it has admitted only commissioned command and political officers, with the status of at least deputy company commander. A third of the teaching time is devoted to technical military subjects and most of the rest goes to military pedagogy and psychology and practical instruction on party work. Between 1939 and 1975, 100 doctoral and 1,400 candidate degrees were awarded by the academy, and it also has a large correspondence program.[81] Many other senior political officers study at major command academies, including the Frunze and General Staff academies and the Military Institute.[82]

How successful has this educational program been? Although performance has always fallen short of objectives, the result has not been the unchanging predominance of military ignoramuses preoccupied with ideological questions, as has often been assumed by Western analysts. The school system of the 1920s was reasonably successful. In 1927, 60 percent of company-level political officers had military preparation equivalent to platoon commanders. Training of senior personnel was undoubtedly unsatisfactory at this time and well into the 1930s (only one in five politotdel chiefs in 1931 had a higher education). The purge and the huge expansion prior to 1941 made preparation inadequate at every level (in command ranks as well as the MPA). In May 1940 only 8 percent of political officers had a higher military education; 77 percent were graduates of schools and courses, and 15 percent were without military training of any sort.[83] Technical competence was further diluted by the vast wave of wartime reservists and civilian recruits. In mid-1942 about 80 percent of all regiment commissars were cadre political officers with a formal military education; by two years later, in the tank troops which had expanded most rapidly, this figure was down to 13 percent.[84]

It is important to realize that the level of formal training has improved dramatically since the war. In 1953 about 40 percent of regiment zampolits and division politotdel chiefs had a higher military or military-political education; by 1960 the proportion was up to 70 percent. In 1962, 20 percent of all political officers (including 98 percent of politotdel chiefs) had a higher education; by 1965 this stood at 25 percent. This compares favorably to the proportion of all military officers with such qualifications.[85] By 1976, 99 percent of the chiefs of political organs and 80 percent of all cadre political officers at the regiment level (including, evidently, propagandists and heads of clubs as well as zampolits) had completed a higher education. So had 60 percent of all company zampolits, an unprecedented achievement reflecting the arrival of the graduates of the new MPA schools. (By way of comparison, somewhat over 50 percent of all commanders have a higher military education, including 90 percent of regiment commanders and virtually all at higher levels.)[86] In addition, one of every four political officers is certified as an engineer, and it is becoming increasingly common for them to have technical "class qualification" (for performing a specific task or handling a piece of equipment). In the air force, for example, about 90 percent of all squadron, regiment, and division zampolits are certified as pilots or navigators.[87]

This is not to say that political officers have not tended to bring to their work rather different dispositions from those of most military officials. The party worker obviously must have some taste for ideology. More important, he must be prepared for a career that, as official prescription has emphasized, is above all work with people. Not every political officer has the "warmth and soulfulness" (*dushevnost'*) expected in theory,[88] but he is not likely to be a man with no interest in psychology and human relations.

Yet, although political officers may have somewhat different aptitudes and are still not usually the equals of commanders (at equivalent levels of administration) in terms of formal military preparation, the gap is not so great as to prevent understanding, collaboration, and shared attitudes toward the outside world. Even for earlier periods, the evidence of interchange between political and other ranks cautions against any tendency to divorce the MPA from its military milieu. In recent years the trend toward specialized military training has gone so far that there is frequent comment on the tendency of political officers to neglect ideological study and even political work in favor of the acquisition and excercise of technical virtuosity. Like commanders, political workers are often castigated for "taking refuge in their great work loads" to avoid ideological study, or for "merely register[ing] in groups of Marxist-Leninist preparation and visit [ing] classes rarely."[89] It is obvious that those political officers who choose technical over ideological improvement are responding (like commanders) to the incentives conveyed to them from above. One MPA official realized this when visiting a former Lenin Academy classmate, now zampolit of an air regiment, who was ignoring his ideological growth on the grounds that his superiors were little interested in it:

It seems to me that Viktor Vasil'evich is right. Many senior officials have almost ceased to be interested in how their subordinate political workers improve their knowledge of Marxist-Leninist theory, study military pedagogy and psychology, or perfect their methodological skills. If the political worker successfully completes his flying program, this is considered completely sufficient for praising him and holding him up for example at conferences and seminars. So much do some comrades lose taste for party-political work that you hear from commanders, "I have plenty of first-class pilots in the regiment, but no real deputy for political affairs."[90]

Personal Interaction

The final attribute to be expected of an effective monitoring agency —lack of personal interaction between its members and those of the operating organization—is also strikingly absent in the case of the military party apparatus. In fact, intense communication and often personal friendship have flourished between political and command colleagues, and little has been done to discourage them.

The classic case is the growth of friendship between the stormy Civil War commander, Chapaev, and his commissar, the Moscow intellectual Klychkov, depicted in Dmitrii Furmanov's famous novel *Chapaev* (with Klychkov a surrogate for Furmanov, who was the commissar of Chapaev's cavalry division). The initial barriers between the two men are far greater than for later generations of command and political officers, but shared work and hazards make them "close friends and inseparable workers."[91] After his comrade's death in battle the aggrieved commissar writes the novel as a eulogy.

The military press contains frequent references to the presence of such feelings—usually portraying them in a highly favorable light— but the richest mine of illustrations is the World War II memoir literature. Typical is Marshal Kirill S. Moskalenko's account of how he became close friends with his two military council members in the Fortieth Army in 1942-43, Ivan Grushetskii and Konstantin Krainiu-

kov. "The successes and failures of our army brought us together."
When Epishev (who was to be Moskalenko's colleague in the military
leadership after 1962) replaced Krainiukov in 1943, relations between
him and Moskalenko also "grew into true friendship."[92] Some of the
most poignant cases in the memoirs involve reluctant or emotional
farewells. For instance, when the commander of an infantry corps,
Bondarev, was ordered removed for insubordination, the first to protest was his politotdel chief, Nikolai S. Demin (later to be a senior MPA
official). "I must confess," Demin wrote later, "that the decision to remove Bondarev astounded me . . . I had been in every kind of fine
mess with Andrei Leont'evich. More than once we had, as they say,
died and risen from the dead together . . . I did not want to part with
Bondarev. I had become intimately linked with him."[93]

To be sure, one can also find some relationships between party
workers and commanders that are mediocre or even hostile. But
upon close reading there seems no reason to see these as expressions of
consistent institutional conflict. I have never found a case where a
member of one hierarchy has had poor relations with members of only
the other organization. Commanders who feud with political officers
tend also to quarrel with other commanders, and political officers
who have indifferent relations with their command colleagues are also
unlikely to get along smoothly with fellow political officers.

One also sees commanders (or political officers) who disagree with
one political (or command) colleague but enjoy excellent relations
with others. Marshal Tukhachevskii, for instance, had several disputes with his political officer in the Western Military District in 1924
(a man who was, according to another political worker who wit-
nessed the quarrel, "undoubtedly inclined toward intrigue"), but
Tukhachevskii worked amicably with the officer's successor.[94] It is
even possible for an officer to have poor relations with a colleague
because of his affection or esteem for the colleague's predecessor (as
happened with Demin and Bondarev's successor).[95]

If personal involvement between command and political officers
performing related tasks is common, this has obvious implications for
the kind of information that political officers are likely to transmit to
superiors. Clearly a leadership interested primarily in making that
information as complete and unsparing as possible would take steps to
inhibit fraternization at lower levels. Yet such steps have not been
systematically pursued in the case of the military party apparatus.

One possibility would be for central decision makers to encourage
conflict between political officers and their command associates. But
this course of action has not been followed with any consistency. The
political officer who appeals to his superiors for help in a conflict

with his commander is under most circumstances likely to be rebuked for "not having correct relations" with the other officer, and the fate of his appeal will be uncertain even if it is heard.[96]

The other obvious option would be to disrupt nascent relationships by increasing the mobility of political officers. There is no evidence of consistent pursuit of such a policy for senior MPA officials. From 1948 to 1975 the average tenure of the several dozen most important political officers was slightly greater than that of commanders holding comparable posts (4.9 years as opposed to 4.4). (See Table 12 for specification of posts and year-by-year figures.) In district-level military councils in April 1978, commanding officers had served an average of 3.9 years in their posts; the heads of political administrations were slightly behind at 3.6 years. Fifteen years earlier the order was reversed—political officers had been in their posts an average of 2.9 years, commanders 2.5 years. (It was presumably the lengthier service of political officers in earlier years that led to their somewhat more rapid turnover in the 1970s.)

At lower levels, the rule on rotation of half of all elected party executives at every election which was in effect from 1961 to 1966 had as one of its announced aims the combating of "family circles." Under the rule, the elected party secretaries in the army, as elsewhere, had considerably briefer tenures than before or since.[97] But the rule was short-lived, and it was never extended to appointed political officers. Even at this time MPA spokesmen called for fewer rather than more transfers of cadre political workers. These demands have continued since then.[98]

Conclusion

The characteristics of the political organs are thoroughly at variance with those to be expected of an organization capable of effectively monitoring the army command. Party workers and commanders are joined by a division of labor which harnesses them in pursuit of closely related objectives. Their career paths are often intertwined. Political workers have increasingly been committed to the army for life and equipped with military expertise. And there has been continuous personal interaction between the two hierarchies.

Of relations between the two organizations, General Krainiukov has written: "We political workers acquired a great deal of military knowledge from the commanders [and] the political workers also passed on their experience to the command cadres. A mutual enrichment of knowledge took place ."[99] There is no question that one side—the political apparatus—has been enriched more decisively than the other. The military party apparatus has taken on many of the characteristics of the command structure with which it is integrated in so many ways. What the Soviets call the militarization (*voenizatsiia*) of the political organs goes far beyond the limited sense in which this term is used officially (to mean acquisition of a specialized military education).[100] Militarization has affected not only political workers' work schedules and career expectations but their self-image as well. It is thus perfectly understandable to see General Epishev and other political officers referring to themselves in military terms—as "we military men" or "we military workers."[101] They are soldiers of the party, and they bear special weapons, but they are soldiers nonetheless.

Part Two
The Military Party Organs and Military Politics

Routine Administrative Politics

5

We turn now to military politics—political conflict in which military officers are major participants—in five quite diverse settings. The choice of settings has necessarily been influenced by the availability of evidence. Two chapters—Chapter 5 on routine administration and Chapter 9 on broad political articulations—have an indeterminate time focus, although their main concern is with the post-Stalin period. The three other chapters in Part Two deal with sharply defined periods and can properly be called case studies.

For some purposes this subject matter can be considered as evidence of interest group activity, to use a concept which has gained currency among students of Soviet politics.[1] Such a conceptualization is useful if it reminds the reader that we are analyzing a process in which different needs and preferences (interests) are being articulated and acted upon by aggregates of individuals (groups). No assumption is made that conflict involving groups is the sole determinant of outcomes. And it will be important to bear in mind that the principals are appointed administrative officials whose primary political concerns are those arising in the bureaucratic workplace. They are not members of voluntary associations such as formed the basis for the development of interest group theory in the United States, and whatever their preferences on questions unrelated to their status and functions as officials these are beyond the scope of at least this part of the book.

The first political setting to be surveyed is the routine-bound world of peacetime military administration, the main procedures of which were introduced in Chapter 3. One is struck in observing this activity both by the diversity of military officers' views on organizational questions and by the structure inherent in this diversity. As in Ezra

Suleiman's study of French civil servants, "Behavior . . . is in large measure defined by the function performed . . . by the position of the official in the administrative hierarchy."[2] What is crucial to recognize is that the political attachments dictated by position cut in a patterned way across the formal boundaries between institutions. Not only are the military party organs themselves beset by hierarchical tensions, but these intermesh with the conflicts among the levels of the military bureaucracy as a whole. From the point of view of low-level personnel, superior political organs are part of a general set of senior officials striving to constrain their behavior. From the perspective of higher-level officers, junior political workers belong to a larger body of subordinates resisting compliance with their preferences.

The View from Below: Penalties Reinforced

There is no room in the standard Western image of the MPA as a finely tuned monitoring instrument for the frequent and often intense intraorganizational conflicts which are amply reported in military publications. Most of these conflicts are essentially hierarchical, pitting political workers from one level of authority against political officers working at another level.

General discussions of such strains can be found in almost any period, and the consistency among them is striking. A representative view from below dating from the interwar period is a regiment party secretary's declaration in 1936 that the officials in his division's politotdel (that is the political officers one level above him) were "little concerned with the questions that interest us" and were inflexible and unfamiliar with his regiment's personnel and problems.[3] In the accompanying exchange of letters, a cadre political officer from another regiment portrayed this as a common pattern: "Politotdel instructors rarely give the political workers in the units what they want from them." He expressed only the modest hope that senior officers would "learn to correct shortcomings peacefully, without fuss, noise, and turmoil."[4]

The evidence suggests no fundamental change since then. The junior political officer's greatest source of anxiety continues to be his superiors, particularly superior political officers, and not the commander with whom he works. The interest of those above lies in maximizing his contribution to the attainment of their goals. They evaluate his performance against that standard and hold the key to his job security and career advancement. Unit-level political officers still speak of superiors who "prefer to rebuke lower officials rather than [offer them] practical help,"[5] yet even well-intentioned help normally involves the bestowing of unwelcome sanctions. The most saccharine of reports on the ideal inspector cannot conceal the inherent conflict of interest on managerial questions between him and the inspected. They must show him as a man who is capable of imposing his will and judgment on others, as someone who "sincerely [tells lower officials] where and how they have committed mistakes and what to do to correct them."[6]

This inbuilt tension is aggravated by the rigidity of the discipline to which political officers must submit, which often produces conflict when intermediate officials cannot question misguided or even malicious instructions from above. Thousands of political workers have experienced the frustration felt by the party secretary who was compelled by the political department of his ship formation to hold a meeting on a specified propaganda theme for the second time in less than a week. "The politotdel workers understood, of course, that Chovgal [the secretary] was right. But what could they do when the political administration of the fleet had directed that there be party meetings with such an agenda in each and every subunit? The politotdel workers were afraid to assume the responsibility for allowing Chovgal to dispense with the second meeting." Chovgal convoked the meeting, although in bad humor.[7]

Hierarchical strain is further worsened by the highly formalized nature of vertical communication within the MPA, particularly the attachment to written directives and reports. "You sometimes get the impression," one political officer wrote in 1966 about his superiors, "that some of these people could not live in peace unless they were 'launching' papers downwards."[8] While the flood of paper probably reached its peak during Stalin's reign, there is no doubt that coping with it is still a strenuous and highly resented imperative.[9]

A final irritant lies in the tendency for senior administrators, in an organization which has always placed a high premium on irreconcilability toward shortcomings, to "concentrate almost all their attention on finding faults below" in order to improve their own reputations for diligence.[10] It may often seem more important to uncover a problem below than to help correct it. The regiment political officer writing in 1936 observed that when an official from a superior party organ arrived in his unit, "usually the first thing he tries to do is to . . . find the weakest link in our work and to raise a corresponding 'uproar' about it."[11] This approach, which was certainly encouraged by the general style of Soviet politics under Stalin, remains a topic of frequent discussion. One reads, for instance, of inspectors who "speak about derelictions not with alarm but with a strange pride." Such an official's " 'find' does not upset him. For him it is important, but only as a trenchant 'inspector's fact.' "[12]

Two important points bear emphasis here. One is that senior political officers do not work alone in imposing such priorities. Given their position, their almost invariable collaborators are the command and staff officers from their own level of authority. It is with these men that their offices are tightly integrated, with whom they are jointly accountable to superiors, and with whom they interact from day to day (and indeed "meet many times a day," in the words of a recent story about a division politotdel chief and his commander).[13] Political officers routinely accompany staff officers on inspection trips and exchange information on problems involving mutual subordinates. And because the main medium of political officers' work is information, they make no major material claims on their immediate colleagues.[14] Occasional misunderstandings and disagreements based on personality cannot be precluded. But it is safe to say that the chief of staff of the Baltic Fleet was describing the typical relationship in 1972 when he referred to his office's close contact with the fleet's political administration and to how the two bodies "try to solve similar problems by mutual efforts."[15]

Spokesmen recognize this grouping of interests when they regularly use the behavior of political organs along with that of commanders in illustrations of overbearing or insensitive superiors. A typical criticism is of a division where "the staff and the political department . . . are little concerned with people."[16] There is also repeated comment about the reluctance of political officers to conduct investigative or even educational work among their staff colleagues—"the political organs give little attention to the party organizations of staffs and administrations."[17]

While the specialized concerns of the senior party worker (at the division, army, district, or service level) are different from those of, say, a staff engineer or logistics officer, his general sense of administrative priorities—particularly of the necessity to ensure the maximum contribution from subordinates—is likely to be quite similar. As one reporter put it, "Common threads bind the work of staffs and politotdels organically together."[18] These ties are not flawless, but they far exceed in durability and warmth those linking successive layers of either the political apparatus or the military command. Indeed, Soviet spokesmen have usually judged it less probable that political officers will fail to cooperate with military staffs than that they will collaborate so intensely as to submerge their identity entirely. Even in 1943 a story could relate how the politotdel instructor touring the field with staff officers "often becomes a peculiar kind of appendage to the operations group of the staff of the division or army."[19] Likewise in 1966 the chief political officer in the Odessa Military District could remark on the narrow practicality (*uzkii praktits-izm*) of many political organs. "You look at a plan of work for a field exercise, and you cannot tell for whom it has been composed—for workers of the political organ or for command officers. In it you see scrupulous time estimates, plans for the use of vehicles—everything but thoughtful concern for the spiritual food of the men."[20]

The second point to be clearly understood is that the lower officials subject to constraint by superior political organs are not party workers only, but junior commanders as well, and that this pressure tends to reinforce the administrative sanctions leveled by superior commanders rather than run counter to them. In the 1920s MPA chief Bubnov went so far as to pronounce party discipline "a subsidiary means for the strengthening of military discipline."[21] More recent statements do not rank either type of discipline above the other, but they do emphasize their compatibility and mutual reinforcement. The man who falters in his official duty is culpable in the eyes of both the command and the political organs. Party discipline can be said to be infused with military content.

This fact has been overlooked by Western scholars who stress those outward aspects of "intraparty democracy" that seem to run contrary to the line of military subordination. Foremost among these is the much-vaunted practice of intraparty criticism and self-criticism (*krit-ika i samokritika*) of behavior that violates party norms. In form, permitting the members of any organizational unit to criticize operations poses a threat to its leadership. There might well be a compromising of military discipline if, say, regiment commanders were regularly criticized by soldiers or junior officers at regiment-level party meetings. Certainly there was use of such practice during the Great Purge, and there was a mild recurrence in 1957-58. But, with these exceptions, intraparty criticism has not proved a serious impediment to the military command.

In the first place, commanding officers have little reason to oppose orderly discussion of the affairs of their organizational units. Party meetings can be valuable forums for collecting information from colleagues and subordinates on an informal basis. Many commanders seem to agree that "a businesslike exchange of opinions allows [them to make] use of the rich experience of all party members, of their knowledge and abilities."[22]

Moreover, criticism of leaders rarely has more force than what a Western social scientist would call feedback about decisions already taken. Indeed, if criticism has a consistent relationship to military authority, it has been to buttress that authority rather than contravene it.

One major reason for this is the existence of formal restrictions on the criticism of officers, most important the ban on criticism of orders and the denial to most party organizations in the army of the right of checking of management commonly found in civilian settings. Also of importance are MPA directives imposed after the purge forbidding examination of officers' possible misdemeanors (*prostupki*), for which a formal party penalty may be imposed, by assemblies composed mainly of their subordinates. Under the rule in effect since 1958, most misdemeanors are scrutinized by primary party organizations, but the case of a commander or political officer at the regiment level or above can be considered only by the party commission of the next highest political organ.[23] The only generally approved area for criticism of commanding officers remains their bearing (*povedenie*), meaning essentially their attitude toward their colleagues, and even here the impact is usually quite limited.

Criticism is also subject to informal constraints. A chronic weakness is the permeation of the process by bureaucratic ritualism. The press often carries stories of criticism carried out "for the record" and without lasting effect:

You often meet officers who look upon criticism as a seasonal thing. They respect it one day, but do not even notice it the next. For example, you arrive at a party election meeting in a unit. All the attention is focused on criticism. The Communists are chatting about the significance of party principle, about irreconcilability toward shortcomings. On the walls of the meeting hall you find slogans and posters on criticism and self-criticism. You listen to the speeches of the party leaders from the tribune, and they are thanking the members for their criticism of deficiencies and promising to take immediate, effective measures. In a word, everything is as it should be in form.

However, once the meeting is over and the protocol transcribed, everything goes on as before. The shortcomings remain as they were.[24]

Another informal constraint, which persists despite repeated condemnation, is the willingness of officers at all levels to use their official and private resources to intimidate vigorous critics. There are repeated accounts of men silencing outspoken critics for "undermining authority" or of dissenters being called into officers' quarters for warnings. At least some do not stop short of sabotaging the careers of those few who do make bold criticism. One officer described the situation in 1970 (in an anonymous letter): "If a man behaves quietly and is not an activist in the struggle against shortcomings, some senior comrades give him a good appraisal. But if he mounts businesslike criticism of shortcomings and abuses, and points to concrete culprits, they start to look for shortcomings in him."[25] These tactics, regardless of the risks, have clearly had a cumulative dampening effect. As the author of the letter put it, even the courageous "go limp when it is necessary to speak openly and condemn incorrect actions." Another officer, asked in 1962 why he had failed to raise his voice against poor leadership, replied unambiguously, "I have not yet reached pension age."[26]

It should be recognized that suppression of criticism is by no means a sin ascribed exclusively to commanders. Party workers have no less incentive to resort to it, and judging from press reports they do so no less frequently. Sometimes the political officer acts alone, but it is more likely that he will speak for a broader group which includes commanders and for which the criticism is threatening or annoying. Most official condemnations of suppression of criticism make no distinction between political officers and others, and most of the examples in the press involve both. In a typical case, a politotdel official attending a regiment party meeting was infuriated by comments about the neglect of the regiment's housing stock by the division command and politotdel. He "was clearly offended by the remarks. He saw them as 'undermining authority' and emphatically advised the meeting to conduct itself 'in a proper manner.' "[27]

The most important factor inhibiting the turning of criticism against the grain of military discipline is neither formal circumscription nor the informal limitations mentioned thus far. Rather, it is the view of criticism as part of a general fund of disciplinary measures that parallel and reinforce military authority. Official spokesmen have long insisted that criticism "should strengthen the power of the commander, of his will and word," and even praises of criticism from below will refer to its role in "strengthening the authority of leading cadres."[28] Such statements sometimes mean that commanding officers can lead their subordinates with full authority only when they are sensitive to their grievances and concerns. More frequently, however, they point to the fact that the normal targets of criticism at party meetings are junior personnel. A regiment commander may hear at a party meeting in his command that there are problems with discipline or equipment maintenance in one of his subunits, and such information may imply that he or other senior personnel have been at fault. But there is no question of his specific decisions being scrutinized in detail by a party meeting, or indeed by any agency of the party except one operating at a higher level of the military hierarchy. When one reads of commanders being criticized at party gatherings, it is important to keep in mind that these are usually men holding low-level offices (at a regi-

ment party meeting, these would be the platoon or company commanders and technicians). Where an officer of some standing is
criticized directly and sharply, it almost invariably means that a
directive demanding such treatment has been issued by superior officials (political and command). Even under these circumstances, the
discussion may be perfunctory.[29] Rarely will the active participants in
the discussion be rank-and-file personnel, if for no other reason than
that soldiers and sailors are overwhelmingly outnumbered in party
organizations in the army by officers.

How and why is party discipline normally applied? Acts enforcing
it can range from informal warning from a political officer or party
secretary, through public censure and notation of an offense on a
man's party record, to suspension or termination of his party membership. While failure to live up to the terms of membership in the party
(by attending meetings and so forth) can incur reprimand, the vast
majority of cases reported in the press entail actions that violate military norms as well. Even the exchange of party documents of 1973-75,
which required military officers (like all party members) to justify
their commitment to the party and its goals in a broad sense, involved
conversations with each officer by a responsible MPA official "on
the shortcomings and errors of the Communist in his official duty and
bearing."[30]

Party discipline is sometimes administered for "immoral behavior."
There were a number of reports in the early 1960s of stiff reprimands
leveled for unacceptable sexual conduct, particularly when this involved civilians or the wives of fellow officers. More often, heavy
drinking or alcoholism is the target of this sort of punishment, especially if it impairs working relations or is brought to the attention of
the party organization by a senior officer.[31]

Party discipline is also applied for commision of clearly illegal acts,
usually after these have been dealt with by administrative or judicial
procedure. The severity of the penalty varies with the offense. An
officer who has been discharged or imprisoned for embezzling funds
or diverting labor or materials to his private use (the press provides
numerous examples of this, especially in construction and commercial
units) is sure to be expelled from the party as well. A man who
manages to remain in the army on probation or at a lesser post will
probably escape with either public censure or temporary demotion to
party candidate status.[32]

In most cases given in the press, there is a direct link with military
discipline but the behavior being punished falls short of outright
illegality. Party discipline is routinely invoked for quite specific acts
of dereliction of duty or even for mere inadequacy of performance. In

the Stalin period this supplement to military discipline could be extremely harsh. In 1940 *Krasnaia zvezda* could report favorably on the expulsion from the party of an officer who was late in returning from an excursion to town "by almost two hours."[33] In the modern army the penalty is unlikely to be so draconian. A similar lapse would now occasion a public or private reprimand, or perhaps the assignment of several party members to take shefstvo (patronage) over the wrongdoer. Expulsion is now treated as a remedy of last resort, and there are even reports of "people who have not heeded . . . party reprimands [but] remain for a prolonged time in party ranks."[34] A man expelled for whatever reason also has a much better chance now of being restored by higher political organs—two thirds of all appeals against exclusion in 1974 were sustained.[35]

Whatever its lessened stringency, the direction of party discipline has undergone little alteration. Besides punishing party members on an ad hoc basis for falling down in their military duties, party organizations now hear periodic reports by officers on the carrying out of their military assignments. Once frowned upon, this came into use more and more often in the late 1960s.[36] It is in many ways a modification of well-established past practice. Officers have always been liable to occasional summons by elected party executives (most of whom are themselves officers); typically the session was described as one at which the party bureau or committee heard out (*poslushal*) the suspected offender.[37] The recent change is a systematization of this procedure that implies no new lines of subordination. Commanders deliver reports only to elected party bodies at higher levels, and party organizations have been granted no right to redefine or even to express an opinion on the appropriateness of official duties.[38]

Soviet accounts of how party organizations participate in disciplinary matters are not always clear. Some refer to steps taken by "the Communists" or "party activists" of a military unit, or even by "the members of the party bureau," in very imprecise terms. These steps seem in many cases to be no more than the routine actions of officials who happen to be party members or the occupants of elective party offices. At other times, elected party organs are said to take clear collective action, but there is little or no information about how such actions relate to the preferences and decisions of responsible commanding officers. Consider, for instance, this description of an air defense unit in 1969:

Recently it has become more common . . . for party bureau sessions to hear how individual Communists carry out duties connected with the heightening of combat readiness and the improvement of watch duty. For example, the bureau . . . heard a report by officer Sliuzin on "the work of Communists in the crew of the command point in inculcating in personnel responsibility for vigilant carrying out of watch duty." The reporter and the members of the bureau uncovered deficiencies in the training and education of the soldiers and sergeants of the command point crew. The implementation of the resolution adopted [by the bureau] facilitated the heightening of the responsibility of the Communists of the command point for the carrying out of their official duties. As a result the work of the crew was noticeably improved and the military expertise of the personnel was heightened.[39]

Viewed in isolation, such an account might imply party interference with the prerogatives of regular staff and line officials. Yet such an interpretation would almost certainly be incorrect. Had the party bureau actually felt capable of redefining the crew's objectives, the report surely would have talked about a result other than heightening the responsibility of party members for the carrying out of what clearly are predetermined duties.

In fact, most press reports leave no doubt about the position of the responsible command official, or about the fact that the normal effect of a party action is to bolster that position, not undermine it. It is often specified that the action of the party organization has come at the initiative of the commanding officer himself, as in the regiment where the colonel in charge "first of all took the measures that depended on him" when a problem arose and then "turned the attention of the party activists toward . . . the execution of their duties."[40] Likewise, when one reads that a young air force officer "made a landing approach in a manner contrary to that decided upon by the flight leader" and therefore received a serious reprimand from his party organization, there can be little question about the reinforcing effect of the party action.[41] Many accounts even suggest invocation of a party penalty to be a natural or inevitable consequence of a man's breach of military rules. For instance, when an officer violated commitments to his superiors to improve his performance at artillery practice in 1960, "Ultimately the [party] bureau had to bring him to party accountability. He was assessed a party penalty." Similarly, when a weary company commander ruined a tank exercise in 1972, he "received a disciplinary punishment and, as a Communist, also answered before the party organization."[42]

It cannot be overemphasized that the political organs do not normally impose upon officers standards derived from a set of values external to the military or antithetical to its spirit. Indeed, if there is a single criticism that echoes again and again, it is that party discipline is excessively bound up with general military discipline to the point where party life loses all distinctiveness.

The most common fault found in party discipline in the Stalin era—except for the purge years—was precisely that it mechanically reinforced military discipline. As Konstantin Sidorov, the secretary of the MPA party commission, wrote in 1936, "Many party organizations and party commissions mechanically impose party penalties for each military misdemeanor. Any punishment whatever received by a Communist in the administrative line is matched by a party penalty." Sidorov was careful to stress that he wanted only a change in method in the direction of flexibility and "comradely explanation of mistakes," not an amnesty for offenders.[43]

Sidorov's recommendation has been followed as far as severity of penalty is concerned. But there has been no major change otherwise. The press still refers to a "mechanical approach" to the levying of party penalties on administrative matters, and to the tendency for party organizations to copy (*kopirovat'*) or duplicate (*dublirovat'*) measures undertaken by command and staff officers.[44] The kind of practice reported in 1967 for one regiment appears to be quite typical:

Personal cases have been raised in identical circumstances, following one and the same scheme. Let us assume that an error has been committed in one of the companies. The party committee is silent, as if this was of no concern to it. But then a senior officer punishes the subunit commander (who is as a rule a party member) and a reaction by the party committee follows immediately. The party member is summoned to a committee session, given a strict rebuke, and served with a party punishment. The commander has not been punished as a Communist for his errors and shortcomings, but because he has received an administrative punishment.[45]

The eagerness to integrate party and military concerns is evident in the ideological realm. Marxist-Leninist seminars for officers are said often to "confine themselves to a scrupulous enumeration of current tasks in the unit," complete with imputation of fault by superior officers. Some ideological discussions "are in no way different from official (*sluzhebnye*) meetings" (routine meetings of personnel without party content).[46]

This same characterization is made of meetings of party organizations themselves. As one reporter put it in 1968, "Often party meetings do not differ essentially in agenda or content of the reports and discussion from official meetings." He gave the example of one party organization in the navy where even the election meeting "was in many ways reminiscent of an official conference," with speakers reporting on the grading of exercise books and navigation in stormy seas.[47] In another unit where party meetings were studied for a year, "As a rule it was the commander who gave the report. These reports were no different from his addresses at regular meetings. The discussion was in the spirit of an official meeting. Each Communist gave an account of himself and gave assurances he would devote all his energies to carrying out his duties."[48] It therefore is hardly surprising that the resolutions adopted by political organs and party organizations often contain "points very similar to paragraphs in the orders, directives, and instructions given out by the command."[49]

Spokesmen in the press occasionally object to this phenomenon from several points of view, although this never has been enough to force significant change. There is some disquietude over the authoritarian style of many party meetings, and especially over the effect on members' sense of participation of sessions dominated by "staff orators" (shtatnye oratory) and "planned in advance down to the tiniest detail."[50] Yet there is no indication of official readiness to alter this pattern, which could be accomplished only by quite fundamental departures from both military discipline and the party's "democratic centralism."

There is also occasional anxiety over the inattention to nonmilitary questions at party gatherings. For many party meetings involving a great deal of discussion of matters such as vehicle preparation and shooting practice, "the only thing that is not discussed directly . . . is intraparty work," including ideological campaigns and party recruitment.[51] Here again the problem is implicit in the MPA's whole approach to its mission. Narrow practicality is the natural outcome of intimate involvement in routine military administration. The distinction between this vice and the virtues of concreteness (konkretnost') and goal-directedness (tseleustremlennost') is a fine one, usually too delicate to be made in real life.

But the most commonplace stricture is less drastic. While there is some concern about party resolutions that obligate (obiazut) officers to perform actions covered by their official duties and properly the business of their line superiors, the more usual worry is about resolutions that do nothing but reinforce dispositions the commanding officer has already made. This reflects a general awareness that political officers and party organizations do not always delineate a distinctive contribution to the carrying out of military tasks—an awareness which, however, takes the nature and primacy of these tasks for granted. This was the point of Sidorov's criticism of mechanical party penalties, and it also appears in more contemporary discussions. For instance, when the member of the military council of the Leningrad Military District complained in 1967 about party resolutions that are nearly identical to official orders, his argument was not that such resolutions contradict commanders' preferences but that they go no further than restating commanders' orders and endorsing measures already "taken care of by the training plan."[52] Likewise, the report on the officer belatedly punished by the regiment party committee after intervention from above did not object to the committee's penalizing him but to its allowing him to go without attention for so long that punishment became necessary—to its having failed "to prevent errors, to inculcate in [the officer] a conscientious attitude toward his duty."[53]

This is mild opprobrium indeed, a critique of technique and not of ends. It is as powerful an avowal as any of the degree to which the military party apparatus's operations and interests have become intertwined with those of the army command.

The View from Above: Information Distorted

Central military officials reviewing the shortcomings of subordinates rarely find it necessary to differentiate between commanders and political officers. Officers below make the same kind of identification in many of their statements and actions. At any given bureaucratic location, the commander and party official are likely to be political allies acting together on common interests.

The cooperative political efforts of junior command and political officers can be either assertive or defensive. Assertive or outward-looking group activity appears to be most common on the issue of supply procurement. Although this is the primary responsibility of specialized logistics officers acting under the general supervision of commanders, there are intermittent references in the press to political officers who act as supply expeditors, using personal influence to procure needed materials or favors on behalf of their units and colleagues. For some political officers this can evidently become a full-time undertaking. In 1963, for example, the MPA's journal printed a profile of a battalion zampolit, Tkachenko, who had "earned a reputation as a 'go-getter.' Every time something needs to be found, searched for, or 'beat out,' the unit commander assigns the job to Captain Tkachenko." He had gone on sixty trips in the previous eleven months, "getting accounts, authorizations, and the like into shape," often "compromis[ing] his party conscience and indulg[ing] in machinations." Away three or four days a week on logistics matters, he had been "essentially transformed into a supply specialist" (snabzhenets).[54]

It is difficult to ascertain how common such interventions are at more senior levels. There can be little doubt that political officers above the troop formation level have preferences on supply questions reflecting the interests of the military agencies in which or with which they work. Clear evidence of widely diverging perspectives emerges in discussions such as that held at a conference on the improvement of military living conditions in June 1962. First deputy MPA chief Efimov acknowledged some defects in the work of central logistics organs but insisted that shortcomings were explained largely by the poor work of field agencies, including "a number of political organs and party organizations." On the other hand, the head of the political administration of the Turkestan Military District, Lieutenant-General Nikolai Demin, took the opportunity "to address some critical remarks to several central administrations of the Ministry of Defense," saying they "fail to take into account the problems of water supply and organization of public services and amenities in distant garrisons."[55]

Beyond these general statements, Soviet sources reveal occasional cases of intervention by senior political officers on specific logistics questions.[56] On the whole, however, assistance in the procurement of material supplies does not seem to be a major role in peacetime. The examples I have cited are quite rare (even for junior political officers, whose behavior is amply described in the press), and they are far less numerous than instances of group behavior on other issues. It should be pointed out here that party involvement in logistics was much more vigorous in wartime (see Chapter 7), mainly because supply questions were of far greater urgency when military units were responsible for producing tangible results while at the same time having their material and human assets subject to constant depletion. In the peacetime army most political officers certainly prefer more materials for their units, but few seem to intervene as aggressively in the supply process as Tkachenko, for whom personal aptitude was probably an important factor.

Much more widespread in peacetime seems to be acquiescence by political organs in administrative practices which deplete material supplies or otherwise distort central planners' detailed preferences in order to meet gross performance targets. This seems to be especially common in military organizations specializing in construction or for which construction is a major function. In 1976 the MPA held a special conference to discuss the failure by party organizations within construction agencies to "create an atmosphere of exactingness" toward the economic use of materials and the avoidance of waste and stockpiling. The charge that party officials are moved by "the urge to fulfill the production plan at any cost" is one frequently directed at construction and manufacturing executives—in the civilian economy as well as the military—and it follows a long line of complaints about political officers and party secretaries who "do nothing to correct" hoarding and extravagant use of capital equipment and materials "even though there are shortages of such materials in other places."[57] Comprehensive critiques of administrative malpractice in military construction and retail agencies commonly draw a specific connection between party officials' and line administrators' actions. "One finds," says a typical criticism (written by the first deputy head of the political administration of the Leningrad Military District), "that certain executives are quite prepared in order to fulfill the plan to let 'the small things' suffer. In construction they 'ram through' metre after metre of housing space, leaving future residents without stores and kindergartens. In retail trade, in looking for a high level of turnover, they 'fail to see' the narrowness of selection. Such distortions of leadership are possible only where the political organ and party organization do not take a principled position."[58]

As far as active appeals for materials are concerned, most seem to occur in the construction area. Most of these are directed through private channels within the army and are very rarely reported in the press. Nonetheless, a recent entreaty aimed mainly at civilian agencies is indicative of the vigor with which MPA officials are prepared to pursue sectoral interests if convinced that such action is necessary. The solicitation was published in early 1976 (during the final stage of preparing the current five-year plan) by Lieutenant-General Iakov M. Maiorov, the chief of the political administration of the railroad troops, which bear main responsibility for the eastern leg of the huge Baikal-Amur Mainline (BAM) project in Siberia. Maiorov criticized the slowness of planning and design decisions, demanded more investment in repair facilities, and called on the State Committee for Material-Technical Supply and other civilian organizations to "reconsider their system for supplying spare parts for the equipment on BAM" to take into account the climate and pace of construction. He also proposed more attention to the local construction and materials-manufacturing enterprises on which the project depends: "It would be appropriate to set aside some of the resources designated for the building of major new construction facilities for the development of local enterprises in areas adjacent to the railroad. That way they would be able to give BAM more concrete, metal, ties, and other construction materials."[59]

If assertive group action such as this is rare (except in military construction), quite the opposite is true of defensive group activity. Most political officers would gladly "knock on any door" (to quote one party secretary) in order to improve their administrative units' chances of success, but the fact is that in peacetime military administration it is normally senior officials who knock on doors.[60] They usually do so in quest of a peacetime military unit's main output— information, mainly information about the unit's state of combat readiness. The chief producers of this output (the command and political officers in charge) do indeed pursue a common interest, but primarily one in preserving their discretion in making decisions and in maintaining a favorable image of their joint performance in the eyes of superiors.

Discussion of the party apparatus's capacity for distorting the upward flow of information recurs through decades of the military press. During the 1936 debate on the political organs, for example, MPA chief Gamarnik declared categorically: "Many political workers are less concerned with making their units model ones than they are with showing them in the best light."[61] Another senior official agreed with observations by junior party workers about hierarchical friction but placed the blame squarely on subordinates whose information about their work could not be relied upon. "In a number of cases commissars refuse to provide this information, and the instructor must literally 'tear it out.' "[62]

It is easy to find virtually interchangeable comments in the more recent press. Some discussions single out party workers for withholding or warping information. For example, one reads a political administration inspector describing how, although he would prefer frank statements from lower-level political officers, "unfortunately I am usually forced to hear the reverse . . . In giving information, the comrades stress the positive. Talk of shortcomings is cursory and general, without details."[63] More often, no line is drawn between party workers and other officers: "Some commanders, political workers, and party and Komsomol secretaries, not wanting, as the saying goes, to let the litter out of the hut (*vynosit' sor iz izby*), do not always give objective information to superior officers and political organs. They try to present the situation as better than it actually is."[64]

What are the inducements for such collaborative effort? The formal subordination of political officers at the division level and below to the corresponding commanders no doubt inhibits the upward flow of information, as does the commander's superiority in informal status (which is especially pronounced in comparison to party and Komsomol secretaries as opposed to cadre political officers). Personal timidity and a concern for safeguarding organizational routine are also of some weight. The man who raises his voice before superiors about the deficiencies of his colleagues must reckon on those colleagues' later hostility and, whatever his original personal relationship with them (which is often quite an intimate one), he can expect a disruption of their working association. Even in 1938, at the height of the purge, one can find criticism of "unprincipled commissars who, out of a reluctance to spoil 'good-neighborly' relations with commanders, cover up shortcomings in combat training." Similar phrases are used in the modern press.[65]

Probably the most substantial factor is the sharing of operational responsibility by the commander and the party official. Both are vitally concerned with their unit's success, are judged in terms of this success, and have a powerful interest in presenting performance in as favorable a light as possible. Neither is likely to evade reproach for errors even if the other man is mainly to blame. (Superiors will usually reason like Trotsky during the Civil War, for whom, "if the regiment is poor, it must mean that the commander and the commissar are [both] poor.")[66] And both officers may also with perfect sincerity perceive the objective truth in a way very different from superiors. What strikes the inspector from the military district's political administration (or staff headquarters) as poor performance or negligence may well seem to the regiment zampolit (or commander) to be justifiable or even inevitable due to factors beyond the control of the regiment's leadership (among them the actions and expectations of the district leadership).

To these self-interested calculations and perceptions are often added nonrational attachments to the organizational unit—feelings which the political officer, one of whose main duties is fostering the solidarity of the fighting team, may be even more likely to develop than others. In 1936, for instance, one reads of the head of a division politotdel who, "worried about guarding the 'honor' of his formation, . . . does not always report on defects in work to superior political organs." Thirty-six years later a regiment zampolit could explain his failure to report a breach of discipline in almost identical terms—"by the fact that he 'had not wanted to injure the honor of the entire collective.' "[67]

There are several avenues for persuasion and misinformation of superiors. The most common is through one of the formal bureaucratic channels for submitting plans, reports, and requests to higher political organs and staffs. For example, political officers are often said to file greatly inflated plans for upcoming measures and projects (exactly the opposite of behavior in Soviet industry, where managers and party officials tend to project artificially low performance at given capacity because targets represent tangible material outputs). "Of course our plans are sometimes unrealistic and monotonous," one

party secretary told an interviewer in 1965. "But you have to understand our position. If we propose a curtailed plan, we get scolded. So
what do we do? We just include more measures in it."[68]

Political officers are also accused of "looking through their fingers"
at illegalities and arranging with commanders to settle disciplinary
matters "behind closed doors."[69] They are frequently berated as well
for exaggeration and even outright fabrication of results of combat
training and socialist competition. (The whole socialist competition
program, with its elaborate quantitative indicators, almost invites
such a response.)[70] Most of the periodic denunciations of simulation
(*ochkovtiratel'stvo*, literally "eyewash") are directed equally at political officers and commanders. One reads in 1938 of commissars
and commanders composing misleading reports "with brotherly effort"; in 1947 about party workers' reports on their units' performance
being "worked over, decorated, and glazed"; in 1956 about political
officers who "are inclined to exaggerate the results of their work,
tolerate sham, and close their eyes to serious errors in work"; in 1961
of party organs that "dress up reality, gloss over shortcomings, and
commit simulation and deceit"; in 1966 about political officers providing "nonobjective information that varnishes and fancies up the
truth"; and in 1975 about the efforts in political reports "to avoid
the 'rough edges,' oversights, and unresolved questions" in which
superiors are interested.[71]

One mode of misinformation deplored with particular vehemence
concerns the personnel files maintained on individual officers. Military authorities have repeatedly expressed exasperation at the unobjective nature of these documents, especially the attestation (*atte-
statsiia*) which summarizes the professional and personal attributes of
each officer being considered for promotion or reassignment. These
criticisms are often quite sweeping. In 1947 a report insisted that "the
majority of attestations have no relation whatever to reality," and in
1972 one cadres official declared that the attestation is "usual[ly] a
useless scrap of paper."[72] So seriously has the situation been viewed
that in 1971 there was a public debate on the merits of replacing attestations with competitive examinations.

The important point for our theme is that the military party organs,
far from acting as a corrective to such distortions, are universally
acknowledged to contribute to them as much as commanders and staff
officers. Political organs participate in composing and reviewing each
attestation, and they also keep a special reference (*kharakteristika*) on
each party member which is periodically updated by the secretary of
the man's party organization. In the special circumstances of the Great
Purge and the several years following it, political officers were fre-

quently said to write artificially negative evaluations to protect themselves from possible suspicion of "lack of vigilance."[73] Since that time (and before it as well), the common complaint has been of attestations and party references that idealize their subjects because of personal friendship, concern for preserving good working relations, or reluctance to admit defects in a subordinate or colleague that could imply prior indulgence on the part of the man writing the recommendation. Reports on attestation—whether written by general troop commanders, officials of the main cadres administration of the Ministry of Defense or its subsidiaries, or MPA officials—usually make no distinction whatever between political and command officers as originators and condoners of unobjective information. A typical discussion will lament the frequency of unreliable recommendations, then go on to say, "To a great extent this is explained by the fact that the political organs also tend to adopt *the same position* [as commanders]."[74] Sometimes a special point is even made of emphasizing party officials' predilection for partiality. Some of the most piquant illustrations of favoritism have been from references written by political officers for advancement of colleagues within the MPA itself—"even cases where a weak official is positively characterized only in order for [his referees] to get rid of him."[75]

Occasionally, misinformation by bureaucratic groups can spill over beyond the channels of formal communication. The political officer (or commander) may then resort to active and sometimes quite ingenious tactics—coalition building, trading of favors, personal vilification, and others—to maintain his area of discretion and manage the flow of information to superiors. While there are very real limits on such tactics set by prudence and conscience, they are employed frequently enough to be subject to repeated official warnings and to remain a persistent focus for discussion in the press.

Normally the immediate target of influence is a member of the party officials's own organizational unit, who must be persuaded not to take a complaint or an unflattering piece of information to higher authority. We read, for example, of one political officer agreeing to remain silent about a commander's falsification of training results in return for silence about his own recent drinking spree in a nearby town; of a regiment zampolit who "tried to convince other officers [in the regiment] 'not to make noise' " about an untoward incident in maneuvers involving regiment personnel; or of a party secretary striking a junior officer's criticism of the unit's leadership (and of the secretary himself) from the record of a party meeting and then "tak[ing] every occasion to find fault with [his] work."[76]

Should a member of his unit manage to appeal to a superior agency, the political officer's strategy is often to discredit the dissenter in the eyes of those superiors. In 1967, for instance, a pilot disturbed by poor safety precautions taken by the command of his fighter squadron wrote a letter of complaint to a newspaper. When a correspondent asked the squadron zampolit about the letter, he was informed tartly that the pilot "has cast a slur upon our entire squadron, which by the way is an excellent one. He has slandered us. He has set himself up against the collective." "He is a mudslinger," the party secretary agreed. "He has turned hairsplitting into a principle."[77]

External investigators are sometimes opposed by more strenuous means. The politotdel instructor who wrote in 1936 about having to "tear out" information from lower-level political officers gave the following illustration:

> I ran into a number of serious defects in the . . . unit where the pompolit is Amokin. I found it necessary to bring this up at one of the unit's party meetings, and I also wrote about the matter in the military district's newspaper. In his speech at the meeting, comrade Amokin directed a thousand caustic remarks at me and declared that I had done nothing but look for defects without helping them in their work. The pompolit, unfortunately, was supporting the comrades in the unit who had displayed the shortcomings. I remained, as they say, "in the minority." It is understandable that such an attitude toward the instructor does not bolster his authority or create a healthy setting for his work.[78]

Usually, however, a recalcitrant political officer will not hazard this use of open forums in which superiors, with their well-established prerogatives, are not likely to remain in the minority for long. A favorite tactic is to accuse the investigator in private of ignorance of the real situation in the unit in the hope that he will decline to pay the cost of probing further, or to suggest to him that he is jeopardizing overall performance and perhaps his own position and that of intermediate leaders by undermining authority in the low-level work unit. Sometimes such a policy will succeed. In 1973, for example, a party secretary and his associates are said to have convinced a division politotdel that poor results in their work could be attributed to objective factors. As the story about the incident pointed out, the politotdel's acquiescence "inevitably gives rise to the thought that certain officers in the political organ are not inclined to make public an embarrassing breakdown in combat training in a previously outstanding subunit."[79]

Should the superior agency not be amenable to persuasion that its interest lies in acquiescence, the hierarchical tension will be resolved by the imposition of a settlement on the superiors' terms. If the affair is reported in the press (and the vast majority of such incidents are, of course, unpublicized), it will be described in the kind of ominous language used in a 1965 story about a naval zampolit who "cast aspersions" on an inquiry into living conditions at his base: "The interference of the fleet political administration was necessary for, as the saying goes, putting everything in its place."[80]

The Great Purge

6

The Great Purge of the late 1930s seems the antithesis of administrative routine. Its roots lay outside the army, and any complete account of them would have to consider variables as diverse as Stalin's personality, Bolshevik history, and Russian culture. This chapter has the limited aim of analyzing the penetration of the nationwide terror into the military establishment. However overwhelming the impetus behind it, the workings of the purge were a political process which individuals and groups assisted and opposed. The military's party workers figured prominently in the process. From the beginning, the purge's embrace of them was as crushing as its grip on commanders. Violated in the same manner as the army command, the military party organs also responded in fundamentally similar ways. Some commissars facilitated the purge, some resisted it, but most strove simply to survive it.

The Purge Unfolds
The Great Purge was in form a deliberate verification of Communists' fidelity to the party's program and leadership and of their right to remain in its ranks. It was the sequel to a series of purges, most recently those of 1929-30 and 1933-34, which had had limited effect in the army. The earlier one had expelled 11.5 percent of the party as a whole but only 4.7 percent of military commanders and 2.8 percent of political officers. The later excluded or demoted 6.7 percent of military members, a quarter of the party average, and on this basis it was announced in 1934 that the army organizations were "the party's healthiest."[1]

In substance, however, the Great Purge in the army was a sustained act of externally managed terrorism. The key instigative role was assigned to the secret police, not to the regular line of MPA officials. Moreover, the grounds for doom were now almost entirely arbitrary. Some of those arrested during the preparatory phase (before the spring of 1937) may have once sympathized with one or another of the intraparty oppositions of the 1920s.[2] But by the time the terror unfolded in full, the executioners selected their victims with little or no regard for genuine political commitments and, indeed, with frequent reference to a theory of political motivation (Stalin's concept of the political hypocrite—*dvurushnik*) which cast most suspicion on those who appeared to be cleanest. The purge was a bludgeoning, not a surgical operation. The absence of standards pointing to where the club would next draw blood disarmed the political apparatus as thoroughly as the military command and left it equally open to the blows and the infection that ensued. Far from being a measured action by the party's organs in the army in the name of the party and its values, the purge was a crude assault *upon* the party apparatus as well as upon the army command itself.

No doubt the official terrorists were aware of the MPA's lack of zeal in the earlier screening of party ranks, especially in relation to the purging of officers. The MPA had endured strenuous censure during the checking and exchange of party documents in 1935-36, the antiphony to the mass terror. Political officers were accused of taking a "purely technical attitude" toward the exchange and conducting it with intolerable haste.[3]

Nothing was left to chance once a reluctant Central Committee endorsed a new, expanded purge at its spring plenum in 1937. The announcement on June 11 of the treason trial of Marshal Tukhachevskii and seven associates, the sign that all restraint was abandoned, was preceded by a three-month campaign of public vilification—one in which the MPA was a primary target. It was in fact against a political officer, the anonymous chief of a division politotdel, that the first accusation against a military man was leveled in *Krasnaia zvezda* of March 9. His principal sin, significantly, was "suppression of criticism" of himself and his deputy. As other charges followed, they actually outweighed in number and gravity those made against the command. While the campaign was in part a recital of familiar complaints about the political organs' bureaucratism, increasingly it came to focus upon their attitude toward the purge. The imputations of "complacency," "lack of self-criticism," and "lack of party-mindedness" were often quite specific. By June 11 *Krasnaia zvezda* had printed explicit attacks upon the heads of thirteen district-level political administrations, the deputy chiefs of three others, the secretaries of eight party commissions, and the director of the Tolmachev Military-

Political Academy; dozens of other alleged offenders were unnamed. Stalin's address to military leaders in early June announcing the discovery of a "counterrevolutionary military fascist organization" within the Red Army attacked "a number of commanders and political workers," among the latter the head of the political administration of the Leningrad Military District, Iosif Slavin.[4]

It was natural, then, for the transition from verbal abuse to mass force to apply as much to the party organs as to the military command. Symbolic of the turn was the fall of Ian Gamarnik, the head of the MPA since 1929 and a plainly marked victim from the beginning. Confined to bed for most of May by diabetes, he appeared for only the May Day parade, a tearful farewell to Tukhachevskii (departing for his last command in the provinces), and one session of the Moscow party conference. The noose tightened on May 10 when Gamarnik was relieved of his status as First Deputy People's Commissar of Defense. On May 31 Marshal Bliukher visited him at home, depressing him further with news about spreading arrests, and NKVD agents then sealed his offices. Informed later that day that he had been dismissed as MPA chief, he shot himself, preferring suicide to certain arrest.[5] *Pravda's* note on his suicide on June 1 stated that he had been "entangled with anti-Soviet elements and evidently in fear of exposure." From then on Gamarnik rated a star role in the official fantasy about military plotters. He was identified as a coconspirator in the June 11 communique and mentioned no fewer than ten times at the Bukharin trial in 1938. His wife was shot, and his grave was desecrated, like those of many of the fallen commanders. Even Gamarnik's memory was contaminated: a pilot who had once flown him to the Far East and a man for whom he had written a recommendation to military academy were considered ripe for expulsion from the party on those grounds.[6]

The removal of Gamarnik and his associates meant the destruction of one of the army's main buffers against the terror. The MPA leadership was soon to be arraigned for having at this time "defended the spies in every possible way" and attempted to "interfere with the unmasking of enemies of the people."[7] For good reason did word of Gamarnik's death "make a painful impression" on General Staff and other senior officers. They had ample reason to sense "that some great misfortune was moving toward us."[8]

It was a time of unrelieved misfortune for the MPA itself. As the arrests unfolded, the press aired sweeping execrations about how it had "not mobilized the vigilance of party organizations" against actual and prospective enemies, about the "many examples of political carelessness and blunting of vigilance" in its ranks.[9]

The evident aversion of the political organs to the bloodletting encouraged a trend which was already evident—consignment of the brunt of the task of "unmasking enemies" to the secret police apparatus, the NKVD, which had begun selective arrests in the army as early as the autumn of 1936. Editorials and speeches lauding the NKVD and its chief, Nikolai Ezhov, began to appear in the military press in June. It was the NKVD, with Stalin's personal encouragement, that fabricated the thousands of cases against military officers (among others) and assembled them on lists for his signature.[10] And it was the NKVD that was assigned the actual apprehension of designated enemies.

Reference to the experiences of prominent military casualties drives home this last point. All were to be expelled from the party after their arrests, but not one is known to have been subject to prior repudiation by the party organization or agency in whose jurisdiction he fell. Clearly the task of besmirchment was not one with which the military party apparatus could be trusted. In recognition of this inadequacy, many victims were seized quickly and surreptitiously, without party officials even being informed the arrest had taken place. Tukhachevskii, for example, disappeared between sessions of a party conference in the Volga Military District; no one was notified of his fate. Robert P. Eideman, the head of civil defense, met a similar lot in Moscow, and the commander of the air force, Iakov Alksnis, was swallowed up on his way to an evening diplomatic reception. Elaborate stratagems were devised to catch some victims off guard and away from possible support. Frequently the man was first relieved of his command, then arrested in transit or while waiting for new duties. Iona Iakir and Ieronim Uborevich, the commanders of the Kiev and Belorussian military districts and defendants at the Tukhachevskii trial, were arrested on trains taking them to an announced conference in Moscow preparatory to their reassignment. Aleksandr Sediakin, the head of air defense, was taken in July 1937 while on route to a new post in Baku.[11]

The NKVD terror machine did not function without aid from allies at the apex of the defense establishment. At least five senior officials are known to have actively furthered the purge: Kliment Voroshilov, the People's Commissar of Defense throughout this time; Petr Smirnov, successor to Gamarnik in the MPA and the head of the autonomous People's Commissariat of the Navy after December 30, 1937; Mikhail Shaposhnikov, the first chief of the separate MPA of the navy (not to be confused with Marshal Boris Shaposhnikov); Efim Shchadenko, the head of the army's main cadres administration from late 1937 onward; and Lev Mekhlis, who followed Smirnov in the MPA.

Voroshilov's role was complex. His public statements contained praise of the purge. He refused outright to help the officers accused in June 1937 and even wrote insulting epithets on Iakir's pleas for mercy for himself and his family. Nonetheless, he did act unobtrusively on behalf of some of the accused. He saved one former member of the dismantled guerrilla training staff by assuring Ezhov the officer was a little man he could deal with himself, and he interceded to rescue ten high-ranking artillery officers from disgrace in December 1937.[12]

Smirnov had come under heavy verbal fire in the spring of 1937 for complacency in his post as chief political officer in the Leningrad Military District. Notwithstanding this, by the last week of May he was in the Belorussian Military District, apparently involved in the beginnings of the purge there, announcing to a hushed party conference that Uborevich was under arrest and had "already confessed everything."[13] About his activity as head of the MPA, little is certain except his loud advocacy of vigilance. His tenure coincided with the greatest destruction there, and he cannot but have had a hand in it. One commissar who saw him in the autumn of 1937 for reassignment did later picture Smirnov sympathetically in his memoirs, a courtesy this man does not extend to Mekhlis.[14] Smirnov's involvement in terrorizing the navy in 1938 is clear. As Nikolai Kuznetsov, who took over the naval command in 1939, put it later, Smirnov "considered it his main task to 'cleanse the fleet of enemies of the people.' As a result we lost many valuable officers."[15]

Shaposhnikov was evidently a willing collaborator of Smirnov. But neither man seems to have displayed the energy sought by their superintendents in the NKVD and Stalin's entourage. Both Smirnov and Shaposhnikov disappeared from public view in the summer of 1938 and were shot before the year's end. In November 1938 Smirnov's post was given to Mikhail P. Frinovskii, an NKVD stalwart who in turn vanished in early 1939 and relinquished command of the navy to Kuznetsov. Shaposhnikov was not replaced until May 1939.[16]

Shchadenko, like Smirnov and Shaposhnikov, was a career political officer. He had some command experience and a reputation for high-handedness, but his main claim on high office was his personal acquaintance with Stalin, with whom he had served in the Civil War while on the military council of the First Cavalry Army. In late May 1937 Shchadenko arrived in Kiev as the new member of the district military council, and forthwith began "extremely energetic activity toward compromising command and political personnel who opposed the mass arrests of cadres."[17] He returned to Moscow in late 1937 to head the main cadres administration, and under him the army's key bureau for assigning personnel became an integral part of the purge mechanism. The tone of Shchadenko's stewardship is indicated by his agency's treatment of Andrei T. Stuchenko, who was peremptorily summoned, interrogated coldly about associates now exposed as saboteurs (including a former colleague arrested for "exterminating numerous horses" by contaminating them with pneumonia), and ordered to provide the information on the accused preferred for NKVD indictments.[18] When Aleksandr V. Gorbatov (like Stuchenko, a future general of the army) was naive enough to ask for his help in 1937, he was promptly arrested in a Moscow hotel room the whereabouts of which he had told no one but Shchadenko.[19]

Finally we come to Mekhlis. He could not have brought to his mission a psychology more fitted to the task. "An odious figure," "this cynical despot," "an unprincipled man whose sickly vanity overshadowed everything else"—even the superlatives of the memoirs pale before the genuine evil of the man.[20] Mekhlis was the inquisitor par excellence, a vigilante in combat fatigues. He went about the business of routing supposed enemies with passion. The reader can almost hear the rising tone and feel the tightening cadence in his speeches announcing discovery of yet another cluster of subversives. He frankly embraced the NKVD as allies in the cleansing process, as "our truest friends and assistants."[21]

Mekhlis's catalogue of friends was a narrow one indeed. In reserve or reticence he saw criminal conspiracy; in opposition he sensed high treason. But it is important to realize that he saw enemies everywhere, not least of all within the MPA. Mekhlis terrorized his own subordinates with the same vehemence he applied to the military command—perhaps even more. In 1940 he was to look back with pride on having personally scoured the MPA, an organization which "has for almost all its history . . . been headed by enemies of the people."[22] He had no compunction about exposing political officers to ridicule or handing them over to arrest and probable death. Most were dispatched by the simple refiling of a personal dossier, but Mekhlis was capable of revealing the "rotten interior" of a quivering corps commissar in front of hundreds of officers attending a district party conference.[23]

Mekhlis and the purgers were little concerned with the external rubric of commissar or commander. Their definition of internal worth differed fundamentally from the conceptions of many of Mekhlis's subordinates, and these responded in ways that also largely ignored external designation. The ensuing struggle was not without its heroes.

The Sequence of Terror
The iron broom of the purge swept through the military party apparatus with virtually the same ruthlessness as the command and staff

organs. Quantitative estimate of the destruction is difficult. Most Western computations have placed the attrition rate among commanders at between a quarter and a half. The incidence among political workers was certainly comparable to this and was probably closer to a half than a quarter. Even at the end of 1937 the political organs were lacking "almost a third of their authorized numbers" despite massive promotions; the worst shortages, of 50 percent or more, were above the level of division.[24] And 1938 was by all signs still worse. It was, as one report judiciously proclaimed it in October, "the year of . . . mass promotions of new cadres," with "thousands and thousands of fresh people" moving into senior posts—and thousands of others moving out.[25]

Between May 1937 and September 1938 every single one of the original members of military councils and chiefs of political administrations of military districts perished (as did all district commanders). Most political workers at the corps, division, and brigade levels went down (compared to all corps commanders and almost all brigade and division commanders). Even Voroshilov was astonished at the turnover at a meeting of corps commissars in August 1938: "You are all new, unfamiliar faces!" At the regiment level, about a third of the commissars were arrested (compared with about half of the commanders). Many political officers in the military education system were also liquidated.[26]

This comparable destruction was meted out in comparable sequence. If one traces the purge's progress through some of the most important segments of the MPA, one finds that commissars usually fell victim at almost the same time as their command colleagues, sometimes even beforehand. The terror treated commander and commissar with deadly equality.

1. *Central organs.*   Central MPA offices in Moscow were the first to be smashed, and at the same juncture as the high command. Gaik A. Osepian, Gamarnik's deputy, was arrested the same day as Gamarnik's suicide. Most of his peers were swept up by midsummer, when I. Rachkov, Gamarnik's former secretary, arrived at a party meeting at MPA headquarters to be met with hostility by "a circle of unknown faces." The only man he recognized, inspector Kruglov, was so anxious to dissociate himself from the Gamarnik regime that he moved that Rachkov be expelled from the party for having "worked all these years with enemy of the people Gamarnik." The motion was adopted unanimously—as was a second resolution excluding the accuser Kruglov on identical grounds—and Rachkov was arrested soon thereafter.[27] Anton Bulin, who was made Gamarnik's second deputy in late May and was briefly his acting successor, survived a little

longer. He took over the main cadres administration of the People's Commissariat of Defense in June, but his "rotten liberalism" resulted in his seizure and replacement by Shchadenko, apparently in late November 1937.[28]

2. *Schools and academies.* Most accounts show political officers under attack at the same time as instructors and administrators. The MPA's own schools were hit hard. Boris M. Ippo, the head of the Tolmachev Academy, was dismissed in May 1937 for political errors and disappeared after a brief posting to the Central Asian Military District. That summer the academy got a political department staffed by fresh cadres which supervised, with NKVD assistance, "the liquidation of the consequences of the sabotage . . . of the Gamarnik-Bulin bands."[29] Students were ordered to write denunciations of former colleagues. One "fabricated fifty-three slanderous denunciations" before being ousted from the party for "supervigilance" in 1938 after the arrival of a new director, Fedor B. Bokov.[30]

3. *Kiev Military District.* Mikhail P. Amelin, the head of the political administration, "took hard the arrests of men he knew well. He was especially depressed by the news of Iakir's arrest." His transfer to another district was announced at the same time as Iakir's, but he was arrested on June 19 and shot September 8. Shchadenko and the NKVD moved in on his departure.[31]

4. *Belorussian Military District.* Bulin left his post as political administration chief before Uborevich's arrest. His successor, Pismanik, was immediately attacked in the press and disappeared in early June. The new military council member, Avgust I. Mezis, followed him to prison late in 1937, at least a month before Ivan P. Belov, the new commander. The NKVD moved swiftly through the political organs. The nine officers rounded up in the Fifth Mechanized Brigade in the first half of July included the chief of its politotdel and five of its six battalion commissars.[32]

5. *Moscow Military District.* Commander Belov departed for the Belorussian post in mid-1937 and was succeeded by Marshal Semen Budennyi, who was untouched by the purge. Senior party workers did not fare as well. Lazar N. Aronshtam, the head of the political administration, was arrested in May 1937. Both his successor, Mikhail G. Isaenko, and the new military council member, Benedikt U. Troianker, fell in November. They were followed by Zaporozhets (the future chief of the MPA) and Semen E. Kolonin, both of whom managed to survive the purge.[33]

6. *Khar'kov Military District.* Commander Ivan N. Dubovoi was arrested August 21, 1937. His military council member, Sergei N. Kozhevnikov, was investigated simultaneously, jailed in September,

and shot in January 1938, more than six months before Dubovoi. Kozhevnikov's successor, Konstantin I. Ozolin, was also under detention by the end of 1937, and followed Dubovoi to the firing squad by only four days in the summer of 1938.[34]

7. *Pacific Fleet.* Commander Mikhail V. Viktorov was promoted to chief of Soviet naval forces in June 1937 (only to go under in 1938 after Smirnov's arrival). When the purge came in December 1937, the member of the fleet's military council, Georgii S. Okunev, was one of the first to be caught up, a month before commander Grigorii Kireev.[35]

8. *Northern Fleet.* Senior political and command officers were doomed together in a bizarre sequence of events in May 1938. The head of the political administration, P. P. Bairachnyi, was summoned to Leningrad by Mikhail Shaposhnikov and promptly seized. Four days later commander Konstantin Dushenov and the new political chief, P. M. Klipp, were also called to Leningrad, this time by Smirnov. After several false starts caused by NKVD maneuvering along their prospective path, Klipp and Dushenov were arrested together at a train station outside Leningrad. Other arrests followed.[36]

9. *Far Eastern Army.* The NKVD swept through the party organs long before commander Bliukher's removal in August. Grigorii D. Khakhan'ian, the member of the military council, was recalled to Moscow in the autumn of 1937. Despite an appeal to Mekhlis for aid "as an absolutely clean and dedicated son of my party and country," he was taken into custody in February 1938 and shot a year later.[37] His associate as chief of the political administration, Vainerose, was arrested and replaced by P. I. Mazepov in April 1938. Although Mazepov survived, as late as five days before Bliukher's arrest in October (while on vacation in Sochi) the press was reporting about a "group of enemies" in the army's political administration.[38]

Three Political Options

The purge interlude was one of dreadful pressure and limited alternatives. "It was a frightful time," Stuchenko recalled. "People began to fear each other. Anything could occasion arrest: national origin, failure at one's work, even the incorrect use of a word."[39]

In such an atmosphere there were three political options available, which can be called the strategies of withdrawal, offense, and active defense. The crucial point to understand is that the distinction between party organs and military command had no bearing on the choice or execution of strategy. Each option was open to members of both hierarchies equally, and each exacted its price from both. Each option was fraught with its own mix of anxieties, rooted for commander and commissar alike in the uncertainty about standards for determining political virtue (and hence survival).

Under the withdrawal strategy, a man could try to maximize the physical, emotional, or administrative distance between himself and possible accusers or apprehenders. This is perhaps the normal response to extreme political repression in any society, and it permeated Soviet military life in 1937-38. Officers returned from service in the Spanish civil war to find friends' doors closed in their faces; commanders' wives ostracized the families of the fallen at military stores and gathering places; students left military academies for months to wait out the storm.[40]

The withdrawal option found numerous reflections in party work. There was a decline in enthusiasm for normal administrative rounds, as many political officers "lost taste for party work and turned into narrow desk-sitters," avoiding "contact with the masses" and doing paperwork in their offices.[41] Another trend, singled out for opprobrium only in the spring of 1938 and again from the late summer onward, was for higher political organs to "mechanically confirm" or "rubber-stamp" expulsion decisions made below rather than question them and leave themselves open to accusation of lack of vigilance.[42] Other political officers tried to curtail communication of any sort with other political organs. Typical was the regiment party secretary who, "dwelling on the mistakes" of the division politotdel, "came to the absurd conclusion that the party leadership of the regiment should consult less often with the politotdel."[43]

The most widely used withdrawal tactic related to party admissions. If the press had complained after the resumption of admissions in November 1936 of indiscriminate "campaignism" (kampaneishchina) in recruiting, by the summer of 1937 the finger was pointed at the opposite extreme, "overinsurance" (perestrakhovka). It was obviously hazardous to certify for admission a man whose frailties were as yet unknown or who might turn to denouncing his sponsors as proof of political ardor. One political officer is said to have told an applicant, "You work well, but I am afraid to recommend you nonetheless."[44] Despite official pressure, the MPA continued to hold up applications until the purge spent itself. Although the party Secretariat ordered the admission into the party of 20,000 military Komsomol members in 1937, MPA headquarters and a number of political administrations interfered and only 7,000 were taken. Admissions totaled only 13,158 in 1937; even in August 1938 some 40 percent of applications were still unexamined.[45]

A second political option in the maelstrom was assumption of the open offensive. A man might safeguard himself and even promote his career by playing the role of unmasker of the suspect and hounder of the wavering. The occasional individual would internalize the code of vigilance and denunciation to the point of continuing to live by it even after it was no longer necessary for survival or advancement. Even in 1941 Nikolai Vashugin, the regiment commander elevated in 1938 to member of the military council of the Leningrad Military District, could lecture a subordinate on enemies remaining to be rooted out and leave the impression of suspicion so intense that he "seemed not always to trust himself."[46]

The phenomenon of strategic denunciation came to widespread attention after the January 1938 Central Committee plenum. An editorial in *Krasnaia zvezda* castigated "careerists who are striving to distinguish themselves and be promoted to [the posts of] those excluded from the party, or trying to protect themselves from possible accusation of being insufficiently vigilant, by means of unfounded acts of repression against party members." The same issue gave a number of illustrations of what it called "speculation in vigilance." Yet it also reported a Mekhlis speech which chided supervigilance in one breath but vowed in the next to "continue the work of annihilating enemies to the end."[47] This official duplicity, and the continuing availability of short-term rewards to the hypervigilant, lasted until late 1938.

The offense option was open to all and costly to all. There was no distinction between commissar and commander in the welter of accusations and counteraccusations. To be sure, one can easily find instances of commissars accusing commanders. One regiment commissar, Romanovskii, hearing that one of the senior commanders in his division had known Iakir in the Civil War, procured his expulsion from the party on grounds of "links with enemies of the people." But this same commissar also demanded the ouster of an instructor in the division politotdel (for having a brother-in-law who was a concealed enemy) as well as of dozens of other officers, command and political. Furthermore, the man who eventually had him removed for "careerism" was another party official, politotdel chief Gavrilov.[48]

An offensive strategy could also be followed by men who were not party workers, and could be employed by them against party officials as well as against others. When the deputy chief of the army's cavalry maintenance department, Artamov, decided to become an informer in 1938, he composed cases against all seven of his colleagues and ordered his subordinates to write autobiographies detailing their errors.[49] Similarly Kresin, the commandant of the Zhitomir military hospital, denounced to the police every hospital official "who had tried to criticize shortcomings in the work of the hospital and its director," including not only his supply officer and a senior physician but the hospital commissar and the secretary of the party bureau.[50]

The third strategy available was that of active defense. In this option, men elected to unite with associates and friends to take positive action against those who accused them from above or below. Ad hoc coalitions formed and reformed as men grasped desperately for support, all the more despairingly if other strategies had failed.

Party workers often formed such alliances with fellow political officers. Mekhlis was especially incensed with Ivan I. Sychev, the head of the political administration of the Belorussian Military District in 1938 (the fourth man to hold that post in less than a year), who strenuously refused to cooperate with investigations of the district's political workers, particularly those who had sympathized with the so-called intraarmy opposition to unitary command in the late 1920s. In announcing Sychev's removal in June 1938, Mekhlis said that when MPA headquarters had demanded the names of former adherents of the opposition, Sychev "gave a positive recommendation to the overwhelming majority of these rotten people, some of whom were soon arrested by the NKVD, and demanded that they remain in party-political work in the army." "Sychev's basic profession," Mekhlis went on with an air of injury, "has been the profession of saving fallen cadres."[51]

The Sychev pattern was in one sense atypical. It was not unusual for political officers to align themselves with fellow officers against the purge, but it was uncommon for these comrades not to include commanders. The normal variant of the strategy of active defense involved groupings or coalitions containing both political and command personnel.

Commissars chose such alliances for a number of reasons. Intangibles such as elementary decency and friendship assuredly played a part. It is hardly surprising, for example, that Gamarnik, a man of obvious integrity, would be perceived by the NKVD as an obstacle. This is even less surprising in light of Gamarnik's friendship with a number of the doomed commanders, including Tukhachevskii, Iakir, Bliukher, and Dubovoi, all of whom were frequent guests at his home. Gamarnik was especially close to Iakir, with whom he had served in the Civil War and kept in touch in the 1920s when they both were working in the Ukraine. After 1929 Gamarnik was one of Iakir's three most intimate friends, and to a colleague "it often seemed as if . . . they were brothers."[52] Personal bonds of this kind were not easily fractured, and neither was political officers' more diffuse solidarity with the army as an institution. This was the kind of attachment that moved deputy MPA chief Osepian to refuse to replace his military uniform with civilian garb upon arrest. "I am a commissar of the Red Army," he is said to have declared to his NKVD captors, "and I have no costume but my military uniform."[53]

But underlying these considerations was a solid fundament of self-interest. Two tangible interests were entailed. The first was the joint stake of commanders and political officers in safeguarding the routines of military administration which were being so seriously disrupted by the purge. There were recurrent reports in the press of commissars trying to stifle pressure from below for actions that would undermine the command and, by extension, themselves. When sailors confronted one commissar with what they termed "facts of enemy work" involving commanders on his ship, the commissar refused to proceed and even "tried to prove the harmfulness of such accusations." His argument mirrored his vital concern with order and stability: "In his opinion, [the accusations] would erode the authority of leaders and weaken discipline in the unit."[54]

A second and even more serious issue was involved—the likelihood of political officers' joint implication in alleged misconduct, a perverse extension of the principle of joint responsibility for organizational performance. In the eyes of the accuser, a normal working relationship implied complicity. If one man was an enemy, then the other had "links with the enemy" or was "tangled up with the enemy." From the political officer's point of view, unmasking of his command colleague was all too apt to lead to exposure of himself as well. Even if the commander's sins were private, the commissar could be faulted for not having brought these to light earlier. Vladimir N. Bogatkin recognized the strength of this logic when the commander of the Siberian Military District, to which he had recently been named as military council member, was marked for liquidation in 1938. Confronted with two NKVD officers carrying an order for the commander's arrest, Bogatkin ordered them out of the district headquarters, declared the commander to be an honorable Communist, and made a penetrating observation on his own conundrum: "This way [if the commander is arrested] you will number *me* among the enemies of the people today or tomorrow." The next day Bogatkin flew to Moscow and defended the commander. "He went to the very highest institutions and had the unjust decision changed."[55]

The tactics available to a defensive coalition were several. Those with the most fortitude (or the greatest faith in Soviet justice) could choose to face their accusers openly, attempting to disprove or defuse the charges. A vivid illustration is reported in the memoirs of Lieutenant-General Andrei Ia. Vedenin, eventually to become commandant of the Kremlin but in 1937 the chief military recruiter in Viaz'ma, in Smolensk oblast. Vedenin was bullied and interrogated at a party conference electing members of a local party committee by the head of the Viaz'ma NKVD office, Us, and the chief of the NKVD department in the division garrisoned there, Rostovskii. After the swaggering NKVD officers posed a long string of ominous questions about Vedenin's background and conduct, it was a political officer, Fedor Stebenev, the division's commissar, who came to Vedenin's defense:

"Both comrade Rostovskii and comrade Us have a very glib attitude toward this extemely serious business," Stebenev said. "We hear little questions and comments, but it all comes to nothing. They see shade on a clear day. Comrade Vedenin is in our party organization and we, the Communists of the staff and politotdel of the division, know him well as an honorable Communist."
    "Are you sure?" Rostovskii screamed.
    "I am sure," Stebenev replied firmly.
    "How so?" Rostovskii said menacingly . . .
    "What stupidity!" the division commissar said, getting angry . . . "It is necessary to vouch for a good comrade. I stand up for comrade Vedenin and move that he remain on the list for secret election as member of the *raikom* [raion party committee]."

The vote went against Vedenin.[56]
    The most common defensive tactic was undoubtedly the less valorous one of stalling and inertia. Commissars and elected party officials were frequently berated for "ignoring signals" or "shelving signals" about the hostile activity of fellow officers. In April 1938, for example, Mekhlis complained that commissars in the central apparatus of the people's commissariat "are not struggling for the final cleansing of hostile filth." He singled out Novikov, the commissar of the veterinary administration, who "ignores signals about deformities in the administration." Two months later he found the same fault with Iustus, the secretary of the party bureau of the transport and warehouse administration, "a typical silent man."[57]
    But it was not always feasible to remain silent. The political officer was often drawn into sharp conflict with other members of his organizational unit, frequently rank-and-file Communists or junior officers who were motivated by fear, ambition, or sheer taste for blood to pursue the victim to the end. For instance, regiment commissar Baturin was reported in 1938 to be rejecting strictures against the regiment commander, Alekseev. "Baturin connives with Alekseev and protects him in every possible way." He was said to have tried to disorient and threaten soldiers wanting to have the commander expelled and to have organized group drinking sprees for waverers.[58] In the

Poltava Military School, even after enemies had been "uncovered by the NKVD," the politotdel chief and his deputies refused to allow students to discuss the alleged deviations at party meetings. When a group of students persisted in pressing the issue, the politotdel had a resolution passed denouncing them as slanderers.[59]

In conducting these defensive maneuvers, the political organs had limited but not negligible tactical resources accruing from their formal and informal powers and prerogatives. In the Vedenin incident, for example, commissar Stebenev was able to draw up a special pass allowing Vedenin and his wife (who worked in Stebenev's office) to travel to Ivanovo to collect evidence disproving slander about his family. Stebenev also sent several members of the division party commission to Central Asia to refute NKVD contentions that Vedenin had procured defective horses while garrisoned there.[60] Powers of military and party discipline could also be used to structure the arena of struggle and constrain the more unruly combatants. An accusing soldier or sailor could simply be ordered out of the commissar's office, in the hope that the word would not reach the NKVD.[61] Rights of personnel assignment and promotion were available as well. Gamarnik and Bulin were stated, for instance, to have "attempted to chase out of the party and Red Army" men who sympathized with the purge. The administration and party leadership of the military publishing agency are alleged to have cashiered thirty dissenters in the second half of 1937, and the political administration of the Baltic Fleet penalized partisans of the terror by delaying their promotions and accession to higher ranks. In other cases, political officers transferred or helped transfer men who had come under fire to safer jurisdictions.[62]

Success in the strategy of active defense was contingent upon timing, personal connections, and sheer good fortune. Bogatkin, the commissar who saved the commander of the Siberian Military District, survived to become a senior official of the MPA and to die in a bed in 1956. Commissar Stebenev managed to clear Vedenin's name only to find himself the target of a separate NKVD investigation for conspiring with Vedenin. He was reinstated, but not until he had been expelled from the party and dismissed from his job. For some others, no strategy was of avail.

For most Soviet officers, political and command, the purge was a time of frightful waiting no matter what personal strategy was adopted. But it was not a wait without end, for by 1939 the worst of the violence was over. Nor was it a wait without rewards. The man who was able to parlay retreat, aggressive opportunism, or active defense into safety was likely to find his circumstances vastly improved by the time the executioners' swords had been sheathed. While the purge brought disaster to its victims and anxiety to all, it also conveyed opportunity to the survivors, pulling thousands into positions they might have never attained in a lifetime of service. Official spokesmen courted the new promotees (*vydvizhentsy*) with the claim that they had not been advanced earlier because of the treachery and insensitivity of leaders who had "cultivated the numbing system of gradual promotion."[63]

The purge's promotions were anything but gradual, they were no less numbing in a political and moral sense. Some of the most obvious beneficiaries were in the MPA, where the "thousands and thousands of fresh people" included officials who had leapt over whole rungs on the career ladder. One man began 1938 as a politruk and by October was commissar of an infantry corps; another rose from commissar of a warehouse to member of the military council of the Kalinin Military District.[64]

Even more conspicuous were the avenues to the top afforded to military commanders. In May 1937 Pavel V. Rychagov was a model test pilot whose press biography emphasized his prowess as captain of his unit's hockey team; by April 1940, now a colonel-general (*six* ranks higher than before), he was the head of the entire air force.[65] Konstantin Rokossovskii, back to command an army in 1940 after several years of imprisonment, saw around him officers who had risen to "heights about which these comrades had never dreamed."[66] Nikolai Kuznetsov, who went from assistant ship commander to head of the navy in three years, had "dreamed, of course, of commanding a ship. I did not think of more. But . . . my climb became extremely swift. This could be explained by the stormy wave of forced transfers."[67] Entire classes from the new General Staff Academy achieved "dizzying upward flights."[68]

It was all too natural for officers to suspend moral judgment on a wave which, for all its turbulence, was pitching them forward at dazzling speed. In so doing, many became part of the wave itself. As Admiral Kuznetsov wrote later, with all the chastened wisdom of hindsight, "It is too simple and too easy to explain everything purely in terms of the cult of Stalin's personality. Many of us were guilty, even if only of remaining silent when the situation demanded that we speak our minds. Many paid themselves for such passivity when their turns came."[69]

World War II
Decision Making

7

While inquiry into the politics of the war is well justified by the magnitude of the events alone, attention is also attracted by the unique evidence provided by the memoir literature. Notwithstanding the impediments of censorship, faulty and selective memory, and sheer bulk of information, the memoirs allow direct analysis of high-level military politics in a way not possible for any other period.

Such an analysis shows the individual participants to have moved away from the question of personal security, which the purge had jeopardized so gravely, to a much more normal set of issues. It reveals far more extensive political conflict than most visions of Stalin's Russia would lead us to expect. Despite the memories of recent terror and the long shadow of Stalin, military officials vigorously pursued the resources and opportunities necessary for discharging their organizational missions. The military party officials who are the focus of our attention were under considerably more pressure than in peacetime to intervene in the making of decisions on matters of military operations and the allocation of material and human resources. But the alliances forged in such interventions were fundamentally similar to those depicted in earlier chapters.

Preparing for the Storm

It is useful to begin with the dispute on the eve of the war over how to prepare for attack, a conflict that can be probed in more depth than any during the war itself. The issue stemmed from Stalin's refusal to act upon the information from numerous sources throughout the spring of 1941 that German aggression was impending. His apparent motives were several: fear of provoking Hitler, mistrust of informants, faith in diplomacy for at least postponing war, perhaps belief in German attempts to disguise their intentions. This was probably the worst misjudgment of Stalin's career, but erroneous or not it was official policy to which the entire military establishment, party apparatus included, had to respond.

Central Military Leaders. Decades later official histories and many memoirs were to criticize roundly the People's Commissariat of Defense and the General Staff and their heads, Semen K. Timoshenko and Georgii K. Zhukov, for failing to react adequately or to convince Stalin to respond to the warnings. Such criticisms tended to take insufficient account of some of the high command's actions—persuading Stalin to allow mobilization of half a million infantry reserves in March 1941, moving five armies into western districts in mid-May, establishing skeleton headquarters for several fronts, making improvements in airfield camouflage.[1] But on the whole there is no doubt that the high command allowed its deference toward Stalin to outweigh its professional misgivings about the real dangers of the German buildup. Some generals withheld evidence concerning German preparations, others (including Filipp Golikov, chief of military intelligence and a future head of the MPA) passed it on to Stalin but with judicious disclaimers of their own credence in it.[2] As Marshal Grechko testified in 1966, Stalin's intuitions "did not meet with consistent and effective objections from responsible military comrades and were often supported and reinforced by them."[3]

Military executives also acted, unwillingly or not, as a conduit for pressure on officers below for compliance with Stalin's edict. The General Staff several times ordered the pullback of troops from border regions, which meant that most were up to 400 miles from the frontier when war came. The high command also prevented air and ground interference with German overflights, and as late as the morning of June 22, with German bombs already in the air, it was prohibiting retaliation and permitting only limited reconnaissance.[4]

The military party organs were naturally involved in this official program of restraint and fully cognizant of the hazards of opposing a policy emanating directly from Stalin. Under their guidance the military press faithfully reflected the official position that war was not forthcoming. Many senior political officers probably thought like Shirokov, the MPA lecturer in Aleksandr Rozen's novel *The Last Two Weeks*, who demands that a distressed division commander, Zimin, trust in Moscow to the last and "assume they will take appropriate measures." When Zimin persists in probing, Shirokov orders silence and announces he will go ahead with a lecture based on the famous

TASS communique of June 14 denouncing rumors of war. Shirokov shares Zimin's concern but finds his own behavior dictated by his post and rank: "I understand, Sergei Sergeivich my friend, with all my heart and soul! If I were in another skin, I could fight for every last word. But . . . I have to follow orders."[5] In a similar event in real life, a group of MPA inspectors arrived in the Baltic Military District in mid-June and took officers to task for "talking too sharply about war with Germany." The evening before the attack the group was still blithely holding meetings "at which officers and soldiers were told insistently that there would be no war and that conversations about it were provocations."[6]

However, the picture is more complex than this kind of episode suggests. Even though MPA leaders, like the high command, generally complied with the Stalin policy, they were more than passive executors. Some were disturbed enough by the discrepancy between public propaganda and their own perceptions and responsibilities to attempt to change or circumvent official policy.

The prime illustration is the conduct of the senior party official in the army, MPA chief Aleksandr Zaporozhets. This career soldier complained repeatedly to civilian leaders about the country's lack of military preparedness. In February 1941 he protested to Andrei Zhdanov, the Central Committee secretary in charge of ideology, that Soviet propaganda was "imbued with a pacifist tone" and only "weakly infused with the military spirit." Another letter deplored the prevalence of "the simple-minded thesis that we are strong and the capitalists are afraid to attack us" and demanded a more realistic attitude. "There is no sober estimate in our propaganda of the Red Army's power. This leads to the harmful attitudes of 'hurrah patriotism' and 'cap throwing.' Reports and articles often toss about unthinkingly epithets such as 'great and invincible' and 'irresistible force.' All this disorients our troops and blunts their vigilance."[7]

Zaporozhets also raised questions about explicit aspects of military policy. In April he wrote a letter to Stalin, Molotov, and Malenkov, "based on the opinions of commanders and political workers and on personal observations," pointing up the failure to expedite work on fortifications on the western frontier. Another report to the same three attacked the poor outfitting and preparation of front-line artillery units and blamed the army's artillery administration, then under the irrepressibly incompetent leadership of Stalin's Civil War comrade, Marshal Georgii I. Kulik. In yet another letter, in late May, the MPA chief criticized the erratic pace of airfield construction in the border region, a task which was a direct responsibility of the NKVD.[8]

Nor can Zaporozhets' counterpart in the navy, Ivan Rogov (another career military man, and the head of the independent naval MPA until 1946), be seen as an apologist for the official line. Rogov called on navy commander-in-chief Kuznetsov in late April or early May to voice concern about the "complacent character" of official attitudes and promised "to instruct the political organs to heighten preparedness and explain to the sailors that fascist Germany is a most likely enemy." On June 16 or 17 Rogov met in Kuznetsov's office with other naval leaders and implored them "to raise the navy's preparedness, to assume the likelihood of an attack."[9]

This attitude—which was as far as can be ascertained *more* critical of the Stalin line than that displayed by senior commanders—was conveyed to lower echelons by at least some of Zaporozhets' and Rogov's subordinates. Representative of these was Il'ia I. Azarov, the head of the naval MPA's organization-instruction department, who was sent by Rogov in early June to brief political officers in the Black Sea Fleet during a major exercise. On June 14, aboard the cruiser *Krasnyi Kavkaz*, Azarov was asked by the dumbfounded ship captain to explain the TASS communique to the crew. He told the commander the announcement "put us in an absurd position" and was "completely at variance" with his "personal conclusions based on materials to which he had access because of his official position." After some trepidation Azarov (who had served in the navy since 1924) addressed the sailors and, far from parroting the TASS statement, he frankly contradicted its main thesis. "Fascism remains our foulest enemy," he announced. "The TASS report must not demobilize us. *We are military men* and must understand that the war raging in Europe is approaching the borders of our Motherland."[10]

Field Commands. For senior officers in the field, far from Moscow but directly in the Germans' path, the incentives for circumventing official policy were far greater. During the last week of peace the commanders of each of the five frontier military districts (Leningrad, Baltic, Western, Kiev, and Odessa) attempted precautions ranging from concealment of equipment to the positioning of large formations closer to the border (a move which succeeded only in the Odessa district). But wariness of reaction from above meant that these mild preparations were invariably combined with refusal either to challenge Moscow directly or to countenance disruptive initiatives from below. So while Mikhail P. Kirponos, commander of the Kiev Military District, did sanction some precautions, he strictly forbade his air commander to overstep directives on aircraft interception, warning him this was a question of state policy and beyond question. Kirponos's party colleague, Vashugin, concurred and urged "caution and more caution."[11] In this atmosphere district commanders resorted to near-conspiratorial methods to protect themselves—F. I. Kuznetsov in the Baltic Military District by issuing his mobilization orders in sealed envelopes which could be opened only with his permission, Dmitrii G. Pavlov in the Western district by refusing to commit any of his directives to writing, and Iakov T. Cherevichenko in Odessa by assuring subordinates that the bustle in his headquarters was merely "staff exercises."[12]

The commander below thus faced certain resistance by intermediate officials to any attempt to prepare openly for the coming battle, opposition which was likely to include political officers, such as Vashugin, whose distance from the top was less than his. On the other hand, the commander's allies were also likely to embrace party workers from his own level.

Although political officers in the field were by no means unanimously opposed to inaction, there is ample evidence that many strongly preferred a more forward policy. This was partly a derivative of direct observation of the threat. As Petr V. Sevast'ianov, then a division zampolit in the Baltic Military District, wrote in his memoirs, he "would have had to be simultaneously blind and deaf not to understand the meaning of these [German] maneuvers and exercises."[13] Observation gained force from the professional commitment which most political officers shared with commanders. "We know who Hitler is and who our 'friends' are," the member of the military council of the Sixteenth Army, Aleksei A. Lobachev, is said to have told a superior. "Like you I am all for diplomatic successes, but diplomacy is one thing and political work in the forces is another."[14]

Military party officials desiring greater readiness pursued a number of strategies. Some incorporated danger signals in political classes and lectures.[15] Some passed on to superiors information, collected from defectors and other sources, about German rehearsals.[16] Others elected to collaborate with commanders in conducting or permitting precautionary measures such as readying equipment or repositioning front-line officers and troops.[17]

It is not difficult to see how such actions could bring political officers into conflict with their superiors. When, for instance, Ivan V. Zuev, the young military council member of the Eleventh Army in the Baltic district, authorized preparatory moves, a "special commission" was dispatched from Moscow and accused Zuev and the army commander of "exaggerating the danger and creating unnecessary tension." Undeterred, Zuev shortly afterward approved the readying of the army's signals equipment for use and reminded his colleagues that "Whatever happens [in Moscow] . . . we are responsible for the inviolability of our borders."[18] Sevest'ianov, the political officer whose division was in Zuev's army, found himself in similar circumstances when the party member of the district military council, P. A. Dibrov, passed on an order to remove forward units' ammunition so as to make them incapable of "responding to provocation." Like his commander, Sevast'ianov wondered if the district leaders had "lost their heads," and the two of them decided not to give the order to their men.[19]

Frequently political officers openly took the position of advocate of preparations, pushing cautiously but audibly for whatever adjustments were possible. In the Fourth Army in the Western Military District, for example, politotdel chief Sergei S. Rozhkov (who had earlier been careful to stifle "noises" from subordinates about imminent attack) was the most insistent critic of the "self-satisfied" outlook of the General Staff and district commander Pavlov. He was joined by the member of the army's military council, F. I. Shlykov, who had also repeatedly found fault with Pavlov and his political officer, Aleksandr Ia. Fominykh. In the final days of peace Shlykov unsuccessfully urged district headquarters to evacuate the Brest garrison and endorsed the appeal to Pavlov by the head of a division politotdel for permission to assume defensive positions and withdraw officers' families.[20]

By the last hours before the Soviet counterattack, the military party organs behaved like a chain of hyperactive neurons, spasmodically transmitting and amplifying the despairing entreaties of soldiers for the right to fight for their lives. With all hope of a reprieve gone, political officers flailed at their superiors and uttered threats of outright insubordination. Many found themselves on the same razor's edge as Andrei G. Rytov, later to be the chief political officer in the air force but then the zampolit of an air division in the Baltic Military District. When Rytov alighted at the newly bombed Libau airfield early on June 22, he was met by the overwrought airfield zampolit and warned that without authorization the pilots would fight anyway and he would "answer for the consequences together with them." After a futile appeal to Dibrov and a similar entreaty from a regiment political officer at the Riga airfield ("I am a pilot myself and I fully understand . . ."), Rytov finally agreed with the division commander to give the signal for battle without further delay.[21]

Moscow and the Front

Once the fray was joined, opinions about decisions again coalesced across institutional borders. The main lines of cleavage in the fierce bureaucratic politics of the war were dictated by hierarchy and territory, not by the boundary between army and party or between military command and MPA. The most salient cleavage of all was between center and periphery, as can be demonstrated by examining the workings of the military leadership and the behavior of two of its most conspicuous members, Zhukov and Mekhlis.

The analysis of the supreme command is inextricably bound up with the analysis of Stalin, who unlike Lenin in the Civil War assumed direct responsibility for strategic leadership. By early August 1941 he was Supreme Commander-in-Chief, People's Commissar of Defense, and chairman both of the State Defense Committee (in charge of the overall war effort) and of Supreme Military Headquarters or *Stavka*.[22] He communicated directly with front-line commands and indirectly through the General Staff and special plenipotentiaries. Stalin remained, of course, General Secretary of the party, but unlike Lenin he was unencumbered in his military decisions by any larger party constituency. The Central Committee, which met throughout the Civil War and several times resolved major military controversies, convened only once and did not touch upon military questions even then.

Soviet evaluation of Stalin's military performance has been influenced by the general state of receptiveness toward criticism of him and his regime. This receptiveness peaked in the late Khrushchev years and has been tempered since 1966 by strictures against "one-sided appraisals of the work of Stavka and . . . Stalin."[23] Although the new line has not implied a return to the obsequies of Stalin's lifetime, public criticisms of him and his associates are now much more restrained and balanced than before.

Within these limits, two other variables have had an effect. One has been war periodization. Criticism of Stalin was always most unsparing for the first eighteen months of the war, when Moscow's essential goal was to stem retreat whatever the human cost. But even before Khrushchev's fall in 1964, and continuing since then, there have been numerous testimonials, including some by men who were derogatory of Stalin's early role, to his military leadership in the period of mounting victories after Stalingrad.[24]

The second and more important variable has been wartime location. Until 1964 the memoir literature was dominated by soldiers who had spent the war—like Khrushchev, then the head of the Ukrainian party and a member of several military councils—in positions at the front. While it is mistaken to see these men as a single faction maintaining unity one or two decades afterward, they did share during the war a remoteness from central decisions and a vulnerability to central miscalculation which were easily translated later into a common critical stance.[25] Since the spring of 1965, however, the recollections of officers who were an integral part of the wartime high command have been allowed to appear. If Marshal Sergei S. Biriuzov's 1963 characterization of Stalin as "an office recluse" divorced from the field embodies the frustrations of a front-line officer, then Zhukov's 1969 judgment of him as "a worthy Supreme Commander-in-Chief" reflects the pride of a partner who shared in Stalin's decisions and (at least for a while) in his glories.[26]

The image of Stalin that emerges from this recent material is of neither the superman of the early hagiography nor the whimsical ogre plotting strategy on a globe in some of the Khrushchev-period portrayals. He is pictured as an attentive and reasonably competent military decision maker with "a naturally analytical mind, great knowledge, and an acute memory,"[27] gaining in skill as the war wears on. He stands, moreover, at the center of a cohesive military leadership that was, in the words of Sergei M. Shtemenko, the head of the General Staff's operations administration from mid-1941, "not cut off from life [but] holding both the planning of the war's campaigns and the leadership of operations firmly in its hands."[28]

Outright fear was certainly one cement of this central grouping. It was fear that bound the General Staff to Stalin's nocturnal schedule and brought marshals scurrying into his office, papers in hand, at the ring of his personal secretary Poskrebyshev. Even Stalin's recent defenders have taken pains to specify that, if dissatisfied, "he could become abusive and unjust."[29] There could be no illusions about the permanence of the trust of a leader who had only several years earlier allowed thousands of officers to be destroyed for imaginary crimes. As one Stavka officer who narrowly escaped in 1937 testified, "Once someone stumbled, [Stalin] did not spare words. You would wait for that irrevocable Stalinist phrase, 'I do not need this worker—remove him.' "[30]

Yet it would be highly misleading to ignore the bonds other than intimidation that tied Stalin to his close military associates. The diverse demands on his time forced delegation of authority to military subordinates for such matters as drafting resolutions and elaborating plans, and this delegation clearly gave them great influence over outcomes.[31] In the decisions he took himself, Stalin relied heavily on information and counsel provided by his military colleagues, particularly the General Staff (which has often been described as Stavka's "working organ"). It was this agency, staffed entirely by professional soldiers (and particularly its operations administration, which reported to Stalin three times a day), that was the only organized channel of battlefield information, that provided the detailed maps from which Stalin planned operations, and whose reports were normally the basis on which orders of the day were formulated.[32]

This is not to say that Stalin's mind was always open to this counsel. At several of the low points of the first year of the war, he "took decisions unilaterally," without consulting even his closest military confidants.[33] He also consistently shunned advice on the political or economic ramifications of strategic decisions or "when his memory told him he had been in a comparable situation in the past," especially in the Civil War.[34] However, on most questions he expected to hear, indeed actively sought out, the opinions of his associates. As Shtemenko recollected, "Stalin repeatedly asked, 'What does the General Staff think?' or, 'Has the General Staff examined this question?' And the General Staff always gave its opinion."[35] According to Zhukov, Stalin "knew how to listen" to his generals, "correctly took the advice of our outstanding military specialists," and often "changed his personal opinions and decisions" at their urging.[36] To this must be added the fact that Stalin's relationship with the high command had a personal dimension as well. The postwar fates of some members of the Stavka group should not obscure Stalin's evident admiration and even affection for many of them during the war, particularly for the wartime Chiefs of General Staff—Zhukov, Boris Shaposhnikov, Aleksandr Vasilevskii (like Stalin a former seminarian and in 1949 to become the second professional head of the armed forces), and Aleksei I. Antonov. This admiration was often warmly reciprocated and was reflected in later tributes to Stalin's strengths.[37]

With the high command as a generally cooperative group, the main strain on most issues lay between it and the rest of the military establishment. To commanders *and* commissars at the front, the Stavka group was above all a source of constraint and uncertainty. What the front saw as a timely maneuver, Moscow might well judge an overdue (or premature) one; what the front saw as a need, Moscow might interpret as an extravagance; what the front saw as commitment to an assigned task, Moscow might dismiss as parochialism. Differences of substance were reinforced by style, as field officers chafed at waiting long hours for telephone calls and at taking orders from officials often junior in rank and experience.

Stavka pressure was not always exerted through the impersonal medium of the telephone line. In a pattern common in Soviet wartime administration, Stavka routinely sent representatives (*predstaviteli*), individually or in groups, to verify performance and enforce central priorities at the front. The Stavka representative, usually an officer from the General Staff or another central agency, brought the field officer both anxiety and opportunity, but primarily the former. One general who saw the Stavka presence as reducing field staffs to "wander[ing] around like tourists" may have been overstating the point, but the sense of grievance was genuine.[38] As Biriuzov recalled, the man from Moscow "often . . . complicated the work of the front staff, interrupted its rhythm, introduced excessive tension into it . . . stood guardian over the front commanders." With no firm demarcation of prerogatives, much "depended on the character, abilities, and tact of the Stavka representative."[39] Not only a buffoon such as Kulik would lack tact in a wartime setting. Even as diplomatic and erudite a representative as Vasilevskii posed a threat to field officers because of his mandate and intention to "subordinate the interests of the particular front to general interests . . . to the priorities of the Supreme Commander-in-Chief."[40]

Yet, at the same time, the man from Moscow could be of considerable use. "The most influential representative," as Biriuzov observed, "could always 'squeeze out' material resources, ammunition, fuel, and in isolated cases reserves for the front entrusted to him, at the expense of others."[41] But for this to happen the Stavka legate would first have to be "squeezed" himself, convinced that the front's needs were urgent and consistent enough with the high command's priorities so that he would not jeopardize his standing with Moscow by vouching for them. Failing this, the front commander's only recourse—not one to be taken lightly—was to go over the Stavka representative's head, to "phone Stalin to protest and complain that he was being 'robbed.' "[42] Either way, an adversary and bargaining relationship inevitably developed between Stavka man and field officer, and the manifestations ranged from disagreement over fine points of planning to shouting contests over cases of supposed insubordination.

Zhukov: The Stavka Commander. Zhukov, the future Defense Minister, was with Kulik and Shaposhnikov one of the first Stavka representatives dispatched on the opening day of the war. As a member of Stavka, Chief of General Staff (until July 30, 1941), the only Deputy Supreme Commander-in-Chief (from August 26, 1942), commander of five important fronts, and Stavka representative on a number of others, Zhukov was clearly Stalin's foremost military adviser and plenipotentiary.

Zhukov's historical reputation was to be eclipsed during the Khrushchev period along with that of other members of the Stavka group, but the disfavor was made much more complete by his personal political demise in October 1957. Once the most serious of the 1957 accusations were withdrawn in 1965, discussion of Zhukov's wartime role came to follow the general pattern. His actions and style were defended energetically by Stavka officers with whom he had collaborated in planning and supervising operations—particularly Shtemenko, Vasilevskii, and Marshals Aleksandr A. Novikov and Ivan Peresypkin, the wartime heads of the air force and military communications. He was also supported by several officers who served with him on the First Belorussian Front in the last six months of the war, when senior Stavka figures were given direct charge of major fronts (and the potential conflict with front staffs was lessened). Among these officials was Lieutenant-General Konstantin Telegin, a career political officer and a member of the front's military council, whose defense of Zhukov's management of the Berlin operation was the first openly favorable appraisal of his wartime performance.[43]

Even allowing for October 1957, Zhukov's unreserved defenders have been outnumbered by his critics (most of whom, particularly since 1965, acknowledge his skill as a strategist). Predictably, most of his detractors have been officers from the field for whom Zhukov was the most palpable element of a distant high command, obliged to implement Moscow's decisions even when he had reservations about them. Invariably they have remarked on how Zhukov's organizational role was powerfully reinforced by a personality that was imperious and intolerant. While depictions of the darker side of Zhukov's character were most acerbic during his period of political disgrace, they did reflect a genuine perception and they did continue to be expressed after his return to favor. There is consensus that Zhukov was given to "sharp expressions and high notes" and "did not choose courteous words" in his demands and orders.[44] Even Rokossovskii, a longtime acquaintance and one of the most tolerant of the marshals, could write in memoirs published seven years after Zhukov's rehabilitation: "Great exactingness is a necessary and important quality in the military leader. But he must always combine iron will with attentiveness to his subordinates and a willingness to rely on their opinions and initiative. [Zhukov] did not always follow this rule . . . He was unjust and, as they say, hot-handed."[45] This could easily be supplemented by numerous detailed accounts of how Zhukov insulted, dismissed, and intimidated particular front-line officers.[46]

It is in this context, as part of his general disregard for subordinate officials, that Zhukov's attitude toward the political organs should be evaluated. There is no factual basis for a Western historian's contention that Zhukov's crudeness was especially reserved for party workers.[47] Certainly several political officers later recounted embarrassment at Zhukov's hands.[48] But they were equally critical of his treatment of commanders, and it is commanders who have borne the most convincing witness to his high-handedness. I know of no occasion when Zhukov singled out a commissar for abuse. If at times he saw party workers as adversaries, it was along with commanders, never apart from them.

For example, when Zhukov arrived by special plane to take command of the Leningrad Front in September 1941, his wrath did not discriminate between the two hierarchies. Incensed by one army's performance, he dismissed both its commander and its political officer; in another army, he threatened both with the firing squad. The front's chief engineer later attested how Zhukov, who bullied him and his political colleague into attempting a near impossible assignment, "did not treat the other senior officers of the front any better. He threatened *nearly all of them* with the tribunal."[49]

This pattern is even better exhibited in a later incident. In July 1944 Zhukov, now Stavka's representative on the First Belorussian Front, confronted the commander of the Sixty-fifth Army, Pavel I. Batov, and Batov's military council member and close friend, Nikolai A. Radetskii. As Batov describes it:

We had just finished shaving and cleaning our boots when we heard a vehicle pull up on the road and brake sharply in front of our hut. Radetskii looked out the window. It was Zhukov. We rushed out onto the porch. I had intended to greet the Stavka representative, but things went differently.

"What are you doing shaving and covering yourself with Eau-de-Cologne? Why haven't you taken [the nearby town of] Baranovichi?"

Somehow we managed to get Zhukov into the hut. There he continued the dressing-down. In my long military service I had never had to experience such a humiliation. Radetskii kept a stone face. Finally I managed to report that our units were progressing well and taking the town hour by hour. But the reply was no better than before.

"The commander is reporting correctly, comrade marshal," Radetskii said. Zhukov paid no attention. "The commander is reporting the truth," the military council member repeated. The abuse was then shifted to him. This intolerable scene finished with Zhukov ordering Radetskii to go to Baranovichi and not to return until the town was taken. Kicking aside a stool, Zhukov exited and slammed the door. A heavy silence reigned.[50]

Mekhlis: The Stavka Commissar. Lev Mekhlis's brief second term as MPA chief (from June 21, 1941, to June 12, 1942) was almost as trying for the army as his first. He infused a Stavka role with the mentality of the professional enforcer. His coarseness tempered by neither compassion nor expertise, he seemed at times "purposeful to the point of fanaticism," as if driven to compensate for boundless ignorance with boundless energy.[51]

Mekhlis's special currency was again suspicion, the coin in which he had dealt with such zeal as chief overseer of the Great Purge in the military. So mistrustful that he insisted on deciphering his own coded telegrams, he was able to make one general shudder—even three years after his eviction from the Stavka circle—simply by taking notes on a conversation. Mekhlis could without raising his voice accuse an officer who had volunteered to cross enemy lines of scheming to return to his family; or demand that a squadron commander be court-martialed when he imagined that the man's bombers were attacking Soviet positions; or have a division commander cashiered after leading his troops out of encirclement because the tattered officer objected to being called a bandit. He could during a meeting with a wounded General Gorbatov nod coldly in appreciation of a remark that Gorbatov "obviously learned little at Kolyma," the icy camp region where he had been held after being arrested in the purge.[52]

Mekhlis was assigned a prime punitive function in the opening months of the war, leading an inquiry into Moscow's air defenses and playing a part in the decision to execute Western Front commander Pavlov.[53] In September 1941 he was sent to the Northwestern Front as a Stavka representative. Noticing that one general's army was floundering, he "reported to Stavka on his behavior and at this the career of the army commander ended."[54] Following brief excursions to the Reserve and Western fronts, Mekhlis arrived on the new Volkhov Front in late December and, as front commander Meretskov remembered, "drove us on hour after hour" to carry out ambitious offensive plans.[55]

Mekhlis's star as Stavka plenipotentiary culminated on the Crimean Front in the spring of 1942. Reaching it in March, he forthwith "began to reshuffle leading cadres," and within a month he was dominating meetings of the military council with his "strident tones."[56] He interfered in "literally every operational matter," even instructing front engineers on which spare engines to place in refitted tanks (he had personal lists of both).[57] All this ended abruptly in May when the front crumbled; within a month Mekhlis was demoted in rank and replaced in the MPA by Shcherbakov.

Tempting though it may be to seize upon Mekhlis's conduct as unambiguous support for the image of Soviet military politics as dominated by antagonism between party organs and command, such an interpretation would be incorrect for several reasons. First, even the Crimean affair has aspects that contradict the standard image. Mekhlis was, after all, dismissed at Stalin's behest, as were front commander Dmitrii T. Kozlov and military council member Fedor A. Shamanin. Kozlov has fared no better in historical treatments than Mekhlis. A former subordinate has faulted Kozlov for lacking the courage to rebuff Mekhlis,[58] and Vasilevskii has accused him and his staff of criminal negligence and disobedience of Stavka orders. As for Mekhlis, Vasilevskii condemns him not so much for interference as for acquiescence in Kozlov's delinquency, and this was precisely the tone of Stalin's telegram dismissing Mekhlis for being a passive spectator rather than a responsible representative of the center.[59]

Second, while the travesty in the Crimea was not to be the last exhibit of Mekhlis's high-handedness, he did at times act more like a political ally of the commanders with whom he was working. Even in the Crimea, his help in getting outside assistance for front engineers repairing tanks "was simply beyond calculation," and on other sectors he vigorously "beat the bell" for artillery and ammunition for his fronts.[60] Mekhlis's style was irreversibly mellowed by the Crimean experience. According to Marshal Meretskov, the catastrophe "taught him . . . that questions of tactics and military art were not his work," and as a member of the military council of the Volkhov Front in the winter of 1942-43 (no longer Stavka representative) Mekhlis "occupied himself mainly with political work and with organizing the supply of everything we needed," exploiting in the latter capacity his special relationship with Stalin.[61] To be sure, there were strict limits to Mekhlis's identification with front officers even after his removal from the Stavka elite, as is demonstrated by an extraordinary episode reported by Meretskov. After "using insulting language" to defend Meretskov from Stavka representative Voroshilov, Mekhlis was so aghast at his temerity that he composed a letter to Stalin which "sternly condemned his own behavior and suggested that he deserved severe punishment for insulting a superior officer."[62]

A third and crucial qualification about Mekhlis is that, as in the Great Purge, commanders were not his only victims and opponents, any more than commissars were Zhukov's. He was resented and in some cases resisted by other party workers for the aloofness and arrogance that saw him think nothing of replacing a front-line political officer without notification or keeping another waiting three days at his office door for an audience.[63] Given his low opinion of political officers other than himself, it is no wonder that on the Crimean Front the commissars of a tank brigade and a tank repair unit were as scornful of Mekhlis's ineptitude as any other officers were; nor is it surprising that Khrushchev considered him a nitwit.[64] The commissar who voiced his objections was no more to be tolerated than a troublesome commander. Mekhlis would, as he did to Telegin in late 1941, excoriate the offender for "looking at the situation purely from your own parochial point of view" or he would, as Rytov more vividly remembered it, "throw thunder and lightning" at the insufficiently pliant subordinate.[65] There was no middle course for anyone. The tempest could be averted only by the complete submission which, to the great relief of both the army command and party apparatus, Mekhlis was no longer in a position to demand after the long spring of 1942.

Groupings in the Field

The inference should not be drawn from the preceding section that officers at the front did nothing but react to forays by emissaries of Moscow. The constant pressure from the German armies—an authority whose judgment was even more final than the NKVD's in 1937, but against which a deliberate strategy could be worked out—gave the normal perception of common interest possessed by command and party officials working at particular locations an acuity not usually found in peacetime. Clusters of like-minded commissars and commanders were in fact political actors in their own right. They could be initiators as well as responders, pushing for positionally defined needs on three major types of issue—security, operations, and supply.

Security. A prime military interest was in containing the activity of the secret police in the military forces. This concern was generally efficacious, although officers on all fronts had to contend with "special departments," subordinate to NKVD headquarters and empowered to suppress real and imagined deviance, as well as occasional excursions by NKVD bosses and NKVD detachments operating to safeguard the field army's rear.

The memoirs are understandably silent about the private understandings which military officials—commanders and political workers —struck with NKVD monitors. But inasmuch as conflict and tension were built into the arrangement, the evidence suggests that political officers shared and channeled the general military disquietude as much as they had during the purge. There were times when party workers directly confronted NKVD officials, as when Shlykov, member of the Fourth Army's military council, scorned the claim by the commandant of the Brest NKVD border detachment to have detained two dozen spies and provocateurs in the first three days of the war and told him bluntly he was interfering with military operations.[66]

Normally, MPA functionaries acted more discretely to limit NKVD encroachment. Characteristic was the success of Rytov, as commissar of an air division in 1941, in using private pressure with superiors to save a pilot arrested after spending five days in enemy territory following a forced landing. Rytov had been brought into the case by the commissar of the flyer's regiment, who "knew [the pilot] well and . . . sympathized with him."[67] Similarly Telegin, as member of the military council of the Moscow Military District, was able to rescue the district aviation commander from retribution for delivering a reconnaissance report fancied to reflect poorly on NKVD performance in the area. Following a telephone conversation with Beria "so sharp that it rattled the membrane" on his telephone, Telegin interceded with an unnamed Central Committee secretary (probably Shcherbakov, who was also a member of the Moscow military council) and had the meddling ended.[68]

Operations. It was military commanders who dominated the process of making strategic and operational decisions at lower and intermediate layers of the military hierarchy. It was also command and staff officers who were the prime source of information and (often conflicting) advice to Stalin and the political leadership during the making of peak-level decisions, who were flown to Moscow for planning and bargaining sessions and left to work out the fine points of decisions with General Staff officials, and who were given the lion's share of the credit for triumphs on the battlefield.

Political officers did participate to some degree in most decisions, and this participation was welcomed by most commanders. It had long been asserted that the military party organs would "help ensure commanders' attention to political factors" during the making of wartime operational decisions.[69] Although these pronouncements did little to define political factors, they and common assumptions about the MPA's control functions lead one to look, at the very least, for some special sensitivity by commissars to overall war aims. The search is not a productive one. Party workers in the field were, of course, wholly committed to victory and to the principle of central determination of strategic goals. But they saw no inconsistency between this and the energetic pursual of the interests of the operational units which they managed. They were no more amenable than commanders to dictate from above and no less insistent in demanding compliance from below.

This is amply illustrated by the wrenching hierarchical conflicts early in the war over the pace of retreat. Some party workers may have felt a particular responsibility for implementing Stavka's demands for suicidal resistance (like politruk Zotov in Konstantin Simonov's novel *The Living and the Dead*), but clearly most did not. Some equaled or even surpassed commanders in advocating unauthorized retreat. In the Fourth Army, for instance, it was military council member Shlykov who adamantly resisted compliance with a June 22 order to attack near Brest, and the counterargument was actually left to the commander.[70] In the Fifth Paratroop Brigade fighting near

Kiev in September 1941, commissar Fedor Chernyshev convinced his comrades to retreat without permission. When the chief of staff recommended caution, Chernyshev replied, "Let them shoot us! Better that we three die than the whole brigade perish senselessly."[71]

Some of the most brutal disputes over operations pitted one party official directly against another from a different plane of responsibility, frequently with one or both defending the preferences of command colleagues. An incident related by Lieutenant-General Nikolai K. Popel' gives some sense of how acute these hierarchical conflicts could be. Popel' was serving in late June 1941 as the chief political officer in the Southwestern Front's Eighth Corps, commanded by Dmitrii I. Riabyshev. When the corps failed to carry out a front order to surrender some hard-won territory and recapture the city of Dubno, the member of the front military council (Vashugin) arrived at corps headquarters along with a sizable group of front-level officials, including the chairman of the military tribunal. After rejecting Riabyshev's arguments, Vashugin accused the commander of outright treason:

"The field tribunal will listen to you, traitor. Here under the pine we will listen to you, and here under the pine we will shoot you." . . .

I could not restrain myself and stepped forward: "You can accuse us of whatever you want, but take the trouble to hear us out first."

"Oh, so it is you, the staff defender of the traitor." Now a stream of abuse descended on me. Everyone knew that the member of the military council could not stand being interrupted. But I had nothing to lose. I used this as a weapon . . . Angrily I said, "I don't understand what kinds of considerations must have motivated those who force us to give the enemy territory we won in battle."

[After an inconclusive argument, Vashugin gave the corps commander twenty minutes to consider the front's order.] "I order you to begin the offensive immediately. If you do not, I will remove you from your post and turn you over to the tribunal."

[Vashugin] dictated an order and signed it so that black blobs of ink flew. He turned to me: "Capture Dubno by evening and you will receive a decoration. Fail and we will expel you from the party and shoot you."

In my breast the feeling welled up, "Ugh . . . you are such a master at not caring a whit for human beings! You want me to attack for the sake of a decoration and beat the fascists for fear of being shot." But I answered curtly, "Yes sir," and turned about exactly as regulations specified.[72]

This scene is very reminiscent of Zhukov's encounter with Radetskii and Batov, only this time the superior official is a political officer rather than a commander. It could be multiplied many times over by examples from all periods of the war.

Again, it is important that the impression not be left that political officers espoused the strategic interests of their organizational sub-units only when challenged from above, as Popel' was (or, for that matter, Vashugin, who was under enormous pressure from Stavka). Party officials frequently took the initiative, singly or in concert with their command colleagues, to press for the operational interests of their sectors in the limited ways available to them. Nowhere does this come into clearer view than in the wartime activity of Khrushchev, who, while not a typical political officer, was quite typical in his assiduous advocacy of his sector's concerns. This fact can be gleaned from both friendly and hostile reports. It is known from numerous accounts that, as the member of the military council of the South-western Sector (a command layer intermediate between Stavka and the front level) in 1941, Khrushchev backed the appeals of the sector and front commands for permission to fall back on Kiev and later to withdraw from it.[73] In May 1942 he persuaded Stavka to permit his Southwestern Front to undertake an ambitious offensive on Khar'kov, then pressured Vasilevskii and Stalin by telephone to call off the offensive when the Germans counterattacked.[74] While member of the military council of the Stalingrad Front, Khrushchev, in the words of front commander Andrei I. Eremenko (written in 1961), "warmly supported me . . . irrevocably brushed aside everything that did not help our cause," including interference by Stavka representatives.[75] When assigned to Nikolai F. Vatutin's Voronezh Front in 1943, Khrushchev fully upheld with Stavka (according to Zhukov, an unfriendly witness) Vatutin's plan, which was ultimately rejected, for a pre-emptive blow against German forces on their front leading to an all out offensive.[76] In September 1943 Khrushchev also convinced Zhukov and Stalin to redraw front boundaries to transfer the coveted assignment of recapturing Kiev to his and Vatutin's front.[77]

Supply. Political officers have tended to remain outside the competition for supplies in peacetime. The situation was starkly different in wartime, when most political officers soon discovered of supply matters that "the success of operations . . . largely depended on this."[78]

To begin with, every front and combined-forces army had in its military council a political officer (the so-called second member) who was directly charged with overseeing logistics work. Many of his duties involved internal management, but he also participated in efforts to procure assistance from beyond the army's or front's boundaries. A standard such official at the army level was involved day-to-day in "soliciting from the front's logistics organs fuel, shells, cartridges, wheat, groats, and meat" as well as arranging for transport of materials, fresh troops, and the wounded.[79] These functionaries were sufficiently effective that lower-level logistics officers "sometimes bypassed their direct superiors and turned directly" to them to ease particular shortages.[80] While this may have troubled some senior logistics administrators, the arrangement was apparently valued by those below whose overriding interest was in the fact rather than the mode of delivery.

But the entanglement of the military party organs in supply questions did not end here. It was in fact typical for the political officer at all levels to find he "had to concern himself with [supply] day and night."[81] So intense was this involvement that there were complaints at party conferences of political officers who were enthralled with logistics matters to the point of "forget[ting] about their basic calling."[82] This preoccupation is well reflected in a regiment commissar's offended reply to Rytov's casual inquiry about his work load: "What do you mean, what do I do? Does food have to be brought? It does. Do gasoline and ammunition have to be procured? They do. Almost all our vehicles are laid up. Who else is going to take care of that?" Rytov could respond with only a weak reminder that the commissar's main job was to provide spiritual food.[83] The expectation that the political officer would act as a supply "pusher" (as Rytov himself frequently did, notwithstanding his remarks to the other commissar) was sufficiently ingrained that a man who did not play the role might well evoke suspicion. At Stalingrad Khrushchev could explode at a division commissar who had declined to request help for his shivering and hungry troops: "No complaints? No complaints, you say? You are fooling yourself, and now you are trying to fool me."[84]

For those relatively few MPA officials who concurrently held high posts in the local party organs (like Shcherbakov in Moscow and Zhdanov in Leningrad), some conflicts between military and civilian supply priorities were unavoidable. Zhdanov, for instance, had to suspend transport of artillery shells over the "road of life" across Lake Ladoga in January 1942 in favor of food for starving civilians.[85] But such conflicts were by no means common, and they implied no inhibition when it came to bargaining with external agencies. Few political officers simultaneously held high civilian office. Those who did tended to observe two simple rules: "priority for the front," that is for military over civilian needs; and reluctance to choose among competing claims from one's own sector, passing on with approval all demands for material and human resources. Zhdanov, to take an obvious example, was anything but restrained in pressing for his front's needs (this despite the fact that he was not only the civilian party boss in Leningrad but a member of the party Politburo). The Red Army's chief of logistics for most of the war, Andrei Khrulev, later recalled with some chagrin how Zhdanov "generally thought that everything necessary [for the Leningrad Front] should be brought in from outside the blockade."[86] A touring Stavka official would soon find this out. Nikolai N. Voronov, the commander of Soviet artillery troops, had barely deplaned at Leningrad in late 1941 when Zhdanov took him aside and "insisted that Leningrad receive more ammunition."[87] That first winter alone Zhdanov helped persuade Stavka to transfer the Fifty-fourth Army to Leningrad from the adjacent Volkhov Front, accused the member of the military council of the Baltic Fleet, Nikolai K. Smirnov, of being a kulak for reluctance to share provisions and fuel with the Leningrad Front, and got the hard-pressed Karelian Front to send a major food store.[88]

Pressure for supplies could be exerted in a number of ways. In the first place there were the regular channels of the MPA's own communication network. One of these connected commissars with the second military council member above. Thus, when a brigade logistics officer told his commissar in 1942 of an acute scarcity of ammunition and fuel, "of course it was [the commissar] who had to go to see" the member of the army military council.[89] Another routine channel was through the multitude of periodic reports to superior party organs, which could be made to reflect the needs of the reporting organizational unit. For instance, Mikhail Kalashnik, a future deputy chief of the MPA and then the head of the Forty-seventh Army's politotdel, recounts that in a number of political reports in 1942-43, "we wrote at the request of our supply workers that the army was short of warm clothing." The superior political administrations in turn "promised us all possible assistance in procuring uniforms."[90] Appeals through less formal channels within the MPA were also possible. Commissars could turn to superiors on an emergency basis "to help push a matter through" concerning materials or manpower, and there was also the rarely utilized option of intervening (as Zhdanov did with Smirnov) with party officials in a parallel agency, such as another army or front, which controlled a valued resource.[91]

In most cases, however, the search for supplies quickly led party workers to go outside the MPA to other parts of the military establishment. (Obviously, even an appeal initiated inside the MPA, such as Kalashnik's, would eventually have to be passed on to a military agency capable of accommodating it.) Initiative here was normally reserved to logistics officials and commanding officers (the latter were invariably involved in appeals for troop reserves). Since most major pieces of correspondence at the level of army or above were cosigned by the political officers in military councils, the support of the party organ for a major request could be taken for granted by the recipient of the appeal. Beyond this, the most common form of participation for military party officials was to apply supplementary pressure in support of an appeal already made through normal military channels. For example, several hours after the military council of the Fourteenth Army on the Leningrad Front requested the command of the Northwestern Sector to transfer several divisions to it in August 1941, the member of the army military council (Gennadii Kupriianov, the first secretary of the Karelian party committee) telephoned Voroshilov, the commander of the sector, "in order to argue our request in detail."[92] Kupriianov was unsuccessful in this appeal, but his success the week before in working his way up the ladder of military authority to the Supreme Commander-in-Chief must have given him reason for hope:

[Valerian A. Frolov, the commander of the army] telephoned me in Suoiarvi from Murmansk, told me of the critical situation near Kestenga, and asked me to get in touch with the commander of the Leningrad Front, M. M. Popov. "I just phoned him and asked for a division," General Frolov said, "but the commander categorically refused. Perhaps he won't refuse you, as a secretary of the [Karelian] central committee."

I immediately got through to Popov. He heard me out attentively and said that he could well understand our situation but was in no position to help. "It is even worse around Leningrad," Markian Mikhailovich replied to me. "I have no reserves."

Then I phoned . . . Voroshilov. He listened to my request, said that he had no reserves either, and advised me to try Stalin. "Ask him for the Eighty-eighth Division, which is in Arkhangel'sk and is at the disposition of Stavka," Kliment Efremovich advised.

I was put through to Stalin extremely quickly. I reported to him the situation in the Kestenga area and asked him to transfer the Eighty-eighth Division to us . . . [Stalin queried Kupriianov as to how the division could be moved.] I assured him that we could manage to transport the division in no more than two days. Then Stalin said he would immediately issue an order for the division to be transferred to the authority of the Fourteenth Army.[93]

A political officer could also take it upon himself to press supply questions with superior military authorities on his own initiative. Some of the examples recorded in the memoirs are marvels of ingenuity. Kupriianov, for instance, while in Moscow for an abortive Central Committee plenum in October 1941, called on the head of the army's artillery administration, Nikolai D. Iakovlev, and asked him for "twenty wagons of shells above our approved limit." He also visited logistics chief Khrulev and "requested that he reserve for us two and a half thousand more food rations." He took advantage of a Moscow trip the following June (for a Supreme Soviet session) to seek out Vasilevskii and ask him for reinforcements (including eight infantry divisions, four tank battalions, and fresh engineering and artillery troops) for the Karelian Front's planned offensive.[94] General Rytov managed to slip a petition for more aircraft for his division into a telephone call congratulating Marshal Novikov on his appointment as first deputy commander of the air force in 1942.[95] The member of one army military council, Semen I. Mel'nikov, personally commandeered a fuel allotment at First Ukrainian Front headquarters in July 1944 and astonished his command colleague by making his way back, fuel and all, at the head of a tank column.[96]

A final possibility was for the political officer to turn for supplies to a promising source outside the military hierarchy entirely. A common procedure was to send party workers as plenipotentiaries to particular origins of supply, such as a major munitions plant, where they sometimes found themselves competing with representatives of other fronts or even of Stavka.[97] The political officer could also forage for materials on a more sweeping scale. A good example of the latter practice is the member of the Leningrad Front military council, Terentii F. Shtykov, who personally scoured "the central USSR" in 1941 and 1942 looking for food and other vital materials and "hurried to the site . . . and communicated directly with local political and public organizations" in the event of a snag.[98] Whenever possible, prior ties to civilian organizations were exploited. A number of second members of military councils were deliberately recruited from party or state agencies in the locality or an adjacent area so as to make such "mobilization of local resources" easier,[99] but many other political officers were involved in similar activity. Brezhnev, as first deputy chief of the Southern Front's political administration in 1941, repeatedly exhorted the Dnepropetrovsk party machine, in which he had worked before the war, for material help to the front's forming armies.[100] Khrushchev used his connections in the Ukraine and the Stalingrad area in campaigning for construction materials and emergency labor assistance for his fronts.[101] Kupriianov procured rifles and heavy guns from the warehouses of the Karelian NKVD and obtained scarce signals equipment and technicians from the republic's communications administration.[102]

The ultimate civilian target for an entreaty for supplies was the Central Committee Secretariat in Moscow. Yet it would seem that such petitions were quite rare. This was partly because of central party offices' sheer distance from the front and their lack of a clear mandate to interfere in military matters. But also important was the long-standing insulation of the MPA from the activities of the civilian administrative departments of the national party apparatus. It was one thing for Khrushchev to solicit Central Committee assistance,[103] but quite another for an obscure political officer, with probably no experience of national party management, to attempt to do so. Nevertheless, these barriers did not prevent some political workers from going to the top. Witness this account by General Popel' of how the First Guards Tank Army, in which he was chief political officer, sought help in 1943:

Telegrams would arrive from near Torzhek, Kalinin, almost from Moscow: "We are without fuel and food; we are awaiting instructions." What was needed, of course, was not instructions but precisely the fuel and food itself. But how could you throw these across many hundreds of kilometers? Where could you turn? [The commanders] and staffs of the group and army were occupied with directing operations. The logistics workers themselves were calling for help. The front would brush us aside, saying we were an independent entity and should act like one.

When all the usual channels had been exhausted and the usual curses uttered, Shtykov [the member of the military council of the army group] would stand up from his desk and pick up the high-frequency telephone. "We have no alternative," he would say, and then he would call the party Central Committee.

In the most pressing and desperate cases we ran to the Central Committee for help and immediately received it . . . A convoy would appear with gasoline, bread, and food concentrates.[104]

If more party functionaries did not follow this lead, it was not for lack of commitment to the needs of their military units.

The Zhukov Affair

8

No political event involving a Soviet soldier since the war has been as dramatic as the Zhukov affair of 1957. Without warning, the country's foremost military officer and the first to sit in the highest council of the party was evicted from office and pursued into disgrace by an indictment amounting to a bill of high treason. The military party organs had ostensibly played an important part in his fall—the resolution condemning Zhukov was formally entitled "On the improvement of party-political work in the Soviet Army and Navy."

Scholars have been unanimous in seeing the Zhukov affair in institutional terms, as a head-on political collision between the army under Zhukov and the party (including the party's organs in the military). Not only was Zhukov a genuine threat to Khrushchev's ascendancy within the party Presidium, writes Carl Linden, but the civilian politicians "probably also saw in Zhukov *a menace to party rule as such.*"[1] An American biographer has characterized Zhukov's dismissal as the outcome of "a struggle between army and Party," and Merle Fainsod described it as "a reassertion of Party primacy over the armed forces."[2]

This interpretation of Zhukov's fall is in drastic need of revision. A more useful understanding would emphasize Zhukov's personal history and peculiar position in the party elite and would de-emphasize elements of institutional conflict. Western analysis has relied almost exclusively on the official indictment of October 1957 and has in fact amounted to little more than summary or even literal quotation of the charges. My evaluation of this and other evidence yields quite different conclusions. The key portions of the indictment, far from being a reliable guide to Zhukov's conduct displaying him as a threat to party supremacy, turn out to be contrived and fraudulent. The portions that are truthful are those that give least credence to the thesis of a frontal clash between army and party. Although special attention should be given to the military party organs' role in the controversy, this can be attempted only after some other central aspects of the affair are thoroughly explored.

Zhukov's Rise and Fall

Georgii Konstantinovich Zhukov's climb from peasant origins had seemed the quintessential Soviet success story. A former NCO in the imperial cavalry, he joined the Red Army in October 1918, entered the party five months later, and fought in the Civil War in Budennyi's First Cavalry Army. His rapid rise was aided by Budennyi's patronage, by the vacuum created by the Great Purge, and by the talents he clearly exhibited when he led forces against the Japanese in Mongolia in 1939.[3] Zhukov was appointed chief of the General Staff in January 1941 and a candidate member of the Central Committee the following month. The day after the German invasion he was named to Stavka, and his wartime service as Stalin's chief military aide reached a climax when he personally received the capitulation of Nazi Germany on May 8, 1945.

This first stand in the limelight was brief. In July 1946, after heading the occupation administration in Germany and Soviet ground forces, Zhukov was abruptly demoted to command of the Odessa Military District (later the Ural district) and expelled from the Central Committee. What Khrushchev later called Stalin's "sickly suspicion" had lighted on Zhukov as early as December 1944, when Stalin rejected artillery regulations he felt Zhukov had promulgated without appropriate consultation and ordered him "henceforth not to act hastily in resolving serious questions."[4] Evidently led on by the intrigues of civilian associates like Beria and Malenkov, Stalin soon began "to tell all kinds of nonsense" about his former colleague.[5] Zhukov's name had sunk so low by 1948 that a foreign Communist could be assured that his demotion had been for looting jewelry in occupied Berlin.[6]

Within days of Stalin's death in March 1953, Zhukov was back in Moscow as First Deputy Defense Minister. In February 1955 he succeeded Nikolai Bulganin as minister, becoming only the third professional officer to hold that post (after Marshals Timoshenko and Vasilevskii). By 1957 Zhukov had also accumulated unprecedented party standing. He was reinstated as a Central Committee candidate in 1952, made a full member in September 1953 (filling the vacancy left by Beria), and designated a candidate member of the Presidium in

February 1956—the first career officer to sit on the Presidium or Politburo until Marshal Grechko in 1973-76. In June 1957 Zhukov attained
the summit of full Presidium membership, at the same Central Committee plenum that ousted the "antiparty group" led by Malenkov and
several other of Khrushchev's opponents.

Only four months later it was Zhukov's turn to fall. On October 26
he was peremptorily summoned from a visit in Albania to a Presidium
meeting at which his fate, presumably decided beforehand, was
quickly voted on. Several hours later TASS announced his replacement as minister by Marshal Rodion Ia. Malinovskii, the commander-in-chief of the ground forces. On October 28-29 a full Central
Committee plenum convened and, with the concurrence of leading
officials from the military, stripped Zhukov of his party posts and
passed a resolution recording the main charges against him. On
November 3, after several days of denunciatory meetings, *Pravda*
finally carried a communique on the plenum and several elaborations
on the accusations, most important a lengthy article by Ivan Konev, a
first deputy minister and the head of Warsaw Pact troops. Also
printed was Zhukov's own acknowledgment of how he had become
"profoundly aware" of his errors and would "eliminate [them] completely."[7] Details were added later, but the substance of the arraign-
ment was never altered.

Zhukov and the Presidium

Although the indictment contained no reference to the private relations between Zhukov and his fellow members of the Presidium,
neither this silence nor the continuing scarcity of evidence means that
these relations can be disregarded. It seems clear that Zhukov was left
in an exposed position by the competition within the small group at
the apex of the party on which his rise had been thoroughly dependent. If like most Presidium members Zhukov was indebted to Khrushchev, he could also lay claim more than most to a personal debt in
return. In 1953, Zhukov had been the one to arrest Beria at the order
of civilian leaders, including Khrushchev.[8] In June 1957, according to
unofficial sources, Zhukov had headed a "committee of initiative"
pressuring the Presidium majority to allow the entire Central Committee to vote on Khrushchev and had ordered military aircraft to fly
an unspecified number of committee members to Moscow for the
plenum.[9] To be sure, Khrushchev's 1957 coalition was assembled
primarily of civilians, through accepted party channels, and without
military force; and there is no indication that anyone considered
Zhukov a direct rival to Khrushchev for the top post. Nevertheless,
Khrushchev may have seen him as an unreliable supporter against

other potential adversaries, including Bulganin, the head of government (who had initially voted with the opposition in June 1957 but remained in office until 1958). Zhukov's presence on the Presidium could thus be construed as both a reminder of Khrushchev's vulnerability and a temptation to any nascent opposition faction.

Quite possibly this perception was augmented by more strictly personal calculations. Zhukov was a man of strong personality with achievements that had, by admission of his official obituary two decades later, "earned [him] widespread popularity and the deep respect of the Soviet people" in a way his more drab associates might well have envied and distrusted.[10] Khrushchev in particular may have felt upstaged by Zhukov's heroic stature and even by his personal acquaintance with President Eisenhower. Zhukov in turn was perhaps less inclined than others to accept the leader's ebullient style. We know, for instance, that as early as May 1956 Zhukov was contemptuous of Khrushchev's alcohol-inspired exuberance at a Kremlin reception.[11]

It is therefore at least plausible to argue that the logic of the small-group relations within the party leadership provided sufficient momentum for Zhukov's dismissal. This is a credible explanation, and it has been dealt with to some degree by most Western specialists. But is it the entire explanation? Was Zhukov no more than a victim of palace politics, like dozens of others before and after? The answer of the official indictment was an emphatic no. It maintained that Zhukov's actions had juxtaposed him completely to the party and its values. Since this position has formed the basis for Western analysis, we must now turn directly to the allegations.

Five charges were leveled. Zhukov was said to have plotted the actual overthrow of the regime, disagreed on policy matters with civilian leaders, sponsored a cult of his own personality, administered the army in a nonparty manner, and attacked the military party organs. We will go through the indictment charge by charge, placing emphasis on the two accusations, the first and fifth, which received most attention from Soviet authorities.

The First Charge: Bonapartism

There is little direct evidence on the crucial accusation that Zhukov had "pursued a policy directly toward . . . liquidation of the leadership and control of the army and navy by the party, its Central Committee, and the government." The implication of outright disloyalty was strengthened by opaque allusions over the next several years to Zhukov's Bonapartism. Malinovskii told the Twenty-first Congress in 1959 that party leaders had "opportunely discerned . . . Zhukov's striving to tear the army away from the party, and dealt a sharp blow to this latter-day 'Bonaparte.' "[12] At the 1961 congress, Khrushchev spoke darkly of Zhukov's "juxtaposing the Soviet Army to the party leadership," and Malinovskii even of his "Bonapartist aspirations toward a personal seizure of power."[13] The most literal adherence to the coup scenario came in Khrushchev's memoirs, published in the West more than a decade later, in which he insisted that in 1957, "we were heading for a military coup d'etat . . . We couldn't let Zhukov stage a South American-style military take-over in our country."[14]

There is by now abundant circumstantial evidence to allow confident dismissal of this charge. The most important indication is the complete lack of correspondence with the way in which Zhukov was treated. Not only was he not arrested, but the plenum actually instructed the party Secretariat to assign him other work. He remained in military service (without assignment) until March 1958, then was officially retired on a substantial pension to the same Moscow apartment building to which Khrushchev was sent after Khrushchev's own fall in 1964. Zhukov was never demoted from the rank of marshal, although there was ample precedent (and for lesser misdeeds).[15] Nor was he ever excluded from the party or his expulsion publicly demanded (in clear contrast to the antiparty group).

Within months of Khrushchev's removal, the terms of even this mild exile improved radically. The clear implication is that Zhukov's basic sin had been against Khrushchev and the former Presidium majority, not against party rule. All references to Zhukov's Bonapartism ceased, and in May 1965 he appeared in full uniform on Lenin's tomb for the celebration of the twentieth anniversary of victory. His memoirs began in serial form the next month and were issued as a book in 1969, in an enormous printing of 600,000 copies (which most bookstores sold out in hours), reissued in expanded form in 1974, and widely translated and sold abroad. In his last years Zhukov again basked in official favor and received a number of public awards, including his fifth and sixth Orders of Lenin. An interview in 1971 portrayed him working quietly in his dacha on the new edition of his memoirs and engaged in "voluminous correspondence" with schoolchildren and members of Communist youth organizations.[16]

Zhukov's death on June 18, 1974, brought the few remaining honors denied him in life. His *Pravda* obituary noted his outstanding services to the regime and remarked of his nonmilitary activities only that he had participated actively in public life. After "an endless stream of thousands and thousands of people" passed by his body, he was buried with full state ceremony (in distinction to the muted farewell to Khrushchev in 1971).[17] Of the sixteen Politburo members who signed the obituary, two (Brezhnev and Mikhail Suslov) had been full members of the Presidium that ousted Zhukov, three had been candidates, and all but four had sat on the Central Committee. Brezhnev and Suslov (who gave the speech attacking Zhukov at the October 1957 plenum) helped lift his ashes into the Kremlin wall in what seemed almost an act of atonement. Later in 1974 came the final mark of respectability, the affixing of Zhukov's name to his native village and district, a nearby collective farm, streets in Moscow and Leningrad, the senior air defense academy, and scholarships in a number of military schools.[18] Clearly these are not the gestures an authoritarian regime would make toward a traitor.

If official treatment of Zhukov is utterly incompatible with the first charge, so is that of other members of the high command. Had Zhukov actually been planning a South American-style coup, one would expect him to have had collaborators. Khrushchev's memoirs claimed that Zhukov had been "voicing Bonapartist aspirations in his conversations with military commanders," but at no time did the leadership place specific officers under suspicion.[19] Not a single man was arrested, and there was no unusual replacement of senior officers before or after the plenum.

Table 12 puts changes in senior command posts in 1957-58 in the perspective of turnover since the end of postwar demobilization in 1948. While the rates of change for 1957 and 1958 (29.3 and 27.5 percent) are somewhat higher than the average (22.5 percent), neither is close to the maximum recorded. The 1957 figure is eighth (behind 1956, 1949, 1960, 1953, 1967, 1968, and 1951), and 1958 ranks tenth. Turnover for 1957-58 is not significantly above the mean for Khrushchev's years in power (26.6 percent) and it is in fact marginally lower than for the parallel two-year period in the next decade (1967-68), when no one has suggested the high command was under the slightest political suspicion.

A glance at specific cadre replacements in 1957-58 shows that most had no believable relation to precautions or reprisals against a military conspiracy. The most important source of turnover was Marshal Malinovskii's promotion, which created a chain of vacancies beginning with his ground forces command and working through the group of forces in Germany and the Leningrad, Ural, and Transbaikal military districts. (Without these changes, turnover in 1957-58 would be almost precisely equal to the average.) Another change was caused by the death of a district commander in March 1958, one by the assignment of another general to head the ministry's cadres administration in mid-1957, one by the appointment of a new Deputy Defense Minister in charge of radioelectronics in early 1957, and several more by the consignment of three district commanders (all war heroes in their mid-sixties, none touched by a breath of scandal) into semiretired status as ministry inspectors in 1958.[20] Command of the air force was also changed in January 1957 (in favor of the same man whom the incumbent had replaced eight years before), and Deputy Defense Minister Rokossovskii was temporarily moved to the Transcaucasus district in October 1957 to heighten the Soviet profile in the Middle East.[21]

This leaves unaccounted for five senior officers demoted soon after Zhukov's dismissal. Their fates may bear some relation to his, although there is no positive proof of this. About Vice-Admiral Valentin A. Chekurov, the commander of the Pacific Fleet since 1956, we know only that he was replaced in February 1958, at the age of fifty-one, and never heard from again.[22] General of the Army Aleksandr A. Luchinskii was relieved in the Turkestan Military District in December 1957 (by the man Rokossovskii displaced in the Transcaucasus); in early 1959 he also lost his candidate status in the Central Committee, the only officer except Zhukov to do so prior to the next regular party congress in 1961.[23] The three other demotions were all of deputy ministers, each of whom had served with Zhukov during the war—Marshal Vasilevskii, relieved in December 1957, and Colonel-Generals Vasilii E. Belokoskov and Vasilii I. Vinogradov, in charge of construction and logistics respectively, who were replaced by younger men in mid-1958.

The most that can be said is that perhaps these officials expressed reservations about Zhukov's removal. Luchinskii and Vasilevskii, in particular, were not listed among peers who joined in the condemnation at the plenum, and Luchinskii's later appearance at a denunciatory gathering in Tashkent was simply noted in the press without comment.[24] It should be pointed out, however, that three of the five men did receive reassignment (Vasilevskii in 1959; Vinogradov, who served as deputy to his successor until 1960; and Luchinskii, who became deputy chief inspector). Two of the five can be ruled out by geography from participation in a Moscow-based plot (Chekurov in Vladivostok and Luchinskii in Tashkent). And none was ever accused of complicity in Zhukov's schemes or is known to have been detained, reduced in rank, or expelled from the party.

It is equally important to recognize that throughout 1957-58 the men in those posts strategic to any serious bid to overturn the regime by force were not changed. This applies to the General Staff, the center of military planning and communication, where Marshal Vasilii D. Sokolovskii remained in charge until 1960 (as did his two first deputies). The equally sensitive troop commands in the Moscow area, all of which changed in 1953 during the showdown with Beria, went

Table 12. Turnover among senior military commanders and political officers[a]

Year	Commanders			Political officers		
	Positions for which information available	Positions in which officer changed	Percentage turnover	Positions for which information available	Positions in which officer changed	Percentage turnover
1948	33 of 38	7	21.2	19 of 37	3	15.8
1949	36 of 39	15	41.7	27 of 37	5	18.5
1950	35 of 38	2	5.7	26 of 35	15	57.7
1951	36 of 38	11	30.6	25 of 36	5	20.0
1952	36 of 38	4	11.1	26 of 36	4	15.4
1953	38 of 39	14	36.8	27 of 37	12	44.4
1954	39 of 40	7	17.9	28 of 37	2	7.1
1955	43 of 43	11	25.6	33 of 37	11	33.3
1956	42 of 42	18	42.9	33 of 35	6	18.2
1957	41 of 41	12	29.3	34 of 35	17	50.0
1958	40 of 40	11	27.5	34 of 35	17	50.0
1959	40 of 40	4	10.0	35 of 35	4	11.4
1960	40 of 40	16	40.0	35 of 35	11	31.4
1961	38 of 38	7	18.4	35 of 35	6	17.1
1962	38 of 38	8	21.0	35 of 35	6	17.1
1963	38 of 38	9	23.7	35 of 35	4	11.4

Year						
1964	38 of 38	10	26.3	35 of 35	3	8.6
1965	36 of 36	7	19.4	35 of 35	2	5.7
1966	36 of 36	3	8.3	35 of 35	5	14.3
1967	38 of 38	12	31.6	36 of 36	5	13.9
1968	39 of 39	12	30.8	37 of 37	3	8.1
1969	39 of 39	11	28.2	38 of 38	6	15.8
1970	40 of 40	4	10.0	38 of 38	6	15.8
1971	40 of 40	5	12.5	38 of 38	7	18.4
1972	41 of 41	10	24.4	38 of 38	3	7.9
1973	41 of 41	6	14.6	38 of 38	3	7.9
1974	42 of 42	4	9.5	38 of 38	6	15.8
1975	42 of 42	5	11.9	38 of 38	12	31.6
Mean			22.5			20.8

Sources: Press references, obituaries, official biographies, and historical works.

a. Command positions include Minister of Defense (of War 1950-53); deputy ministers; commanders of military and air defense districts, fleets, and groups of forces; chief of General Staff Academy. From Naval Ministry of 1950-53, only minister and fleet commanders are included. Political positions include chief and deputy chiefs of MPA; chief political officers in force branches if not included among deputy MPA chiefs; members of military councils of military districts and equivalents; chief of Lenin Military-Political Academy. Chief of political administration of Naval Ministry was counted as deputy chief of MPA. Figures are not included for three military districts for which continuous existence of five years could not be determined. Position was considered to have experienced change if the officer was replaced or if the position was created or liquidated.

without turnover as well. Marshal Kirill Moskalenko stayed as head of the Moscow Military District until 1960, and the commands of the city, Kremlin garrison, and air defense district also remained in the same hands.

The Second Charge: Policy Adventurism

Little conclusive has come to light on the allegation of concrete policy disagreement between Zhukov and civilian leaders. The plenum simply declared him "inclined to adventurism both in the understanding of the most important tasks of the Soviet Union's foreign policy and in the leadership of the Ministry of Defense." The term "adventurism" surfaced in several later pronouncements, but it was quietly dropped after 1964.

It is intriguing to speculate about use of a word which later became a favorite term of opprobrium for Chinese conduct, especially in foreign relations. Could Zhukov have espoused a more assertive foreign policy in a way that alienated civilians? We know that it was at this time that Chinese leaders, impressed by Soviet missile technology (the first Sputnik was launched October 4, 1957), were beginning to exhort Soviet policy to the left, and that they made a strong plea to this effect at the conference of Communist parties in Moscow the week after Zhukov's ouster. We can assume that Zhukov was involved in negotiating the agreement to provide China with nuclear assistance, signed October 15 (and revoked in 1959), and it is quite conceivable that he advocated closer cooperation. We know also that thousands of Soviet military advisers were currently in China, and that the two senior field officers demoted after Zhukov's fall (Chekurov and Luchinskii) had commands where collaboration with the Chinese must have been extensive.

All this must remain speculation, however. Other commands adjacent to China went unchanged in 1957-58.[25] The Chinese have never claimed any affinity with Zhukov, and such a tie seems improbable in light of his rehabilitation after 1964. More important, Zhukov had foregone a sterling opportunity to promote "adventurism" in June 1957 when he opposed the antiparty group, one of whose ostensible objections had been to Khrushchev's betterment of relations with the West. Zhukov may have changed his mind after June, or agreed with the group on foreign policy while opposing them on other grounds. But there is not a hint in his public statements of any sympathy for the deposed faction's policies, and he repeatedly underlined his support for the easing of international tension.[26]

It can scarcely be doubted that Khrushchev and Zhukov rated military needs rather differently against other national priorities. But this is not to say that opinions were juxtaposed along institutional lines. On the party side, Khrushchev's own views on defense spending and policy were not without their ambiguities.[27] To the extent that he was compelled to defend his efforts to reduce the military burden, Western scholars have long been aware of how this was mainly against a wide array of civilian opponents in the party and state bureaucracies.[28] The party apparatus in the army backed precisely the kind of energetic defense effort to which Zhukov was committed.

As for the army, it is Khrushchev himself, in his memoirs, who does most to dispel any notion of a bellicose military under Zhukov challenging a peace-seeking party: "I respected Zhukov for his intellect and for his common sense . . . Unlike so many thick-headed types you find wearing uniforms, Zhukov understood the necessity of reducing our military expenditures [and] demonstrated a realistic approach to the questions of establishing some sort of reciprocal arms control with the United States. In short, Zhukov was exceptionally perceptive and flexible for a military man."[29]

Whatever Zhukov's status as voice for military concerns, there is nothing to show that he was "the one leading figure who could, in any real sense, 'speak for the Army,'" or that he was dismissed because he stood for promilitary programs that were to suffer later.[30] One is hard pressed to identify a single important policy bearing upon the army that changed drastically in or soon after October 1957. Zhukov advocated heavy defense investment, yet so did his successors; the general trend in military spending under Zhukov, of reallocating resources from manpower to weapons development and procurement, continued unabated after his ouster. Likewise Zhukov appears to have favored rehabilitation of military victims of the Great Purge (as did most political officers). But this process also persisted and even intensified after his departure; the most important forum for military discussion of the purge, *Voenno-istoricheskii zhurnal* (Journal of Military History), began publication only in 1959.

The Third Charge: The Personality Cult

According to the plenum resolution, Zhukov had lost his "party-minded simplicity," acquired "the conceit that he was the sole hero" of the war, and encouraged the propagation of "a cult of his own personality" by "fawners and sycophants." The resolution may have been alluding to (but did not specify) facts such as the erection of a bronze bust of Zhukov in his native village in late 1953 and the publicity given his role in the battle of Moscow during fifteenth anniversary celebrations in December 1956.[31] The only details came from Marshal Konev, who outdid the resolution in denouncing Zhukov's vanity and particularized several manifestations of the cult, including a painting of him on a rearing white charger in Berlin ("like St. George the Dragonslayer on an old icon"). In debunking the Zhukov myth, Konev also reviewed that he termed Zhukov's many errors and blunders during and immediately prior to the war.

The cult charge illuminates two important aspects of the Zhukov affair. The first is the polemical exaggeration and even outright falsification infusing the indictment. The clearest example is Konev's discussion of Zhukov's "large share of the responsibility" for the army's lack of preparedness in 1941. He singled out Zhukov's haphazard deployment, as Chief of General Staff, of mechanized formations, large armored groups supported by air power, "without regard for the prospects of providing them with the proper equipment and specialized cadres." It is difficult to conceive of a more tendentious summary of the episode and Zhukov's role in it. The Soviet Union had pioneered in the development of mechanized formations in the early 1930s, but they were hastily disbanded in late 1939 at the insistence of the chief of tank troops, Pavlov. Zhukov had no part in this decision (he was in the Far East) or in the decision to begin reassembly in mid-1940 after the German victories in Europe with similar formations. In December 1940 a conference of senior officers in the General Staff resolved to accelerate the program, and this occurred largely under Zhukov's supervision over the next six months. If the new formations were poorly organized, this was clearly the fault of the prior decision to dismantle them and not of Zhukov, who advocated careful redeployment in December 1940 and vigorously sought resources for them later.[32]

So casual a violation of historical fact can only inspire doubts about other parts of the indictment hitherto accepted in the West. But the cult charge also illustrates a second point about the Zhukov issue—how, rather than neatly dividing army against party, it cut across both institutions.

Konev's article captured the central tension in Soviet historical treatment of the war over the relative contributions of Stavka and the front commands. He was not simply a mouthpiece for a vindictive party. Not only did Konev bear a long-standing personal antipathy to Zhukov (amply demonstrated in accounts of the drive on Berlin in 1945), he also articulated anti-Stavka and anti-Zhukov sentiments that were broadly based within the army.[33] His assertions that Zhukov had no special role at Stalingrad and that the basic weight of planning and organization lay at the front level could elicit great sympathy from other commanders who had spent the war in the field. This kind of disapproval certainly extended to officers other than

Zhukov (like Vinogradov, deputy chief of logistics during the war, whose work at Stalingrad was said by one marshal in 1962 to have "done us more harm than good").[34] Likewise Zhukov's later declaration that the decisive role at Stalingrad "indisputably belonged to Stavka and the General Staff" spoke for another broad coalition.[35] As was noted in Chapter 7, Zhukov's reputation was to be upheld after 1964 by several former Moscow colleagues. Vasilevskii, the most important, had known him since the early 1930s and worked closely with him at both high points of his career. Vasilevskii was mentioned by Konev as having benefited along with Zhukov from the reworking of a film about Stalingrad, and he was to write Zhukov's *Pravda* eulogy in 1974 with obvious feeling.[36]

Furthermore, these respective opinions were shared by many senior party officials. Konev's stand reflected the memories and interests not only of field commanders but of many current and former political officers as well. Among the latter was Khrushchev himself, who had disagreed on a number of occasions with Zhukov and other Stavka officers (including Vasilevskii and Vinogradov) and who complained in his memoirs about Stavka "celebrities" whom he was "never very pleased to see."[37] On the other side of the line, it should be remembered that it was a career political officer, Telegin, who wrote the first public defense of Zhukov in 1965. And Zhukov in turn did more than anyone in the 1960s to restore the wartime reputation of Stalin, the supreme commander but also, of course, head of the party. Zhukov was willing to distinguish the tyrant who banished him to Odessa from the military leader with whom he had worked successfully earlier.

Conflicting recollections of the war may thus have been a source of quite direct tension between Zhukov and Khrushchev. It is likely that the following words in Vasilevskii's memoirs could have been written equally well by Zhukov: "I had good relations with Khrushchev . . . in the first postwar years. But they changed sharply when I was unable to support his claims that Stalin did not know the particulars of operational and strategic matters and was incompetent as Supreme Commander-in-Chief. To this day I cannot understand how he could say this . . . Khrushchev must have known how great was the authority of Stavka and Stalin on questions of military leadership."[38]

The Fourth Charge: Personal Crudeness
While the charge about Zhukov's personal crudeness and "unfounded dictums" as defense administrator is probably the most reliable part of the indictment, it is also that which most directly concerns his transgressions against other military officers.

This image of Zhukov is fully consistent with the picture of him as a wartime leader available from the memoir literature. Colored as these impressions were by Zhukov's wartime status, they also reflect basic lines of his personality. Zhukov reports in his own memoirs that even as a young cavalry officer in the 1920s he was "criticized for excessive exactingness" and lack of patience and tact. He claims he reacted only when others displayed bad faith but concedes that "Some did not understand this, and I in turn was apparently not tolerant enough of human weakness."[39]

Nothing indicates that Zhukov's indulgence of human weakness increased after he became Minister of Defense. While we know little about his behavior toward his ministerial colleagues and subordinates, there is no reason to suppose that he was any less imperious than during the war. One memoir passage depicts Zhukov dressing down (in front of other officers) the head of the air force, Marshal Pavel F. Zhigarev, for his command's slowness in developing helicopters.[40] Descriptions of Zhukov's crudeness (*grubost'*) published at the time of his dismissal, even if somewhat overstated, seem essentially authentic. There is an obvious parallel with Stalin's personality (indeed, one must wonder whether this was not one of the reasons for Stalin's high regard of his abilities). It would have been entirely in keeping with past performance if, as Marshal Biriuzov claimed in November 1957, Zhukov as minister "refused to listen to the opinions of others and did not consider it necessary to consult with them or discuss suggestions coming from below."[41] Many of the most critical accounts in memoirs were later written by men who held high military office in 1957 and joined with evident satisfaction in Zhukov's denouncement.[42]

There were undoubtedly some who did not share this judgment and paid a heavy price. But this only further accentuates the way Zhukov evoked a differentiated response. Zhukov's army was not a monolith mobilized behind an unchallenged leader.

The Fifth Charge: The Attack on the Military Party Organs

The final charge is of special relevance to this book. It proclaimed that Zhukov had "pursued a policy directed toward the curtailment of the work of the party organizations, political organs, and military councils" within the army. Some specifics emerge from the Konev essay and later statements. Konev stressed that Zhukov's decisions had "reduced the party organizations to the status of purely educational organs" and "led to the violation [of] the good and sound tradition of close communication" with local party agencies. In 1961 MPA chief Golikov submitted that Zhukov had "slighted and dis-

paraged" the party organs and encouraged dissension between command and political officers.[43] The authoritative history of the MPA in
1964 contended that Zhukov had "attempted to limit the rights" of
party organs and military councils, secured the liquidation of a
number of political organs and the curtailment of their training facilities, and terminated the political instruction of officers.[44]

Again, the accusations must be read with great caution. It is not
adequate merely to quote them and presume that they are true. Since
1964 much of the indictment has been toned down or even eliminated.
The 1968 edition of the MPA history, for instance, gives a much
briefer list of inadequacies in party work and declines to ascribe responsibility to Zhukov, stating only that he was said at the time to
have "undervalued party leadership."[45] Many other discussions of the
plenum make no mention of Zhukov.

It does appear that there was more than routine concern in late 1957
about the state of political work in the army. The press carried an unusual number of reports on it, and a ten-day conference of MPA propaganda officials ended shortly before Zhukov's departure for Eastern
Europe. A deputy head of the Central Committee's propaganda and
agitation department, Vasilii I. Snastin, attended and may well have
reported disquieting signs to the party leadership.[46] (It is noteworthy
that Snastin's superior, Suslov, the secretary in charge of ideology and
a man not normally involved in military affairs, gave the main report
at the plenum.) For whatever immediate reason, the Presidium on
October 19 discussed a report by MPA chief Zheltov and called for
improvement, but apparently without blaming Zhukov (who was still
abroad). Only a week later did the decisive Presidium meeting tie defects in political work specifically to Zhukov.[47] We cannot know
exactly why so direct an association was drawn between Zhukov and
the MPA's deficiencies. But there is evidence enough to suggest that
the short-term exigency of justifying Khrushchev's disposal of his
former ally was paramount.

Zhukov seems to have had well developed but thoroughly conventional ideas about party work. He had an excellent opportunity to
observe it in the early 1930s when he spent two years as party secretary in the army's administration of combat training.[48] If during the
war he was sometimes brusque with individual political officers, it
was only as part of his general impatience with subordinates. As Defense Minister, Zhukov several times contributed to the discussion of
party work. The thrust of his remarks was that political officers
should contribute more directly to military performance by improving
their military expertise and making greater efforts to reinforce discipline and relate political education to combat training. In April

1956, for example, Zhukov criticized "declarative and paradelike" party work and demanded that the MPA display more concern with "questions . . . related to the practical tasks standing before the forces."[49]

Western observers have misinterpreted these comments by reading them in isolation and overlooking the extent to which they were typical of many at the time. Such pronouncements were quite common by the autumn of 1953, well before Zhukov's promotion to minister, and many of the most forthright were made by the leaders of the military party organs. For instance, in October 1954 the head of the MPA's propaganda and agitation administration, Lieutenant-General Mikhail A. Mironov, used language that was virtually interchangeable with Zhukov's: party workers "must pay more attention to the military education of the personnel, explain more profoundly the demands of regulations and instructions, and more actively carry out military-technical propaganda"; reinforcing commanders' authority must be "an object of special concern."[50] Similar imperatives can easily be found in the statements of Zheltov and other MPA officials, and most of this discussion would indeed be commonplace at any period.

It is not surprising that some political officers were displeased with these strictures, although few could have objected to them in principle. The head of the political administration of the navy, Vice-Admiral A. V. Komarov, observed in 1956 that when changes began "there were among the senior political workers of the navy a certain number of skeptics who doubted the appropriateness of such a reform of their work . . . Clinging to old methods that had been outdated for years, they continued to trample in the same place and essentially hindered implementation of the reform."[51] If any voiced reservations, it is not at all improbable that, as one political officer claimed in November 1957, Zhukov "crudely belittled" them, much as he treated anyone who stood in his way.[52]

Let us look briefly at several of the specific allegations relating to the political organs for which enough is known to make a judgment about veracity.

1. The 1964 history of the MPA accused Zhukov of abusing the military councils and in particular the political officers who sat on them. This is perhaps the most difficult charge to verify. The language of the 1964 text is extremely ambiguous on this point, and the charge was dropped in all post-Khrushchev accounts. It may reflect Zhukov's personal indelicacy toward political officers and other council members as much as any other factor.[53]

2. Zhukov was said, by Konev and others, to have tried to remove

the political organs from practical training. This charge is very doubtful. The onus of Zhukov's public comments was to reprimand the
political organs precisely for their insufficient practicality. In March
1957 he personally sponsored the revival in the army of socialist competition and strongly criticized the earlier abandonment of it.[54]

3. Zhukov was blamed for a decline in party strength in the army, a
reduction in the number of political organs and officials, and curtailment of MPA educational facilities. His responsibility for any of
these developments is unlikely. The numerical reductions were due
mainly to demobilization, limp MPA recruitment efforts (remedied in
1958), and party-wide attempts to limit the number of full-time
officials which were generally praised even during Zhukov's period of
disgrace.[55] Zhukov had no discernible convictions on the training of
political officers. The only major change in practice in the 1950s was
the abolition of secondary MPA schools, and this occurred in 1951,
when Zhukov was commander of the Ural Military District.[56] Zhukov
was to be criticized in 1959 for forcing abandonment of correspondence study at the Lenin Academy. Yet this program had been
singled out as the worst in the entire army in 1954, and surely this was
not due to Zhukov. The 1959 report, moreover, castigated Zhukov
for terminating correspondence courses at two other establishments
which trained military engineers, not political officers.[57]

4. Zhukov was said to have hampered the ideological instruction of
commanders and ordered an end to mandatory political classes for
them. Zhukov may well have had preferences along this line, as do
many Soviet officers. But it is certain that the post-Stalin reform was
fully implemented before Zhukov became minister and was approved
of by the military party organs themselves.

Except for wartime, Soviet commanders had always been required
to attend formal political sessions. Beginning in mid-1953, however,
the MPA pursued a "principle of voluntarism" whereby officers were
given the option of studying independently and attending only
lectures and seminars on political themes. By October 1954—four
months before Zhukov's promotion to minister—most officers were
under the new system.[58] "Soviet officers and generals have grown
ideologically," one MPA official declared in justification. "It is
necessary that each of them have the opportunity to define his method
of study according to his own judgment."[59] A similar argument was
being advanced for changes in political education for civilians at
about the same time.[60]

If any single factor impeded the new procedure, it was the haste of
the political organs to extricate themselves from it entirely, even to the
point of declining to check performance or organize support activities.

As early as 1954, one reads of "many [political officers] who are completely uninterested" in political study or "have interpreted the principle of voluntarism in Marxist-Leninist study as allowing them to remove themselves completely from the ideological education of our cadres."[61] A number of retrospective accounts also assigned "a significant degree" of the blame to the MPA itself.[62] Obligatory classes were reinstated in December 1957, but criticisms have appeared regularly since that time of the military party organs' lack of zeal in implementing the program.

    5. A final example is Zhukov's alleged accountability for the paucity of communication with local party organs and other civilians. The charge ignores the long history of this pattern and flies in the face of detailed descriptions of it decades before 1957. Zhukov did not design the system, and there is no indication that he altered it significantly. He was not responsible for civilian indifference to relations with the army on the local level, and the October plenum certainly did not alter this attitude. Five major civilian newspapers surveyed for the six months after the plenum printed an average of only two stories on military life during the entire period.[63] After October 1957 several senior political officers spoke publicly of the need for local officials to display more initiative if ties were to become more intimate, and indeed most civilians seemed to take this need for granted.[64] On the military side, the coolness toward ties with civilians has always been abundantly shared by the MPA. It makes far more sense to note the inattentiveness of "certain commanders *and* political organs" to this question, as one article did in 1954 (and as most Soviet discussions do at any time), than to ascribe the entire fault to Zhukov or to the army command.[65] On the whole, the propaganda drive for consolidation of ties seems to have brought no permanent result. By January 1958 there were already reports of "attempts to reduce this work to a short-term campaign."[66]

Before leaving the MPA, we should briefly review the impact of Zhukov's fall on its personnel and operations. A look back at Table 12 shows clearly that for the party organs—unlike the command—1957 and 1958 were years of exceptionally rapid change in personnel. Turnover in top posts was 50 percent each year, the second highest figure since 1948 and two and a half times the mean. This was a rate almost double that in the high command. By the end of 1958 only three posts (in the air force, Kiev Military District, and Northern Fleet) had the same political officer as at the beginning of 1957, and several positions had had more than one change. Moreover, the changes were much more likely than in the command to involve retirement or demotion. MPA chief Zheltov was given a lateral (and short-lived) transfer to a civilian post (head of the administrative organs department of the Central Committee, a less prestigious posting by most Soviet standards). His replacement, Golikov, was another career soldier—and curiously a man whom Khrushchev depicts in his memoirs as a coward and complainer.[67] Two of Zheltov's deputies left the MPA altogether, and the third (Lieutenant-General Fedor P. Stepchenko, who had accompanied Zhukov to Eastern Europe in October 1957) was demoted to the same Odessa Military District to which Zhukov had been consigned in 1946. Whereas only ten commanders (of forty-one) left the top group in 1957-58, twenty-one political officers (of thirty-four) were removed by transfer, retirement, or demotion.

It cannot be said whether this house cleaning resulted from direct resistance to Zhukov's removal. Zheltov is unlikely to have done so, judging from the timing of his report to the Presidium, but other MPA executives (Stepchenko, for example) may have behaved differently. Whatever these men did, it is evident that many were unable to avoid being tarred with the same brush as Zhukov. And whatever the regime said about Zhukov's responsibility for the political organs' poor performance, its actions show that it looked to the MPA for much of the blame. Aside from personnel changes, it was on the MPA that most of the ameliorative structural alterations designed to "rejuvenate" party work were performed in 1958-60 (measures such as the intensification of party recruitment, replacement of some politotdels by elected party committees, and transfer of primary party organizations down to the battalion level).[68] Most of these amendments were superficial and short-lived—and subject to glib distortion in the press[69]—but they were indicative of the party leadership's awareness of the MPA's own shortcomings.

This impression is confirmed by the progress of the campaign against the "Zhukov style of work" in lower military echelons. It evoked no clear sense of grievance or mission among MPA officials. Rather than purposive action against well defined culprits, one finds "a certain unjustifiable oscillation, slowness, waiting for some sort of extra instructions."[70] The distinct sensation given by accounts of party gatherings on the plenum is of contrived crisis, with officials avoiding the plenum for familiar and more innocuous topics. At a party conference in the Northern Fleet, for instance, "many speakers began to depart from" the subject of the plenum. One party secretary "devoted most of his speech to criticism of the [fleet's] logistics organs for sending too little paint to keep the interior of his ship in order and for poor repairs to communications equipment."[71]

This confusion was partly the result of the vagueness of the indictment. But equally important was that at the implementation stage the military party organs were as much as the command the target of the campaign, as is normal in Soviet military politics. Thus when the navy's newspaper reported on insensitive leaders two days before the communique on the plenum, it gave as an illustration, not a commander, but a party official who had "become convinced of his infallibility."[72] Other examples followed until the issue was laid to rest in mid-1958. Political officers were expected to find public fault with one another's work, and in January 1958 the chief political officer in the Moscow Military District could be taken to task for making a speech in which "he did not pronounce a single remark critical of superior political organs."[73] Not infrequently, offending party workers were castigated together with their command colleagues.

If the military party organs were held jointly culpable, they also acted jointly with the command to contain the corrective campaign. To structural innovations such as the relocation of primary party organizations, political officers reacted with their usual conservatism and were roundly accused of "repeating old mistakes," "preferring the old, familiar scheme," and "fail[ing] to fill the new organizational forms with innovative and richer content."[74] As to the wave of officially inspired criticism, again and again the press reported on party workers siding with commanders against it. One example will suffice. At a party conference in the Northern Military District, a junior officer from the district's vehicles administration criticized the administration leadership, particularly its chief, for crudeness and errors. Two days later the party secretary of the organization pronounced the speech a slander on the entire work unit and called a party meeting to discuss it at which he and the commander accused the junior officer of "all the deadly sins" and of "vulgarizing criticism" and had a resolution adopted condemning him. Word of the incident was said to have reached the district political administration, but it had taken no action.[75]

If too much about the Zhukov episode remains unknowable to allow a perfect reconstruction, enough is now known to say that the image of it as a clash between party and army is a serious misinterpretation. This eminent military professional was also a lifelong Communist who wrote in his memoirs of having "tried to subordinate all my thoughts, aspirations, and actions to my duties as a party member."[76] If Zhukov's character had a darker side, it was as much apparent to his fellow soldiers as to his colleagues in the party leadership. On the party's part, assessments of Zhukov were complex and susceptible to change. The party's organs within the army were neither the outraged victim nor the pliant instrument of official retribution. They behaved, as they normally do, as an integral part of the military establishment, sharing its aspirations and faults.

This reassessment sheds some light on the enduring problem of analyzing elite-level politics in the Soviet Union. It reinforces T. H. Rigby's admonition to distinguish with care between conflict among leaders and conflict among societal groups and institutions.[77] It also reminds us to be aware, as Grey Hodnett has urged recently, of the importance of political contingencies.[78] It was, after all, only a combination of contingencies—such as Zhukov's personality, his status as a national hero, and his arrival in the Presidium as part of a precarious leadership coalition—that produced the outcome in 1957. The experience of Marshal Grechko in the 1970s was very different largely because the contingencies of the case were so different. Grechko's character was to all appearances benign, he was without claim to heroic stature, and he came to Brezhnev's Politburo together with several other senior politicians and after nearly a decade of unprecedented stability at the top.[79] In the end, only death removed him from the inner circle.

These findings may point to a more general conclusion. The recent and necessary search by Western scholars for general and invariable elements of the Soviet system, particularly ones that can be compared with those of other countries, should not desensitize us to more personal and variable features. If the Zhukov episode has a broad lesson, it is that these latter facets of Soviet politics continue to merit serious consideration even as specialists attempt to integrate their work further with the mainstream of social science research. In the Soviet field as elsewhere, the science of politics is incomplete without the arts of biography and history.

Public Demand Articulations

9

Although most civil-military interactions in the Soviet Union take place in closed settings, there is also an important arena of public discussion and demand making. For army officers, even more than for most officials, freedom to voice policy preferences and suggestions in the press and other public forums increased greatly after the death of Stalin. Certain subjects have remained essentially out of bounds for comment and criticism, notably the actions of individual holders of top party and military offices and the specifics of weapons development and arms transfer programs. Yet, on the whole, officers have been able since the mid-1950s to make much more detailed and comprehensive policy recommendations and to be far more frank than before in documenting their grievances and concerns.

This chapter examines the articulation of key military concerns during the comparatively open policy discussions of the post-Stalin years. In contrast to preceding chapters, we find here that military spokesmen are relatively united in viewpoint. We find also that party officials in the armed forces are on most questions in overall agreement, and moreover that their basic views are shared with military commanders.

This last statement does not mean that officials in the MPA are completely lacking in distinctive political preferences. The interests of all political officers were engaged during the several major redefinitions of their authority under Stalin, and to a degree these interests conflicted with those of the military command as a whole. Even though the terms of its integration with the command have been fixed for decades, the MPA continues to relish its status as a party institution. When MPA chief Aleksei Epishev refers to the political organs' "enormous role" and to their being "conductors of party policy in the armed forces," he is speaking of a mandate in which—however it is embodied in concrete action—the military party apparatus takes great pride and which it would not see diluted without resistance.[1] Yet the fact is that the acceptance of this mission among all military officers (and among civilian party leaders) is so complete that MPA officials can feel little anxiety about it being jeopardized. To read controversy into every similar statement about what is basically a cooperative relationship (or into equally incontrovertible declarations by commanders about edinonachalie) is gravely to underestimate the Soviet capacity for repetition of the obvious.

Within the existing and stable institutional framework, the political organs have iterated broad preferences for policy that are strikingly similar to those of the military establishment as a whole. Political officers are conductors of existing party policy, like all military officers, but they also transmit military opinions as to what party policy ought to be. Like senior commanders, MPA officials concentrate their persuasive effort in three main areas—establishing the priority of the defense effort, discussing certain details of defense-related policy, and urging the inculcation of promilitary attitudes among the population.

Priority for National Defense

If there is a dominant theme in military commanders' pronouncements on national affairs, it is the insistence that the Soviet state make the allocative choices that enable them to perform their basic function of defense of the national territory. Like professional soldiers elsewhere, they have been inclined to take a pessimistic view of the international environment and to argue from this for acknowledgment of the defense effort as the first claimant upon societal resources and energies. Such opinions have not produced frontal civil-military conflict, as there is a wide range of views among civilians concerning the urgency of foreign threats to Soviet security. Since the passing of Stalin, military leaders have consistently occupied a position on this spectrum which is perceptibly more alarmist in its appraisal of external dangers than the civilian party executive. It is much more extreme than the point of view of some other civilians (particularly scholars working in academic research institutes specializing on foreign policy problems).[2]

The military party apparatus was a major channel for private pressure on the leadership to prepare adequately for war in 1941. It would be surprising if it did not give public expression to similar opinions concerning preparedness in a general sense. If a marshal or general heading a major military command is predisposed by training, role, and professional interest to see the world through the eyes of the soldier, the same is no less likely to be true for a Grishanov (the head of the naval political administration, who has served in the navy since 1932), a Gorchakov (Grishanov's counterpart in the strategic rocket forces, a military man since 1937), a Mal'tsev (the director of the Lenin Military-Political Academy, a graduate of the General Staff Academy who joined the army in 1933), or even a Epishev (who has spent all but nineteen of the years since 1930 in military uniform).[3] In fact, the record allows little doubt that political officers' perceptions of the needs of defense, and their reminders to national leaders of those needs, have been at least as unflagging as those of the high command.

Like senior commanders, officials in the political organs record their views on national priorities primarily by communicating an impression of the external environment. This impression is most commonly conveyed in formal essays on foreign policy themes carried in MPA publications intended mainly for military consumption, in particular *Kommunist vooruzhennykh sil* (which began to appear in 1960). But it can be traced also in contributions by MPA officials, including the staff of the Lenin Academy, to civilian newspapers and journals, as well as in addresses to national and regional party meetings, academic conferences, and other public gatherings.

This discussion is usually guarded and the references to Soviet policy oblique, but the argument is clear nonetheless. As is the case with most conservative Soviet analysis, MPA spokesmen have tended gradually over the last two decades to lay less stress on the inherently predatory nature of Western societies or on their absolute domination by a monolithic capitalist class and to say more about contention among economic and political circles in the West (among them the military-industrial complex). Still, the almost invariable conclusion is that it is aggressive circles and forces which maintain the upper hand and that such forces will remain tractable for Soviet policy only if it remains firm and vigilant against any political or military eventuality. Typically, background analysis of this sort is combined with a review of current world events (a provocative statement by an American politician, a flareup of tension in the Middle East, a meeting of the NATO council) which "convince us again and again of the necessity . . . of strengthening our defense in every way, of attention to it as our primary problem."[4] Explication of Chinese intentions and behavior is also used to support similar conclusions, although this occurs somewhat less frequently.

At times MPA statements go beyond contextual analysis and vague exhortation to make measured but perceptible criticism of trends in official policy. This usually comes in the guise of comment about the tone of propaganda, for which the MPA bears responsibility within the army, but the broader implications are often quite unmistakable. If anything, political officers take more liberties than commanders in expressing promilitary viewpoints in this area, perhaps because their own propaganda duties confer extra legitimacy on their opinions. In June 1963, for example, we find Epishev taking the floor at a Central Committee plenum on ideological questions, at which other speakers covered a wide range of topics, to enunciate an obviously military concern: "In [the party's] propaganda work, the question of the struggle for peace is sometimes considered in isolation from the necessity of consolidating the country's defense capability. Often only one side of things is stressed, namely that we do not want war, while we neglect the education of people in the spirit of vigilance and readiness to crush any aggressor with arms in hand."[5] Statements of this sort are sometimes phrased more sharply, and they may go rather further in pointing out the negative consequences of insufficiently militant propaganda for the state of awareness of the Soviet population. Consider, for example, this declaration during the discussion of foreign policy following the escalation of the Vietnam war by Mikhail Kalashnik, a deputy chief of the MPA and its main spokesman on ideological matters from 1958 to 1972:

Our propaganda has frequently manifested a certain one-sided interpretation of questions of peaceful coexistence, the prospects for averting war, and so on. The political, economic, ideological, and military diversions of imperialism have only weakly been unmasked. We have not always focused attention on the growth of the danger of war, on the fact that peaceful coexistence is a form of irreconcilable class struggle, and an extremely sharp one at that, and that the defense of peace demands unremitting vigilance, all-round preparedness, and a firm resolve to struggle against the enemy with all the means at our disposal, to ruin the plans of the atomic maniacs, to bind their hands. All this can only disorient those among our people who are insufficiently prepared and encourage pacifist attitudes among them.[6]

The MPA's commitment to military preparedness, like that of the high command, tends to be particularly conspicuous when the civilian leadership's perceptions of foreign and domestic priorities are in a state of some flux. This occurred during the debate in the several years following Stalin's death over the desirability of improving relations with the West and diverting resources from defense-related industry to the consumer economy. As best as can be ascertained, the MPA allied itself firmly with the military command and those in the civilian party and state apparatus who favored the traditional priorities. MPA chief

Zheltov (who had been serving in the army since 1924) used the "aggressive policy of the imperialists" to justify an unremitting defense effort and "the development . . . above all of heavy industry."[7] At this time and later it was in the pages of *Krasnaia zvezda*—a Ministry of Defense newspaper, but one under the direct supervision of the MPA—that Western specialists were able to detect many of the most promilitary statements in the discussion.

MPA leaders responded in like fashion to Khrushchev's January 1960 proposal (which was never implemented) to reduce the defense budget substantially and demobilize 1.2 million troops. Senior political officers, like commanders, publicly endorsed the proposal, but they did so in a tone of professional reserve and with the interjection of clear notes of caution. When MPA chief Golikov addressed the Supreme Soviet the day after Khrushchev's speech, he warned that "we cannot forget that there are still significant aggressive forces in the world. This obliges us to raise the military capability of our army and navy still higher."[8] Similar comments continued for several months.

The MPA has articulated military unease in more trenchant fashion during the period of accommodation with the West beginning in the late 1960s. The public discussion of Western (particularly American) motives following the opening of strategic arms limitation talks in 1969 found political officers unequivocally in favor of dealing with the West only from a position of strength and of continuing to improve the country's military position during and even beyond the period of negotiations. Immediately prior to the Twenty-fourth Party Congress in 1971, Epishev published articles in *Pravda* and *Izvestiia* expressing strident disapproval of initiatives toward the West on any terms except those favored by the military establishment. Epishev's broadsides contained not a trace of the belief in the complexity and reasonableness of Western intentions that apparently induced the Brezhnev leadership to pursue detente. He depicted the West as deliberately accelerating the arms race, preparing to "cast socialism from the heights of world influence which it has won," and presenting an even greater challenge to Soviet well-being than before. "Changing its strategy and tactics, imperialism has retained all of its aggressive nature. In its inability to halt historical progress, it is capable, in Lenin's definition, of 'every kind of savagery, atrocity, and crime.' . . . In a situation where imperialism, in its efforts to regain the lost initiative, has become even more aggressive and adventuristic, Lenin's words about the need to keep our army 'fully ready for battle and increase its military potential' are particularly appropriate."[9]

The concern behind these pronouncements was undiminished by the series of limited arms control and other accords with the United

States beginning in 1972, although the tone of the discussion was moderated somewhat (particularly after the inclusion of Defense Minister Grechko in the Politburo in April 1973). Senior commanders have foregone few opportunities to urge civilian leaders to "keep our powder dry" while pursuing the Brezhnev "peace program."[10] Epishev and his colleagues, on their part, have continued to refer to the strengthening of Soviet military capabilities as an immutable law and cautioned that "underestimation of military questions or a weakening of the armed forces in a revolutionary movement invariably leads it to defeat."[11] *Kommunist vooruzhennykh sil* has printed detailed statements about growing imperialist aggressiveness, which means that the danger of war "continues and is even intensifying," dark references to illusions about the USSR's adversaries, and admonishments against attempts by the West and its apologists to convert the Soviet love for peace into "abstract pacifism." Contributors do not blush at pointing out the implications for the army's claim on resources: "Imperialism reckons only with force, and this immutable fact retains its significance. A unilateral slackening in the USSR's defense power might call forth sharp changes in the policy of the ruling circles of the imperialist states . . . Life dictates the necessity of untiring concern for strengthening . . . the Soviet Armed Forces."[12]

The Content of Military Policy

In addition to espousing overall primacy for defense needs, the leaders of the army's party organs have put forth views on particular aspects of defense policy. Most of their comments about military management and programs relate to the MPA's specialized responsibilities—matters of discipline, morale, and the like—and do not touch on institutional questions on which civilian decision is necessary. Still, on quite a number of military issues, MPA articulations, ones which essentially reinforce the views of the military command, are clearly visible. They are especially common in four important issue areas.

First, the political organs have endorsed military preferences as to the style of decision making to be adopted by civilian leaders in military affairs. While in no way questioning party leaders' right to the final say on policy (any more than commanders have done so), they have supported freedom for military officers to make policy recommendations (especially on matters of strategic and other military theory) and have provided some of the most trenchant criticisms of Stalin's suppression of creativity. Epishev was airing a general military grievance in 1963 when he castigated Stalin for having "unilaterally taken decisions on all the most important policy questions" in the military realm and for a personal cult that was a "serious brake" on military thought.[13] So was General Zheltov, director of the Lenin Academy and former head of the MPA, when he wrote in 1965 about how, "when Stalin was hailed as the sole creator, no one besides him could say a new word in working out important problems of military theory."[14]

Since Khrushchev's removal, senior political officers have been especially strict in their judgment of the erratic style of decision associated with his rule. This, again, has been a general military viewpoint, and it has probably been expressed most forcefully by army commanders. Roman Kolkowicz is correct to point out the importance of an article published in February 1965 by the Chief of General Staff, Marshal Matvei V. Zakharov, whose comments on "dilettantism" by persons lacking even "rudimentary knowledge of military strategy" were a thinly veiled attack on Khrushchev (presumably inspired, above all, by the Cuban missile crisis).[15] Yet it is important also to point out that Zakharov's misgivings about the actions of the civilian party elite were vigorously supported by senior officials in the party organs within the army. At precisely the same time as Zakharov's article, the essay by Zheltov appeared and contained precisely the same sort of criticism. Zheltov took issue with "subjectivism and disorganization, all types of premature and hasty decisions and actions divorced from reality" in military affairs, and insisted that the constant threat of war "demands strategic perspicacity and exceptional discretion" from Soviet leaders.[16]

A number of articles in the MPA's journal, most of them by lecturers in the Lenin Academy, have elaborated on this argument, demanding a rational or scientific approach to military policy making and putting great emphasis on the desirability of deference to military advice and expertise. The language often echoes Zakharov's: "Scientific leadership of the forces is inconsistent . . . with subjective arbitrariness in decisions . . . Subjectivism is particularly harmful for the armed forces. The army has its specific features." The connection between scientific leadership and respect for professional military counsel is often drawn clearly. "The more the political leadership relies on the conclusion reached by military science," one political officer wrote in 1969, "the more effective its decisions will be, the more the unity of political and military leadership will be attained. Lenin often stressed the importance of specialized knowledge and the role of specialists in leading any cause, including the defense of the country."[17]

A second important kind of articulation has concerned the necessity of specific contributions from nonmilitary sectors of society to the cause of national defense. The general argument, as Epishev stated it in 1972, has been that defense "is not the concern of the military alone

[but] encompasses all areas of social life: the economy, culture, politics, and ideology."[18] Political officers' suggestions about resource allocations in favor of the defense sector have already been cited; their concern for the instilling of military values in the population will be discussed in the final section of this chapter. But the several other arguments for civilian cooperation most frequently assayed in the press, usually directed at quite specialized audiences, should be mentioned here. In every case MPA statements closely parallel those of the military command.

1. MPA officials often demand greater efficiency and adaptability from defense production and research establishments, as well as greater political and economic support for these organizations. "At the current level of development of military technology, the problem of maintaining military-technological superiority can be solved only by mobilizing all of the country's economic, scientific, technical, moral, and political forces."[19]

2. Military party workers advocate that economic planners pay greater heed to stockpiling of strategic materials and dispersal of productive facilities so as to minimize the impact of an enemy nuclear strike.[20]

3. The MPA has long appealed for increased attention to civil defense and related programs. Its leaders have called for "more concern for bettering mass defense work at enterprises, collective and state farms, and institutions of higher education," and have criticized slack efforts on the party of DOSAAF, the major paramilitary organization.[21]

4. The MPA has insisted on greater attentiveness by local authorities to the housing and service needs of soldiers. Because of their morale-related duties, individual political officers press for satisfaction of such needs when the occasion arises (and are said to furnish "major assistance" in convincing local agencies to honor their commitments).[22] But senior military party officials also speak out on a more general level. In 1965, for instance, one finds Colonel-General Pavel Efimov, the first deputy MPA chief, complaining in *Izvestiia* about local organs that "have an unobliging attitude toward the legitimate requests of soldiers and their families." He enumerated failures to answer letters of complaint, delays in construction of nurseries and kindergartens for military families, and shortages of acceptable housing for reserve and retired officers.[23] (The last is perhaps the most common shortcoming in local civilian performance cited in the military press.)

5. Political officers have also taken part in criticism of civilian ministries for inadequate servicing of the army's needs in the area of

consumer goods. Their responsibility for morale probably makes them more sensitive than most military officials to deficiencies in this area (just as senior MPA functionaries make the sharpest criticisms of shortcomings on this score within the military bureaucracy itself). Thus, when a conference was held on provision of the army with consumer products in 1969, the most straightforward statement of the military position was made by the deputy head of the MPA's administration for organizational-party work (and a deputy MPA chief since 1975), Major-General Mikhail G. Sobolev. After conceding that the military had to take its own steps, Sobolev appealed directly to the civilian agencies:

It would obviously be difficult for [this question] to be resolved by the efforts of military trade workers alone . . . Of course, a very important role must be played by the ministries and departments connected with the supply of the armed forces with goods and daily necessities . . . Significant amounts of goods are being assigned to military trade, but life goes forward. Allow me to suggest that the supply of the army and navy with goods does not yet measure up to their growing demands. There are, for example, serious shortcomings in the provision of the army and navy with goods of a military nature. The Ministry of Light Industry of the USSR does especially little to produce emblems, stars, neckties, soldiers' belts and number plates, boots, military headgear, officers' shirts, and certain other items which are essential primarily for servicemen. Often goods of low quality are sent into our trade network. We can include here several kinds of cloth lining treated with unreliable dyes, emblems for epaulettes which quickly deteriorate, Polius refrigerators and Belka washing machines which often must be removed from service, and a number of other goods.[24]

In a third area of defense-related policy, military party officials have been involved in discussion of the relationship of military instruments, particularly nuclear weapons, to foreign policy. They actually took little public part in the intense debate of the strategic implications of nuclear technology which followed Stalin's death. This exchange, conducted mainly among commanders, culminated in the rejection of Stalin's dictum on "permanently operating factors" which determine the outcome of all wars and, implicitly, downgrade the skill with which weapons are used. It is noteworthy that no political officer offered a defense of the Stalin position. The only MPA official to enunciate a detailed viewpoint, deputy chief Sergei S. Shatilov, identified himself clearly with innovators who argued that the Stalin doctrine left the Soviet Union unprepared to cope with a surprise attack which in the atomic age could deal it a decisive blow.[25]

Since the fall of Khrushchev, MPA spokesmen have taken a leading role in military efforts to establish nuclear war, for all its destructiveness, as a final but real resort for attaining policy objectives. At the Twenty-third Party Congress in 1966, Epishev chastised unnamed proponents of "false and confused opinions" about the consequences of the use of nuclear arms and demanded that the country face any potential conflict with "the spirit of optimism, of firm confidence in our powers and in the inevitable defeat of any aggressor."[26] The same year General Kalashnik denounced "philosophers, military historians, and publicists" who are excessively concerned with the destructive power of nuclear weapons and lack "unshakable faith in victory over aggressors who dare to unleash nuclear war."[27] A number of articles in *Kommunist vooruzhennykh sil* have developed the theme in detail, but perhaps the most outspoken statement was made in 1974 by Rear-Admiral V. V. Sheliag, a Lenin Academy professor and author of several MPA texts on military psychology. Sheliag excoriated "reasonings about the fate of civilization, about the fact that in nuclear war there will be no victors" and cautioned against the blandishments of foreign powers and their ideologists who are seeking "to bully the countries of socialism with the thermonuclear bugbear (*zhupel*), . . . to impose on the peoples 'peace' on the condition of maintenance of imperialist dictate."[28]

Political officers are not unanimous in their views on such questions, any more than are military commanders (who were responsible for some of the "false and confused opinions" belittled by Epishev). Not all MPA spokesmen are as emphatic about the prospects for victory in a nuclear conflict as men like Sheliag, whose main professional expertise is in the area of troop motivation and who presumably feel responsible for assuring soldiers and the populace at large that wartime sacrifices would not be in vain. Some seem even to harbor quite contrary opinions. According to a former Soviet sociologist, a research institute attached to the MPA concluded in a secret study undertaken in 1971-72 that nuclear war would result in "mutual destruction and ruin" and advised a major Soviet effort to pursue arms control negotiations and abandonment of the project to develop a "clean" atomic bomb.[29] It is safe to say, however, that inasmuch as there is a range of military opinion on this issue, senior officials in the political apparatus cluster toward the "hawk" end of the spectrum.

As far as nonnuclear conflicts are concerned, political officers (like senior commanders) have since 1965 insisted openly that the Soviet Union make strenuous preparation for contained local wars fought by conventional means at the initiative of the West, of the type which earlier Soviet theory tended to argue (particularly during the polemic with the Chinese leadership) would inevitably escalate to global conflict. Recent MPA statements have warned against the "absolutization of nuclear weapons" and the "underestimation of the prospects for conventional warfare and the role of local wars in the aggressive plans of imperialism," and some have asserted that local wars are more probable than before in an era of strategic parity between the two superpowers.[30] MPA officials have not endorsed outright use of the army to export social revolution, but they have increasingly pointed to Soviet strength as an umbrella which "objectively aids the growth of the national liberation movement and prevents the export of counterrevolution and neocolonialism." Like civilians who think along similar lines, they have contended further that detente with Western states casts not the slightest doubt on the justice of national liberation struggles or the Soviet Union's obligation to support them.[31]

The fourth and final series of major policy questions on which senior political officers have taken a forthright public position has related to the balance of forces and fighting capabilities in the Soviet defense posture. It is of interest that during the early debate over the fundamental issue of whether the country should have a standing army or a militia, most party workers in the army sided with their military colleagues in advocating retention of as large a cadre force as possible. MPA chief Ivan Smilga was a particularly ardent backer of a professional force. "Soviet Russia is better off with an 'expensive' standing army and an effective guarantee of peace than with the risky route of experiments with a militia, which will deprive us of a military capability for many years," he told a national conference of political workers in December 1920. The conference overwhelmingly approved his resolution calling for a moderate sized but well trained standing army.[32] The commissars of the Field Staff and Main Staff, D. I. Kurskii and V. G. Sharmanov, both supported proposals by staff members for retention of a million-man standing army and only a gradual and partial transition to a militia system. Gusev, Smilga's successor, was also a strong proponent of a standing force.[33]

In more contemporary Soviet politics, where the existence of a standing army is assumed but opinions differ about which parts of the professional establishment deserve priority, political officers appear to divide to some extent, as commanders do, along service lines. The statements of, say, Admiral Grishanov, the head of the political administration of the navy since 1958, reflect that service's claim to a mission, resources, and prestige. Many of his assertions—that the Soviet Union is a great naval power, that the navy is both a symbol and a guarantor of that status, that the navy is technically sophisticated and "ready to carry out independent and complex combat assignments far from its bases"[34]—closely resemble declarations about the navy's growing importance made by its commander, Admiral of the Fleet Sergei Gorshkov, and other naval leaders.

The memoirs provide additional evidence of strong service loyalty among some political officers. We know, for example, that Efim Shchadenko, a senior political officer of the interwar period with long experience in cavalry formations (including service as member of the military council of the famous First Cavalry Army), was "a man simply in love with cavalry."[35] He once clashed directly with Tukhachevskii when the latter tried to persuade him of the future importance of machines and armor. "The main thing now," he informed Tukhachevskii, "is horses. The decisive role in future war will be played by cavalry."[36] But Marshal Zhukov describes in his memoirs the very different outlook of the commissar of an armored regiment, A. S. Zinchenko, who told Voroshilov in 1936 that he would feel himself "a good for nothing commissar of a mechanized regiment if I doubted the great future of tank technology." He advised Voroshilov "to be more bold in developing mechanized forces."[37] Branch loyalties such as these will perhaps gain in salience as the graduates of the specialized MPA schools instituted in 1967 rise through the ranks.

Members of the MPA's central apparatus, who do not have immediate ties to any particular service but almost always have had lengthy experience in the dominant ground forces, tend to take the same line as other central defense administrators—pressing Soviet leaders to develop all services and arms "harmoniously" and to allow only incremental changes of emphasis among them. Thus, in the wake of Khrushchev's 1960 proposal, which would have drastically curtailed conventional forces while enlarging missile capability, MPA spokesmen were quick to join with other officers in underlining the continued relevance of mass armies and urging caution in implementing this or any similar plan. Epishev was echoing the opinions of Defense Minister Malinovskii and other senior commanders when he decried "the reasoning of certain theorists about the necessity of repudiating the creation of mass armies" and insisted that despite the growing import of nuclear technology, "the role of mass armies is also increasing."[38] (Epishev's views were no doubt influenced by his wartime service in conventional armies and by his training at the Tank Troops Academy in the 1930s. This same academy was headed in the mid-1950s by Marshal Golikov, Epishev's predecessor as head of the MPA, and it was to be named in honor of Malinovskii after his death in 1967.) Since Khrushchev's removal, senior political officers have frequently restated the necessity of simultaneous strengthening of all services. They have opposed "overestimation of one or another type of weapon or military technology, or of one or another branch of the armed forces," and have advocated "the development of all services and arms . . . so that our army and navy will always be ready to wage victorious war with nuclear weapons, with conventional means, or with both together."[39]

In the very limited public discussion of the merits of particular weapons systems, military party officials have virtually no role. Nor do they seem to participate in private decisions on such matters (or, it might be added, in negotiations on arms control and military assistance questions with foreign soldiers and civilians). Subject to ultimate control by the civilian leadership, these matters are left to military engineers and commanders and to civilians with the appropriate expertise. Where MPA views have been aired quite openly has been on the general question of the need to develop and deploy advanced military hardware. Clearly military party workers do not see their specialized role as jeopardized by increasing technical sophistication and complexity. They have gone out of their way to emphasize that political education and solidarity cannot guarantee military effectiveness and that it would be "extremely harmful and dangerous" to attempt "to compensate with moral force for shortcomings in the technical aspects of the military power of the armed forces."[40] Political officers have insisted that technical modernization is inevitable and desirable, and indeed that its greater demands on personnel will make political work more necessary than ever before. Even Kalashnik, whose main duties were in the propaganda realm, could write a stirring call for greater prowess in military technology and end it with a fitting quotation from Lenin about how any successful army must possess "every type of weapon, every means and instrument of struggle which the enemy has or can have."[41] The MPA has no difficulty whatever in subscribing to the standard military view of weapons development as an open-ended process spurred on by enemy capabilities and the push of technological imperatives. As one political officer put it in 1971 (during the exchange of views concerning arms control talks), "The supply of technology cannot stand still any more than the development of the military art can—especially now, under conditions of stormy renewal and perfection in all spheres of human activity, including military affairs."[42]

The Propagation of Military Values

Most Soviet military men are obviously concerned with the public image of themselves, their mission, and the values they seek to embody. They often demand in extremely frank terms that Soviet leaders and citizens acknowledge this image in favorable terms and that the regime propagate military values through its systems of mass communication and education.

The interplay of interest on this issue can only be misunderstood if one assumes a dichotomy of preferences between the military command and the MPA. Consider, for instance, two manifestations of the army's quest for a positive image discussed by Kolkowicz. He refers to several blunt reviews of military memoirs and histories published in 1961-62 by Ignatii S. Prochko, a lieutenant-general whom he describes as "an ardent champion of the military and a fearless critic of Party hackwork among historians." He also cites a tribute to Soviet military honor and the social utility of the officer corps, written in 1963 by Nikolai I. Makeev, the editor-in-chief of *Krasnaia zvezda*, as typical of a military point of view which is "resisted and rejected by the party functionaries" in the army and elsewhere.[43] These articles appear in a rather different light when one inquires into the identity of the authors. Both Makeev and Prochko are in fact party workers. General Makeev, the editor of the principal military newspaper since 1955, is a member of the MPA's bureau; Prochko, who died in 1971, spent his entire career in the MPA, rising to become the senior political officer in the artillery troops.[44] This is not to deny that either man was an "ardent champion of the military" but rather to affirm that the army's party organs participate fully in the championing of military values.

On the question of the army's historical reputation, there is no evidence that the preferences of political officers have deviated significantly from the military norm. Political officers are chided as often as commanders for writing unobjective memoirs that inflate their achievements and those of colleagues. Thus Prochko, as a defender of objectivity, felt compelled to criticize both commanders and MPA officials for self-serving accounts that undermine the credibility of the memoir literature—a criticism that has been made many times by commanders as well.[45]

On the specific historical issue of treatment of the Great Purge, MPA performance has also been little different from that of other military men. Some political officers who had played a major part in it or benefited in especially dramatic fashion assuredly had profound reservations about any frank discussion of the issue, reservations which some commanders (who were no less likely to have participated and profited) must have shared. But, on the whole, senior MPA officials—whose ranks had been scoured as viciously as the military command and who had as much to lose from any repetition of the experience—pushed openly for rehabilitation of purge victims until the mid-1960s. A variety of forums were used for the purpose, including articles about individual political officers or commanders, discussions in memoirs, historical works, and even public commemorative meetings.[46] Some political workers went so far as to evince a sense of special responsibility for restoration of the reputations of military victims of the purge and of Stalin's other excesses. In July 1956 it was the head of the MPA's propaganda and agitation administration, Major-General Nikolai M. Mironov, who castigated military journalists for being timid in demystifying Stalin.[47] In 1962 Epishev prodded historians to take a more critical view of the former dictator and to "reveal to the very end the enormous harm which Stalin wreaked on the cause of military development."[48]

There is nothing to suggest that most political officers welcomed with particular eagerness the moratorium on open discussion of the purge imposed under Brezhnev. Senior MPA spokesmen joined in the repudiation of criticisms of Stalin that could be interpreted as downgrading Soviet military achievements or the Soviet system as a whole.[49] But senior political officers have continued to make those restrained references to Stalin's errors, on the eve of the war in particular, that are still permitted.[50] The refurbishing of Stalin's military reputation since 1956 has been accomplished, not by the MPA, but primarily by distinguished commanders who worked with him during the war.

On the broader question of the status and propagation of military values in Soviet society, the political organs' stand has been sharp and unambiguous. Their leaders have repeatedly expressed concern for the inculcation, especially in young people, of "military-patriotic" ideals and have openly called for cooperation from artists, the official media, and government and party agencies. So relentless has the MPA's pressure been that the novelist Mikhail Sholokhov described it to the Twenty-fourth Party Congress in the same breath as the same efforts of Defense Minister Grechko—citing "comrades Grechko and Epishev" for their insistence on military-oriented contributions from artists.[51] Indeed, one can go further and say that the military party apparatus has been the most forceful articulator of the military viewpoint. If on many issues the MPA seems mainly to restate general military viewpoints which commanders are in a better position to pursue, on this question political officers have taken the initiative. They have consistently displayed more activism than the command, and the energy with which they have sought civilian compliance has increased over the last decade. This commitment seems to reflect an intense personal concern on Epishev's part, but it stems in a more general sense from the MPA's overall preoccupation with using communication and persuasion to further military goals.

Many of the MPA's demands have been simply for a greater volume of coverage of military life in civilian communications. The calls are at times broad and diffuse, but they may also be addressed to specific groups or organizations. Writers have been the most frequent target group, beginning with the protest to the second congress of the Union of Soviet Writers in December 1954 by a ranking MPA official, Lieutenant-General Petr A. Lapkin, that "very few books" had been written on military themes.[52] In 1957 the head of the faculty of party history in the Lenin Academy, Major-General N. M. Kiriaev, implored social scientists at a national conference to "create serious works on the history of the Great Patriotic War," and Kiriaev's faculty later faulted the journal *Voprosy istorii KPSS* (Problems of Party History) for its dearth of articles on the army.[53] Several years later, MPA chief Golikov turned to the film industry, demanding that it act promptly to replace war films centered on Stalin and withdrawn from circulation in the mid-1950s. He also proposed (without effect) that the Union of Soviet Journalists organize military sections or commissions in its central and local organizations as a focus for more extensive coverage of military news.[54] From the beginning of his term in 1962, Epishev has demanded that military questions be given "greater resonance in our literature, theater, film, television, radio, and press."[55] Explicit calls by his subordinates appear quite frequently.

MPA spokesmen have voiced demands concerning the content as well as the volume of public treatment of the army. Censure of artists who portray the military in an unflattering light is probably the most usual expression of this kind of concern. Often the criticism is quite sweeping. Epishev has inveighed against authors who betray "intimations of pacifism" in their work by overemphasizing the sufferings and terrors of war or portraying heroes who "daydream in fear of death" rather than go boldly to face the enemy. Such artists and others who distort the life of the modern army "wittingly or unwittingly belittle the enormous significance which military service has for the cause of building Communism."[56]

But strictures against artists can also be very specific. In 1958, for instance, the head of the political administration of the Leningrad Military District, Lieutenant-General Vasilii K. Tsebenko, took the Leningrad magazine *Zvezda* to task for printing articles containing "serious distortions" of military life and scolded the magazine's editor from the podium of a city party conference. In 1961 *Kommunist vooruzhennykh sil* castigated the same publication for carrying a story in which a Soviet officer was depicted as crass and uncreative. Two years later *Zvezda* was again under fire from the chief political officer in the Leningrad district (now Major-General Fedor A. Mazhaev), along with the magazine *Neva*, the major local film studio, and a number of individual artists who had treated military themes incorrectly.[57] Other illustrations can be found with ease.

MPA criticism often extends to the official media, and even to state and party authorities. For instance, Epishev's insistence that the press and electronic media treat military issues "more profoundly and intelligently" is an obvious reprobation of journalists and editors, and presumably of the civilian party officials who supervise them.[58] Epishev has also attributed distortions in artistic treatment of military questions, not only to writers and artists but to "the inadequate demands made of the author by press organs, publishing houses, and film studios."[59]

The educational system has been a particularly frequent object of MPA calls for improvement. By the late 1950s political officers (as well as commanders) were asking at regional party conferences and in other forums for greater efforts by civilian agencies in specific localities "to better inculcate in our young Soviet men love for our armed forces, to foster in the young our glorious heroic traditions, to be especially concerned about the preinduction preparation of youth."[60] By the mid-1960s MPA executives were speaking in more general terms about the failure of the school system as a whole to prepare future soldiers at an early age. Typical is this observation by first deputy MPA chief Efimov in 1965:

It would be desirable if [local party and government organs] were more concerned about the military-patriotic education of school pupils. Surely it is precisely in the schools that the person forms and develops those qualities that are especially necessary to defenders of the Motherland—Soviet patriotism, readiness for heroic deeds, fortitude, courage. It is a good thing when the schools propagate the timeless feats of our soldiers in the battles for the Motherland, convincingly demonstrate the sources of the victories of the Soviet people in the Civil and Great Patriotic wars, lead classes and circles for young friends of the army, navy, and air force. Unfortunately, such work is carried out in not nearly all of our schools. It often has an episodic character and suffers from dryness. Too little attention is yet paid in the schools to the physical hardening of our youth. Thus the young men called into the army have a hard time at first in carrying out a soldier's duties.[61]

Pressure such as this was no doubt taken into account in 1967 when courses on basic military training were introduced into secondary schools.

Frequently the political organs have taken upon themselves direct responsibility for what can only be termed public relations projects designed to improve the military's image. It is the MPA and its subsidiaries which organize and publicize most anniversary and commemorative occasions involving the armed forces. Political officers have authored many of the army's most widely circulated image-building volumes.

Increasingly the military party organs have taken their public relations and mobilizing efforts directly to individuals and organizations with the resources to broadcast the desired message more widely. The most common device for suasion and browbeating of this sort has been the public meeting for artists and cultural officials. The first of these apparently was held in 1958, when the MPA hosted a conference for delegates to the first congress of Russian Republic writers, with Kalashnik delivering a pitch for more literary production on the war and the modern military.[62] In 1960 the MPA sponsored a meeting with writers at its headquarters at which Golikov demanded "new works on the glorious defenders of the socialist Fatherland."[63] In 1966 the MPA and Ministry of Defense arranged a national "conference on problems of the military-patriotic education of Soviet youth," highlighted by a table-thumping speech by Epishev, and over the next decade the MPA and its subsidiaries organized a number of meetings on military-patriotic literature.[64] In April 1977 the MPA and Ministry of Defense staged the most ambitious assembly of all, a meeting on patriotic education dominated by an extremely specific and critical address by Epishev and attended by the elite of the cultural establishment—including the heads of the major artistic unions and of the central theater and film organizations, the editor of *Literaturnaia gazeta*, and even the head of the party Secretariat's culture department.[65] Later that year the MPA was said to be developing close contacts with writers' organizations.[66] It has also continued to expand a reservoir of material and honorific inducements for individual artists. Since 1968 the MPA has sponsored (together with the Union of Composers) an annual contest for the best military-patriotic song. In the 1970s it has initiated prizes and diplomas for military essays and novels put out by the military publishing house, for military-related essays printed in the republican and local press, and (conjointly with the central film production agency and the Union of Cinematographers) for films on martial themes.[67]

None of this is activity which challenges the self-esteem or interests of major civilian elites. There are many in positions of authority outside the army who are quite receptive to military and MPA entreaties for a freer hand in infusing the arts and mass media with martial themes. (Among these, surely, is General Secretary Brezhnev himself, a wartime political officer who has recently appropriated the military rank of marshal and has spoken with enthusiasm of the army's role as a socializing device.) The point is, however, that latent sympathies must be converted into active cooperation and large nonmilitary organizations with diverse interests must be convinced to reorder their practical priorities. The very assiduousness of military solicitations shows that compliance cannot be taken for granted, and indeed it may indicate a perception that certain large-scale trends in society are working in the countervailing direction.

What is impressive about the MPA's campaign is its facility in appealing not only to the widespread pride in the army's past accomplishments but also to the anxiety felt at numerous points in the political system about declining public regard for many of the heroic values which the military in some sense personifies. Clearly this anxiety has been heightened by the far greater openness of Soviet society to extraneous information and ideas in recent years. Political officers are striking a responsive chord outside as well as inside the army when they admonish writers and officials, "The illumination of the problems of duty before the Motherland, before the people, before one's own conscience—this is a theme which will never grow old. This is all the more so now, when the propaganda organs of the imperialist states attempt to disorient our youth, to envenom its consciousness with the poison of apoliticism and skepticism, to propagate the theory of generational conflict, to implant the cult of a consumer's attitude toward life." The eloquent point of their argument is that it is precisely the virtues found in the soldier that civilian society needs at a time of uncertainty "that show the way to the overcoming of egoism . . . to the realization of Communist ideals."[68]

Conclusion

Evidence from military politics provides considerable support for the central contentions of scholars who have attempted to apply group models to the Soviet system—that aggregates of opinion and interest do exist in the Soviet Union and that those who hold these opinions possess sufficient leeway in defending and furthering their interests to justify reference to the overall political system as being characterized by some degree of pluralism. Fragile groupings of interest were at work in the armed forces and MPA even during the Great Purge, when power in the system as a whole was most highly centralized and was exercised in the most arbitrary fashion. Bureaucratic coalitions were highly active in the environment of wartime decision making, a setting which was far more fluid than the purge and indeed much more characterized by political contention than most interpretations of the Stalinist system (many of which are modeled implicitly on the purge experience) would have us believe. Personal and other attachments were of great importance to the course of the Zhukov controversy. Routine political action by aggregates of officers is also quite evident within the peacetime military bureaucracy, where such activity has not changed greatly since Stalin's death, as well as in the area of public discussion of broad policy goals, where much more straightforward debate has been possible in recent decades.

In some cases it is probably accurate to refer to the process we have observed as one of resistance group politics, to use William Odom's phrase.[69] Yet Soviet military bureaucrats have done more than resist the dictates of superiors, civilian and military. Within the bureaucratic milieu, command and political officers have taken the initiative to satisfy their subunits' needs in areas such as supply and operations. In the realm of public discussion, senior military and military party officials have come to speak in quite unmistakable terms about military doctrine, civilian decision style, spending priorities, the image of the army, and other important policy matters. Obvious differences in the direction and intensity of opinion have existed on major and minor questions of concern to army officers (differences among officers and between them and some civilians), and this range of viewpoints has found expression in political discourse and has been tolerated by political leaders. It would be misleading to equate the pursual of such opinions with open advocacy of constituent interests by voluntary political organizations in a Western society, but evidence from the military sector would indicate that Odom is mistaken when he refers to "the absence of interest articulation in the Soviet system." Nor do my findings support his view that members of the party "can be counted on to subvert the . . . self-interest" of the organizations and organizational subunits within which they work.[70]

The evidence presented here cautions against efforts to categorize the actors in Soviet group politics in terms of a single pattern or standard. Recent Western analyses of opinion groups which coexist with occupational groups and even of "non-institutionalized, ad hoc lobbies" spanning Soviet institutions are quite suggestive in approaching military politics.[71] Clearly military opinion should be analyzed in relation to specific issues, and one should be aware of the likelihood that the structure of interest groupings will vary from one issue to another —and concomitantly that an individual party or military official will belong simultaneously to a number of "groups." On some major issues most military officers do share broad preferences on policy outcomes. Yet on many questions some of the most intense conflicts are within the army itself. And on virtually every issue military views find resonance in other institutions, including the several administrative branches of the party.

However, it is important that in accepting intraorganizational diversity and cleavage we not lose sight of structural factors altogether. Franklyn Griffiths, for example, uses the "informality" of Soviet politics to justify almost total rejection of the group approach in favor of examination of "tendencies of articulation," broad images of policy alternatives which are properties of the political system as a whole.[72] To push the point this far is, to my mind, to confuse informality with formlessness. The members of major Soviet organizations do share and pursue some common interests, and these interests can be very important ones if the issues examined in the present chapter are any guide. And, even if political alignments do not usually parallel the boundaries of formal organizations, such alignments are normally *not* without structure. Moreover, this structure is not without relation to the structure of institutions—or, at least, of administrative institutions such as the army and the party. The point is not, as Griffiths puts it, that the Soviet organization is "internally fragmented" and "loses a great deal of its significance" for politics. Rather, we should be aware that even if the organization as a whole is not the unit of action on a given issue it is likely that considerable political significance will be possessed by particular subunits (not fragments) of bureaucratic organizations, often acting in concert with related subunits of others. Thus, to illustrate from the subject matter of this book, there may be little coherence of opinion in either the MPA or the military command on a particular issue, yet there still may be discernible communities of interest shared and acted upon by political officers and commanders working at particular locations in the bureaucratic field. Institutional structure is not irrelevant to the shape of political conflict—it is simply that in determining the composition of bureaucratic groups (opinion groups containing nonbureaucrats may be a different matter) the elements of organizational structure that often matter most are not external boundary but hierarchical location and task allocation.

An examination of military politics testifies to the inadequacy of any analysis of Soviet politics which denies the importance of conflict. It also underlines the care that must be taken to define the structure of that conflict. Whatever the evidence says about the army command, it underscores the existence of patterned political contention within the party and its administrative apparatus and the linkages between that pattern and conflicts involving other actors in the political system. It suggests that we devote more attention to how the political life of the party reflects not only its vanguard or governing role in society but many of the fundamental tensions and contradictions within the social and institutional fabric itself. The party does not stand apart from these strains, and indeed on many issues to speak of "the party" at all, as if it were a unitary actor, is to build distortions into the discussion. The central party leadership deals with conflicts from its own vantage point, but on many issues other strata and segments of the party machine pursue much narrower interests and ultimately contribute to the very problems of choice and integration which the party elite faces.

Party secretaries who attempt to manage the flow of information to senior officers, commissars protecting commanders from the purge, members of wartime military councils telephoning Moscow to plead for reinforcements, veterans recollecting joint service at the front, MPA executives lecturing writers on respect for the army's image—in each situation officials in the military party organs have been shown to share key interests with the command officers with whom they work and to pursue those mutual interests against other, similarly mixed coalitions. This dynamic is consistent with the findings of Jerry Hough, the only scholar who has subjected civilian party administration to intensive examination. In the appropriations process within the industrial economy, Hough found that most conflicts "arise between one group of industrial and Party officials who support one project and another group of industrial and Party officials who support another project." In the more centralized process of allocating resources to major sectors of society, the specialized functionaries in the central party apparatus "may come to have a vision of the political world more similar to that of their counterparts in the government than to that of their nominal colleagues in other departments of the Central Committee."[73]

If officials in the military party organs possess a vision of the political world fundamentally similar to that of military commanders, then many of our notions about the structure of Soviet military politics must be changed. But where does this leave our ideas as to the second broad concern of this book, the persistence of that structure over time? Here, as we move from military politics-as-usual to the question of why this kind of politics is usual, even more thoroughgoing reassessment of customary interpretations is required.

Part Three
Army-Party Relations
Reassessed

The Army in Soviet Politics:
Capabilities
and Participation

10

Why has the structure of army-party relations in the Soviet Union persisted without the kind of disruption found in so many other societies, particularly those undergoing rapid economic and social development? Why has the military been a loyal instrument of civilian authority? To approach this question it is necessary to stand back from the detailed workings of military administration and politics and to reflect upon the Soviet experience in comparative perspective. The logical place to begin is with the issue of political capabilities. Can it be said, in light of the evidence of earlier chapters and of other information, that the Soviet Army has been capable of being anything other than politically quiescent? Is it a lack of coercive or ideological potential that explains the fact that the military has not usurped civilian power?

The Army's Coercive Capability

Comparative Analysis. A glance at the roll call of military takeovers and regimes testifies to the distinctive, indeed unique, political capabilities of modern armies—meaning, for practical purposes, of the officer corps of these armies. Armies are organizations with an exceptional potential for exerting broad and profound political influence, up to and including the displacement of governments and assumption of rule. They do not always use these capabilities, but they have resorted to them frequently enough that no analyst (or government) can disregard them.

An army's basic political advantage is its high coercive capability. It has weapons, usually most (or the most powerful) of those in the society, and if effectively trained and managed it has the organizational coherence to use them. Employed capably by its officers, a unified military establishment can normally assume physical control of the state's central apparatus within hours.

This coercive capability is not absolute or invariable. Most attempts to usurp civilian power involve substantial risk and uncertainty. A successful insurrection usually entails careful planning, secrecy, and decisive and skillful tactics (in particular, active participation by strategically situated, middle-level troop commanders, especially in the area of the capital city). The absence of any of these factors may signal defeat for even the most highly motivated conspirators.[1]

Ultimately, military officers' coercive capability must be measured against the political forces or institutions which their troops and weapons are opposing. It is sufficient for our purposes to say that this measurement has often been in officers' favor. The extreme case has been in the frail states of postcolonial Africa, where "a little coercion goes a long way" and lightly armed battalions have carried out coups.[2] History has provided no conclusive test in a modern society with an industrial economy, established institutions, and mass political participation. The sociologist Gaetano Mosca may have been overstating the point in arguing that the modern army "will have no difficulty in dictating to the rest of society," but a more guarded affirmation of military potential would not be inappropriate.[3] Although the armed forces did not assume power, civilians did back down in the only instance in this century in which a unified military command confronted the civilian leaders of a modern liberal democracy (France, 1958). In perhaps the nearest case to this (the Ulster crisis of 1914), a showdown was averted by civilian retreat and the coming of war. The experiences of Germany in World War I and France and Japan in World War II suggest that military-dominated coalitions can provide at least minimal direction to complex societies. Armies have conquered and retained power in a number of societies on the threshold of full modernity, among them Spain, Greece, Portugal, Argentina, and Chile.

Governments can pursue a variety of counterstrategies against actual or potential military threat. They can repress military dissidents through legal or extralegal means, create nonmilitary security or guard forces, or play military factions off against one another. The record of these devices is uneven, although one can readily identify insurrections which might have been at least deferred by judicious use of one method or another.[4]

A military organization's coercive capability can also be inhibited or negated by three extragovernmental factors. First of these is the influence of foreign governments. Both Britain and France, for example, restrained military rebels in dependent states in Africa in the 1960s, and the United States did the same in South Vietnam. In Eastern Europe, the Soviet Union presumably exercises such a power over the armies of its allies.

A second potential limitation on coercive capability comes from armies' own internal divisions. Most debilitating are sharp hierarchical rifts between officers and troops, which usually result either from military defeat (as in Russia in 1917) or from a general perception of officers as belonging to a group whose holding of any public office is illegitimate (as with the mutiny against Belgian officers in the Congo in 1960). Such breakdowns of discipline are rare. Normally, enlisted men have been "so much potter's clay in the hands of their commanders."[5] More likely to be severe is discord within the officer corps over the desirability or direction of forceful participation. Such fragmentation was one cause of the Russian officer corps' impotence in 1917. It was also behind the collapse of the 1961 revolt by French officers in Algeria and the ouster of an officers' regime in Sierra Leone by rank-and-file troops in 1968.[6]

The third possible extragovernmental constraint is mass resistance to military power. While there are several modern cases of widely based public action defeating small and primitive armies and deposing the regimes they support, usually these have not had permanent effect. A popular uprising destroyed the Bolivian army in 1952, but twelve years later a reconstituted army ousted the revolutionary regime. Mass demonstrations and a general strike prompted the resignation of the Sudan's military government in 1964, only to have soldiers return to power five years later. The 1948 revolution in Costa Rica dismantled the army and converted its main barracks into a museum, but against even such a tiny force the rebellion could succeed only with foreign assistance.[7] Public opinion will, of course, be a practical consideration for any military government, and unpopular military regimes have even abdicated power to civilians without violence when these regimes have experienced internal conflict over personalities, ideology, or a major policy failure (as in Pakistan, Greece, and Portugal in recent years). But anticipation of unpopularity or civilian opposition is unlikely to prevent the inauguration of army rule in the first place.

It seems clear, then, that under most circumstances armies have unique coercive capabilities. As Eric Nordlinger observes, soldiers almost inevitably "have enormous potential or actual coercive power. A united officer corps is virtually always capable of maintaining a civilian government in office, or taking control itself."[8] General Hans von Seeckt's pronouncement to the German cabinet in 1923, "Gentlemen, no one but I in Germany can make a *Putsch*," was no empty boast.[9] For most united and resolute military elites acting with good political sense and without foreign constraint, a seizure of power is an eminently feasible operation.

The Soviet Case. Soviet military officers have never used or threatened to use force in politics. But what we must ask is whether they have had the capability to do so. Has the army had the capacity to coerce other actors in the political system? Has military takeover and rule ever been a feasible prospect for the Soviet Union?

Certainly the army possesses the organizational resources essential to a seizure of power. It has generally been large, disciplined, and impeccably equipped. No other organization comes close to matching it in raw physical power. None of the three extragovernmental factors outlined above seems likely to negate its coercive capability in a crisis. There is no foreseeable restraint from a foreign power. Internal dissolution of the army or fragmentation of the officer corps are possibilities, particularly during a future war, but cannot be assumed to be inevitable. Neither has occurred in the past. The state of discipline has been high and, as Roman Kolkowicz rightly stresses, officers have "a firm sense of solidarity" on issues that affect their core interests.[10] As for mass resistance, nothing we know about Soviet political culture suggests this would be widespread or effectual. Centuries of authoritarian government do not seem to have produced a feel for open political participation or resistance to dictate from above. A military regime would likely earn at least a period of grace from a populace with, in Alexander Solzhenitsyn's phrase, a "habit of obedience."[11] What happened after this period would depend on the army's internal cohesion and on the mix of policies its leaders chose to pursue.

Therefore, any discussion of the Soviet military's coercive capability should hinge on the efficacy of governmental constraints, those applied by civilian leaders. It is precisely the organization we have examined, the military party apparatus, that Western scholars have seen as the regime's indispensable lever of constraint over the officer corps. This is not, I would argue, an assertion which is consistent with the evidence. The military party organs probably do *not* fulfill that role of efficient monitor and controller of the army command imputed to them by Western analysis. It is difficult to regard them as the key regulator of the civil-military relationship.

Certainly many of the original commissars acted as extensions of the party into a hostile milieu. Certainly the MPA's program of political education has helped inculcate the regime's values. However, we have seen how the political organs' principal role has long since shifted from surveillance of commanders to management of the army in cooperation with them; how their capacity for acting as a flawless conductor of civilian leaders' preferences has been eroded by the tendency of their members' work assignments, career patterns, specialized training, and personal affiliations to mesh with those of command officers; and how they have been subject to many of the same internal stresses and conflicts as the military command. Most military party officials have taken part in politics as members of location-based groupings or coalitions involving members of the military command. On issues where commanders are relatively united, the MPA has tended to share and articulate military preferences.

To be sure, one cannot draw from evidence about "within-system" politics automatic inferences about behavior under the very different circumstances of a military confrontation with the central party leadership. Some political officers would side with civilian party leaders no matter what the conditions—but so, no doubt, would many commanders. It is improbable that support for the civilian elite would be significantly greater in the political apparatus than in the command hierarchy, particularly if action could be justified in terms of basic party values. Military discontent would probably grow over the kinds of routine and middle-level issues analyzed in Chapters 5 to 9. There is nothing to suggest that political officers would be more immune than commanders to radicalization on such issues.

Illustrations from two other Communist systems are suggestive in this regard. In China, the political organs supplied both victims and victors in the military's political entanglements of the last decade and a half. Commissars fell in the Cultural Revolution, the factional disputes that followed it, and Lin Piao's unsuccessful coup of 1971. In Bulgaria, a number of senior political officers were implicated in the military-civilian plot the Zhivkov regime claimed to have unearthed in 1965. As a result, a deputy head and a former head of the army's political administration were convicted of conspiracy and the incumbent chief was dismissed.[12]

Reference must also be made to a second possible arm of governmental constraint, one given limited attention in this book—the regime's security forces and secret police. Under Stalin, militarized security and border troops constituted a sizable army in themselves, administering a vast detention system and guarding frontier areas, transport facilities, and government buildings. Militarized units of the KGB and MVD still amount to at least a quarter million men, most of them deployed in border regions. They numbered two or three times that many during World War II.[13]

Within the army itself, there has also been since early in the Civil War a network of secret police organs—the so-called special departments (*osobye otdely*) of the KGB and its predecessors. It was this self-contained hierarchy that administered the Great Purge and the arrests of former German collaborators and prisoners-of-war at the end of World War II. These organs still exist, and they and the central and local KGB offices to which they report retain an official punitive function. The KGB is empowered to investigate "cases involving betrayal of the Motherland, espionage, terrorist acts, diversions, and some other especially dangerous state crimes" in the army; its special departments are also charged with "liquidation of cases involving leaking of state and military secrets."[14] The personnel, methods, and resources of the KGB outposts are virtually invisible in the press, and a detailed study from open sources is simply not feasible. According to a Western study based on interviews with defectors, the special departments are exempt from most military orders, have custody over nuclear weapons, and were responsible for the arrests of several sympathizers of dissident groups (mostly young officers and soldiers) in the late 1960s.[15] One of the few published biographies of one of their officials (who died as head of the special department of a naval fleet) mentioned his "strictness in the struggle with actual enemies of the Motherland" and also praised him for being "particularly tactful in re-educating Soviet citizens who had inadvertently fallen under the influence of bourgeois ideology."[16]

What has been the significance of these forces in ensuring the officer corps' political quiescence? Without dismissing their influence, it is possible to argue that their role has not been decisive, at least since 1953. Even for Stalin's lifetime, it is far from certain that police terror played an indispensable part in maintaining either overall political stability or the docility of the military command. Stalin's Russia may well have been one of those "systems of terror . . . supported by authority, consent, and tradition" analyzed by Eugene Walter.[17] The terror of the 1930s was not a rational instrument of political control; it struck down friends as well as potential enemies, the true believers along with the fellow travelers. Stalin's officer corps was loyal, but this might have been in spite of, rather than as a result of, the terror.

Moreover, whatever one thinks about the several decades when terror was in indiscriminate use, one is still left with the fact of military officers' quiescence in other periods, before and since. Western specialists agree that security forces were drastically reduced in numbers and powers after 1953. Within the army, the special departments now appear to concentrate on genuine counterintelligence activity. There is no evidence that they pose a major presence in military units or staffs or that they carry out effective, continuous monitoring of daily activities. That they no longer apply force on a wide scale is evidenced by the absence of arbitrary arrests or dismissals since Stalin's death. In that time the secret police have had "less political power and influence" than the military, and this disparity could only increase during a serious political crisis, when the army's far greater size, access to means of violence, and popularity would weigh more heavily.[18] The power of the police would doubtless complicate any bid for power (probably constricting the circle of conspirators and thereby the initial base of any military regime), and it might produce a struggle for supremacy among armed factions reminiscent of earlier episodes in Russian history. But it is at least arguable that this power is no absolute guarantee against such a bid taking place.

It is thus plausible to maintain that the Soviet Army possesses a coercive capability sufficient to allow it to seize supreme political power in a way not fundamentally different from that followed by soldiers in other societies. At a minimum one can agree with Robert Conquest that the military "may be capable of intervention."[19] Success would require intelligent strategy and tactics, and these would be shaped by the particular context of Soviet politics. Forceful action would be feasible, as in any society, only if most military officers were willing to participate in it or at least to acquiesce in the outcome. But, given these conditions, it can hardly be said that the chances of success for an officer insurrection would be less than those that faced the founders of the Soviet state in 1917.

The Army's Ideological Capability

Comparative Analysis. Military officers have a second outstanding political capability—for investing their actions with wider ideological meaning. The man on horseback has rarely ridden into politics without theoretical accoutrement justifying his cause. For some, ideology has been primarily an instrument for self-glorification and recruitment of support. A Sudanese officer could glibly defend his colleagues' use of the word "revolution" to describe their 1958 coup by explaining that the army, as "parent" of the event, was "free to call it by whatever name we please."[20] But other soldiers have taken ideology very seriously indeed.

Clearly, specific military ideologies must be examined in a national and historical context. They depend on circumstance, political culture, and the native and foreign ideas absorbed in military training and interaction with the civilian milieu. Although certain motifs are widespread—notably nationalism and verbal revolutionism—the range of orientations is remarkably broad. Arab officers have generally claimed to be social reformers and supporters of Arab unity. The new military rulers of Ethiopia see themselves as Marxist-Leninists, while some other African armies have been inspired mainly by indigenous warrior traditions. The military in Latin America has often been influenced by corporatist ideas. The French military rebels in Algeria did not blush at claiming to defend "all the free world."[21]

Whatever this diversity in specific ideologies, military officers have shared one crucial claim—to a special right or obligation to implement the given convictions. This traditionally is grounded in certain beliefs about the unique nature of the military institution and profession.

First, military leaders usually view their organization and occupation as having a distinctively national orientation. Since the army defends the entire community and draws on all segments of society, it is seen as, in von Seeckt's words, "a striking embodiment of national unity," rising above ties to any particular region, class, or group.[22]

Second, the army has a service orientation. "It has no other interest and no other task than service to the state," one general wrote of the German army in 1930.[23] Moreover, the service soldiers provide is an indispensable one, necessary for the very existence of the political system. "In our hands lies the state," one young German officer could claim in 1925. "Its face is our face. We are the bearers of the state."[24]

For many military leaderships, the product of intense ideological commitment and this self-defined national and service orientation has been self-righteousness and contentment with the purity of their motives. "The army has only one worry here, the national interest," one of the architects of the French military's 1958 rebellion confided at the time. "It is an enormous advantage."[25] It is a great advantage indeed, for the military can thereby make serious political choices but also deny their consequences. Few politicians except one in uniform would find it possible, as General Maxime Weygand of France did at the Pétain trial in 1945, to "dare anyone to find a political act in my life."[26]

The Soviet Case. Like all military men, Soviet officers might appeal to the rationale of military professionalism in justifying a forceful intervention in politics. No doubt most of them have seen no contradiction between the demands of their professional code and those of Soviet citizenship and membership in the party, and they insist that it is precisely by carrying out professional duty that they best discharge their obligations as Communists. As Marshal Nikolai Krylov said in 1963, "We men of the military profession look upon our military work as work for the victory of Communism, for the attainment of our party's program."[27] But would this synthesis always hold? Would ideology invariably uphold civilian authority?

Even Soviet leaders have never claimed that ideology is the sole determinant of their actions. One can easily find statements ranking it below other concerns, as with Khrushchev's declaration that "before people are to concern themselves with ideology and politics, they must eat, drink, be clothed, have housing."[28] Among Western scholars, there is a long tradition of skepticism as to the overall significance of ideology in Soviet politics, although this was until recently a minority position. Doubters have always been able to point to the frequent availability of ideological arguments to both sides in a political dispute and to the existence of policies that manifestly contradict ideological tenets. Some of the most critical scrutiny has come from students of Soviet philosophy and science, fields where the practical dilemmas of relating theory to practice are faced most squarely. Loren Graham, for instance, has found Soviet ideology "flexible almost to the point of evanescence" and therefore an unreliable predictor of performance.[29] David Joravsky's studies of biological controversies have led him to conclude that theoretical ideology has served mainly to justify pre-existing policy preferences and has been largely irrelevant to major decisions.[30]

It may well be, then, that ideological qualms have not kept Soviet officers from political intervention simply because they do not take these beliefs seriously. One can only be strengthened in this supposition by Soviet statements about the continuing ideological indifference of many commanders. "We still have officers," reads a typical complaint, "who . . . have not grasped the soul of Marxist-Leninist science. Approaching political study formally, they assimilate only formulas, only the letter and not the spirit of the theory. Therefore they are incapable of drawing from it the necessary practical conclusions."[31]

Even if we assume that Soviet state ideology is internalized by most officers and taken seriously as a guide to action, it is very doubtful that the ideology would have great power to prescribe practical conclusions in the sphere being considered here—the choice of political leaders. Soviet ideology has never given a clear and definitive response to the question, who governs? The party, of course, governs Soviet society, but this fact merely reformulates the question at another level—who governs the party? And this latter issue has always been resolved pragmatically, by utilizing various formulas of legitimacy and tactics of rule. Lenin used personal prestige and public persuasion, Stalin relied on mastery of party organization and police terror, and Stalin's successors have combined organizational weapons with policy appeal. Even Stalin did not attempt to adorn his particular mix of means with ideological sanctity, arguing that "the forms of our state change and will change depending on the development of our country and changes in the external setting."[32]

It is not hard to imagine an army coup being rationalized as merely another change in form of party leadership. Stalin himself carried out a "coup d'etat by inches" in consolidating his power, with repeated recourse to force implemented by an organization (the secret police) outside established party institutions.[33] A less gradual coup by soldiers, probably involving far less violence, is not unthinkable. Although its makers would face certain problems in justifying their actions to themselves and to others, their task would be no more exacting than it was for the makers of the mature Soviet system five decades ago. Their argument could follow the line of Stalin's defense of "extraordinary measures" in 1924: "Democracy must be evaluated in terms of the situation . . . There can be no fetishism on questions of intraparty democracy, for the installation of intraparty democracy . . . depends on the concrete conditions of time and place."[34]

Military action could achieve further credibility from several other circumstances. In the first place, it would not necessarily lead to permanent army rule. It could be followed by policy and personnel changes and a return to a civilian regime. Officers might at first intend such a return even if they reassessed this commitment later. If so, they would be acting in a fashion which is quite typical in the Third World countries, where only about 10 percent of recent military regimes have come to power with the intention of governing for more than several years.[35]

Second, forceful military action could be carried out in league with sympathetic, opportunistic, or intimidated civilians, the most important of whom would inevitably be lifelong Communists. Whether or not civilians were involved in the establishment of military government, they would almost certainly be used as administrators, advisers, and legitimizers afterward.

Third, military rebellion need not be explained or even conceived as a blow against the party, but as a choice made by part of the party and in its best interests. It would not have to entail renunciation of all or even many of the party's public purposes and symbols. Officers could retain the party's ultimate objective of a classless society as well as many of its immediate goals, particularly rapid economic growth. They could rationalize their rule as a search for a more suitable leadership formula, or as a return to a version of an earlier formula (such as the revivified Leninism recently advocated by some Soviet intellectuals).

Finally, there are some aspects of the extant ideology which could be used to sanction military intervention. Rule, at least temporary rule, by an armed elite professing its devotion to the public interest would not be inconsistent with the vanguard strain in Leninism. Soviet leaders have long compared the party and its followers to an army, and the literal transposition of this metaphor into central political institutions would not be unthinkable or unexplainable. Military leaders could wrap themselves in particular cloaks already available to them. The army has always been uniquely identified with nationalism—"the personification of Soviet patriotism," as *Pravda* called it in 1968—and its history has also been said to be "inseparable from the revolutionary traditions of the working class, from the traditions of Bolshevism."[36] This is inspiration and material enough for the apologists of a future military regime.

The case for the ideological tenability of army intervention is reinforced by events in other Communist systems. Ideology did not inhibit the authors of the 1965 conspiracy in Bulgaria. In North Korea, there was an attempted coup in 1958, led by a deputy chief of staff, and there is said to be a good chance of the Kim Il-sung dictatorship being succeeded by a military-dominated (but still Communist) regime.[37] Ideology did not stop Lin Piao in China, who evidently took Maoism more seriously than did Mao. Even Lin's opponents have paid tribute to his facility in manipulating ideology. As Chou En-lai said in 1973, Lin's group "never showed up without a copy of 'Quotations' in hand and never opened their mouths without shouting 'Long live [Mao].' "[38]

Military Participation and the Routes to Military Rule

The argument has thus far done nothing more than raise a possibility. It suggests that the Soviet military establishment has been at least capable of playing far more ambitious roles in politics than it has, and that these could conceivably be extended so far as to include seizure of supreme power in society.

This kind of possibility has been recognized by some Western analysts (among them Kolkowicz, according to whom the army represents the greatest single threat to the regime), but it has been seen as pointing in quite a different direction.[39] Most studies have argued that a military challenge to the party has been possible and that therefore the party has imposed institutional controls (particularly the MPA) which in turn have been effective in preventing that potential from being realized. I began, on the other hand, with an examination of what has been reputed to be the main agent of institutional control, and found the behavior of that agent to be rather different than has previously been thought. There is, I would argue, reason to believe that the military continues to possess major unexpended political capabilities. This gives rise to a further question: why have Soviet officers not exercised these capabilities?

It is necessary here to conceptualize the main subject of concern in the study of Soviet military politics in a more meaningful way than has been common in previous scholarship, and in a fashion which encourages comparison with other national experiences. Western students of the Soviet military have been preoccupied with the process of *control*—the way in which the party is said to use bureaucratic checks and other means to deny army leaders the capability of challenging its overall supremacy in society. The concept of control process predisposes the analyst to make several assumptions about his subject matter. The first is the assumption of an essential dichotomy in the identity of the actors—one actor (the military command) which is subject to controls, and another (the party, including the military party apparatus), which is the author and beneficiary of the control procedures. The second presumption is that political action should be conceived of in dichotomous terms. Either control is being exerted or it is not; the possible gradations between the two poles seem of little importance. The third tendency is toward unidimensional analysis. One issue—who is to have mastery in the relationship?—is paramount over all others.

A more appropriate approach is to orient the analysis toward military *participation* in politics rather than the process of civilian (in this case party) control over the military. Such a concept is more consistent with the evidence of earlier chapters of this book, which can far better be seen as demonstrating participation by commanders and party officials in military politics than as displaying the exercise of surveillance and control by a tightly integrated party apparatus. It should not be taken to imply that Soviet officers' political behavior has been free of practical constraints. It suggests, rather, that regime constraints alone have not been sufficient to prevent a challenge to civil authority, and that an understanding of why such a challenge has not been mounted can be reached only by examining officers' actual and potential roles in politics.

The concept of participation predisposes us to make more useful assumptions about military politics, and thus to ask more useful questions, than does the concept of civilian control. First, it makes no presumption that the main actors should be put into dualistic categories. It leaves open the extent to which officers and civilians will take part in politics as aggregates. (Participation can involve individuals, ad hoc groupings, stable groups, or entire institutions.) It has room for internal differentiation on both sides of the civil-military boundary and also for the kinds of cross-institutional connections and alliances that were highly visible in earlier parts of this study. Second, the focus on participation encourages analytic flexibility. It can easily make allowance for gradation and variation in civil-military or party-army relations. And third, it brings more than one level of complexity to the analysis. While permitting disciplined discussion of the question of ultimate supremacy, it also encourages consideration of the many ways in which an army's relationship to politicians can change without its officers escaping civilian control entirely—indeed, without supremacy as such ever becoming an issue.

Military participation in any political system can be thought of as having two distinct and continuous dimensions—*scope* of issues concerned, and political *means* employed. Besides clarifying what are two quite separate facets of political activity, such a distinction allows for covariation on the two dimensions and thus for the occurrence of discrete patterns of military politics which would be unintelligible using a unidimensional analysis.

The scope of military participation in politics is narrowest when confined to internal military matters of intense concern only to army officers and usually capable of resolution within the boundaries of the military establishment. Of rather broader scope are what can be termed institutional issues. These bear directly upon officers' ideological self-image, material well-being, status, and professional concerns but can be decided only with the participation of civilian elites outside the military. From here, the scope of participation can range through progressively more general issues, having less and less relevance to the military's normal institutional concerns. Intermediate issues touch in some way on the interests of some army officials but are of primary concern to other specialized segments of society. Societal issues are the broadest of all, affecting all citizens and dealing with the basic goals and needs of society as a whole. In the realm of education, for example, the determination of the overall objectives of the education system would be a societal issue; the treatment of military themes in civilian curricula an intermediate issue; the nature of officer training an institutional issue; and the fixing of responsibility for, say, poor performance by the graduates of a naval school an internal issue.

Wide variation is also observable—from society to society, from officer to officer, and from issue to issue—in terms of the means which officers utilize in politics. In internal military politics, as in politics in any bureaucratic context, most officers use primarily official prerogatives such as rights of decision and command, disciplinary powers, and control over information. Officially assigned or delegated prerogatives are also important in relations with civilians, since normally these define not only officers' rights of decision within the army but the extent to which they will be expected to participate together with civilians in determining and implementing policy on issues of institutional and even broader scope. In dealing with civilians, means can also include provision to politicians of expert advice which draws on officers' specialized experience and knowledge, with no necessary expectation that this advice will be taken into account. Some military leaders employ techniques for political bargaining in which they exchange valued goods with other political actors (such as the complex tradeoffs with legislators and private corporations concerning military procurement and location policies in the United States). The ultimate means is utilization of the armed forces' unique political resource, force. Obviously this instrument cannot be employed without qualitatively changing the structure of political authority in society.

Figure 1 captures the possible combinations on these two dimensions of political participation, dividing each dimension into four seg-

Figure 1. Patterns of military participation in politics

Means used	Scope of issues			
	Internal	Institutional	Intermediate	Societal
Official prerogative	1	5	9	13
Expert advice	2	6	10	14
Political bargaining	3	7	11	15
Force	4	8	12	16

ments defined by the terms already introduced. Cell 1, involving the resolution of intraorganizational issues by means of official prerogatives and sanctions, seems to be found within the military establishment of virtually any society. As one moves down the table from here, military participation entails use of progressively more assertive means; as one moves to the right, it concerns increasingly inclusive issue-areas. Cell 11 is the most extreme pattern commonly found in modern societies. Here military leaders use political bargaining as well as expert advice and official prerogatives; they also exert influence in a number of intermediate issue-areas not involving the army's primary concerns as an institution. Cell 16, the ultimate point on both dimensions, represents outright military rule—the arrangement so common in modernizing countries but never found or even approached in the Soviet Union. Although the threshold of army rule is not always easy to draw, and although such rule can take many forms, a convenient criterion is military officers' influence in choosing political executives. Military rule exists when officers have successfully exerted a claim to decide who shall hold executive office in the state. To define military rule is essentially to identify what other scholars might call the absence of civilian control. But to do so in terms of two facets of political participation encourages clarity of thought about the pattern of behavior and—equally important—about the causes of it.

For an army not previously in power to come to rule, assuming that it is capable of forcefully expanding its political participation, military participation in politics must thus change on one or two dimensions. The precise avenue of change can be conclusively analyzed only in a national and historical context, but one can make a general distinction between two broad routes toward military rule. They differ as to which dimension of political participation expands first. In the first pattern, which I call military intervention, it is means which escalate initially. In the second pattern, military involvement, it is scope which first increases. These can be seen as alternative pasts or hypothetical futures for Soviet military politics, but first it is essential to sketch how either path comes to be pursued by any military elite.

Military Intervention. The *Oxford Dictionary* defines "intervene" as "to come in as something extraneous." When an army intervenes in politics, its assumption of rule is its (that is its effective leaders') first serious introduction to the full range of societal issues. It arrives because officers have expanded the means they use in politics and come to employ force rather than bargaining, advice, or delegated prerogative to further what are essentially narrow institutional interests. Only after the choice of forceful means has been made—and in some cases only after their actual use—does the intervening army address itself to questions unrelated to its institutional benefit.

The initial scope of military participation in the intervention route is, then, a circumscribed one encompassing primarily institutional concerns which cannot be satisfied within the military establishment itself. (It is assumed here that strictly internal issues will be resolved without force as long as civilians rule; Cell 4 is for practical purposes an empty set.) The main determinant of this narrow scope is the acceptance by military and civilian elites of military professionalism, the ethic that defines the military calling in terms of its expertise, responsibility, and corporativeness.[40] But often professionalism also turns out to be the main ingredient in officers' resolve to escalate the means they use to have their way within this bounded range of issues. The classic justification for intervention is that offered by a French colonel during the Algerian crisis: "If we . . . became interested in the political problem, it was not because of a taste for politicking; it was because of the demands of our professional duty."[41]

The process of intervention can in theory be halted at Cell 8, with officers using force to have their way only on institutional issues and showing no interest in an outright challenge to the ruling regime or in acceptance of responsibility for all problems facing society. In reality, however, Cell 8 is an unstable and unlikely end point. Since the use of force (or the commitment to employ it later) normally calls into question the very basis of civilian authority, it is almost certain to evoke counterforce from the civilian government and necessitate a resolution in favor of one side or the other.

The movement of a military group toward forceful intervention commonly brings at least some discussion and decision on extrainstitutional questions. Indeed, it is possible that the military will already be participating on a number of intermediate or even societal issues— in which case the path toward military rule is somewhat of a hybrid of the two types I have distinguished here. Whatever the starting point, once an army has employed force it has no option but to make broad policy choices. In doing so, the intervening officers' attitudes toward systematic change may range from hostility to passionate enthusiasm. In Thailand, army rule has been "conservative and in some respects reactionary," and this description applies well to recent military governments in Greece and Chile and to the Franco regime in Spain.[42] In other societies, officers have initiated far-reaching socio-economic change and developed an elaborate savior theory justifying the new universality of their interests. In much of Latin America, for instance, armies have supported "a modern economy and social structure as the necessary supports of a modern military organization" and have taken action against traditional elites opposed to modernization.[43]

The sequence in which the scope of issues broadens varies greatly from one case to another, as does officers' eventual stance toward the rest of society (a stance which may not be agreed upon by all officers and which is susceptible to change in any event). The important point to recognize here is how in the intervention route these broader concerns, and the choice of violent means, evolve from an original preoccupation with quite circumscribed institutional grievances.

The 1952 coup in Egypt shows this relationship clearly. Although they were later to develop complex theories of Arab socialism, the Free Officers group began with a concern with the immediate impact of the old regime on the army itself. "One looks in vain for a clear view of the role these officers envisaged for themselves even as late as 1951, other than resisting the King's abuses of their profession. One also finds few indications of any political program or plan of action."[44] A general program did emerge, but as President Sadat, an officer in the original group, explained later, it developed from the officers' bitter personal experience in King Farouk's ragtag army: "My political ideas grew out of my personal experience of oppression, not out of abstract notions. I am a soldier, not a theoretician, and it was by an empirical process that I came to realize my country needed a political system which responded to its essential needs."[45]

Several other illustrations of military intervention help make the point. When the Young Turk rebellion began among Turkish officers in 1908, "there was nothing to distinguish it at first from the mutinies which had become so commonplace in the preceding year." Only when officers rejected as inadequate the sultan's proposals for improving their fighting and living conditions did they raise the banner of reform for all of Turkish society.[46] In modern Spain, military discontent found initial expression in "councils of military defense" first formed in 1916. If army leaders were later to don the mantle of national regeneration, the original councils' "basic goal was not national reform or political justice but simply recognition of the Officer Corps as a corporate entity deserving of special perquisites, equitable rewards, and public recognition."[47] The military group that overthrew the South Korean Second Republic in 1961 also began with narrow aims. It was only after civilians denied claims to higher salaries, dismissal of incompetent senior officers, and an end to corruption in military procurement that "a limited 'military purification' movement . . . acquired the revolutionary objective of overthrowing the Second Republic and everything that was symbolized by it."[48]

Military Involvement. In the second route to supremacy the army begins by being involved—"entangled . . . implicated . . . included," in the words of the dictionary—in broader and broader areas of policy. Only after this expansion of scope to include issues far exceeding the bounds of a military organization's normal institutional competence do officers escalate the means of their participation to include force.

Most armies are involved in political decisions in at least several intermediate issue-areas. (This is certainly true in the Soviet Union.) But how is it that officers come to participate in a great many such intermediate areas and, ultimately, in the resolution of issues of societal scope? Here several distinct types of involvement can be identified, in each of which the military is pulled into more inclusive political participation by forces in the political environment.

First, officers can be involved in national politics by the consequences of earlier intervention. If this has created civilian opposition, the army may return to politics out of fear of the consequences of rule by antagonistic civilians. The hostility between the two sides can easily become "self-perpetuating and self-reinforcing," as in the lengthy conflict between Argentine military officers and supporters of Juan Peron.[49]

A second type of military involvement is induced by private groups who appeal to the army to act forcefully to support their causes. In Brazil, for instance, "civilians who form the politically relevant strata of . . . society have always attempted to use the military to further their own goals." Successful and attempted coups have followed extensive "civilian solicitation to act," with the army widely perceived as a moderator or balancer of competing social interests.[50] Pressure from other groups can become acute when the armed forces are compelled to coerce or pacify them by government instruction. The sheer necessity of maintaining order may then pull officers into broader decision making, whatever their initial sympathy with the disorderly. In Nigeria, for example, the use of the army to quell disorders during a general strike and election campaign in 1964 "tended to blur the line between professional and political matters" and "drew upon [the army] political pressures from the outside to allocate values."[51]

A third kind of involvement process finds the officer corps pulled into societal politics by the force of nonprofessional but politically relevant roles played by military leaders. Typically these roles are ascriptive, revolving around kinship, friendship, or communal group. The armies of Latin America *caudillos*, in which success depended on personal standing with the boss, were involved in politics in this way until well into the twentieth century.[52] The Russian military was involved in the negotiations leading to the abdication of the tsar in 1917 because many of its highest officials were members of the royal family. In Nigeria, the entry of the army into national politics in 1966 was closely bound up with the intensification of regional and tribal tensions throughout the society. At least some officers perceived their participation in terms of communal rather than professional identity, as they "were increasingly caught up in a spiral of mutual fear and suspicion" centering on communal affiliation and permeating all of Nigerian life.[53] Similar involvements have been reported in other African countries and occurred in Cyprus in 1974 and in Lebanon in 1976. Some scholars have seen evidence of a trend in this direction in Yugoslavia, and it is often predicted that the military's role will increase if communal strife breaks out after President Tito's death.[54]

It is the fourth type of increasing military involvement that is most widespread. In this sequence, it is not private groups or nonprofessional roles that draw officers into politics, but the civilian government itself. This pattern can occur in a variety of circumstances. In the least likely case, the government actually invites the army to replace it entirely in a confession of its own inadequacy to govern. The Burmese regime is said to have done this in 1958, after the governing party split, and the military takeover in Pakistan the same year occurred under similar circumstances.[55]

Normally, however, the government involves military officers by assigning them decision-making roles that encompass a number of broad societal issues yet fall short of supreme power. A common variant has been for this to occur in wartime. The "unexpected involvement of the army in social and economic affairs" in World War I Germany, culminating in the Ludendorff dictatorship of 1916-17, occurred in this way. Uprepared for total war, the government in effect abdicated much of its authority to the army in fields such as economic planning, armaments production, local administration, and even labor relations and food distribution. "It was simply assumed that all matters connected with the conduct of the war fell within the exclusive domain of the military authorities. They were placed in a position from which it was relatively easy for them and even necessary for them to expand their power."[56] The same virtual abdication has been noted in France's colonial wars and in anti-guerrilla struggles and civic action programs in Latin America.[57] The rise of the military-industrial complex in the postwar United States has been a limited experience with this pattern—military participation expanding into policy areas such as science and education during a period of national mobilization against an external enemy.

Mao's China demonstrates a different variant of government-induced involvement, in which the moving factor is factional conflict within a civilian-dominated leadership. Long seen as a model Maoist institution, the People's Liberation Army was brought into often violent national and local political struggles in the late 1960s as the ally of one party faction grouped around Mao and his then designated heir, Lin Piao. The army "did not intervene in politics against the wish of the political leadership, but rather was brought into the political arena by this leadership."[58] By the end of the Cultural Revolution, soldiers were in charge of most local party committees and constituted more than half of the national party leadership. It was under these circumstances that Lin and a number of military and civilian collaborators, apparently alarmed by a downturn in their fortunes, made an unsuccessful bid for supremacy.

The Importance of Institutional Interest. There is no philosopher's stone for understanding military participation in politics. No single scheme can substitute for detailed analysis, and no one variable explains all situations, the Soviet one included. However, assuming that military capabilities are sufficient for successful interference, there is one factor that deserves particular attention—institutional interest.

The importance of this variable for understanding intervention should be clear enough. Officers intervene against civilian authorities when their perceived interests are being denied or threatened by civilian policy. As Nordlinger has written (using a somewhat more diffuse definition of intervention), "by far the most common and salient interventionist motive involves the defense or enhancement of the military's corporate interests."[59]

The relation of institutional interest to military involvement is less immediately apparent. Involvement is a salient pattern which demands attention in its own right. Yet it is normally not enough to bring about military rule. It is much less likely than intervention to do so, mainly because the irrevocable commitment to use force comes at the end of the involvement process but nearer the beginning of intervention. Furthermore, it is much easier than in the intervention pattern for an army well along the involvement route to move, or be moved, back in the direction of minimal participation.

When the military does seize supreme power after a process of involvement, this is usually only because its core institutional interests have become engaged. Even when an individual officer or group reaches for power out of involvement considerations, it is necessary to mobilize the support of colleagues and subordinates for whom corporate self-interest is usually prime. We can briefly illustrate these points for the three main types of involvement leading in the direction of military rule (leaving aside the reactive type, where involvement is explained by prior intervention).

Some armies may take the advice of private groups urging political action, but most clearly do not. Even an officer corps receptive to outside appeals must decide which groups to favor, and here institutional interest tends to come into play. In Brazil, for instance, where private appeals have been numerous, "often . . . the threat to institutional self-interest or survival is the key factor in finally creating officer consensus" on action.[60]

Likewise, the pressure of ascriptive identities such as kinship or ethnicity is rarely enough on its own to prompt forceful action by officers in a modern army. Most latter-day caudillos were in fact abandoned by their officers once their armies had been professionalized. Even where communal passions are aroused, as in Nigeria, the effect of communalism is often channeled in part through the military's own hierarchy and status system. Ibo officers, for example, seem to have been as much concerned with the effect of anti-Ibo discrimination on their own career prospects as with communal relations in the country as a whole.[61]

Finally, it is also uncommon for government-induced involvement to be sufficient to cause a full-scale military assumption of power. The Burmese government's offer of power to its armed forces in 1958 remains a historical oddity, and even here the offer appears to have been hastened by the realization that otherwise the generals would seize control on their own initiative (as they did four years later).[62]

Military establishments involved in societal politics by government direction or abdication in wartime are often persuaded to retreat after the military emergency has eased. In France, officers returned to their standard roles once the Algerian conflict was over and the government was able to assure them that their budgetary and other interests would be safeguarded.[63] In Latin America, the only politically involved armies to carry out coups in recent years were ones whose corporate interests were jeopardized. Even in Peru, where the military regime inaugurated in 1969 was vehement about its broad developmental aims, an anti-guerrilla struggle convinced army leaders of the need for reform only because of its direct implications for institutional survival. As in Brazil, where the armed forces intervened but did not promote reform at all, "the officer corps believed that [existing] conditions were ultimately a threat to the military institution itself."[64]

In China, where military involvement was rooted in disputes among civilian factions, Lin Piao's coup attempt failed to elicit broad support among officers who did not see their basic interests as being at stake. Even before the attempt, the PLA was beginning to withdraw at civilian insistence from the numerous political heights it had occupied during the Cultural Revolution. The party has now revoked much of its earlier gift of power without military resistance, although the scope of army influence remains far broader than in the Soviet Union.

Military Participation in Soviet Politics
Before being in a position to explain why the Soviet military has not expanded the scope and means of its political participation, it is necessary to sketch the actual pattern of that participation. This will mean

going beyond both the traditional statements by Western scholars about the process of party control and the selective analysis of particular points of army-party contact. Figure 2, depicting in a very rough way the frequency with which Soviet officers take part in the kinds of political action described in this chapter, will be useful as a tool for classification and summary. The fact that the figure is fixed in time reflects not only the limitations of summary descriptions but also, to some extent, my conviction that many of the crucial features of civil-military relations have been remarkably stable over the years. Such major changes in the parameters of participation as have taken place will be treated in the text. What are more important in comparative terms are the changes that have not occurred, changes in the array of military roles in politics whose possible direction and form the analytic scheme employed here helps illuminate.

Earlier portions of this study should leave no doubt that the internal politics of the Soviet military establishment is quite vigorous and that frequent and often successful participants in it are military commanders. Cell 1 in Figure 2 (where individual officers and bureaucratic groupings use official powers to deal with routine internal issues, usually in conflict with other commanders and political officers) is thus the one within which most day-to-day political participation is located. Some political activity on internal issues also involves expert advice and bargaining tactics (Cells 2 and 3), but the frequency of use of these instruments is much lower, as is to be expected in any stable organization.

It is also evident that some officers, mainly men of senior rank and position, take part in the resolution of institutional issues—those which are of primary concern to military officials but cannot be dealt with by them alone. The civilian leadership retains the prerogative to make final decisions in the military realm, as in all others, but clearly it delegates much of this authority to officers and has at most times exercised its own authority in consultation with them.

Professional soldiers have been entrusted with managing the Ministry of Defense at its highest level for most of the time since Marshal Vasilevskii's appointment as minister in 1949 (excepting Bulganin's second term in 1953-55 and Dmitrii Ustinov's term beginning in April 1976), and at most other levels since the Civil War. Thus it is military commanders, as agents of civilian leaders, who make most of the routine decisions—with some participation by the political organs—concerning matters such as military training, living conditions, weaponry, and strategy (these fall into Cell 5). Even on the minority of institutional issues resolved by civilian party leaders, senior officers supply much of the information used in making choices and are con-

Figure 2. Incidence of military participation in Soviet politics

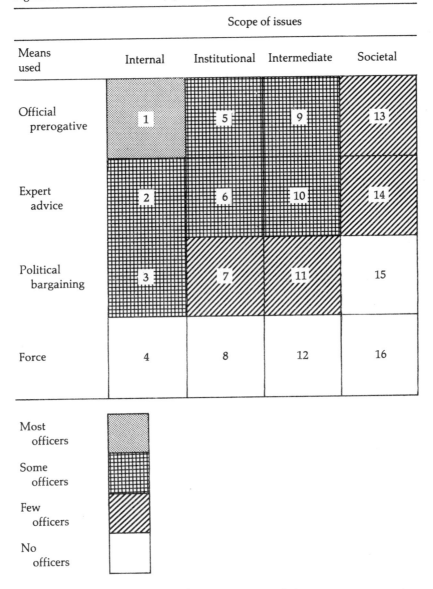

sulted on outcomes in much the same way as their counterparts are in Western societies. There is considerable evidence that such consultation was common even in Stalin's lifetime. Since his death officers have been able to proffer considerably more by way of advice in public forums. Perhaps more important, the seeking of military advice in private has come to be acknowledged as a matter of party policy. In the words of a recent Soviet text, "Before deciding one way or the other on questions of military development, the party Central Committee and Politburo carefully study the state of affairs in the army and navy and consult with (sovetuiutsia s) the high command and the most important specialists of the armed forces."[65] Such participation is formalized to some extent through military membership in bodies such as the Council of Ministers, the Defense Council (a collegium for discussing military policy, chaired by Brezhnev and given legal status in the 1977 constitution), and the Military-Industrial Commission (which deals with defense production at the top level). But less formal channels of access (classified in Cell 6 rather than 5) are probably of equal importance.[66]

That the acknowledgment of specialized competence has been the main resource of Soviet officers in dealing with civilian politicians should be apparent from many of the cases analyzed earlier. One should note that special weight is lent to officers' counsel by the fact that the expertise underlying it is not widely shared outside the military establishment. Notwithstanding party apparatus, KGB, Foreign Ministry, and defense industry involvement in some aspects of military affairs (and the evident growth of military competence in several civilian research institutes in recent years), the military seems to control far more of the information relevent to making policy in its specialized realm than do its counterparts in the West. Although civilian decisions are ultimately shaped by values and perceptions over which the army has no control, civilians do not have the substantial non-military sources of military information found in American politics. There are no Soviet equivalents for the Central Intelligence Agency, the Arms Control and Disarmament Agency, or private consulting firms such as the RAND Corporation.

Soviet officers' status as experts is further reinforced by the high degree of instability and danger which civilians have perceived as inhering in the milieu—the international environment—in which military decisions take effect. The tendency of Soviet leaders to resolve such uncertainty on the side of safety has clearly made them more receptive to military advice than to that of most other skill groups. Khrushchev's remarks to President Eisenhower in 1959 display this receptivity well:

Some people from our military department come and say, "Comrade Khrushchev, look at this! The Americans are developing such and such a system. We could develop the same system, but it would cost such and such." I tell them there's no money; it's all been allotted already. So they say, "If we don't get the money we need and if there's a war, then the enemy will have superiority over us." So we discuss it some more, and I end up giving them the money they ask for.[67]

It is neither necessary nor possible to establish here that deference to military opinion has always been the party leadership's response. The important point is that most of officers' participation in national politics is directed at attaining such deference by capitalizing on their qualifications as specialists and experts.

As in the United States, there has been some spillover beyond Cell 6 in both the means and the scope of military participation. On the means dimension, the political primacy of the party executive has precluded the direct appeals to an independent legislature which are open to the American military. Yet this is amply compensated for by the fact that Soviet soldiers have been represented on the political decision-making bodies of the ruling party. The thirty military members on the 1976 Central Committee were by far the largest contingent from any bureaucratic constituency. The Minister of Defense is currently a member of the party Politburo, and there is also a substantial military presence on regional and local party committees.

An additional resource which supplements officers' persuasiveness as tenders of expert advice is the army's elaborate system of public relations and image building, of which the efforts of the political organs described in Chapter 9 form an important part. Although this system is viewed with overall favor by civilian leaders (and serves to propagate broad party values as well as military ones), it cannot but serve to legitimize military counsel in the eyes of present and future civilian elites. Promilitary propaganda is especially effective when it resonates with deeply felt memories of past struggles and triumphs. If the army's "endless columns" could five decades ago make old revolutionaries "stand and weep," as a party congress was told at the time, much the same is true for many Soviet citizens today.[68] Not infrequently military achievements and military goals are discussed with an air of reverence. Significantly, the current party program refers to defense as a sacred duty of the regime.

Some military executives seem also to have benefited from informal connections with civilian politicians. In some instances these have been personal relationships based on friendship and common experience—such as the ties between Stalin and his former Civil War colleagues (Voroshilov, Budennyi, Kulik, and others), or the link sometimes seen between Brezhnev and Marshal Grechko. One can also assume the existence of less personalized linkages with civilians involved in defense research and production, who along with their organizations inevitably share key interests with their military customers.[69] Recent Central Committees have contained a dozen or more executives from the eight armaments production ministries as well as at least that many persons with extensive administrative experience in the area.

As in most consultative relationships, there has been no sharp line between advice solicited by civilians and prodding at the military's own initiative. Stalin preferred to seek out policy-relevant information on his own, "question[ing] the military chiefs in minute detail about the situation in the field, about their concerns, demands, wishes, and shortcomings."[70] Yet, as the evidence on the war makes plain, he also expected military officials to bring their concerns to him, and he quite frequently was responsive to those concerns. Khrushchev may have grumbled in his memoirs about military pressure or even intimidation of the party leadership, but there is no indication that he sought to prevent soldiers from speaking their minds on military issues. "I don't reproach the military for that—they're only doing their job."[71]

If the means of military participation have not fallen entirely within the two minimal categories, the same is true of scope, which has encompassed a number of issues not of a strictly internal or institutional nature. The presence of officers on most collegial party organs assures army leaders some voice in the discussion of issues of societal scope, and the stability of this representation seems sufficient to warrant recognition as a prerogative of high military office (hence the entry in Cell 13). A small number of soldiers are also in a position to tender expert advice on such questions in both formal and informal forums (Cell 14).

More significant is participation in making and implementing policy on intermediate issues touching both on military interests and on those of other segments of Soviet society. Military participation here is specialized according to issue and actor. Only a minority of officers participate on any given issue (as is true in internal military politics), and they are not necessarily coordinated in their actions or consistent in their preferences. These intermediate issues should be specified here, since many have not been discussed in this book and most have been ignored in Western analysis. They fall into three main categories.

First, senior military officials have made known their preferences as to the share of societal resources and energies to be devoted to the army and its mission. Public articulations on this question are highly visible, as was seen in Chapter 9, and they are undoubtedly made with equal force in private. There are differences of emphasis among officers from different services and backgrounds, and military claims have considerable backing from elements in the military party apparatus and, often, from some civilians. Such claims necessarily have at least indirect implications for the shares of other groups.

Second, military officials have sought to secure specific contributions to the defense effort from civilian organizations, a fact which implies some military participation in realms of decision entrusted primarily to civilians. There have been, for example, major military demands on several branches of science, and this along with the ties to defense industry, the planning establishment, and the space program has produced what has justifiably been called a military-industrial complex comparable to that in the United States.[72] Military officers collaborate widely with civilians on matters of civil defense (a program which has expanded significantly since the mid-1960s), civil aviation (whose head carries senior military rank), maritime navigation (some elements of which are used to collect military intelligence and transport naval cargoes), and diplomatic representation abroad (which is interwoven with KGB and military intelligence activity). The army's officials also bargain at several levels with civilians providing it with routine goods and services. Ministry of Defense headquarters are known to negotiate agreements with the Ministry of Oil Refining and Petrochemical Industry (for fuel and lubricants), with the Ministry of Agriculture (for use of farmland), with the railroads (for use of main and spur lines and rolling stock), with food processing ministries, and with the Ministry of Trade, Ministry of Light Industry, and other consumer goods producers (for supply of clothing, consumer durables, and other items). At the local level, housing is sometimes leased from civilian authorities, conscription call-ups involve close contact with local health and school officials, and public safety issues bring army officers into regular contact with police officials. Annual contracts must be reached with republic and local agencies to provide military retail and service outlets with perishable foods, leisure and household goods, and a range of other commodities.[73]

Finally, military officers, usually in quite specialized agencies, participate in several areas of mainly civilian jurisdiction into which the army has been allowed to extend efforts of its own whose principal aim is to augment military capabilities. While officers' prerogatives in these areas are clear, their status as experts in policy formulation is less clear than in the internal and institutional realms and the opportunities for bargaining are probably limited to senior officers with good access to civilian decision makers. Three issue-areas stand out: construction, transport, and education.

The army has long participated in civilian construction projects on a considerable scale—partly, it seems, in order to enhance its own capacity and partly to compensate for civilian deficiencies. It has helped in postwar reconstruction of industrial plants (after 1945 a number of generals occupied senior posts in construction ministries), in land reclamation and irrigation projects, and in the erection of government buildings, large-scale recreational facilities, communication lines, and housing. In Moscow alone, soldiers (usually specially drafted construction troops, who are visible in large numbers on the capital's streets) have built Moscow State University, Sheremet'evo airport, office and commercial establishments, and whole blocks of multistorey housing.[74]

In transport, too, military construction has been a major enterprise. Construction troops are involved in building and maintaining some civilian roads. The specialized railroad troops make up a major construction force. Between the wars (when they were controlled alternately by the army, the railroads, and the secret police), they laid down lines in the Donets basin, Urals, Siberia, and other regions. In the thirty years after 1945 they constructed 27,000 kilometers of track and 13,000 other facilities. All facets of military and civilian transport were tightly integrated during World War II, with generals temporarily heading the People's Commissariats of Transportation and Communication, and one assumes that there are elaborate plans for reintegration in any future conflict. Even in peacetime, military use of trunk and spur rail lines, airports, canals, harbors, and other facilities has necessitated complex negotiation over terms of access. The most important service which soldiers provide to agriculture at harvest time is also in the transport realm.[75]

The army has always had some involvement in paramilitary training, although the main actor in this area has been DOSAAF, a voluntary organization not subject to formal military control. A major policy innovation came in 1967, when a system of basic military training for predraft-age youths was inaugurated. It is administered by civilian ministries and departments of education, but with substantial military participation. Military instructors, mostly reserve or retired officers, now work in secondary and vocational schools and in many workplaces. Military and MPA contacts with artistic and youth groups have increased in the last decade as well, as part of the broadened program of military-patriotic education.[76]

These extensions in the scope and means of participation could be analyzed in much more detail, but enough has been said to trace their outlines and to make the central point in comparative terms—namely their limited character. Most military participation in Soviet politics has been confined either to intramilitary matters or to exercising delegated powers and providing civilian leaders with advice on institutional questions. There has been some extension of scope into several nonmilitary spheres, and of political means into bargaining and use of connections with civilian politicians. But there has been no movement in the direction of military rule. Army officers have displayed no inclination either to employ force to further their aims or to shift their attention to issues of societal scope. They have repeatedly acknowledged, in theory and practice, the party's right to resolve basic issues of governance and development for society, including issues bearing on their specialized function. As Marshal Grechko phrased it in 1974, *"Only the party*, armed with Marxist-Leninist theory, is capable of comprehending every political, economic, social, and military phenomenon and event, of profoundly analyzing all of our social and political life, and of setting the proper course for resolving the complex problems of building Communism, defending its just cause, and consolidating world peace."[77] It is this deference which now must be explained.

Explaining the Army's Political Quiescence

11

Why has military participation stopped so far short of forceful interference in Soviet national politics? If the Soviet military is thought to have been incapable of assuming any larger role—because of the effectiveness of institutional controls or for some other reason—no further analysis is required. But if the argument about the army's coercive and ideological capabilities is taken seriously, our discussion must turn directly to the two dimensions of political participation and the two hypothetical routes for expanding it. Again, the discussion is best pursued in explicitly comparative fashion.

Barriers to Military Involvement

Military involvement has been defined as the path toward military rule which begins with expansion in the scope rather than the means of officers' participation in politics. This broadening of scope toward societal issues can result from any of four factors: prior military intervention or involvement; pressure from nongovernmental groups; the pull of nonprofessional, usually ascriptive, roles; and inducement by the civilian government.

Little need be said about the relevance of the first factor to the Soviet Union. The regime's early decision to disband the tsarist army in favor of a new force precluded any possibility that it would inherit military involvement from its predecessor. Since then, there has been no way for the military to be involved in national politics by an earlier intervention because there has been no such intervention to begin with.

Nor has pressure on officers to act emanated from other groups in society. Soviet politics has, of course, never been characterized by open contention among private groups. Political demands have been made only in the context of unquestioning acceptance of the system's fundamental premises. Civilian supremacy has been such a basic premise from the start, and any appeal for military assistance would be a categorical violation of the "rules of the game" and tolerable only if the game were breaking down. None has occurred. The army has not had to cope with private demands for interference because the structure of the political system has virtually foreclosed the possibility of this kind of demand.

Officers' insulation from group pressures has been reinforced by the sparingness of their use in coercing the regime's domestic opponents. The suppression of actual and potential opposition has been assigned since the Civil War almost entirely to specialized security forces not under military command (in the present-day KGB and MVD). The army has been used as a supplement to the security police in dealing with ethnically based insurgencies (in Central Asia in the 1920s and the Ukraine in the 1940s) and against occasional threats to public order. Such missions have not been without strain for the military men involved, as is clear from a recent account of the employment of troops against striking workers in Novocherkassk in 1962 (when one officer committed suicide rather than order his men to fire).[1] Nonetheless, these have been infrequent and limited experiences. The Soviet claim that after 1921 the army essentially lost its internal functions is basically accurate.[2] This has made Soviet officers far less likely than their counterparts in many developing countries to "perform tasks on the margin of moral behavior" in coercing their fellow citizens,[3] and thus less vulnerable to symptoms of anxiety about the legitimacy of civilian authority.

The third potential contributor to involvement, the pull of ascriptive attachments, has also been of little consequence thus far. The military has not been involved in societal politics by personalist leaders, as in nineteenth-century Latin America, or by senior officers' family ties to the civilian elite, as in pre-1917 Russia. Nor have regional or ethnic antagonisms drawn officers in. Communal relations have never approximated the mistrust and hatred that engulfed the Nigerian military in 1966.

The fourth type of military involvement—at the initiative of the civilian regime—is the most common of all. Yet it, too, has never applied in the Soviet Union. Unlike a number of other Communist regimes, Soviet leaders have had a highly refined sense of the specificity of the army's task and of its place in national development. Whatever the requirements of citizenship and membership in the party, Soviet officers have almost always found that their active political participation is encouraged only on questions related to their professional function as specialists in the use of violence against external enemies.

The army has indeed been involved in several extrainstitutional issue-areas. But it is important to realize that this role enlargement has been quite restrained in comparative terms and has been subject to deliberate civilian check and scrutiny. Even on most major functions in direct support of the army's basic mission, among them weapons production and paramilitary education, the regime has been careful to assume the burden of decision and to delegate most practical work to civilian organizations outside the military establishment. Such organizations may share many of the military's values, but they are not subject to the direct control of soldiers.

The defense production ministries, for example, are substantial institutions in their own right, and their principal executive and overseer for most of the time since 1941 (Ustinov) has recently assumed command of the Ministry of Defense. In the field of paramilitary training, William Odom's study of Osoaviakhim, the interwar predecessor of DOSAAF, shows how it served party leaders as a means of restricting the military's authority and pre-empting its expansion into important policy areas.[4] A similar rationale applies to the innovations in basic military training, civil defense, and military-patriotic education since 1967, changes which some Western observers have been too quick to equate with increased influence for the military itself. In each field new programs pursue the regime's military goals (increasing military capacity without damaging economic growth) but do not sharply expand the area of policy in which army officers make binding decisions. It is civilian education ministries which are primarily responsible for the new basic training network, and DOSAAF (an essentially self-financing organization independent of the Defense Ministry) continues to play the major role in inculcating military-related specialties outside the armed forces. Although active and retired officers are involved in military-patriotic education, it is managed mainly by the national youth federations and by school authorities and is under control of the local party organs. And in the civil defense area, except at the national level (where the program's formal chief is a uniformed officer, Deputy Defense Minister Aleksandr T. Altunin), all formal authority and most practical responsibility are vested in civilians. Again, as is never the case with intramilitary activity, program implementation is supervised by local party and government authorities.[5]

Political communication between military and civilian leaders except at the highest level has been inhibited by the professionalization of military careers, including careers in the military party organs, and by the specialization of the military policy sphere and the envelopment of it in an aura of secrecy. Stalin discouraged almost all lateral communication short of his own person. According to Khrushchev, "Stalin never gave us a chance to get to know military people unless we had specific business with them." Even Politburo members were not allowed to ask questions during discussions of nuclear weaponry, and after Stalin's death they "gawked [like] a bunch of sheep seeing a new gate for the first time" at a presentation by a rocket designer.[6] Clearly, important elements of this pattern persist. It is now well known that at the strategic arms limitation talks in the early 1970s Soviet civilians were so lacking in information possessed by their military colleagues as to be prone to factual errors during negotiations. At one session the ranking military delegate, Nikolai V. Ogarkov (since 1977 a full marshal and chief of the General Staff), asked Americans not to disclose technical information to the Soviet civilians, even about Soviet military capabilities, saying such facts were strictly the affair of the military.[7]

This compartmentalization does not rule out all military input on broad political issues. Yet on societal questions military officers speak as only one constituency among many, and at the peak of the decision pyramid there has been a consistent practice of limiting their voice—again in distinction to a number of other Communist systems. No professional officer has ever been a Central Committee secretary (although two former secretaries, Bulganin and Ustinov, have served as Defense Minister). One nonprofessional marshal (Bulganin) was head of government, and another (Voroshilov) was chief of state. But no career soldier has ever held either of these posts or belonged to the Presidium of the Council of Ministers. Only two professional officers (Zhukov and Grechko) have sat, briefly, on the Politburo, and each has done so as an individual politician, with no implied right for the army to participate as an institution in the making of political decisions outside its specialized field. As Zhukov's dismissal shows and Ustinov's appointment to succeed Grechko in 1976 confirms, even this sort of representation is subject to the vicissitudes of change within the leadership and is in no way defined as an institutional entitlement. Grechko's recent term on the Politburo, throughout which his public remarks continued to focus on defense and security issues, is best seen as reflecting his personal authority and, perhaps, the military's right to consultation on military-related questions. That right seems in no sense jeopardized by arrangements since Ustinov's accession.

The contrast with Chinese practice in this regard, one rooted in different revolutionary experiences and attitudes toward military organization, is evident from even a casual comparison. In China there has always been considerable overlap between peak civilian and military offices, and this has gone hand in hand with extensive military participation in making political and economic decisions in all realms. The contrast between the two models is clearly recognized in Soviet analysis, which in recent years has shown, even allowing for polemical flourish, something approaching incomprehension that any Communist regime could consider proper a military role as expansive as the PLA's. The PLA is said to have been assigned functions that are simply inappropriate; its role has "nothing in common . . . with the historic significance and functions of the military organization of a socialist state."[8]

The pattern of role specialization and bounded political scope is also highly evident at the local level, once again in obvious contrast to China (where senior commanders headed many local party committees after the Cultural Revolution and soldiers are much more involved in local production and education than in the Soviet Union). Contacts between the military and the local party organs have been far less extensive than some Soviet rhetoric (and some Western analysis) implies. There was nothing preordained about this. Even though the army's political extraterritoriality was firmly established on most points by the end of the Civil War (see Chapter 1), it was maintained only by deliberate policy choice. It might have been seriously eroded, for example, if Trotsky's plan for use of the army to militarize labor (in effect to merge economic and military management) had been realized. As it was, the several labor armies were poorly supplied, preoccupied with their own organizational difficulties, and hampered by "parallelism and friction" with civilian economic agencies.[9] The labor armies were disbanded in 1921, and in 1924 the autonomy of the army and MPA from most local decisions was confirmed. Within several years observers could even note "an insufficiency of communication, involvement, and familiarity of the party leadership of the military units with local party, soviet, trade union, and other work."[10]

The mold was strengthened by Stalin's emphatic opposition to any military voice on major local issues. Despite peasant resistance, little use seems to have been made of military units in the collectivization of agriculture. Stalin made it clear that military leaders should deal with local officials only on questions directly bearing on military functions. His attitude toward the army's local role was summarized in his icy response to the joint plea by the Ukrainian Military District command and the heads of three regional party committees in 1933 for help for Ukrainian agriculture: "They [military and civilians] are not to be in cooperation. *The military should occupy themselves with their own business* and not discuss things that do not concern them."[11]

There has been no major change of approach under Khrushchev and Brezhnev. Some contacts and interdependencies do exist at the local level (and existed under Stalin). But these are quite circumscribed and Soviet leaders show no tendency to encourage their development for either political or administrative reasons. Nor do army officers themselves seem anxious to press for more intense contacts. Commanders and political officers alike have done little to involve local party and state organs in their work. Indeed, the military has at times been reluctant to apply pressure on local civilians even concerning issues closely related to the army's specialized tasks. On the question of preparing young men for military service, for example, some command and political organs "do not keep in touch with the organization of classes in DOSAAF schools and clubs, and rarely raise before local party and soviet organs questions the resolution of which would improve the level of specialized training and ideological hardening of draft-age youth."[12] Concerning local supply of consumer goods, some military trade officials "do not meet their suppliers for years on end" and even fail to obtain delivery of goods already contracted for because they "do not insist on having their orders filled."[13]

It terms of military administration, self-sufficiency continues to be the dominant pattern. The growing importance of road and air transport and the expansion of the army's network of state farms have evidently diminished military dependence on logistical support from local civilians.[14] Military officers have welcomed this trend and made no effort to reduce it. Illustrations of military autarchy carried to the point of irrationality and wastefulness abound in military publications. We read, for instance, that some garrisons prefer to generate their own electric power even when they can obtain it locally at half the price.[15] The occasional use of soldiers to drive harvest vehicles brings "well-known difficulties."[16] New military retail outlets continue to be concentrated in large cities, despite the duplication of civilian facilities, because "military clients and construction agencies do not maintain close working contacts with local executive committees."[17] Logistics officers "tend to plan the shipment of loads from areas where the Ministry of Defense has raw material or machinery stores, even when these are 'twenty-nine lands' away and the necessary [materials] are, as they say, right under their noses—[in civilian warehouses] close to where the recipient is located."[18]

Chapter 10 distinguished three variants of the government-induced pattern of military involvement. The first—in which a civilian government invites its armed forces to replace it entirely, as in

Burma—is hard even to imagine in Soviet politics. The regime has wanted nothing as much as the right to govern and has never displayed the slightest urge to abdicate this prerogative to the army or any other institution.

Nor has either of the other two variants—greatly expanded military participation in wartime or involvement at the behest of a leadership faction—been operative. There was a significant expansion in the scope of the army's activity during World War II, as the impetus of mobilization pushed it into areas such as communications and transport management where it had had little role before the war. Nonetheless, civilians remained firmly in charge of overall coordination, as is evidenced by the failure to name a single military officer to the State Defense Committee, which supervised war mobilization. Moreover, the regime rescinded most of the increment to military scope by the end of the war, presumably because of its determination that officers occupy themselves with their own business. For example, Marshal Peresypkin, who was head of both civilian and military communications from July 1941 onward, relinquished his civilian post in July 1944. The army's logistics chief, General Khrulev, who had been appointed People's Commissar of Transport in March 1942, gave up this responsibility only eleven months later.[19] The city defense committees, joint civil-military bodies in charge of local mobilization, were also dissolved in 1944-45.

The Soviet military has also been under little pressure to follow the path of the Chinese army toward expanded participation as the ally of one side in a civilian factional dispute. Leadership factions have generally fought their battles within regular party arenas. No leader has chosen to appeal for open military support, although several have probably had the opportunity to do so.

During the conflict over Lenin's succession, Trotsky, who was formal head of the army until a year after Lenin's death, declined to do what Mao did in China four decades later. Soviet history might have been very different had he tried to commit the military to his cause, but Trotsky "was convinced that a military *pronunciamento* would be an irreparable setback for the revolution, even if he were to be associated with it."[20] Similar restraint was exercised during the struggle to succeed Stalin. It should be clear from evidence already presented that neither Marshal Zhukov nor the army played a decisive part in the triumph of Khrushchev and his allies. Military representation on the Central Committee actually dropped by almost half at the Twentieth Congress in 1956 (to 7.1 percent), in clear contrast to the huge increase in military standing, into the 50-percent range, in China after the Cultural Revolution. Whatever military leaders' limited role in palace politics up to 1957, it was abruptly terminated with Zhukov's dismissal and the inauguration of a sixteen-year hiatus in military representation on the Politburo.

All in all, then, there has been little sustained inducement for Soviet officers to follow the route of uncontrolled involvement in national politics. For a variety of reasons having to do with basic features of the Soviet political system and specific policy choices, the scope of military participation in politics has been confined to a point well short of universality.

It should also be emphasized that even if one or more of the factors conducive to greater involvement had been at work, a movement toward military rule would not have been the necessary result. An officer corps satisfied that its institutional interests were not in jeopardy might well have withstood pressures from private groups, ascriptive feelings, or even civilian politicians to move decisively into national politics. For instance, had Trotsky issued a call for active military support—for occupation of the Kremlin, for example, or arrest of Stalin or Zinoviev—army leaders would have had to consider whether their best interests and those of the subordinates whose cooperation was essential would be favored by complying with such an order. Officers would have been unlikely to commit themselves to the use of illegitimate force, the decisive step on the path to military rule, unless their corporate interests had been engaged.

Interest and Intervention

Intervention, the second major path to army rule, entails escalation of the means which military officers use to promote or defend their normal range of institutional interests. I have argued that, despite practical and ideological constraints, the Soviet military has probably been capable of staging a successful intervention. There is no way of knowing the exact form this might have taken in the past or may take in the future. The locus of initial military disaffection, the timing of the decision to employ force, the methods used to attract officers' support, the tensions within the officer corps, the response of the regime and of its coercive apparatus, the relation to the aspirations of other segments of society, the ideological coloring given to rebellion or ultimatum—all of these would be contingent upon circumstance and interrelated in complex ways, as is likely with a military attempt to usurp civilian authority in any society.

Rather than speculate about the particulars of a possible intervention, the analysis should consider the broader set of conditions under which—given our knowledge of the determinants of intervention in other societies and our appraisal of the capabilities of the

Soviet Army—it can be argued that such an action would be conceivable. We can assume that, as in other political systems, intervention would occur after a protracted process of politicization of the majority of officers and of their estrangement from the civilian regime. This alienation would be available for mobilization for the purpose of forceful political action by the high command, by a formal or informal group situated elsewhere in the army, or by a civil-military coalition of some kind. (As is generally true in politics, feelings or deprivation could be harnessed effectively or ineffectively and could be used to support a number of courses of action.) It can be presumed that the solidity of civilian obstacles to the use or threat of force would make it likely that only widespread, profound, and cumulative dissatisfaction could move officers to support illegitimate action as a reasonably cohesive unit. (Even in such a case the military would not act as a monolith, any more than it has in less turbulent contexts.) The magnitude and mix of the grievances needed to push a sufficient number of officers over the brink cannot be discerned with precision. Nonetheless, certain general statements can be made about the interaction which might produce such a sense of discontent—that between officers' interests and the party policies that affect them.

Unable to interview senior Soviet officers, I have had to make inferences about what they are interested in from their public statements and from other data, including data on officer preferences in other societies. Not all this information, or indeed of the information on policy output, is satisfactory, and not all officers are alike. Statements about the conjuncture between military preference and civilian policy must thus be phrased in probabilistic rather than absolute terms, and allowances must be made for differences among individuals and over time.

On most internal issues and a number of quite narrowly defined institutional questions the preferences of Soviet officers display considerable variation according to rank, station, and other attributes. Without assuming complete uniformity of opinion, this section will deal with issues that are of intense concern to most members of the officer corps, on which generalizations about corporate or institutional preference can be proffered with reasonable certainty (subject always to modification for particular groups and individuals), and that are capable of resolution only by decision of politicians outside the army. The institutional preferences or interests of military officers on such issues will be divided along four dimensions of value—ideological, material, status, and professional. On each dimension we will examine Soviet policy and compare it to practice in other societies. Brief consideration will also be given to the sequence and combination of policy outputs.

What such an analysis shows is that party policies on most institutional issues and at most times have indeed been consistent with the apparent preferences of most officers. Stalin's claim that in the Soviet Union the army was "loved, respected, and cared for [as] nowhere else in the world" possessed, for all its bluster (and irony in relation to some of his own actions), a residue of truth.[21] On the whole the army and its leaders have been quite well cared for. Their interests have been dealt with in such a way as to make the military, as Marshal Malinovskii characterized it in 1958, "profoundly grateful" to the regime.[22]

Ideological Interests. If army officers have subscribed to a wide range of ideological beliefs, they have displayed more consistency concerning the form of government commitment to ideological values. Two preferences stand out, each related to the military's specialized function.

The first is for openness and declarativeness by civilian leaders in the pursuit of ideological goals. Although government failure in this respect is never the sole cause of military discontent, it is often an important contributing factor. Military officers have generally favored explicit adherence to a public philosophy, on the grounds that this lends import to their work and provides a basis for mobilizing the soldiers under their command. Officers, as de Gaulle said, require "an ideal to serve them as a rallying point, to kindle their enthusiasm, and to give them greater stature."[23]

Second, officers have strongly preferred that governments realize their ideological goals through enhancement of the unity and prestige of the nation-state they serve. This, too, is a predictable concomitant of military professionalism. As John Stuart Mill argued, it is understandable that national awareness should be "deepest and strongest" among soldiers, to whom foreigners "are men against whom [they] may be called, at a week's notice, to fight for life or death."[24] Officers have thus been predisposed toward strong nationalism in foreign policy and firm centralism in domestic affairs, opposing concessions to regional or ethnic minorities in countries such as Spain, Pakistan, and Burma. Their stance is likely to be unclear only when there is uncertainty about the boundaries of the nation or when the officer corps itself is divided along communal lines.

The Soviet regime's performance has generally been consistent with both of these interests. On the first score, it has hardly been reluctant to give the military an ideological rallying point. Many officers, especially in the early years, responded by embracing the official ideology as an article of intense individual faith. In 1926 the director of the Marx-Engels Institute felt it necessary to scold a military audience for containing "hot-headed men who in their sleep and in their waking hours dream only of the beautiful day when they will fight and destroy the entire bourgeois world."[25] Even during the purge, ideology retained sufficient vitality to comfort some of the victims. It could tide Serpilin, the regiment commander in Simonov's *Days and Nights*, through four years in prison during which "he never once blamed the Soviet regime for what had been done to him. He considered it a monstrous misunderstanding, a mistake, an absurdity. And Communism remained for him a sacred and unsullied thing."[26]

This language of personal salvation is evidently of far less moment to some modern-day officers who feel, as one marshal remarked wistfully in 1969, "a certain incomprehensible skepticism" about the ultimate purposes of their work.[27] Yet, even in a postrevolutionary era, the party's secular morality does seem to add meaning to the lives of many military men. One need not accredit the official accolades about officers' boundless devotion to Communist ideals to realize that many find the party's ethic of service and sacrifice a congenial one and want these values preserved against the acid of unbelief and worldliness. On a more practical level, ideology remains a useful torch for kindling the enthusiasm of conscripts who must be taught to fight and risk death.

Party performance relative to the military's second ideological interest—national unity and prestige—has been equally positive, and perhaps more enduring. In domestic politics, the officer corps' natural tendency to support the regime's centralist policies has been accentuated by its domination by ethnic Russians and the two other Slavic nationalities, Ukrainian and Belorussian, most prone to Russification. While comprehensive statistics are not available, Table 13 shows that Russians have been heavily overrepresented among senior officers, with Ukrainians and Belorussians making up most of the rest and four minor nationalities (Armenian, Osetin, Polish, and Jewish) also overrepresented in most periods. All others—including the Central Asian peoples whose share of the Soviet population is increasing rapidly— have been radically underrepresented.[28]

The Russian and Slav-dominated officer corps—perhaps the most thoroughly Russian of all the Soviet elites—has had little cause for complaint about the party's success in reunifying almost all the former Russian lands and combining theoretical federalism with practical concentration of government power. This is a course military leaders have consistently supported (and can be expected to support in future), out of both principle and military expediency (as "a foundation of the might of our multinational armed forces").[29]

In relation to the external world, party performance has also been such as to meet with military approval. Officers have obviously de-

Table 13. Nationality of senior military officers (by percent)

Nationality	All marshals and equiva- lents 1935-75 (N=144)[a]	Senior commanders					Soviet population 1970
		1958 (N=40)	1962 (N=38)	1966 (N=36)	1970 (N=40)	1974 (N=42)	
Russian	71.5	60.0	57.9	58.3	62.5	64.3	53.4
Ukrainian	18.8	25.0	21.1	25.0	25.0	26.3	16.9
Belorussian	3.5	2.5	7.9	5.6	7.5	7.1	3.7
Armenian	2.8	2.5	5.3	5.6	0.0	0.0	1.5
Osetin	1.4	5.0	5.3	5.6	2.5	0.0	0.2
Polish	1.4	2.5	0.0	0.0	0.0	0.0	0.5
Jewish	0.7	2.5	2.6	0.0	0.0	0.0	0.9
All others	0.0	0.0	0.0	0.0	2.5	2.4	22.9

Sources: For column 1, published biographies in a variety of sources. Nationality was positively determined for 110 officers. For 25 whose surnames end in -ov, -ev, or -in, nationality was assumed to be Russian; the same assumption was made for 3 others (I. D. Cherniakhovskii, S. A. Krasovskii, G. E. Peredel'skii), any of whom could be Ukrainian, Belorussian, or Polish. Six officers were assumed to be Ukrainians (I. R. Apanasenko, Ia. N. Fedorenko, V. K. Kharchenko, O. A. Losik, I. I. Pstygo, S. M. Shtemenko). For columns 2 to 6, various editions of Deputaty Verkhovnogo Soveta SSSR (Moscow, Izvestiia) and other biographical sources were used. For only 3 men in these columns could nationality not be positively ascertained—A. T. Chabanenko (assumed to be Ukrainian), A. V. Gerasimov (assumed to be Russian), and A. V. Gelovani (assumed to be Georgian). Column 7 was calculated from Izvestiia, April 17, 1971, p. 2.

a. Marshals and equivalents include 2 political officers. Senior commanders occupy same posts as in Table 12.

rived great satisfaction from the transformation of Russia from the weak sister of Europe into a leading continental and world power, all the more so because this has been bound up so closely with military accomplishment. "Naturally," reads a typical military statement (in Zhukov's memoirs), "one feels great patriotic pride in that social system thanks to which we were able to overtake and surpass militarily, in the shortest imaginable time, . . . the world's most developed states."[30]

Material Interests. Officers' material interests are rather more amenable to analysis than their ideological concerns. One obvious and basic material interest is in sheer physical safety. Officers have acted against governments or political movements that jeopardize this fundamental value. For example, it was fear of extinction that prompted officers to resist the 1965 pro-Communist rebellion in Indonesia and to oust the Sukarno regime for its seeming tolerance of the insurrectionaries. "If we hadn't killed them," one officer is said to have declared, "they would have killed us."[31]

A second interest has related to salary and living conditions. "It is true," von Seeckt observed, "that the soldier does not serve for the sake of his pay. [B]ut a state acts very imprudently if it does not relieve its most loyal and valuable servant, as far as possible, from the daily anxieties of life."[32] Concern over such mundane issues as remuneration, clothing, and sanitation has often been the starting point for officers' radicalization. Rebellious Spanish officers early in this century were embittered by their "utterly insufficient" pay.[33] Material grievances, including a sharp decline in relative salaries, were "undoubtedly significant" in politicizing French officers in the 1950s.[34] Pay for the South Korean officers who staged the 1961 coup "had no relationship to expenses," and before the 1960 takeover in Turkey officers' salaries "lag[ged] far behind the rapidly growing cost of living" and often had to be supplemented by demeaning extra employment.[35]

A third material interest has been in material security after discharge or retirement. Pensions are one means of security, and their inadequacy has been a common source of discontent, as in many of the cases just recited. In Spain, where retirement incomes were barely enough for subsistence, "the resentment aroused by this treatment found expression in political rebellion."[36] Alternative employment has been another form of security, and this is most readily available in circumstances of low unemployment, interchangeability of military and civilian skills, and active government efforts to assist former officers. None of these conditions pertained in South Korea before 1961, where many poorly trained officers who wanted to quit the army "had little or no skill that could secure satisfactory employment" and the government was indifferent to their plight.[37]

How has the Soviet regime's performance been on these three kinds of material interests? It has undoubtedly been poorest in terms of the first issue, physical safety. The great majority of Soviet officers have lived securely. But many did fall victim to officially organized or sanctioned terror under Stalin. At least a quarter of all officers were arrested or dismissed without justification during the Great Purge, and many of these were executed or perished in camps. After the war many officers returning from German captivity were incarcerated and several members of the high command fell casualty to political intrigue. Of the twelve military men (including four political officers) elected to the Central Committee between 1925 and 1934, nine were killed in the purge. All told, five marshals or equivalents were executed or died in confinement during Stalin's reign, and another nine are known to have experienced arrest, expulsion from the party, or arbitrary demotion.[38]

I have no wish to downplay the needless suffering and tragedy implied in these figures. Nevertheless, the negativeness of the record should be qualified in several ways. First, it should not be forgotten that lethal arbitrariness was confined in time. Physical insecurity has not been a permanent characteristic of military life, and it is fair to say that, at least as far as military officers were concerned, the excesses of the decade after 1937 were a deviation from general Soviet practice. The army fared relatively well before the Great Purge, and there have been no known killings of officers since the execution of a former chief of staff of the air force, Sergei A. Khudiakov, in 1950. In the second place, amends were made, however inadequate, to at least some of those who suffered. Many officers—perhaps a majority of the purge victims, although we have no statistics—went from prison or camp to wartime commands. Of the nine marshals and equivalents who survived arbitrary treatment, eight were later given major posts and five (Gorbatov, Nikolai Kuznetsov, Meretskov, Rokossovskii, and Stuchenko) became full or candidate members of the party Central Committee. A third and cardinal point is that even at the height of the terror the regime was performing positively for many officers on other dimensions of interest.

Regime performance in terms of the second material interest—pay and living conditions—has been much more clearly favorable. The starting point was conspicuously unpromising. Living conditions after the Civil War were so poor in some garrisons that they resulted in "disease, death, and crime."[39] Pay was low (Voroshilov claimed that Soviet officers did not "dream of the salaries of generals in imperialist armies"), and as late as 1925 about 70 percent of officers were quartered "extremely badly."[40] All of this improved rapidly from the mid-1920s onward. Salaries, for instance, rose by 20 to 30 percent a year and by even more in the mid-1930s; the spread between junior and senior ranks also widened markedly.[41] Other rewards and privileges were added in short order, and by 1945 the regime could justifiably claim to have done "all [it] can to steadily improve the conditions of life of our generals and officers, to heighten their material well-being, to free them from the tiresome burden of routine worldly concerns."[42]

To be sure, performance has fallen somewhat behind promise. Like all Soviet citizens, officers have chafed at the shortcomings of an underfinanced and overbureaucratized consumer economy. Their access to consumer goods has been complicated by gaps in supply (particularly of articles for officers' families), by poorly trained sales personnel, and by the standard Soviet practice of gauging economic success by quantitative rather than qualitative indicators (meaning that military stores prefer to stock and sell large and expensive items even if the demand for them is not great). Despite repeated campaigns for improvement (the latest of them centering around an army-wide conference on living conditions in December 1977), fresh fruits, vegetables, and dairy products are still missing from many military shelves and dining halls. There are complaints about lack of services and repair facilities in officers' housing, especially outside the large towns (a problem that was considerably worsened by the transfer of large forces to remote areas adjacent to China in the 1960s). Quarters for young officers are sometimes shabby, overcrowded, and short on furniture, showers, and "the amenities of normal life and work."[43] It is no wonder that a survey of military cadets in 1969 found that almost half of those in their graduating year expected future difficulties in living conditions (bytovye trudnosti).[44]

Nevertheless, these irritations should not overshadow the fact that Soviet officers clearly occupy a privileged material position. Most of the disabilities they face are felt more acutely by civilians, and most diminish markedly with progress through the ranks. Many officers have undoubtedly felt like the young lieutenant who chose a military career in the early 1960s because "in the army, as nowhere else, there is a salary, clothing, a pension, and all the rest."[45] In the mid-1950s, the last time for which exact information on salaries is available, officers earned two to four times as much as civilians with comparable qualifications and responsibilities. Western analysts agree that this differential has narrowed, but also that a military career still offers pronounced material advantages, especially at senior levels.[46] A survey of Leningrad secondary school students in the mid-1960s showed widespread awareness of these advantages, as students rated military officer eighth of eighty occupations in terms of expected salary benefits.[47] In addition to high pay, officers enjoy numerous other perquisites—orderlies for officers ranking colonel and higher; a separate commercial network (Voentorg) with relatively plentiful consumer items, sometimes at reduced prices; cheap lodging and, often, preferential access to desirable urban apartments; interest-free loans for building houses and cottages to officers with ranks of major and above and twenty-five years' experience; free health care, special clinics and sanatoria, and other personal services; individual garden plots after twenty years; discounts and special accommodation on civilian transportation, varying with rank; and a special tourist organization which served 200,000 officers in 1976.[48]

Turning briefly to the third category of material interest—security after retirement or discharge—we also find generally forthcoming policy performance. Officers have been among the several pension elites of Soviet society, with pensions rising from 50 percent of salary after twenty-five years' service to 75 percent at thirty-four years. There is no statutory ceiling on these payments, and they can be received in full along with other income. Service-related disability pensions are usually 75 percent of salary.[49] Officers from the highest echelons can acquire personal pensions that are very generous indeed. Zhukov is said to have retired in 1958 at the equivalent of $1,375 a month, almost twenty times the minimum wage.[50] Besides pensions, generals and all officers with twenty-five years' service have the right to retain their military housing. Since 1953 local soviets have been required to set aside for reserve and retired officers 10 percent of all new housing allocated by ministries (an obligation which not all have fulfilled without prodding).[51]

Securing alternative employment for officers discharged prematurely was not a major problem before the war, when the officer corps was expanding steadily, or during postwar demobilization, when the 1.2 million officers released were mostly wartime recruits and included only 2.5 percent of all officers with a higher military education.[52] Dislocation was somewhat more severe during the demobilization of the late 1950s and would have been much worse had Khrushchev carried out his abortive force reduction plan of 1960, which would have released 250,000 officers, all professionals. In preparation for the crisis, legislation in early 1960 guaranteed all demobilized officers admission to civilian universities without entrance examinations and provided travel allowances, retraining stipends, supplements to civilian wages (the amount to be determined by the Ministry of Defense), and preferential access to housing in large cities.[53]

The discharged officers of the late 1950s were apparently assimilated with reasonable success into civilian employment. As of January 1960 some 96 percent of the officers demobilized in the Moscow and Leningrad military districts in the previous six years had obtained employment, almost half of them in responsible posts comparable to their prior military appointments. Although Defense Minister Malinovskii cited "not a few cases" of failure, he was able to claim that the problem had been successfully managed.[54] Since 1960 no major cohort of officers has entered retirement prematurely. The opportunities to supplement pensions have been considerably increased by the expansion of paramilitary education and civil defense since the mid-1960s.

Clearly the regime has been sensitive to the political implications of early release of officers and has devoted considerable resources to remedies. Its task has been eased by the dynamism of the economy and by the chronic shortage of labor, especially of technically proficient workers and administrative personnel. Also useful has been the increasing interchangeability of military and civilian skills which has accompanied the army's modernization. By 1974 half of all officers were engineers or technicians—70 percent in the missile forces, the service most likely to be curtailed by arms control agreements—most of them thus possessing expertise easily transferable to the civilian economy in any future demobilization.[55] Many undoubtedly would find, like one reserve captain employed as an instrument technican at a metallurgical plant in 1957, that his knowledge of military technology "helped me master my new specialty quickly."[56]

Status Interests. Like any group, military officers want favorable status recognition from other members of society. But the relationship between status and political behavior is a complicated one. Since officers' status is determined mainly by complex historical and cultural factors rather than by government policy, failure to achieve high status is unlikely on its own to produce political discontent. Officers with low corporate status have rebelled (as in Nigeria), but so have officers with high status (as in Japan in the 1930s). Conversely, officer corps with similar levels of status (for example in Pakistan and India in the 1950s) have displayed very different political behavior.[57]

What does result from government action, however, is the relationship between officer status and the social standing of the groups from which officers are recruited. An officer whose professional status is lower than that of the stratum into which he was born can easily blame this disparity on the government which brought him into military service.[58] If recruitment policy produces rough parity between professional and original status, the officer is likely to feel neither resentment nor gratitude.

Two kinds of recruitment policy are likely to meet with military favor. One is selection from groups whose status is already high and is maintained at that level by some other aspect of government policy (for instance, policy on land tenure or inheritance of titles or offices), and for whom military service is, as de Tocqueville put it, a way "to find an honorable employment for the idle years of . . . youth." This was the course followed by most European regimes until the nineteenth century and implemented by devices such as deliberate selection of aristocrats and sale of commissions. A second option is to choose officers from social groups of much lower station for whom military status is therefore an improvement on original status. De Tocqueville was the first to note the tranquilizing effects of such a policy, arguing that a man from the lower classes who has risen to an officer's post is likely to be politically conservative. "He has gained a footing in a sphere above that which he filled in civil life . . . He is willing to pause after so great an effort and to enjoy what he has won."[59]

What is the social status of military officers in the Soviet Union? We have limited information on the relative appeal of a military career. One handbook reports three or four applicants for every available place in officer training schools. Secondary school teachers in Nizhnii Tagil surveyed in 1965-67 rated military officer eleventh among thirty prospective occupations for recommendation to their students. On a ten-point scale, officer rated 8.1, close to the 8.3 average for professional and white-collar (*intelligentsiia*) jobs and well above the 7.3 and 4.0 averages for worker and service categories.[60]

The survey of Leningrad students cited earlier has more discriminating data. In terms of overall attractiveness (*privekatel'nost'*), the students gave officer a slightly higher rating than did the Nizhnii Tagil teachers, twenty-fifth of eighty. But they appraised the prestige (*prestizh*) of an army career separately and rated it considerably higher than attractiveness—tenth of eighty, outranked only by careers in scientific research. The main reason for the disparity was the low rating (thirtieth) assigned to creativity (*tvorchestvo*), the quality found to be most closely associated with overall attractiveness. Officers were viewed as having very high status, but as paying for this by accepting infringements on individual autonomy and self-expression.[61]

Military status has perhaps eroded somewhat as Soviet society has modernized, as statements by senior commanders and MPA officials about public attitudes toward the military imply. Nevertheless, the erosion has been slight. The officer corps remains a group held in high esteem, plainly higher than that of the great majority of occupational groups. There seems no reason to doubt Raymond Garthoff's judgment that the status of military men in the Soviet Union is "unsurpassed among contemporary world powers."[62]

While government policy has never fully lived up to commanders' and political officers' expectations, it has certainly contributed directly to military status. The army's place in the official political culture has been second as an institution only to that of the party. The army and individual officers remain immune from criticism in the official media (although the visitor to the Soviet Union hears the occasional private remark that is less complimentary). The regime devotes great effort to idealizing and popularizing the images of the armed forces, of their achievements, of military service, and of military-related and patriotic values and myths.

More significant than the direct impact of policy on military status has been the effect on the relation between officers' professional status and the statuses into which they were born. Through its recruitment and promotion policies, the party has emphatically followed the second path to gratifying officers' status interests—promotion of upward social mobility. A military career has been a major avenue of advancement for men from the lower social strata which the party claims as its natural constituency.

Khrushchev voiced the official version of the policy and its effects in 1958: "Napoleon's saying that every soldier carries a marshal's baton in his knapsack was only a saying. But our generals and marshals have indeed all travelled the road from soldier or worker to marshal or general."[63] This statement is somewhat misleading, as Table 14 shows. The most common origin for senior officers has been peasant rather than worker. Moreover, throughout the interwar period the officer corps included a sizable contingent of survivals from the prerevolutionary class structure—former tsarist officers, among them members of the old nobility, as well as men from commercial, professional, and administrative backgrounds. Such persons were found disproportionately in senior posts.[64]

Nonetheless, the long-term product of policy has been an officer corps dominated by men of humble beginnings, attracted to military service by its status and by the prospects of in-career education (especially important for former peasants) and rapid advancement. By the 1930s men from peasant and working class families (who were given preferential admission to some military schools until the war) were assuming preponderance even in top positions, a tendency accelerated by the rapid growth of the officer corps and the vacancies created by the purge.[65] For many of them the regime and its army made the difference between a life of tedium in village or factory and a career of high prestige and opportunity in a modern sector of society which would have been barred to them under the tsarist system. The majority were peasants. Neither Tukhachevskii, the scion of a landless aristocratic family, not Voroshilov, the son of a railroad worker and a long-time party organizer, was the epitome of the new military elite. Much more typical was Admiral Kuznetsov, a peasant with only three grades of church school when he volunteered for the navy in 1919; or Zhukov, who was born in a decrepit peasant hut, began work in the fields at age six, and labored throughout his teens as a furrier's assistant; or Malinovskii, who was the son of a peasant migrant to Odessa and worked as a boy as an agricultural laborer.[66]

Table 14 testifies to the continuity in the social origins of senior officers, but note must also be made of major changes which have been under way since the war. There is evidence that increasing numbers of

Table 14. Social origins of officers (by percent)

Sample[a]	Social origin			
	Unknown	Peasant	Worker	Other
All commanders, 1921	-	67	12	21
All commanders, 1923	-	52.7	13.6	33.7
All commanders, 1926	-	57.2	16.0	26.8
Platoon and company commanders, 1926	-	61.4	18.0	20.6
Battalion and regiment commanders, 1926	-	46.0	9.3	44.7
Division commanders and higher, 1926	-	31.2	7.3	61.5
Division commanders and higher, 1935-39 (N=60)	3.3	36.7	20.0	40.0
Marshals and equivalents, 1935-75 (N=139)	13.7	47.5	25.9	12.9
General and colonels deceased 1956-75 (N=850)	29.9	33.9	30.0	6.2
All generals and admirals, 1970	-	54.3	24.4	21.3

Sources: For the first to sixth samples, K. E. Voroshilov, *Stat'i i rechi* (Moscow, Partizdat, 1937), p. 153; A. S. Bubnov et al., *Grazhdanskaia voina 1918-1921*, 3 vols. (Moscow, Voennyi vestnik, 1928-30), II, 105. For the seventh and eighth samples, author's biographical files. For the ninth sample, obituaries in *Krasnaia zvezda*, 1956-75. For the final row, *Kommunist vooruzhennykh sil*, 1971, no. 4, p. 31.

a. The seventh, eighth, and ninth samples contain only officers for whom some information on birth could be found (see Appendix A). The seventh sample contains all available officers ranked *komdiv* (division commander) or higher, but excluding men falling into the next two categories. The eighth, ninth, and tenth samples include political officers.

young officers are coming from officers' families, a trend which was noted earlier with respect to political officers. The commander of the Moscow Military District since 1972, General of the Army Vladimir L. Govorov, is the son of the wartime defender of Leningrad, Marshal Leonid Govorov; in 1976 he became the first descendant of any Central Committee member to be elected to the committee. Recent press articles praise this "continuity of generations," describe how many children of officers attend military schools, draw renewed attention to the Suvorov and Nakhimov preparatory schools for officers' sons, and go so far as to speak of "military dynasties" in their second or even third generation under Soviet rule.[67] This may be solid organizational practice, but it carries with it political dangers if the status of the military profession should happen to decline during the lifetime of the sons, as happened in France prior to 1958, thus in effect making the sons downwardly mobile.[68] There is also clear evidence that the overall recruitment base for officers has shifted upward as a result of urbanization and modernization. Partial statistics indicate that only about 30 percent of young officers are now from peasant families, with a similar proportion coming from the families of industrial workers and the rest from low-status service and higher-status intelligentsiia backgrounds.[69] Thus, most officers still are upwardly mobile, but the average improvement in status during a military career is considerably less than for officers recruited in the Stalin era.

Professional Interests. The final category of military interest relates to officers' preferences as members of the military profession. These are held by officers both as individuals and as a corporate group. As individual professionals, officers want access to posts of greater prestige and responsibility within their chosen vocation. The inevitable frustration is best minimized by a government policy of promotion according to standardized rules, based usually on a combination of seniority, formal training, and demonstrated ability. When promotion loses this predictability, and particularly when it is impeded or blocked at some crucial level, officer frustrations flare.

Promotion blockages are complex phenomena, but four common patterns can be identified. These occur when governments: allow domination of high military posts by foreigners, either from a ruler's own nationality (as in Egypt before the Urabi revolt of 1881) or from a more advanced foreign power (as with the British officers in Jordan before 1957); assign high posts by particularistic criteria such as kinship or personal favoritism (as in Spain in the nineteenth century); promote officers indiscriminately to middle and high levels, then fail to retire them after superannuation (as in Turkey before 1960); or create a disproportionately large cohort of middle-ranking officers by stopping or suddenly curtailing growth of the officer corps after an interval of rapid expansion (as in South Korea in the 1950s).[70]

The Soviet regime has managed to avoid each of these pitfalls. There has, of course, been no monopolization of top posts by foreigners. Nor does the evidence suggest major congestion of peak positions by incompetent favorites of civilian leaders. There has been one striking case of cronyism (Stalin's elevation of his former Civil War comrades in the late 1930s), but these men were few in number, and the most egregiously improficient of them were removed from positions of major influence early in the war.[71]

Career mobility has been greatly aided by the dynamics of organizational growth. For forty of the fifty-eight years of its history up to 1976 (1918-21, 1927-45, 1948-55, 1960-61, 1965-76), the military establishment has been an expanding organization (growing rapidly in the first three waves, slightly in the fourth, gradually in the last). It has been in contraction for only fourteen years (1921-23, 1945-48, 1955-60, 1961-65), and in only one of these intervals (1955-60) were sizable numbers of professional officers discharged prematurely.[72] At times of stability or incremental growth, promotion has been without major bottlenecks. During the long swells of expansion in the first four decades, advancement was very rapid indeed. General Gorbatov, who rose from soldier to commander of a cavalry brigade during only fifteen months of the Civil War, later compared his progress to a fairy tale come true.[73] For many, advancement was equally precipitous during the 1930s, when the officer corps grew by 118 percent in the infantry between 1934 and 1939 alone (and by even more in technical arms).[74]

Three specific policy choices have improved officers' career mobility. First, politically inspired purges or premature retirements have twice removed large numbers of senior officers—men from the old army in the early 1920s, the heart of the high command during the Great Purge—and thereby created "room at the top" for ambitious newcomers.

Second, the regime has prudently refused to permit large numbers of redundant officers to remain in service following organizational contraction. Its flexibility in this regard has been aided by the liberality of pension arrangements. When size has stabilized, in the 1920s and again since the late 1950s, it has been only after release of excess personnel. The short-term cost paid by those discharged has worked to the long-term benefit of those who have remained. After the Civil War the army command was trimmed by 55 percent in only one year; as late as 1926 it was actually 7 percent below its authorized strength.[75] A similarly determined curtailment, involving mainly non-career officers, followed 1945. In the 1950s it was mainly military professionals who were discharged prematurely. Although there was some evidence that retention of war veterans was interfering with normal circulation in the 1960s, by the early 1970s two thirds of all officers serving at the regiment level and below were less than thirty years of age.[76]

Third, the regime has chosen to promote and reward its officers in general accord with the kinds of standardized rules preferred by military men. Since the reform of the mid-1920s the army has followed the modern "up-or-out" system of military promotion found in most Western armies, under which officers who fail to reach given ranks by prescribed ages are sent into the reserve rather than being allowed to clog promotion channels for younger men. The age ceilings are sometimes waived for generals and admirals holding major posts but seem to be followed quite closely elsewhere.[77]

During times of organizational stability, and particularly during the last two decades, promotion up to the age limits has followed the standard bureaucratic procedures that officers normally favor, based upon seniority, formal qualification, and assessment by superiors. The main lubricant in this machinery is the medium of informal communication and patronage that exists in most large organizations. It is not difficult to find references to "cases where officers and generals are assigned, not according to their moral and professional qualities, but on the basis of friendly relations, personal ties, and familiarity from joint work in the past."[78] Military promotion is in part a political process, but for most officers the main political stimulus comes from within the military establishment rather than from without. For men at the top of the military pyramid, it is civilian politicians' direct assessment of them which determines ultimate success, but the important point is that (with a relatively small number of exceptions under Stalin) civilians have been interested mainly in professional and organizational competence in making that assessment.[79]

Within the army, so consistently have bureaucratic standards for personnel assessment been applied that some senior officials have felt compelled to deplore their effects on individual incentive and organizational innovation. In 1961, for instance, General Beloborodov, the head of the main cadres administration, criticized "the fundamentally incorrect opinion that military rank comes automatically with the passing of years." But to buttress his point he was able to point to only 200 cases of unscheduled granting of rank in the previous year—this in an officer corps several thousand times that size.[80] Clearly some officers, particularly young ones, have longed in recent years for the more dramatic opportunities of earlier times. Beloborodov's successor noted in 1963 that some young officers "do not want to take into account the peculiarities of peacetime service, when many platoon commanders, technicians, and other specialists must work five, six, or more years in their first posts."[81] But, in general, the routinized and bureaucratized solution adopted has served the interests of most officers as well as any alternative.

In any political system military men have professional interests as a corporate group as well as individually. More than almost any other profession, they are dependent upon government for the means with which to perform their specialized function. For the officer, as de Gaulle wrote, "armed power is something essential and, as it were, sacred . . . Consequently, nothing seems to him more necessary or more urgent than to accumulate the means which will make victory certain."[82]

These means fall into three main categories: leadership, organization, and resources. Officers have rebelled against governments that: lead their armies in flagrant disregard of elementary military rationality (as in the Yemen before 1962, where the king carried the keys to all military weapons stores on his person); fail to assist in the creation of a modern structure of military administration (as in Thailand before 1932), or take actions that threaten its orderly functioning (as with government acquiescence in a sergeants' revolt in Brazil in 1964); or fail to provide the minimal resources (manpower, munitions, transport, and the like) which officers feel they need to carry out their professional task (as with the Ghana coup of 1966).[83] A common precipitant of military intervention on professional issues is war. Government initiation and leadership of armed action requires decisions in which officers' professional interests (and often their lives) are at stake. Officers can revolt against a government which they believe to be preventing victory (as in France in 1958), one which refuses to acknowledge defeat (as in France in 1940 or Portugal in 1974), or one whose incompetence is regarded as responsible for a defeat (as in Bolivia in 1936). A war can also serve to spotlight unsatisfactory government performance on issues of organization and resources (as the losing war in Palestine did for the Syrian and Egyptian armies after 1949).[84]

It would be impossible to assess in full the Soviet regime's performance vis-à-vis officers' collective professional interests without writing a detailed history of Soviet military policy. Nevertheless, the outlines of an evaluation can be drawn. On the whole, policy performance must be appraised as positive.

The regime's record on the first plane—political leadership—is uneven. Least tenable in military eyes were those of Stalin's policies which cost the army dearly in the half decade before 1941. Had the German assault penetrated only a few miles further on key fronts, more officers might have begun to think like the air force general who told friends that if he had realized the full magnitude of the initial disaster he would have ordered the bombardment of Stalin's headquarters.[85]

Still, one must seriously question whether these failures have been at all typical of political leadership in the military realm, even during Stalin's lifetime. Stalin worked amicably with many senior officers during the war. He solicited and often followed their opinions on operational and other questions. Some of his major blunders before the war (such as the decision to disband the mechanized corps in 1939, for which Zhukov was indirectly blamed after his dismissal) were taken at least partly on military advice. The same Stalin who promoted the Kuliks and Shchadenkos also recognized and rewarded the talent of the much larger cohort of Zhukovs, Rokossovskiis, and Vasilevskiis. The same Stalin who kept his generals yawning during predawn strategy sessions also personally imposed the "fantastically short deadlines" for aircraft production that intimidated designers and plant directors into supplying the generals' armies with airplanes ahead of schedule.[86]

If one takes a realistic image of civilian performance in other major states as the standard of judgment, it is reasonable to say that for most of its history the Soviet regime has led its army in a manner consistent with at least the minimum expectations of professional soldiers. Political leaders have generally respected officers' lives, have consulted and frequently deferred to them on specialized policy questions, and have in recent decades permitted open airing of many military concerns. They have been extremely reluctant to commit the armed forces to any sort of foreign conflict, doing so only when attacked or after accumulating a major prior advantage. Most important in the eyes of the generals, the party leaders have never lost a war. Khrushchev's "dilettantism," criticized by military and MPA leaders after his demise, was to some degree at odds with this tradition. It has yielded under Brezhnev to a more cautious style of leadership in which the right of officers to consultation is explicitly acknowledged and the army seems to have more frequent and more secure access to civilian authorities.[87]

On the second plane of professional interest, the regime has amply fulfilled the military's organizational requirements. Its commitment to a regular cadre army has been firm since the early 1920s. It has also supported, since early in the Civil War, a modern system of military command and administration based upon the principles of centralized planning and direction, hierarchical discipline, and assignment and promotion of personnel on the basis of performance. The system of penalties and rewards within the party's own organs in the army has worked largely to reinforce military discipline.

On the final question, of resources devoted to the army's professional needs, the regime's record has been unflaggingly positive. It has lived up to Lenin's commitment to "satisfy the needs of the army first of all."[88] Soviet industrialization created an armaments industry that was to outproduce Germany in World War II and subsequently to rival in quantity and quality the output of a global adversary, the United States, with an immensely superior productive and technological base. Military uses have claimed a share of national income that rose steadily from the late 1920s to a wartime peak of around 40 percent and has never since stood at below 10 percent. Defense industry is undoubtedly the most privileged segment of the economy. Its plants receive the highest resource priorities, laying first claim to investment capital, scientific and managerial talent, materials, and scheduling.[89] Defense industry is the only segment of the Soviet economy which is dominated by customers; military representatives scrutinize all production and refuse to accept items of low quality, a luxury rarely open to the Soviet consumer.[90] Real military outlays per man under arms, a useful index of the intensity of defense allocations, quadrupled between 1928 and 1937, remained at approximately that level for two decades, then multiplied about four times by the early 1970s. In 1973 the Soviet Union ranked on this index fifth of 136 countries surveyed by the U.S. Arms Control and Disarmament Agency, behind only the United States, Switzerland, Canada, and Israel. (The Soviet Union's gross national product per capita, on the other hand, stood twenty-fourth.)[91]

The results are a matter of clear historical record. A regime that came to power in the shambles of a lost war has built and lavishly equipped one of history's most formidable fighting machines. The special world of military-related research has accounted for many of the country's major scientific innovations. At high cost Soviet troops now bestride a third of Europe, Soviet ships ply every ocean, and Soviet rockets bristle at most of the world's great cities. Few could contest Brezhnev's statement that the party "spares neither energy nor resources for defense."[92]

Sequences and Combinations of Outputs. It should be evident from even this summary account that there has been considerable variation over time in policy on each dimension of military interest and in the mix of outputs. This complicates the analytic perspective. In particular, it raises questions about military behavior in several key periods.

One such period is the painful several years after Civil War demobilization. It is quite clear that this time of transition found the officer corps, as Frunze said in 1924 (in a speech so sensitive it was not published until 1966), in "an extremely difficult position."[93] Ideological fervor was at low ebb, material circumstances were straitened, prospects for promotion were dismal, and the troops were poorly armed and trained. The response of many officers was to exit. By January 1923 only 15 percent of the 1918-22 graduates of military schools, most of them from the class of 1918, remained in service.[94] Many simply deserted their commands, joining the "hundreds and thousands of broken men, without occupations, accustomed only to war as a profession," whom Lenin described to the Tenth Party Congress as spreading banditism in the countryside.[95] Even in 1924 the situation was serious enough to warrant what Frunze characterized as a mass demobilization of platoon and company commanders whose frame of mind, he implied, was disgruntled enough to threaten political as well as organizational stability.

This near crisis was mitigated by greatly improved policy performance on pay, living conditions, career mobility, and other issues, beginning with the 1924-25 military reform. This period awaits its historian in the West. But perhaps more puzzling is officers' behavior during another and more terrible period, one which has received more attention from scholars—the Great Purge. Why, one must ask, did the army accept the purge? Most explanations stress the two factors analyzed in Chapter 10 as limiting the army's political capabilities—coercion and ideology. Certainly neither is to be dismissed outright. Secret police compulsion was massive and pitiless, and ideology did reconcile some officers to their doom. Nonetheless, it is difficult to accept that officers were completely impotent on either dimension. A forceful intervention might have been attempted and might have succeeded. (Indeed, it is not far-fetched to suggest that a military conspiracy as ambitious as the one which the secret police claimed existed around Tukhachevskii and his colleagues might have proved successful.) An adequate comprehension of why rebellion did not occur can be achieved only by taking into account the regime's policy performance before and during the purge.

This pattern of policy was of great relevance to the victims, who were among the most obvious beneficiaries of Soviet rule, "men to whom the state had given everything, absolutely everything," as one officer described them.[96] It was due mainly to this fact that most were fundamentally quiescent, joining the ranks of those whom Solzhenitsyn has called the victims "who were guilty of nothing and were therefore unprepared to put up any resistance whatsoever."[97] Not only had they learned to perceive the bosses as benefactors, they had done and intended nothing which a calculating leadership (something the group around Stalin in 1937 obviously was not) could consider deserving of punishment. There were some who read their own destruction into unfolding events (though rarely out of a sense of guilt), but so great was the sense of commitment to the regime that such foresight was rare. Ivan Belov, a senior officer who sat on the tribunal that convicted Tukhachevskii and the others, told a friend after the trial, "Tomorrow I will be seated in their place." Yet even Belov had forgotten his earlier prescience seven months later when, as the commander of the Belorussian Military District (and successor to Uborevich, one of the men he had helped condemn), he, too, was called to Moscow. Pacing the corridor of his train, this good Stalinist simply could not believe that an NKVD van would meet him at the other end. He stared blankly out the window, reminiscing with fellow passengers, returning "over and over again" in bafflement "to the reason for his summons to Moscow."[98]

Policy performance and the loyalty it produced were also of great relevance to the officers who escaped. Like their colleagues who helped swell Stalin's camps, most of them were also "men to whom the state had given everything." Unlike them, they also found some of their interests being served, sometimes in perverse ways, by other aspects of public policy during the purge and even by the purge itself. As Chapter 6 brought out, the terror meant "dizzying upward flights" for those who survived and for the new men entering the rapidly expanding officer corps. The system confronted them with paradoxes at once inviting and cruel. It pulled the able and ambitious upward, yet promised them insecurity when they reached the top; it destroyed the best of one generation of officers, but offered dazzling opportunities to the next; it made individual soldiers tremble, but put the soldiers' institution at the very heart of the national enterprise.

However one appraises the purge experience, the fact remains that for most of Soviet history public policy has been much more consistently considerate of military interests on all four dimensions. Between the mid-1920s and the purge, most officers' ideological interests were being served by the regime's revolutionism and nationalism, their material interests by drastically improving living conditions, their status interests by rapid social mobility, and their professional interests by steady career mobility and investment of much of the increment to national production in military hardware and technology. The picture of policy performance for most of the postwar period is similarly favorable although with a somewhat different mix of outputs. Stalin's death marked a watershed on several scores—notably the security of individual military officers and their freedom to articulate certain kinds of demands—but on many key issues no pronounced change took place in 1953. On some of these the most important changes occurred during Stalin's lifetime; on others, one is struck more by continuity than by change of any kind. Nationalism has now clearly displaced revolutionism as the chief output on the ideological dimension. Material benefits remain high, and for the first time provisions have had to be put into effect for large numbers of retired and discharged officers. Social mobility has declined somewhat for younger officers, but the military elite is still predominantly composed of the sons of peasants and workers. Career mobility is still safeguarded by the army's promotion system, although the spectacular advancements of earlier years are now uncommon. The share of national resources devoted to the military effort has declined, yet the absolute quantity continues to rise and to be applied in ever greater concentration. Stalin's judgment that the soldier's task, defense, is "the basic question for us" has not been revised by his successors. They continue to proclaim defense as "the most important task of the Soviet state," and their actions bear out their words.[99]

It is beyond question that by comparative standards most aspects of this policy performance have been outstanding. It is beyond doubt also that party policies have powerfully affected the army's political stance—more, I would suggest, than any other factor—making it an institution with as strong a vested interest as any in the Soviet order.

It is not necessary to accept Solzhenitsyn's haunting portrait of Major-General Aleksandr Beliaev, his fellow prisoner at the Kaluga Gates camp in Moscow after the war, as that of the typical Soviet officer—Beliaev with "his excellent leather coat, no doubt foreign-made," his expensive cigarette lighter, his haughtiness and his devotion to the regime unruffled even by his arrest on trumped-up charges. A decade earlier or later, Beliaev might have pursued his rounds in a more or less normal setting, like thousands of his fellow officers. Yet the fact that he could retain his faith and sense of privilege in as abnormal a setting as this underlines the need to look for explanations of military behavior that rest on factors other than coercion (which did not intimidate Beliaev) and ideology (which did not interest him). Typical or not, Beliaev's demeanor and experience raise the kind of question about the individual and the formative (and deformative) power of political action that perhaps only a poet can pose properly. "What about me?" Solzhenitsyn inquires. "Why couldn't they have made the same sort of general out of me in the course of twenty years?" His answer, as chilling as the wind that he and Beliaev shared at Kaluga Gates: "Of course they could have."[100]

Civil-Military Relations
and Soviet Development

12

The fact that the Soviet military has not exercised its potential for disruptive political action cannot be explained in terms of party mechanisms for penetration and control of the military command. One can understand the microrelationship between the command corps and the specialized party apparatus which interlocks with it only by taking into account compatible objectives and crosscutting interests. It is in similar terms that the macrorelationship between the army and the party as a whole should be appreciated. There has been ample room for military participation in Soviet politics. The scope of this participation has remained well short of universality because officers have not been subject to the specific pressures which have enlarged it in other societies. And officers have not been motivated to use forceful means to pursue their corporate interests because in many ways these interests have been well served by public policy.

Contrary to the assumption of much Western analysis, army-party relations have not been dominated by unrelenting conflict on the single question of overall political supremacy. Roman Kolkowicz is typical in summarizing the relationship in terms of a central struggle for influence: "As in zero-sum games, where any advantage of one adversary is at the expense of the other adversary, so the Party elite regards any increment in the military's prerogatives and authority as its own loss and therefore as a challenge."[1] I would argue that the relationship between the two institutions has had more resemblance to what conflict theorists refer to as a variable-sum game, one that can produce mutual benefit. The party-army interplay has not produced a single victor, the party, relying for uneasy ascendancy on a repertoire of coercive and manipulative devices. Clearly *both* army and party have benefited from the relationship. The party, on the one hand, has realized important policy goals and has been spared the challenges from an aroused officer corps that have beset civilian regimes in so many other political systems, particularly in modernizing societies. The army, on the other hand, has had its ideological, material, status, and professional interests maintained and enhanced by party policy.

It is not being claimed here that there has been complete unanimity on every issue. On a few scores, outright civil-military tensions are probably of some importance. More commonly, military reservations about policy have been shared with important segments of the party machine. What is crucial to recognize is that such conflicts as have occurred have taken place in a larger setting characterized by consensus on the military's role in society and military satisfaction with key party policies.

The reasons for this substantial congruence of interest have been many, and detailed analysis of them is beyond the scope of this book. Any such analysis would have to delve further than this study, with its focus on military officers and party officials in the military realm, into experiences and attitudes in a wide range of civilian institutions—among them the military-industrial complex and the civilian party apparatus. Ultimately the discussion would have to come to terms with the compatibility between party values and military values. If Robert Michels could be struck in 1911 with how Western socialist discourse was lacking "hardly even a phrase of barrack slang,"[2] the observer of Soviet Communism must be even more impressed with the military imagery in Lenin's and Stalin's writings, with the martial tone of the early five-year plans, and even with how the party's current program refers to it as a great army.[3]

Underpinning this transinstitutional agreement in values and style has been a firm concurrence of practical objectives. Military officers have found the party to be responsive to their major policy concerns. The party, in turn, has given priority to developing military capabilities, primarily because of its instinct for self-preservation. Lenin was not exaggerating when he said that the decision to build the Red Army had been dictated by "urgent, vital necessity."[4] Apart from survival, the regime has always made the same direct correlation between military strength and its ability to pursue a whole range of highly valued objectives in world politics which Frunze saw in the 1920s: "The stronger and more powerful [the army] is, and the more it is a threat to our enemies, then the more our interests will be served."[5] Although the details of military policy are determined by political give-and-take, the process of bargaining and decision has occurred within a context of mutual understanding that a strong army means that the party's own goals will be advanced.

This revised image of Soviet military politics casts light on theories of civil-military relations and on Western approaches to Soviet politics and to political development in general. It is also useful in considering the possibilities for the army's participation in future Soviet politics.

Theories of Civil-Military Relations

In recent years empirical research on civil-military relations has sprouted vigorously. Already stimulated by the cold war and the heightened salience of national security issues in many Western societies, research has been imparted new impetus by the widespread rise of soldiers to political ascendancy in non-Western countries. Yet the accumulation of case studies has not been matched by the development of theory.

Most overviews, particularly those which attempt to explain usurpation of civilian power, continue to focus either on the characteristics of military organizations or on structural or cultural variables at the level of the political system.[6] It is submitted here that neither a military-specific nor a general societal interpretation is satisfactory. Any examination of the military alone can furnish no more than a partial explanation of its roles in politics. "Military explanations," as Samuel Huntington points out, "do not explain military interventions."[7] Yet societal explanations (such as Huntington's own model of the praetorian society) are also fraught with difficulties. If a discussion of the motivational and social structure of the officer corps is excessively narrow, a preoccupation with political culture and the general attributes of the political system is too broad. So inclusive a focus often does little to help us understand why military officers are more active and more successful than other groups in society, why particular armies intervene at particular times, or how civilian institutions succeed in acquiring legitimacy in the eyes of military elites.

No theory of civil-military relations can be complete without careful analysis of the *interactions* between the military establishment and the overall political system and its rulers. In the Soviet Union, interactions across the civil-military boundary have been of vital importance in the evolution of the military party apparatus, the making of political decisions on military issues, and the development of the long-term alignments between institutions. Army-party relations as a whole cannot, of course, be understood without analysis of the army and its leaders or without study of the party's structures and values and the civilian society which it governs. But an exclusive concern with either side or even with both sides in isolation is insufficient. Military participation in politics is a crucial and complex set of civil-military interactions which merit study in their own right. The structure of these has in turn been affected by other, more specific interactions between army and party and between army and society. Some of these interactions (for example, those between army leaders and private groups) have helped to delimit the scope of military participation; others (in particular, the interplay between government policy and the officer corps' policy preferences) have influenced the military's choice of political instruments.

The relation of public policy to officers' interests is the particular civil-military interaction which has had great and perhaps decisive effect on the structure of Soviet military politics. Recognition of the importance of this nexus leads one to question both the once common view of armies as inherently conservative organizations and the more recent tendency, popular in the 1960s, to see them as intrinsically reforming or even revolutionary. Neither prediction holds true in all cases because neither takes into explicit account the interrelationships between armies and political regimes. Armies can be revolutionary, but such a posture is likely to be adopted only in relation to holders of civilian authority who ignore or abuse their core interests. Conversely, military organizations are likely to be supportive of regimes which maintain and enhance those interests. The army is, in the words of the historian Alfred Vagts, "conservative in relation to the order in which it thrives, whether that order be agrarian, capitalistic, or communistic."[8] For this generalization no better evidence can be adduced than the Soviet experience.

The Importance of Choice

While scholars speak of "political development" in a number of senses, most discussions attempt to explain changes in the political process and political institutions by relating them to a broader environment of social change (usually modernization). Many seek also to account for the adoption of a particular style of modernizing change (usually an orderly one) or the arrival at a particular end point. If the argument of this book is correct, it underlines that analysis of government choice and policy output must be recognized as an important part of the effort to understand any of these aspects of political development, in the Soviet Union or elsewhere.

Dankwart Rustow has urged us to examine the "junctures . . . at which a modernizing society must make, by resolution or default, a number of basic choices."[9] These fundamental choices concern the speed, scope, and timing of modernizing change, with which Rustow is primarily concerned. But they have to do also with the *allocation* of the costs and benefits of change. And distributive and redistributive decisions in turn have vital implications for virtually every dimension of politics. By creating and maintaining patterns of privilege and deprivation, they shape bases of government support, help define potential opposition constituencies (which elites may or may not succeed in mobilizing), and mold the agenda of political intercourse.

Soviet development, too, has been drastically affected by allocative choices. However, this fact is often neglected in explanations of political change and stability in the Soviet Union which focus on governmental constraints, controls, and organizational weapons (such as the military party apparatus).

There is no denying the scope and power of public organizations in Soviet politics. Andrei Zhdanov was quite correct in stating in 1939 that the regime has always "attached exceptional significance to organization," and even that this was "the distinctive feature of our party."[10] Public administration has pervaded spheres of political, intellectual, and productive life that have in liberal Western societies been relegated largely (though by no means exclusively) to processes of exchange and competition.

Yet it is true also that organization has not entirely supplanted competition in any of these realms. There is some individual political participation and dissensus within the limits of the one-party system and an appreciable volume of intellectual exchange in which political dictate does not play a decisive part. There is also a vigorous politics within the publicly administered sector, among the various layers and segments of the planned economy and among other bureaucratic organizations and their subunits. There is even, as we have seen, political contention within the bureaucratic apparatus of the Communist party—an apparatus whose degree of purposiveness and integration Western observers have often been as inclined to romanticize as the most facile Soviet propaganda.

Moreover, the ascendancy of organization over market should not be permitted to obscure entirely the allocative choices which Soviet organizations, including the party, have made and abided by. As Zhdanov emphasized, "The organizational principles of Bolshevism are the instrument for achieving its . . . revolutionary program and strategy." Appreciating the importance of organization and its implications for politics does not obviate the necessity of understanding the nature and consequences of the program—the set of choices and priorities in public policy—that organizations have defined and implemented and that ultimately have worked to build and legitimize the organizations. That program, in Zhdanov's day and at other times, has like all programs for modernization had distinct and profound distributive implications, and these have had a critical impact on political development.

No student of Soviet reality needs to be told that regime choices have flagrantly contradicted the preferences of a number of groups—independent peasant producers, religious believers, non-Russian nationalities, and some creative intellectuals, to name only a few of the ones most frequently studied in the West. Nor need the student be reminded that as a consequence the regime has been and has felt itself to be deprived of the support of such constituencies at critical times, has failed to elicit desired contributions from them, and has not been receptive to improving their opportunities to influence its own processes of decision.

The point that bears emphasis here is that there are key constituencies whose interests *have* generally been well served—constituencies which, curiously, often seem to stir less interest among scholars than ones whose interests have been neglected—and that it is for this reason as much as any that the regime has been provided with the support without which it could not continue to govern. The military establishment has not been the only such constituency, but undoubtedly it has been one of the most important. To some degree (less than for most Soviet citizens), officers have had their range of political choice constricted by the party's substitution of organization for the political marketplace. Yet, as members of a privileged segment of society with good bureaucratic representation, they have not had an outstanding interest that would demonstrably gain from greater political competition. So it is with the economic and intellectual realms, where for most officers the advantages of prevailing arrangements far outweigh the disadvantages.

Not all of the regime's military-related policies have been concerned with the army's share of societal resources, and not all have exacted great costs from other segments of society. The specialization of the military's policy role, the deliberate divorce of the army from local politics, the ideological gratification of the early years, the social mobility afforded to officers from peasant and working-class backgrounds—these and other courses of action did not impose clear burdens on others. But many of the essential choices have come only at extremely high direct and indirect costs to the regime and to society. "Everyone knows, comrades," Brezhnev told a military audience in 1968, "how dearly we must pay in resources and energies to support and arm a modern army."[11]

The military case suggests that analysts of the Soviet system should devote more effort to mapping and explaining the societal and institutional bases of the regime's power. The habit of seeing the key features of the Soviet polity as imposed from above and lacking in social roots is a persistent one, as Stephen Cohen has argued, and one which flies in the face of considerable evidence to the contrary for at least some important features of the system.[12] Perhaps Jerry Hough is correct in saying that it is the Western scholar's natural affinity for the dissenting intellectual's view of Soviet reality which has distracted us from the task of analyzing the party's sources of support.[13] Perhaps also we have been misled by the extravagance of many of the regime's own claims about responsiveness and by the redundancy of so many of its instruments of control. Whatever the reasons, there is no longer justification for disregarding William Taubman's advice that we "spend more time investigating the standards by which various groups in Soviet society gauge the effectiveness of their own system, and less time judging it by our own."[14]

The Army and Future Soviet Politics

What can one intimate about the army's political roles in future? The first and most important suggestion is that for the immediate future no major change in civil-military relations is to be anticipated. The determinants of military quiescence are deeply rooted and not susceptible to disturbance in the short run. One should be cautious about interpreting signs of personal conflict or specific irritation as proof of extensive discord between military and civilian elites. Professor Kolkowicz's view that the relationship between army and party is "essentially conflict-prone and thus presents a perennial threat to the political stability of the Soviet state" is belied by much of the evidence presented in this book.[15] In comparative perspective, the party-army relationship has been remarkably free of direct conflict, and the safest prediction is that such confrontation will be avoided in future. The relationship presumably has enough resilience and slack to withstand even quite substantial shocks.

Yet one would be amiss not to take into account the prospects that the military's position may undergo major modification at some point. Whether or not Kolkowicz is correct in describing the army as a present threat to stability, there is no doubt that it possesses in the long run the capacity both for disrupting stability and for taking advantage of unstable conditions created by others. Its coercive capability is unlikely to be greatly curtailed, because even if reduced in size it will remain the organization with the greatest command over means of violence. Nor is its ideological capability likely to decline drastically. The passing of the World War II generation of heroic leaders will dim the military's aura somewhat, but experiences in other societies have shown that soldiers have a remarkable capacity for identifying with grander symbols and codes even in times of peace. Even a return to a more revolutionary variant of Leninism would not be incompatible with increased military participation. The emergence of a Soviet Qaddafi or Lin Piao, a soldier preaching a return to fundamentals which have been compromised by indifferent civilians, is at least conceivable.

The reader should be cognizant of the possibilities for development along both the involvement and the intervention routes. Military involvement, beginning with a broadening of the scope of political participation, would clearly be a strong possibility in the event of drastic disintegration of the political system. Any suspension of controls on open political activity would bring major pressure on the officer corps, from all three potential sources, to take on a more expansive political role. First, the army would be invited to participate on a wider range of issues by specific groups for whom it would be a peerless ally in any unrestrained competition. Second, pressure would come from ascriptive attachments held by officers. The most likely of these to be compelling would be ethnic feelings, which almost certainly would be activated in any less constricted Soviet political process, especially if censorship were abolished and the formation of genuine opposition parties were allowed. (Most senior officers could be expected to side with the Russian majority.) And third, there might also be overtures from the party leadership itself, or some part of it. The regime would stand in particular need of symbolic and coercive assistance if it relinquished its claim to a unique prerogative to rule, enervated its police apparatus, or simply lost control of political events.

Greater military involvement is also conceivable under existing political arrangements. The most probable course is for military influence to increase incrementally at civilian initiative, widening from current beachheads in issue areas such as secondary education, construction, and civil defense. This could very well occur and leave the army at a point of participation far short of outright military rule. One scholar has suggested that American society should "worry not about a sudden takeover by our soldiers but about how to prevent accretions in the scope of military influence in the 'normal' political system."[16] This is also the prospect most likely to confront Soviet civilians.

Such a gradual extension of scope is especially likely if civilian leaders decide to fuse and intermingle military and civilian functions in new areas under the pressure of budgetary and other constraints. One can foresee, for example, that the acute labor shortage predicted for the 1980s may induce experiments in combining military service with economic production (perhaps along the lines of the territorial militia system partially introduced in the 1920s). It may lead also to a greater military presence in the school system and in the workplace.[17]

The range of military participation could be expected to expand more rapidly than this under two sets of particularly propitious circumstances. One would be Soviet entanglement in a war, especially a prolonged conflict, which as in World War II would thrust military matters to the center of the national policy agenda and tend to draw officers into spheres of decision in which they had played only a minor executant or advisory role in peacetime.

The second and more probable scenario would involve a leadership succession crisis or factional struggle in which one or more of the partisans appealed to military leaders for support. Here, as in a wartime setting, the keys to limiting military participation would be civilian restraint and civilians' ability to agree among themselves or at least to confine their disagreements to established arenas. It can safely be said that the probability of such restraint in future is quite high, given the firmly imbedded awareness of the hazards of military entanglement and the apparent absence, at the peak of the political system at least, of grand alternative visions for policy which might motivate contestants to take the risks of reaching for military support.

Army involvement in a palace crisis is certainly more liable to occur if a senior military official is a member of the top party leadership, and this may well be the case when Brezhnev leaves the scene. Defense Minister Ustinov (a career civilian, notwithstanding his new marshal's stars and his decades of experience in defense production) will no doubt be a central participant in selecting the next leader if he is still in office. This is all the more likely if one recalls that prior to his appointment as Defense Minister in 1976 Ustinov had been the party secretary supervising KGB as well as military appointments. Before the succession is resolved Ustinov, who is less than two years younger than Brezhnev, may well be succeeded as minister by a younger professional soldier (most likely either Marshal Ogarkov, the chief of the General Staff, or Marshal Kulikov, the head of Warsaw Pact troops). If the new man is granted Politburo standing, and perhaps even if he is not, he would be a potent force in party councils and an alluring partner for aspirants to the highest post. If the Zhukov experience serves as any guide (and it can be only a partial guide because of Zhukov's unique personal status), this individual will also be vulnerable to the anxieties of his colleagues.

In any event, for involvement to culminate in outright military rule is extremely unlikely unless officers' core interests are vitally threatened by existing or incipient lines of public policy. If officers are drawn into extraprofessional decision making by any of the more probable external pulls, it presumably will be possible to return them to their barracks once the external force has been mitigated, so long as they feel minimal satisfaction with policy performance.

The possibility of military intervention, beginning with the choice of forceful means to pursue institutional interests, will depend essentially on the pattern of policy output. The only inducement to full-scale intervention would be the conflux of a number of policy choices highly unfavorable to military interests. One can envisage, for example, a reformist civilian leadership embarking upon policies of ideological revision, military demobilization, shifting of investment priorities, and accommodation with foreign adversaries such as would alarm military leaders. The combination, as in France in the 1950s, of multiple assaults on officers' key interests with the tensions of waging a difficult war—perhaps a prolonged conflict with China or an embroilment with guerrillas in Central Asia or Yugoslavia—could conceivably bring about intervention, either unilateral or (more likely) in coalition with some civilians. In this event a prudent mixture of government repression and policy adjustment might suffice to narrow and allay military discontent, as de Gaulle managed to do in France. But the outlook for containing intervention short of military supremacy would be much less favorable than for arresting military involvement.

Clearly none of these outcomes is at all likely. Still, none is beyond imagination. Too often, students of Soviet politics have failed to anticipate major changes because of their overreliance on past example and theory. Few, for instance, foresaw that Khrushchev would be an ardent anti-Stalinist and guarded reformer. Fewer still predicted the removal of Khrushchev by his colleagues, the emergence of the dissent movement, the rift with China, or the espousal of detente with the West. Might not an officers' revolution some day reveal observers of Soviet politics to have been imprisoned by the same kind of "authoritarian regime syndrome" which Philippe Schmitter argues to have prevented experts on Portugal from foreseeing the possibility of the 1974 army revolt there?[18]

Yet the forecaster cannot be reminded too often that the Soviet military's outlook, whatever its relation to changing circumstances, is on most substantive issues fundamentally and perhaps irrevocably conservative. Only the need to respond to change beyond the army's boundaries can make it a force for political innovation, let alone transformation. On most basic questions facing Soviet society soldiers are firmly wedded to the status quo. Military leaders can be expected to oppose increased autonomy for national minorities, investment priority for the consumer economy, concessions to intellectuals, and greater openness to the outside world. As for political forms and procedures, the central concern of democratic theory, Soviet officers have displayed indifference to almost every aspect but their own access to national leaders.

If the army has benefited from the party's basic developmental choices, it has also, in accepting these benefactions, made choices of its own. There is no clear standard for judging them. The harshest measure would probably be a moral one, such as that used by Lenin in 1905 to condemn the tsarist military's refusal to side with striking workers against the autocracy. "The army," Lenin declared, "cannot and must not be neutral . . . It is impossible to stand aside from the people's struggle for freedom. Whoever is indifferent to this struggle supports the outrages of the police state which promises freedom in order to scoff at freedom."[19] The Soviet military may have had little part in perpetrating the outrages of the state founded by Lenin, but it also has had little to do with the long and only partly efficacious struggle to contain and reverse them.

The judgment of the onlooker who consents to divorce fact from value should be less severe. Measured by the yardstick of rational response to tangible stimulus and opportunity, officers' behavior has been understandable, if not always admirable. Fixed on its own star, the military has not thought to provide, and is not likely to provide, an alternative to the political order of which it is so integral a part. A modern Russian dissident has written of the imbalance in Soviet development: "Soviet rockets have reached Venus, while in the village where I live potatoes are still dug by hand. This should not be regarded as a comical comparison; it is a gap which may deepen into an abyss."[20] If so, it is improbable that the army, the custodian of the rockets, will be a force for bridging that abyss.

Appendixes, Notes, Index

Appendix A
Biographical Data
on Soviet Military Officers

This book makes frequent use of biographical information on senior Soviet officers. Whenever reference is made to details of an individual's life or career, the note indicates the Soviet source which best illuminates those particulars.

The text and a number of tables also make use of summary information from two bounded sets of biographical data. The first (used in Tables 7, 8, 9, 10, 11, and 14) consists of all biographies printed in full obituary form in *Krasnaia zvezda* between January 1, 1956, and December 31, 1975, of officers possessing ranks from colonel to colonel-general or their equivalents. (For naval officers, the range is from captain first rank to admiral; nomenclature varies somewhat among services and specialties.) Referred to in the text as the "generals and colonels" sample, this set contains a total of 1,237 men, 175 of them political officers and 1,062 nonpolitical officers. Men whose death was mentioned only in a brief announcement (which sometimes gives the year the officer joined the party) were not included in the sample. Also excluded were the several dozen officers for whom no information was provided on the period in which the individual entered military service, as well as those men with military rank who did not have either a higher military education or continuous military service of ten years. There was great variability in the amount of detail provided in the obituaries, ranging from complete accounts of careers to simple mentions of years of entry into army and party and of "long service" in military ranks or work in "responsible posts." Some of the large gaps undoubtedly conceal valuable information, including information on overlap among command, MPA, and civilian careers.

For some purposes, officers from this sample were grouped according to career pattern, and here some judgments had to be made. Men were classified in the career specialty in which they had spent the greatest amount of time. If an officer could not be located in a definite category, he was placed in the largest group, the commanders, which includes officers specializing in troop command and general staff work. The engineering group contains men with careers in military engineering, construction, and communication. The academic group embraces teachers and researchers in military academies and schools and also armaments designers and developers employed in the Ministry of Defense, but not defense industry officials from other ministries (who sometimes have military rank). The other career categories—logistics, medicine (including veterinary service), procuracy, and political work—are well defined and self-explanatory. Table 14, on social origins, uses only those 850 of the 1,237 generals and colonels for whom at least one piece of information on birth (social origin, date, or location) was given in the obituary. An officer for whom a year or place of birth was provided but no social origin was considered to have unknown social origin. As comparison with other samples included in Table 14 suggests, Soviet sources sometimes limit this kind of information in order to conceal middle class and other nonproletarian origins. (This practice seems much more prevalent than outright falsification.)

The second bounded group for whom data were systematically collected (and used in Tables 13 and 14) includes all officers who gained either of the two highest steps on the military rank ladder by the end of 1975. I have referred to these men as marshals and equivalents. The highest ground forces rank, marshal of the Soviet Union, was introduced in 1935, and equivalents for the navy and other services and for some technical specialties were inaugurated during the war. (The highest naval rank is admiral of the fleet of the Soviet Union; in other services it is chief marshal of the service.) The next highest rank in the ground forces, general of the army, was instituted along with other generals' ranks in 1940. A naval equivalent, admiral of the fleet, was established at this time, and equivalents for other forces (marshal of the service concerned) followed during the war.

A total of 144 men were included here, including 2 political officers (A. A. Epishev and E. E. Mal'tsev) and 1 man (F. I. Golikov) who served as head of the MPA but is classified as a career commander. (A fourth political officer, S. P. Vasiagin, was appointed a general of the army in 1976.) Satisfactory biographies could be assembled for 140 of these officers, and information on birth (for Table 14) was found for 139.

This sample does not take in men who have been awarded marshals' and equivalent ranks but have not been career soldiers. It therefore excludes two party leaders (Stalin, the only Soviet generalissimus, and Brezhnev, a marshal), two of Stalin's police officials, the present head of civilian aviation, and one civilian Defense Minister (N. A. Bulganin). (The current Defense Minister, Ustinov, achieved peak rank only in 1976, as did two police officials; they would have been excluded had their elevation come earlier.) Two generals of the army who attained high police posts but spent several decades in the military command (I. I. Maslennikov and I. A. Serov) were included. No biographical information could be found on four men promoted in 1974-75 (O. A. Losik, I. I. Pstygo, I. N. Shkadov, and A. P. Silant'ev), but inferences about their nationality were made for Table 13.

There are several major sources of information on these men and the many others in addition to the 1956-75 obituary group to whom references are made in this study. For many, fairly detailed histories are available in obituaries. For others, entries in encyclopedias are indispensable. The third edition of the *Bol'shaia Sovetskaia entsiklopediia* (Large Soviet Encyclopedia), which has been coming out since 1970, is generally the best such source. It has largely outdated the first and second editions (issued in 1926-34 and 1949-58), each of which, particularly the early volumes of the second, has its peculiar distortions and omissions. The new *Sovetskaia voennaia entsiklopediia* (Soviet Military Encyclopedia), which began to appear in 1976, provides new and valuable information on a number of officers, including political officers; only the first four of the eight volumes were available for this book. For many officers who reached senior rank before or during World War II, histories and memoir accounts are essential sources. Evidence on men who fell in the Great Purge is most readily available from articles of commemoration, most of them published in newspapers or in the indispensable *Voenno-istoricheskii zhurnal* (Journal of Military History). A source notable for its frank treatment of the purge, and useful in some other ways as well, is the *Sovetskaia istoricheskaia entsiklopediia* (Soviet Historical Encyclopedia).

A reliable record of current holders of senior military appointments can be constructed only from the military press. For some of these men, biographical information is provided in the official handbooks on Supreme Soviet deputies (*Deputaty Verkhovnogo Soveta SSSR*, published by the Izvestiia Publishing House at four-year intervals beginning with the 1958 Supreme Soviet). The yearbook (*Ezhegodnik*) of the *BSE* also contains career data on officers selected to the highest party organs and on a few others.

It cannot be overemphasized that these sources must be utilized together. Not only are there systematic omissions of information (the yearbook, for instance, says nothing about either social origin or nationality), there are also omissions and inconsistencies on an individual basis which can be overcome only by checking of all available information. When flat contradictions exist, I have adhered to the latest Soviet source. More worrisome, however, is deliberate and indeliberate concealment of information, which is especially to be suspected when there are lengthy intervals in a man's career unaccounted for. Several men can be used to illustrate this kind of problem.

The career of Mikhail I. Kazakov, a four-star general who was the chief of staff of Warsaw Pact troops from 1965 to 1968, is described in many sources. *Deputaty* mentions that from 1920 to 1925 he served as a political officer, and this experience is described in more detail in *SVE* (and in Kazakov's memoirs). Yet entries in the yearbook and in the third edition of the *BSE* make no mention whatever of this important fact. Likewise, the 1961 obituary of Vasilii E. Belokoskov, who headed military construction from 1949 to 1958, made no reference to political work experience. Only when the second volume of the *SVE* was published in 1976 could one learn that he had worked as a political officer until 1925, rising as high as brigade commissar. In the cases of Kazakov and Belokoskov, the omissions were probably inadvertent, but this is not likely to have occurred with Semen Vasiagin, who has been the chief political officer in the ground forces since 1967. According to the 1966 and subsequent yearbooks, Vasiagin was "in the Soviet Army from 1932 onward"; nothing is said of the posts in which he served until 1941. In the *SVE*, however, we read, "In the Soviet Army from 1932 onward . . . From 1933 onward on party-political work in the NKVD forces, as secretary of a Komsomol bureau, political work instructor and deputy chief of a politotdel, and senior instructor of the main administration of political propaganda of the border and internal troops of the NKVD." His service in the regular army after 1941 is then described.

Appendix B
A Note on Primary Sources

Apart from the career data, it is useful to indicate the primary Soviet sources employed in preparing this study. A wide variety of books were used, as the detailed notes indicate. Particularly extensive use was made of military memoirs, several hundred of which were examined. These provide invaluable information on every aspect of military life and politics, but almost invariably have the major shortcoming of ceasing their narratives in 1945.

An irreplaceable tool, without which this book could not have been written, is the Soviet military press, above all the Ministry of Defense's daily newspaper *Krasnaia zvezda* (Red Star). Scattered numbers prior to 1934 and all issues from that year onward were examined. Also helpful was the navy's newspaper, entitled *Krasnyi flot* (Red Fleet) from 1938 to 1953 and *Sovetskii flot* (Soviet Fleet) between 1953 and 1960. Some use was also made of several limited-circulation military newspapers from the Civil War period.

Nonmilitary newspapers contain much less information on military questions but have been consulted where necessary. *Pravda* (Truth) and *Izvestiia* (News), the daily organs of the Central Committee and Soviet government, were the most useful. Civilian newspapers at the republic and local level were consulted on an eclectic basis, mainly to ascertain statements made by military and MPA officials at civilian party congresses and conferences. They contain much valuable information on civil defense and paramilitary training, but little of this was used directly in this book. More of this kind of information can be found in *Sovetskii patriot* (Soviet Patriot), the organ of DOSAAF, and *Komsomol'skaia pravda* (Komsomol Truth), the Komsomol newspaper, but little information was found which is relevant to the

central themes of this study. The party's central theoretical journal
(*Kommunist*, previously *Bol'shevik*) was useful on specialized questions. *Partiinoe stroitel'stvo* (Party Construction), the central organizational journal under Stalin, printed virtually nothing on the military
or on party work in the military; its successor, *Partiinaia zhizn'* (Party
Life), is only slightly more useful.

On party life in the army, the Main Political Administration's twice-
monthly magazine *Kommunist vooruzhennykh sil* (Communist of the
Armed Forces), published since 1960, is an invaluable if tedious
source. Scattered issues of several military magazines from the Civil
War period were found and used. More substantial files of *Tolmachevets* (the journal of the Tolmachev Military-Political Academy)
and *Sputnik politrabotnika* (The Political Worker's Companion) provided first-rate information on the mid-1920s. From the 1930s, most
issues of *Voennyi vestnik* (Military Herald), a general periodical on
military and military-political affairs, were read, but proved to add
little to information gleaned from *Krasnaia zvezda*. The same can be
said of an MPA magazine published in 1938-40 for propaganda workers, *Propagandist i agitator RKKA* (Propagandist and Agitator of the
Red Army), as well as of this publication's successor in 1940-41, *Propagandist RKKA* (Propagandist of the Red Army). For the last several
decades, several specialized military journals were found to contain
revealing discussions of military party affairs. The best are *Vestnik
protivovozdushnoi oborony* (Air Defense Herald), *Morskoi sbornik*
(Naval Collection), *Voennyi vestnik* (Military Herald, now an organ
of the General Staff), and *Tyl i snabzhenie Sovetskikh Vooruzhennykh Sil* (Rear and Supply of the Soviet Armed Forces). The last journal is also a crucial source on military living conditions and routine
administration, including contacts with civilian agencies at the national and local levels. Of far less value are the several periodicals
published mainly for soldiers and NCO's; almost no reference has
been made to them, although they sometimes give one a sense of
morale and discipline problems.

On questions of military history, the key periodical source is
Voenno-istoricheskii zhurnal (Journal of Military History), published
by the Ministry of Defense monthly since 1959 (and by its Institute of
Military History since 1966). Particularly prior to 1970, it contains
unique information on current policy, organizational history, wartime
campaigns and policy conflicts, and biography. Considerable material on military party work is also found in *Voprosy istorii KPSS*
(Problems of Party History), and less evidence, mostly on general
military questions, in *Voprosy istorii* (Problems of History). Some

valuable historical insights were found in two general historical publications from between the wars, *Krasnaia letopis'* (Red Chronicle) and *Proletarskaia revoliutsiia* (Proletarian Revolution), and for recent decades the occasional gem appears in the literary magazine *Novyi mir* (New World).

Notes

Abbreviations

BSE, 1st, 2nd, or 3rd	*Bol'shaia Sovetskaia entsiklopediia*, first, second, or third edition
Deputaty	*Deputaty Verkhovnogo Soveta SSSR*, handbook of biographies of Supreme Soviet deputies; year of election to Supreme Soviet specified
Ezhegodnik	*Ezhegodnik* (yearbook) of *Bol'shaia Sovetskaia entisiklopediia*; year specified
KVS	*Kommunist vooruzhennykh sil*
SIE	*Sovetskaia istoricheskaia entsiklopediia*
SVE	*Sovetskaia voennaia entsiklopediia*
TIS	*Tyl i snabzhenie Sovetskikh Vooruzhennykh Sil*
Vestnik PVO	*Vestnik protivovozdushnoi oborony*
VIZh	*Voenno-istoricheskii zhurnal*

Encyclopedia citations which do not contain volume and page numbers refer to biographical articles found alphabetically under the name of the individual concerned.

Introduction

1. Gavin Kennedy, *The Military in the Third World* (New York, Scribner's, 1974), p. 3.

2. Samuel P. Huntington, *Political Order in Changing Societies* (New Haven, Yale University Press, 1968), p. 8.

3. On the Vorkuta officers and the recent dissent, see Rudolf L. Tökés, "Dissent: The Politics for Change in the USSR," in Henry W. Morton and Rudolf L. Tökés, eds., *Soviet Politics and Society in the 1970's* (New York, Free Press, 1974), p. 11; Peter Reddaway, ed., *Uncensored Russia: Protest and Dissent in the Soviet Union* (New York, McGraw Hill, 1972), pp. 127-142, 162-167, 171-183.

4. A. A. Grechko, *Vooruzhennye Sily Sovetskogo gosudarstva* (Moscow, Voenizdat, 1974), p. 201.

5. *Pravda*, Sept. 21, 1967, p. 2; A. A. Epishev, *Moguchee oruzhie partii* (Moscow, Voenizdat, 1973), pp. 6-7.

6. V. D. Sokolovskii et al., *Voennaia strategiia* (Moscow, Voenizdat, 1968), p. 451.

7. *KVS*, 1965, no. 4, p. 12

8. *Pravda*, Dec. 26, 1918, p. 3. Soviet sources sometimes distinguish between party "leadership of the armed forces" and a more general "leadership of the country's defense."

9. *Partiino-politicheskaia rabota v Sovetskoi Armii i Flote* (Moscow, Voenizdat, 1967), pp. 134-135.

10. *SVE*, II, 563.

11. The literature is discussed in Timothy J. Colton, "The Party-Military Connection: A Participatory Model," in Dale R. Herspring and Ivan Volgyes, eds., *Civil-Military Relations in Communist Systems* (Boulder, Colorado, Westview, 1978), pp. 53-75.

12. Raymond Bauer, Alex Inkeles, and Clyde Kluckhohn, *How the Soviet System Works* (Cambridge, Mass., Harvard University Press, 1956), p. 61.

13. Roman Kolkowicz, *The Soviet Military and the Communist Party* (Princeton, Princeton University Press, 1967), p. 11.

14. Roman Kolkowicz, "The Military," in H. Gordon Skilling and Franklyn Griffiths, eds., *Interest Groups in Soviet Politics* (Princeton, Princeton University Press, 1971), p. 135.

15. See especially the discussion of civil-military congruence in William E. Odom, "The Party Connection," *Problems of Communism*, 22 (September-October 1973), 12-26; reprinted with an addendum in Herspring and Volgyes.

16. Kolkowicz, *The Soviet Military*, pp. 92-93, 341-342.

17. Thomas W. Wolfe, "The Military," in Allen Kassof, ed., *Prospects for Soviet Society* (New York, Praeger, 1968), pp. 128-129; Erich Wollenberg, *The Red Army* (London, Secker and Warburg, 1940), p. 357; Robert Conquest, *Power and Policy in the USSR* (New York, St. Martin's, 1961), p. 330. A similar image is in Zbigniew Brzezinski, ed., *Political Controls in the Soviet Army* (New York, Research Program on the USSR, 1954); Herbert Goldhamer, *The Soviet Soldier* (New York, Crane, Russak, 1975); Michael J.

Deane, *Political Control of the Soviet Armed Forces* (New York, Crane, Russak, 1977).

18. Kolkowicz, *The Soviet Military*, pp. 123, 330; emphasis added.

1. The Structure of the Military Party Organs

1. Formal designations of the central party organ have been: All-Russian Bureau of Military Commissars (April 1918-April 1919); Political Department (April-May 1919), then Political Administration (May 1919-August 1923), of Revolutionary Military Council of Republic; Political Administration of Red Army (August 1923-July 1940); Main Administration of Political Propaganda of Red Army (July 1940-July 1941); Main Political Administration of Red Army (July 1941-February 1946); MPA of Soviet Armed Forces (February 1946-March 1953), of Ministry of Defense (March 1953-April 1958), of Soviet Army and Navy (since April 1958). An autonomous political organ existed for the navy between December 1937 and February 1946 and again from February 1950 to March 1953.

2. *Partiino-politicheskaia rabota v Krasnoi Armii (Aprel' 1918-fevral' 1919): Dokumenty* (Moscow, Voenizdat, 1961), p. 93.

3. The directives are in ibid., pp. 77, 86-90.

4. Aleksandr Geronimus, *Partiia i Krasnaia Armiia* (Moscow and Leningrad, Gosizdat, 1928), pp. 130-131.

5. On the bureau see *SVE*, II, 563. For a rare report of a bureau session, see *Krasnaia zvezda*, June 5, 1977, p. 2.

6. Indispensable information on structural changes is in Iu. P. Petrov, *Partiinoe stroitel'stvo v Sovetskoi Armii i Flote (1918-1961)* (Moscow, Voenizdat, 1964), and in the same author's *Stroitel'stvo politorganov, partiinykh i komsomol'skikh organizatsii Armii i Flota (1918-1968)* (Moscow, Voenizdat, 1968). Details of current structure (including the names of MPA departments) were gathered from the press and MPA handbooks.

7. S. I. Gusev, *Grazhdanskaia voina i Krasnaia Armiia* (Moscow, Voenizdat, 1960), pp. 112-113; Petrov, *Partiinoe stroitel'stvo*, pp. 207, 306, 468-469; I. V. Stavitskii, "Rol' voennykh sovetov v organizatsii partiino-politicheskoi raboty na frontakh Velikoi Otechestvennoi voiny (1941-1945 gg.)," *Voprosy istorii KPSS*, 1968, no. 2, p. 30; *SVE*, II, 274. Roman Kolkowicz's assertion (*The Soviet Military and the Communist Party* [Princeton, Princeton University Press, 1967], pp. 77, 125) that the title "full-time political worker" (for the first member of the council) is a euphemism for a member of the secret police is simply incorrect.

8. For personnel in politotdels and military units, see especially *Partiino-politicheskaia rabota v Sovetskoi Armii i Flote* (Moscow, Voenizdat, 1972), pp. 62-70. From 1959 to 1967 politotdels in administrative and academic establishments were replaced by elected party committees. Soviet sources do not provide outlines of politupravlenie structure for the postwar period (there is an outline for 1934 in Petrov, *Partiinoe stroitel'stvo*, p. 288), but the functional structure is evident from press references.

9. The 1963 total is calculated from the figure of 4.7 political workers per

1,000 party members in M. Kh. Kalashnik, *Politorgany i partiinye organizatsii Sovetskoi Armii i Voenno-Morskogo Flota* (Moscow, Voenizdat, 1963), p. 17. This figure apparently includes full-time party secretaries, but not "cultural workers" (like librarians and film technicians), who are not commissioned officers. The MPA's maximum size, somewhat over 100,000 officials, was attained in World War II.

10. L. G. Beskrovnyi et al., *Bor'ba bol'shevikov za armiiu v trekh revoliutsiiakh* (Moscow, Politizdat, 1969), p. 138; P. A. Golub, *Partiia, armiia i revoliutsiia* (Moscow, Politizdat, 1967), pp. 176, 179.

11. Figures from Petrov, *Partiinoe stroitel'stvo*, pp. 88, 350; *Istoriia Velikoi Otechestvennoi voiny, 1941-1945*, 6 vols. (Moscow, Voenizdat, 1960-65), VI, 365; Petrov, *Stroitel'stvo politorganov*, p. 338.

12. Petrov, *Partiinoe stroitel'stvo*, p. 388; Petrov, *Stroitel'stvo politorganov*, p. 490; *Krasnaia zvezda*, March 17, 1976, p. 2. Overall party admissions taken from Merle Fainsod and Jerry F. Hough, *How Russia Is Ruled* (Cambridge, Mass., Harvard University Press, 1978), chap. 9. Despite the curtailment, 30 percent of all military Communists in 1975 had been in the party for less than five years (*KVS*, 1975, no. 3, p. 55).

13. A. S. Bubnov, *O Krasnoi Armii* (Moscow, Voenizdat, 1958), p. 128.

14. Jerry F. Hough, *The Soviet Union and Social Science Theory* (Cambridge, Mass., Harvard University Press, 1977), p. 126, gives the average age of party admission in 1975 as 27. Calculations in Chapter 2 of this book suggest the age of party admission in the military may be slightly lower.

15. *KVS*, 1973, no. 3, p. 23.

16. See A. A. Epishev, "Partiinye organizatsii Sovetskikh Vooruzhennykh Sil," *Voprosy istorii KPSS*, 1973, no. 6, pp. 13-14. It is significant, though, that even well before the conscription reform there were complaints about inattention to recruiting soldiers and NCO's. It should be added that re-enlisted soldiers and sailors clearly have higher rates of party membership than conscripts. In 1973, 40 percent of all re-enlisted men with the new ranks of ensign and warrant officer were party members and 20 percent Komsomol members (*Krasnaia zvezda*, Jan. 31, 1973, p. 3).

17. In one military district in 1974, only 35 percent of companies had party organizations, but this was 5 percent higher than the previous year; in 1964, 97 percent of all companies had organizations. *KVS*, 1974, no. 5, p. 27; Petrov, *Stroitel'stvo politorganov*, p. 492.

18. *KVS*, 1971, no. 21, p. 8. As is common in the Soviet Union, formal participation is expected of most members. Practically all party members participated in 1976 electoral meetings (*Krasnaia zvezda*, Nov. 3, 1976, p. 2).

19. *Krasnaia zvezda*, Sept. 30, 1935, p. 3.

20. For a good illustration, see *KVS*, 1975, no. 3, p. 57. Even before Stalin's death one finds a story about two politotdel nominations being rejected in a single division (*Krasnaia zvezda*, Feb. 25, 1952, p. 3).

21. *Krasnaia zvezda*, Nov. 21, 1964, p. 3.

22. Ibid., Aug. 11, 1966, pp. 2-3. Because of their indispensability, party secretaries cannot be transferred from one command post to another without the concurrence of the superior political organ.

23. Petrov, *Stroitel'stvo politorganov*, p. 510. Four percent of these were commissioned officers and 4 percent officer candidates; 15 percent were NCO's, 15 civilian employees, and 62 soldiers and sailors. The highest known proportion for officers is the 22 percent in 1936 (*Krasnaia zvezda*, May 14, 1936, p. 3), a figure inflated by the suspension of party entrance at the time.

24. Statistics in *Krasnaia zvezda*, April 27, 1978, p. 3; April 25, 1974, p. 3.

25. *KVS*, 1977, no. 5, p. 35; in 1974 only 24 percent of Komsomol secretaries were party members (*Krasnaia zvezda*, March 15, 1974, p. 2).

26. I. A. Portiankin et al., *Sovetskaia voennaia pechat'* (Moscow, Voenizdat, 1960), p. 306; *SVE*, II, 563.

27. See especially V. K. Volovich and N. I. Kuznetsov, *Narodnyi kontrol' v Vooruzhennykh Silakh SSSR* (Moscow, Voenizdat, 1973). District-level committees are headed by a deputy chief of the political administration. Sixty percent of activists are party members (*Vestnik PVO*, 1973, no. 7, p. 21).

28. *KVS*, 1964, no. 15, pp. 13-14; 1965, no. 7, p. 26.

29. A. A. Epishev, *Nekotorye voprosy partiino-politicheskoi raboty* (Moscow, Voenizdat, 1970), p. 117.

30. Leaving aside party and state control agencies, which were fused in two periods (1921-34, 1962-65), the major experiments have been the politotdels in machine tractor stations (1933-34, 1941-43), state farms (1933-40, 1941-43), railroads (1933-56), and water transport (1934-56).

31. F. Blumental', *Politicheskaia rabota v voennoe vremia* (Moscow and Leningrad, Gosizdat, 1927), pp. 61-62.

32. Epishev, *Nekotorye voprosy*, p. 103.

33. The biography of the chief political officer in the navy, V. M. Grishanov, refers to him as a member of the Main Military Council since 1967 (*BSE*, 3rd). The MPA does not appear to be represented on the higher-level Defense Council chaired by General Secretary Brezhnev. The MPA chief does sit on the collegium of the Ministry of Defense, an organ which advises the minister on policy questions and contains all his deputies (*SVE*, IV, 235-236).

34. Gamarnik was in fact one of two First Deputy People's Commissars of Defense from June 1934 until May 1937. His five successors up to 1945 were all made deputy people's commissars within several months of their appointments. The same applied in the independent People's Commissariat of the Navy to the two men who headed the naval MPA from 1937 to 1946.

35. *Partiino-politicheskaia rabota* (1972), p. 62.

36. Ibid., pp. 61-62.

37. *SVE*, II, 274.

38. Quote from N. A. Petrovichev et al., *Partiinoe stroitel'stvo* (Moscow, Politizdat, 1970), p. 205, which refers also to "political workers in the *nomenklatura* [confirmation list] of the Central Committee, Minister of Defense, and chief of the Main Political Administration." According to *SVE*, II, 274, all appointments to military councils (which include political officers as well as commanders) are confirmed by the Central Committee "on suggestion of the Ministry of Defense and the Main Political Administration."

39. Petrovichev et al., p. 198.

40. *Obshchevoinskie Ustavy Vooruzhennykh Sil SSSR* (Moscow, Voenizdat, 1973), pp. 24-26.

41. *KVS*, 1964, no. 19, p. 33; A. I. Bedniagin et al., *Kievskii Krasnoznemennyi* (Moscow, Voenizdat, 1974), p. 355.

42. Petrovichev et al., p. 223; *KVS*, 1976, no. 17, p. 43.

43. *Krasnaia zvezda*, March 27, 1962, p. 2. Statistics from this period often exaggerate the increase in commanders' participation in elective organs following the October 1957 Central Committee plenum on military party work (see Chapter 8 for discussion). Officers' domination of elected organs is not a post-1957 or even a postwar phenomenon. In mid-1957 the overwhelming proportion of all bureau members were graduates of military schools, and even thirty years earlier 85 percent of those in elected posts were command or staff personnel (*Krasnaia zvezda*, June 22, 1957, p. 2; April 29, 1927, p. 3).

44. *KVS*, 1969, no. 19, p. 14. In 1977 over 80 percent of secretaries in the strategic rocket forces were unreleased (ibid., 1977, no. 1, p. 40).

45. A. V. Komarov et al., *Leninskie normy—zakon zhizni armeiskikh partorganizatsii* (Moscow, Voenizdat, 1973), p. 83. The 45 percent included 11 percent subunit commanders, 27 percent staff officers, and 7 percent teachers and researchers; 35 percent was unaccounted for. In one formation studied in 1965, 70 percent of secretaries were commanders, mainly platoon commanders (*KVS*, 1965, no. 11, p. 55).

46. *SVE*, II, 564.

47. Both Bubnov and Shcherbakov had secretarial duties in the propaganda realm. Bubnov was made a secretary a year after taking over the MPA but had earlier been head of the Secretariat's propaganda department. Shcherbakov had already been a secretary for a year when he became MPA chief; he also retained leadership of the Moscow party apparatus throughout the war. Four MPA chiefs were also members of the party Orgburo, which had ill-defined duties in supervising party administration prior to 1952—Bubnov, Mekhlis, and Shcherbakov for their entire terms, and Gamarnik from 1934 to 1937.

48. For reference to such discussions in the late 1950s (on revisions in the Central Committee instruction to party organizations in the army), see Petrov, *Stroitel'stvo politorganov*, pp. 429, 446.

49. Petrov, *Partiinoe stroitel'stvo*, p. 206.

50. Kalashnik, *Politorgany i partiinye organizatsii*, pp. 13-14.

51. Petrov (*Stroitel'stvo politorganov*, p. 401) gives this list as of October 1946 and at no point indicates that it has been changed.

52. Ibid., p. 443.

53. This estimate includes the MPA chief and deputies (4 men); heads of MPA administrations, departments, and party commission (10); chiefs of political administrations at service level (7) and in military districts and equivalents (26); chiefs of political departments of army-level commands (15), combat formations (250), military schools and academies (140), central administrations of ministry (20), district-level staffs and administrations (260, or 10 per district), military commissariats (176), and other establishments (100).

This yields a total of 1,008 men. On the command side (assuming parallelism in jurisdiction), the total must be about 100 higher because commanders outnumber political officers by 4 or 5 to 1 on territorial military councils. The Central Committee presumably possesses a nomenklatura in civil defense and paramilitary organs as well, but information is not available on it.

54. The division of labor between the Potapov and Volkov sectors cannot be ascertained. Several "responsible Central Committee officials" whose departmental affiliations are unidentified also attend military meetings.

55. Only Zheltov was a professional political officer, coming to the department in 1958 directly from the post of head of the MPA. The best biography is in *SVE*. For Zolotukhin, see *Voennyi vestnik*, 1961, no. 11, p. 18, and *Krasnaia zvezda*, May 28, 1976, p. 4. For Mironov, see *Ezhegodnik*, 1965, p. 597; for Savinkin, *Ezhegodnik*, 1977, p. 616.

56. I am indebted to Peter H. Solomon, Jr., and Jerry F. Hough for information on the department's size and capabilities.

57. See, for example, Kolkowicz, *The Soviet Military*, p. 89.

58. Iu. P. Petrov, *KPSS—rukovoditel' i vospitatel' Krasnoi Armii (1918-1920 gg.)* (Moscow, Voenizdat, 1961), p. 107.

59. *KPSS o Vooruzhennykh Silakh Sovetskogo Soiuza* (Moscow, Voenizdat, 1969), pp. 168-169.

60. The best discussion is in Petrov, *Partiinoe stroitel'stvo*, pp. 201-206. The key resolution is in *Pravda*, Aug. 15, 1924, p. 5. Until this time the political administration of the most important naval command, the Baltic Fleet, was directly subordinate to the Petrograd party committee.

61. See *Partiinaia zhizn'*, 1957, no. 23, pp. 42-43.

62. "Experience showed that the civilian party organizations could not achieve effective leadership of the Communist organizations in the army. In conditions of evolving battle, the army's party organizations divorced themselves from the local committees and lost contact with them." S. M. Kliatskin, *Na zashchite Oktiabria* (Moscow, Nauka, 1965), p. 248.

63. *Perepiska Sekretariata TsK RKP(b) s mestnymi partiinymi organizatsiiami*, multivolume (Moscow, Politizdat, 1966-), IV, 467; VIII, 649-650. See also Ia. M. Sverdlov, *Izbrannye proizvedeniia*, 3 vols. (Moscow, Gospolitizdat, 1957-60), III, 105-110.

64. *Krasnaia zvezda*, May 16, 1940, p. 3; *Partiinaia zhizn'*, 1957, no. 23, p. 42.

65. *Partiinaia zhizn'*, 1958, no. 3, p. 8.

66. *Pravda Ukrainy*, Feb. 13, 1976, p. 6.

67. *TIS*, 1973, no. 7, p. 63.

68. *Krasnaia zvezda*, Jan. 12, 1978, p. 3. Eleven thousand soldiers were reported on soviets only five years earlier (*KVS*, 1973, no. 7, p. 26).

69. See *SVE*, IV, 267-268.

70. Soviet sources rarely identify the civilians on these councils, but some memberships have been revealed. For example, the first secretary of the Sverdlovsk oblast committee sits on the military council of the Ural Military District; the heads of the Georgian, Armenian, and Azerbaidzhani parties are on the Transcaucasus Military District's council. According to Petrovichev et

al., p. 232, all republic first secretaries and many from the krai and oblast level are military council members.

71. The 1973 figure on total committee membership is from *KVS*, 1973, no. 7, p. 26. Bureau memberships for 1976 taken from the republic press. Information on earlier bureaus is in Grey Hodnett and Val Ogareff, *Leaders of the Soviet Republics, 1955-1972* (Canberra, Australian National University, 1973). Average membership on central committees as of 1972 calculated from *KVS*, 1972, no. 18, p. 74. Partial statistics on membership at the local level are in Jerry F. Hough, *The Soviet Prefects: The Local Party Organs in Industrial Decision-Making* (Cambridge, Mass., Harvard University Press, 1969), pp. 321-331; Joel C. Moses, *Regional Party Leadership and Policy-Making in the USSR* (New York, Praeger, 1974), p. 160. Military representation on the crucial republican bureaus has been quite stable, although the 1976 figure of six full members (in Azerbaidzhan, Belorussia, Georgia, Kazakhstan, Latvia, and Uzbekistan) is down one from the total of seven members and candidates sustained from 1956 to 1971. All military representatives have been commanders with the exception of E. E. Mal'tsev, then head of the political administration of the Transcaucasus Military District, who sat on the Armenian bureau for nineteen months in 1956-57.

72. *KVS*, 1970, no. 15, p. 26; *Krasnaia zvezda*, Jan. 20, 1952, p. 2.

73. *Krasnaia zvezda*, June 14, 1959, p. 1; May 26, 1959, p. 2; Jan. 11, 1966, p. 3; Oct. 20, 1970, p. 2; *KVS*, 1961, no. 3, p. 49.

74. Merle Fainsod, *Smolensk under Soviet Rule* (Cambridge, Mass., Harvard University Press, 1958), p. 73.

75. N. K. Smirnov, *Zametki chlena Voennogo soveta* (Moscow, Politizdat, 1973), p. 147. Currently only the Belorussian Military District coincides with the area of a union republic; all others contain oblasts from one or several republics. Local party organs had "military departments" from 1939 to 1948, but they were concerned entirely with civil defense and conscription. Such matters are now handled by administrative organs departments.

76. A. A. Novikov, *V nebe Leningrada* (Moscow, Nauka, 1970), p. 253. Zhdanov successfully recommended Novikov for the post of first deputy head of the air force; Novikov had worked in Leningrad since 1938.

77. *Khrushchev Remembers*, ed. Strobe Talbott (New York, Bantam, 1971), pp. 70, 88, 144, 173, 204.

78. Fainsod, *Smolensk under Soviet Rule*, p. 73.

79. *Krasnaia zvezda*, July 2, 1947, p. 1.

80. Ibid., May 16, 1926, p. 3; April 14, 1939, p. 1.

81. *Sovetskii flot*, Nov. 26, 1957, p. 2; *Krasnaia zvezda*, Jan. 28, 1958, p. 1; *KVS*, 1960, no. 1, p. 25; *Partiinaia zhizn'*, 1957, no. 22, p. 28.

2. The Roles of the Military Party Organs

1. *KVS*, 1960, no. 1, p. 17.

2. V. I. Lenin, *Polnoe sobranie sochinenii*, 55 vols. (Moscow, Politizdat, 1967-70), VI, 129.

3. N. Podvoiskii, "Voennaia organizatsiia TsK," pt. 1, *Krasnaia letopis'*,

1923, no. 6, p. 64.

4. P. A. Golub, *Partiia, armiia i revoliutsiia* (Moscow, Politizdat, 1967), p. 50.

5. L. A. Beskrovnyi et al., *Bor'ba bol'shevikov za armiiu v trekh revoliutsiiakh* (Moscow, Politizdat, 1969), p. 198.

6. Lenin, XL, 9.

7. In 1928 the first edition of the *BSE* (XII, 323) cited as precedent not only the French revolutionary commissars but those in Italian mercenary forces and in the Russian army of occupation in Manchuria after 1900 (where they were charged with supervising relations with the local population).

8. Robert Paul Browder and Alexander F. Kerensky, eds., *The Russian Provisional Government, 1917*, 3 vols. (Stanford, Hoover Institution, 1961), II, 865, 986-987. The commissars were officially appointed by the Petrograd Soviet until July. Many commissars' reports are in N. E. Kakurin, ed., *Razlozhenie armii v 1917 godu* (Moscow and Leningrad, Gosizdat, 1925).

9. See especially Kh. I. Muratov, *Revoliutsionnoe dvizhenie v russkoi armii v 1917 godu* (Moscow, Voenizdat, 1958), pp. 250-258.

10. G. A. Belov et al., eds., *Doneseniia komissarov Petrogradskogo Voenno-Revoliutsionnogo Komiteta* (Moscow, Gospolitizdat, 1957), pp. 273-274.

11. Podvoiskii, pt. 2, *Krasnaia letopis'*, 1923, no. 8, p. 41.

12. M. D. Bonch-Bruevich, *Vsia vlast' sovetam* (Moscow, Voenizdat, 1957), p. 228.

13. Quoted from an unpublished speech in S. I. Aralov, *V. I. Lenin i Krasnaia Armiia* (Moscow, Znanie, 1958), p. 27.

14. Estimate from L. Spirin, "V. I. Lenin i sozdanie sovetskikh komandnykh kadrov," *VIZh*, 1965, no. 4, pp. 11-12. In mid-1919 Denikin's army contained two thirds of all the lieutenant-colonels, colonels, and generals of the old army; L. M. Spirin, *Klassy i partii v grazhdanskoi voine v Rossii (1917-1920 gg.)* (Moscow, Mysl', 1968), pp. 290-291.

15. A. I. Radzievskii et al., *Akademiia imeni M. V. Frunze* (Moscow, Voenizdat, 1973), p. 10; Spirin, "V. I. Lenin," p. 13; Bonch-Bruevich, pp. 294-302.

16. Iu. P. Petrov, *Partiinoe stroitel'stvo v Sovetskoi Armii i Flote (1918-1961)* (Moscow, Voenizdat, 1964), p. 35.

17. Lenin, XXXVIII, 6-7.

18. L. Trotsky (Trotskii), *Kak vooruzhalas' revoliutsiia*, 3 vols. (Moscow, Vysshii voennyi redaktsionnyi sovet, 1923-25), vol. I, bk. 1, p. 130.

19. *Perepiska Sekretariata TsK RKP(b) s mestnymi partiinymi organizatsiiami*, multivolume (Moscow, Politizdat, 1966-), IV, 420.

20. Ibid., V, 356. Not all commanders were fearful. One general found the effect of his two commissars "not significant enough to be worth describing" (Bonch-Bruevich, p. 304).

21. Trotsky, *Kak vooruzhalas'*, vol. I, bk. 1, pp. 183, 226-227.

22. A. S. Bubnov et al., *Grazhdanskaia voina, 1918-1921*, 3 vols. (Moscow, Voennyi vestnik, 1928-30), I, 246-249; Leon Trotsky, *My Life* (New York, Scribner's, 1930), pp. 401-402.

23. *Vooruzhennyi narod*, Oct. 24, 1918, p. 4; *The Trotsky Papers*, ed. Jan M. Meyer, 2 vols. (The Hague, Mouton, 1964-71), I, 206.

24. S. I. Gusev, *Grazhdanskaia voina i Krasnaia Armiia* (Moscow, Voenizdat, 1960), p. 110.

25. M. V. Frunze, *Sobranie sochinenii*, 3 vols. (Moscow and Leningrad, Gosizdat, 1925-26), II, 180; emphasis added.

26. Trotsky, *Kak vooruzhalas'*, vol. I, bk. 1, p. 42.

27. G. K. Ordzhonikidze, *Izbrannye stat'i i rechi 1911-1937* (Moscow, Gospolitizdat, 1939), pp. 148-149, gives this ratio as of the end of 1921.

28. Spirin, "V. I. Lenin," p. 13.

29. *Voennoe delo*, Jan. 31, 1919, p. 153.

30. V. V. Britov, *Rozhdenie Krasnoi Armii* (Moscow, Gosudarstvennoe uchebno-pedagogicheskoe izdatel'stvo, 1961), p. 187.

31. Petrov, *Partiinoe stroitel'stvo*, p. 39; Spirin, "V. I. Lenin," p. 16.

32. Lenin, XXXIX, 56.

33. N. Movchin, *Komplektovanie Krasnoi Armii* (Leningrad, Izdatel'stvo voennoi tipografii, 1926), pp. 122-145.

34. Bubnov et al., II, 135.

35. Quoted in *Tolmachevets*, 1925, no. 3, pp. 50-51; emphasis added.

36. Trotsky, *Kak vooruzhalas'*, I, book 1, pp. 30, 128. For dramatic illustration of how commissars dealt with discipline problems, see N. I. Kiriukhin, *Iz dnevnika komissara* (Moscow, Voennyi vestnik, 1928).

37. I. B. Berkhin, *Voennaia reforma v SSSR (1924-1925 gg.)* (Moscow, Voenizdat, 1958), p. 33.

38. *Partiino-politicheskaia rabota v Krasnoi Armii (Mart 1919-1920 gg.): Dokumenty* (Moscow, Voenizdat, 1964), pp. 39-40.

39. *Trotsky Papers*, I, 444; emphasis added. See the discussion in Timothy J. Colton, "Military Councils and Military Politics in the Russian Civil War," *Canadian Slavonic Papers*, 18 (March 1976), 36-57.

40. Trotsky, *Kak vooruzhalas'*, vol. I, bk. 1, p. 172.

41. See *Izvestiia Vremennogo Revoliutsionnogo Komiteta . . . Kronshtadta* (the rebels' newspaper), March 5-11, 1921. Kuz'min escaped from the fortress and took part in the final Soviet assault.

42. In N. Podvoiskii and M. Pavlovich, *Revoliutsionnaia voina* (Moscow, VTsIK, 1919), p. 26.

43. K. E. Voroshilov, *Stat'i i rechi* (Moscow, Partizdat, 1937), p. 236; "M. V. Frunze i reorganizatsiia Krasnoi Armii v 1924 godu," pt. 2, *VIZh*, 1966, no. 8, pp. 70-71.

44. *Tolmachevets*, 1923, no. 7, p. 27.

45. Ibid., 1925, no. 2, p. 6.

46. *Polevoi Ustav RKKA* (Moscow and Leningrad, Gosizdat, 1931), p. 46.

47. F. Blumental', *Politicheskaia rabota v voennoe vremia* (Moscow and Leningrad, Gosizdat, 1927), pp. 38-39.

48. V. Triandafillov, *Kharakter operatsii sovremennykh armii*, 2nd ed. (Moscow, Voenizdat, 1932), pp. 50, 163.

49. *Krasnaia zvezda*, Dec. 1, 1962, p. 2; V. D. Sokolovskii et al., *Voennaia strategiia* (Moscow, Voenizdat, 1968), pp. 454-455.

50. Petrov, *Partiinoe stroitel'stvo*, p. 356, referring to the 1941 decree. On the change of 1937, one textbook states that the new commissars "were fundamentally different from the commissars of the Civil War period . . . Then . . . commissars controlled the activity of the commanders, among whom were specialists from the old army. In the new conditions the military commissars helped commanders who were brought up by the Communist party and the Soviet state to lead the troops." *Partiino-politicheskaia rabota v Sovetskikh Vooruzhennykh Silakh* (Moscow, Voenizdat, 1968), p. 28.

51. When official statements refer to officers as being "under the control of the party" (*pod kontrolem partii;* as in *Morskoi sbornik,* 1965, no. 12, p. 10), they normally mean that commanders are basically loyal to the Soviet system and obedient to the civilian party leadership, not that their actions are under minute scrutiny by the military party apparatus.

52. Herbert A. Simon, *Administrative Behavior,* 2nd ed. (New York, Free Press, 1957), p. 176.

53. N. M. Kiriaev et al., *KPSS i stroitel'stvo Sovetskikh Vooruzhennykh Sil* (Moscow, Voenizdat, 1967), p. 214. Antonov-Ovseenko broke with Trotsky in 1927 and later claimed he had attempted to reconcile Trotsky and Stalin. Anton Rakitin, *Imenem revoliutsii* (Moscow, Politizdat, 1965), p. 151.

54. *Tolmachevets,* 1924, no. 1-2, p. 7; no. 4-5, p. 1.

55. Iu. P. Petrov, *Stroitel'stvo politorganov, partiinykh i komsomo-l'skikh organizatsii Armii i Flota (1918-1968)* (Moscow, Voenizdat, 1968), p. 198.

56. Harold D. Lasswell and Abraham Kaplan, *Power and Society: A Framework for Political Inquiry* (New Haven, Yale University Press, 1950), p. 240.

57. Voroshilov, p. 50.

58. Statistics from ibid., p. 445; Bubnov et al., pp. 97-99; Berkhin, p. 261. Of the 14,390 Red Army officers who had at one point fought for the Whites in the Civil War, only 397 were still in service in 1925, among them the future marshal Leonid Govorov.

59. The seventeen who reached the top ranks are A. I. Antonov, I. R. Apanasenko, F. A. Astakhov, I. Kh. Bagramian, S. I. Bogdanov, A. I. Egorov, L. A. Govorov, I. S. Isakov, G. K. Malandin, I. E. Petrov, B. M. Shaposhnikov, F. I. Tolbukhin, M. N. Tukhachevskii, A. M. Vasilevskii, M. P. Vorob'ev, G. A. Vorozheikin, and G. F. Zakharov. Only two, Egorov and Shaposhnikov, received commissions before 1914, and Egorov's career was interrupted because of his (antiregime) political views. Antonov, Egorov, S. S. Kamenev, P. P. Lebedev, Shaposhnikov, Tukhachevskii, and Vasilevskii became post-1921 heads of the General Staff and its predecessor agencies. Bagramian, Bogdanov, Egorov, Govorov, Shaposhnikov, Tukhachevskii, and Vasilevskii became full or candidate members of the Central Committee.

60. Voroshilov, pp. 575-576.

61. *KVS,* 1971, no. 4, p. 31. The proportion of party members seems to decline significantly below unity only at the platoon level. In a typical formation in 1964 all regiment, battalion, and company commanders were party members, but only 60 percent of platoon commanders; in 1963, 90 percent of all company commanders were party members, but in 1978, 20 percent of

company commanders (and 60 percent of platoon commanders) belonged to the Komsomol. Ibid., 1964, no. 10, p. 10; M. Kh. Kalashnik, *Politorgany i partiinye organizatsii Sovetskoi Armii i Voenno-Morskogo Flota* (Moscow, Voenizdat, 1963), p. 15; *Krasnaia zvezda*, Feb. 19, 1978, p. 2.

62. Jerry F. Hough, *The Soviet Prefects: The Local Party Organs in Industrial Decision-Making* (Cambridge, Mass., Harvard University Press, 1969), pp. 171-172.

63. Roman Kolkowicz, *The Soviet Military and the Communist Party* (Princeton, Princeton University Press, 1967), p. 93.

64. The nine who took over twenty years to join the party were Bagramian, Bogdanov, M. N. Chistiakov, Govorov, Isakov, Malandin, Tolbukhin, S. S. Varentsov, and Vasilevskii. All but Chistiakov and Varentsov were officers before 1917. It should not be thought that these were typical experiences. By 1941 the expectation of party membership was so ingrained that when one young officer realized that his division commander (a former tsarist officer) was only then applying for party admission, "It simply would not sink into my head. Here was a man of fifty years, a division commander, and suddenly it turns out that he is not a party member. How could this be?" D. A. Dragunskii, *Gody v brone* (Moscow, Voenizdat, 1973), p. 34."

65. *Krasnaia zvezda*, April 5, 1969, p. 3. Many of these were admitted to the party before leaving military school. One often finds reports of storms (*shturmy*) of admissions shortly before cadets graduate. For example, in Moscow schools "in these [last] two months there are usually as many party admissions as in the ten preceding months" (ibid., July 20, 1965, p. 3). In 1927, 50.4 percent of all military school graduates were party members and 30.5 percent Komsomol members (I. E. Slavin, *Armiia proletarskoi diktatury* [Moscow, Voennyi vestnik, 1928], p. 12). In 1963, 73.6 percent of the graduates of one well-established school were party members (A. I. Babin et al., *Rozhdennoe Oktiabrem* [Moscow, Voenizdat, 1966], p. 324). Virtually all new students are now members of the Komsomol (97.5 percent of those entering naval and infantry school in Leningrad in 1970, according to *Krasnaia zvezda*, Jan. 29, 1971, p. 2).

66. *KVS*, 1965, no. 16, p. 28; *Krasnaia zvezda*, July 6, 1965, p. 1; *KVS*, 1969, no. 12, p. 56. Such concern was perhaps behind the slight decline in party membership among officers in the late 1960s, but as Table 6 shows party membership had again increased by 1974. The proportion of party members among platoon commanders in a typical motorized regiment increased from 27.3 percent in 1971 to 39.2 percent in 1976 (*Krasnaia zvezda*, Feb. 18, 1976, p. 2).

67. *Partiino-politicheskaia rabota v Sovetskoi Armii i Flote* (Moscow, Voenizdat, 1967), p. 74.

68. M. Kh. Kalashnik, *Ideinoe vospotanie sovetskikh voinov* (Moscow, Voenizdat, 1967), p. 74.

3. The Military Party Organs in Military Administration

1. The decree is in *KPSS o Vooruzhennykh Silakh Sovetskogo Soiuza* (Moscow, Voenizdat, 1969), pp. 318-319.

2. *Krasnaia zvezda,* Aug. 29, 1937, p. 1.

3. Iu. P. Petrov, *Partiinoe stroitel'stvo v Sovetskoi Armii i Flote (1918-1961)* (Moscow, Voenizdat, 1964), p. 142.

4. *Obshchevoinskie Ustavy Vooruzhennykh Sil SSSR* (Moscow, Voenizdat, 1973), pp. 22-24.

5. Even the July 1941 decree on commissars concentrated on political work, quoting Stalin to the effect that the commander was to be the head of the unit and the commissar its father and soul (*KPSS o Vooruzhennykh Silakh,* pp. 307-308).

6. *Tolmachevets,* 1925, no. 3, p. 51.

7. Quotations from N. K. Smirnov, *Zametki chlena Voennogo soveta* (Moscow, Politizdat, 1973), p. 35.

8. *Krasnaia zvezda,* Dec. 17, 1940, p. 2.

9. Ibid., May 14, 1938, p. 2.

10. Ibid., April 4, 1938, p. 1.

11. V. N. Eroshenko, *Lider 'Tashkent'* (Moscow, Voenizdat, 1966), p. 43.

12. *Obshchevoinskie Ustavy,* p. 162.

13. *Morskoi sbornik,* 1976, no. 5, p. 11.

14. *TIS,* 1968, no. 3, p. 27.

15. *Krasnyi flot,* May 12, 1946, p. 3.

16. *Izvestiia,* Oct. 12, 1961, p. 4.

17. *Partiino-politicheskaia rabota v Sovetskikh Vooruzhennykh Silakh* (Moscow, Voenizdat, 1974), p. 135.

18. I have no statistics on relative ages, merely a firm impression from the press and other sources. In an extreme case, one young political officer is said to have exclaimed during the war, "How am I to educate my commander if he has twice as much party seniority as I do and has been in the navy for at least a decade longer?" (Smirnov, *Zametki chlena,* p. 75).

19. M. Kh. Kalashnik, *Politorgany i partiinye organizatsii Sovetskoi Armii i Voenno-Morskogo Flota* (Moscow, Voenizdat, 1963), p. 10. This and other sources also insist that commanders are subject to criticism for their personal bearing (*povedenie*) and fulfillment of party duties.

20. *Krasnaia zvezda,* June 5, 1973, p. 1. A typical early statement is in *Krasnyi flot,* May 17, 1946, p. 1. The May 1957 instruction gave the right to direct to all commanders, but in 1958 this was redefined to include only commanders who belong to the party.

21. *KVS,* 1964, no. 19, p. 33.

22. *Sputnik politrabotnika,* 1926, no. 28-29, p. 9.

23. Khrushchev in *Pravda,* Nov. 26, 1957, p. 1.

24. *Obshchevoinskie Ustavy,* p. 25.

25. M. F. Kumanin, *Otpravliaem v pokhod korabli* (Moscow, Voenizdat, 1962), p. 72.

26. *Krasnaia zvezda,* Jan. 5, 1954, p. 2.

27. Ibid., April 11, 1957, p. 3.

28. *Partiino-politicheskaia rabota v Krasnoi Armii (Mart 1919-1920 gg.): Dokumenty* (Moscow, Voenizdat, 1964), p. 166.

29. See, for example, *Krasnaia zvezda*, Jan. 4, 1972, p. 2.

30. See K. V. Krainiukov, *Ot Dnepra do Visly* (Moscow, Voenizdat, 1971), pp. 208-210. Civil War councils did not have the formal right to discuss strategy, but "often operational questions were also discussed collegially [although] the decision remained with the commander." Any council member could cosign the commander's order. S. I. Gusev, *Grazhdanskaia voina i Krasnaia Armiia* (Moscow, Voenizdat, 1960), p. 111.

31. Petrov, *Partiinoe stroitel'stvo*, p. 468.

32. Ibid., p. 367; E. Nikitin and S. Baranov, "Trud o partiinom stroitel'stve v Sovetskikh Vooruzhennykh Silakh," *VIZh*, 1964, no. 11, p. 90.

33. For the striking example of Politburo member Lazar Kaganovich in the council of the Maritime Group of Forces in 1942, see N. Strakhov, "Na voenno-avtomobil'nykh dorogakh," *VIZh*, 1964, no. 11, pp. 70-71.

34. Roman Kolkowicz, *The Soviet Military and the Communist Party* (Princeton, Princeton University Press, 1967), pp. 125-126.

35. *Pravda*, Aug. 29, 1958, p. 4.

36. *KVS*, 1967, no. 8, p. 13.

37. See the comment about Marshal Malinovskii in A. K. Blazhei, *V armeiskom shtabe* (Moscow, Voenizdat, 1967), pp. 100-101.

38. This occurred in the Pacific Fleet in 1969-70 when Admiral M. N. Zakharov, the head of the political administration since 1956, outranked the new commander, Vice-Admiral N. I. Smirnov (who was five years his junior). Zakharov retired in 1971 and died in 1978; Smirnov is now an admiral of the fleet and first deputy head of the navy. Altogether, about 150 nonpolitical officers have attained marshal's or equivalent rank, but only 4 political officers.

39. See V. P. Agafonov, *Neman! Neman! Ia—Dunai!* (Moscow, Voenizdat, 1967), p. 137.

40. P. I. Batov, *V pokhodakh i boiakh*, 2nd ed. (Moscow, Voenizdat, 1966), p. 47.

41. M. Kh. Kalashnik, *Ispytanie ognem* (Moscow, Voenizdat, 1971), pp. 20-21.

42. Iu. P. Petrov, *Stroitel'stvo politorganov, partiinykh i komsomo-l'skikh organizatsii Armii i Flota (1918-1968)* (Moscow, Voenizdat, 1968), p. 414.

43. See Timothy J. Colton, "Military Councils and Military Politics in the Russian Civil War," *Canadian Slavonic Papers*, 18 (March 1976), 41-50.

44. K. K. Rokossovskii, *Soldatskii dolg* (Moscow, Voenizdat, 1972), p. 210.

45. *Khrushchev Remembers*, ed. Strobe Talbott (New York, Bantam, 1971), p. 219. It is noteworthy that even praises of Khrushchev's qualities published while he was in power did not claim that he had exerted primacy in making operational decisions in the wartime military councils on which he sat.

46. In the case of Gorchakov, personal connections as well as current post may have something to do with his high party standing. As the youthful chief

of the politotdel of an infantry division in 1944-45, he worked under the supervision of both Brezhnev (then head of the political administration of the Fourth Ukrainian Front) and Epishev (member of the military council of the Thirty-eighth Army), not to mention the future marshals Grechko and Moskalenko (then commanders of armies). Epishev personally chose Gorchakov to represent his army in the June 1945 victory parade, in which Brezhnev also marched. See P. A. Gorchakov, *Vremia trevog i pobed* (Moscow, Voenizdat, 1977), especially pp. 268-270. For Grushevoi and Brezhnev, the early association is discussed in K. S. Grushevoi, *Togda, v sorok pervom* (Moscow, Voenizdat, 1972). Grushevoi and Brezhnev are the same age, graduated from the same metallurgical institute in successive years, began their administrative careers in Dneprodzerzhinsk and Dnepropetrovsk in the late 1930s, and were both party secretaries in Dnepropetrovsk oblast from 1939 to 1941. After a six-year hiatus, Grushevoi returned to the MPA in 1953 during Brezhnev's brief tenure as its first deputy chief. Since 1976 Grushevoi's candidate status on the Central Committee has been equal to that of the Moscow Military District commander. In only one case—the Pacific Fleet from 1939 to 1948—has the political officer outranked the commander in a district-level command in terms of Central Committee status. The political officer concerned was S. E. Zakharov, a full committee member who was evidently a favorite of Stalin.

47. Krainiukov, p. 207.

48. For a good example see I. I. Fediuninskii, *Podniatye po trevoge* (Moscow, Voenizdat, 1961), pp. 76-77.

49. *Krasnaia zvezda*, Feb. 6, 1963, p. 1.

50. Statistics in Petrov, *Partiinoe stroitel'stvo*, p. 295; *Krasnaia zvezda*, May 13, 1972, p. 1, and Nov. 16, 1971, p. 2; Petrov, *Stroitel'stvo politorganov*, pp. 432-433; E. F. Sulimov et al., *Voprosy nauchnogo rukovodstva v Sovetskikh Vooruzhennykh Silakh* (Moscow, Voenizdat, 1973), p. 188.

51. See *Partiino-politicheskaia rabota* (1974), pp. 271-274.

52. *Krasnaia zvezda*, July 23, 1932, p. 1.

53. See *Partiino-politicheskaia rabota 1919-20*, pp. 110-112, 209-210, 219-221, 517; P. V. Suslov, *Politicheskoe obespechenie sovetsko-pol'skoi kampanii 1920 goda* (Moscow and Leningrad, Gosizdat, 1930), pp. 104-149.

54. The fullest discussion is in K. V. Krainiukov et al., *Partiino-politicheskaia rabota v Sovetskikh Vooruzhennykh Silakh v gody Velikoi Otechestvennoi voiny 1941-1945* (Moscow, Voenizdat, 1963), pp. 523-569. The directive quoted is on p. 566.

55. I. V. Stalin, *Sochineniia*, 13 vols. (Moscow, Gospolitizdat, 1946-52), V, 205.

56. *Krasnaia zvezda*, May 9, 1973, p. 2.

57. Ibid., Oct. 30, 1977, p. 2.

58. *XXV s"ezd Kommunisticheskoi Partii Sovetskogo Soiuza: Stenograficheskii otchet*, 3 vols. (Moscow, Politizdat, 1976), I, 101.

59. Sulimov et al., pp. 140-141.

60. *Vestnik PVO*, 1968, no. 12, p. 10; *Morskoi sbornik*, 1969, no. 9, pp. 5-6. Details on organization over time can be found only in the press.

61. *Krasnyi flot*, April 24, 1947, p. 1; *Morskoi sbornik*, 1969, no. 8, p. 6; *Krasnaia zvezda*, April 11, 1973, p. 2.

62. *Krasnaia zvezda*, June 9, 1934, p. 3; June 11, 1934, p. 3.

63. Ibid., Oct. 30, 1973, p. 2; May 18, 1972, p. 1.

64. Ibid., Jan. 12, 1978, p. 3.

65. Details on organization have been culled from the press.

66. *Izvestiia*, Feb. 21, 1969, p. 3.

67. M. Kh. Kalashnik, *Ideinoe vospitanie sovetskikh voinov* (Moscow, Voenizdat, 1967), p. 18; there have been no announced changes since 1967. On reserve officers, see *Morskoi sbornik*, 1969, no. 10, p. 49.

68. *Morskoi sbornik*, 1976, no. 1, p. 6.

69. *Voprosy partiino-organizatsionnoi raboty* (Moscow, Voenizdat, 1967), p. 62; *Krasnaia zvezda*, June 21, 1966, p. 2.

70. *Propagandist i agitator RKKA*, 1938, no. 15, pp. 2-3.

71. *Krasnaia zvezda*, Nov. 14, 1940, p. 3.

72. *KVS*, 1962, no. 17, p. 15; *Krasnaia zvezda*, Oct. 26, 1962, p. 3; March 30, 1975, p. 2; Nov. 30, 1975, p. 2.

73. *KVS*, 1963, no. 4, p. 38.

74. The criticism is in *Sovetskii flot*, Feb. 14, 1958, p. 1.

75. In *Ideologicheskaia rabota KPSS na fronte (1941-1945 gg.)* (Moscow, Voenizdat, 1960), pp. 49-50.

76. Statistic in Petrov, *Stroitel'stvo politorganov*, pp. 325-326.

77. *Voennyi vestnik*, 1966, no. 2, p. 62; *KVS*, 1963, no. 23, p. 56; *Krasnaia zvezda*, Sept. 13, 1975, p. 2.

78. *SVE*, IV, 523.

79. A. A. Epishev et al., *Partiino-politicheskaia rabota v Vooruzhennykh Silakh SSSR 1918-1973 gg.* (Moscow, Voenizdat, 1974), p. 327; Petrov, *Partiinoe stroitel'stvo*, p. 479.

80. *KVS*, 1971, no. 10, pp. 46-47.

81. See especially V. M. Grishanov, ed., *Voina, okean, chelovek* (Moscow, Voenizdat, 1974); A. S. Zheltov, ed., *Soldat i voina* (Moscow, Voenizdat, 1971); V. V. Sheliag et al., eds., *Voennaia psikhologiia* (Moscow, Voenizdat, 1972).

82. *TIS*, 1967, no. 8, p. 23; *Partiino-politicheskaia rabota v Sovetskikh Vooruzhennykh Silakh* (Moscow, Voenizdat, 1964), p. 91.

83. *Krasnaia zvezda*, Sept. 14, 1971, p. 2.; *Voprosy partiino-organizatsionnoi raboty*, p. 185.

84. *KVS*, 1976, no. 13, p. 51. For a good example of internal advocacy (on behalf of a sailor with a sick mother), see *Morskoi sbornik*, 1965, no. 1, p. 42.

85. *TIS*, 1972, no. 10, p. 13. The twelve MPA chiefs prior to 1942 (including two heads of the independent naval MPA) included six Russians, three Jews, two Ukrainians, and one Latvian.

86. Quotation from *KVS*, 1970, no. 3, p. 24.

87. *Sputnik partiinogo aktivista* (Moscow, Voenizdat, 1965), p. 6.

88. There is a vivid example in D. Kochetkov, *S zakrytami liukami* (Moscow, Voenizdat, 1962), pp. 21-22.

89. *Krasnaia zvezda*, Aug. 9, 1942, p. 1.

90. Ibid., Jan. 9, 1975, pp. 2-3.

91. *TIS*, 1968, no. 6, p. 48.

92. *Bloknot agitatora*, 1974, no. 2, p. 22.

93. See *Vestnik PVO*, 1969, no. 5, pp. 25-27; *Morskoi sbornik*, 1974, no. 1, p. 33.

94. *Partiino-politicheskaia rabota* (1964), pp. 52-53; *Morskoi sbornik*, 1976, no. 5, p. 42.

95. N. M. Kiriaev et al., *KPSS i stroitel'stvo Sovetskikh Vooruzhennykh Sil* (Moscow, Voenizdat, 1967), p. 219.

96. Petrov, *Partiinoe stroitel'stvo*, p. 276.

97. *Krasnaia zvezda*, June 7, 1972, p. 1.

98. *Partiino-politicheskaia rabota v Sovetskoi Armii i Flote* (Moscow, Voenizdat, 1967), pp. 116-117; *KVS*, 1970, no. 2, p. 64; *Vestnik PVO*, 1968, no. 9, p. 13; 1966, no. 4, p. 28.

99. *Krasnyi flot*, Jan.29, 1953, p. 1; *KVS*, 1968, no. 2, p. 57.

100. *KVS*, 1968, no. 2, p. 57; 1970, no. 15, p. 85; *Sovetskii flot*, Dec. 1, 1957, p. 1.

101. *Krasnaia zvezda*, Feb. 23, 1978, p. 3; Feb. 5, 1978, p. 2.

102. Herbert A. Simon, *Administrative Behavior*, 2nd ed. (New York, Free Press, 1957), pp. 125, 140.

103. Kurt Lang, *Military Institutions and the Sociology of War* (Beverly Hills, Sage, 1972), p. 65.

104. Rensis Likert, *New Patterns of Management* (New York, McGraw Hill, 1961), p. 103.

105. Peter M. Blau and W. Richard Scott, *Formal Organizations: A Comparative Approach* (San Francisco, Chandler, 1962), pp. 153, 238.

106. Morris Janowitz, *The Professional Soldier* (Glencoe, Ill., Free Press, 1960), pp. 8-9.

107. Robert K. Merton, *Social Theory and Social Structure* (Glencoe, Ill., Free Press, 1957), p. 199.

108. *Krasnaia zvezda*, July 31, 1957, p. 2.

109. *KVS*, 1964, no. 21, p. 60; *Krasnaia zvezda*, April 17, 1947, p. 1.

110. *Krasnaia zvezda*, Feb. 14, 1936, p. 3.

111. Ibid., June 1, 1947, p. 1.

112. Ibid., Feb. 14, 1934, p. 1.

113. Ibid., May 17, 1961, p. 3.

114. *KVS*, 1963, no. 14, p. 61.

115. *Krasnaia zvezda*, May 27, 1970, p. 3.

116. Ibid., July 28, 1956, p. 3.

117. Ibid., May 20, 1939, p. 2.

118. Ibid., Jan. 26, 1940, p. 1, and Aug. 9, 1956, p. 1.

119. Ibid., June 14, 1966, p. 2, and Jan. 11, 1956, p. 3.

120. Ibid., June 21, 1968, p. 2.

4. The Monitoring Capability of the Military Party Organs

1. The Downs quotations are all from Anthony Downs, *Inside Bureaucracy* (Boston, Little, Brown, 1967), pp. 148-151.

2. *Krasnaia zvezda*, Oct. 28, 1966, p. 2.

3. *Sputnik politrabotnika*, 1926, no. 50, p. 7.

4. See especially Iu. P. Petrov, *Partiinoe stroitel'stvo v Sovetskoi Armii i Flote (1918-1961)* (Moscow, Voenizdat, 1964), pp. 265-275; A. S. Zheltov et al., *Imeni Lenina* (Moscow, Voenizdat, 1966), pp. 76-77; D. A. Voropaev and A. M. Iovlev,. *Bor'ba KPSS za sozdanie voennykh kadrov* (Moscow, Voenizdat, 1960), pp. 109-111.

5. N. K. Popel', *V tiazhkuiu poru* (Moscow, Voenizdat, 1959), p. 36.

6. M. Kh. Kalashnik, *Ispytanie ognem* (Moscow, Voenizdat, 1971), p. 75.

7. Petrov, *Partiinoe stroitel'stvo*, p. 377.

8. *KPSS o Vooruzhennykh Silakh Sovetskogo Soiuza* (Moscow, Voenizdat, 1969), p. 252.

9. Petrov, *Partiinoe stroitel'stvo*, p. 270.

10. Ibid., p. 377. Gordov died in 1951, apparently of natural causes.

11. Aleksandr Geronimus, *Partiia i Krasnaia Armiia* (Moscow and Leningrad, Gosizdat, 1928), pp. 86-88; A. Iovlev, "Pervye shagi po vvedeniiu edinonachaliia v Krasnoi armii (1918-1920 gg.)," *VIZh*, 1968, no. 6, p. 102.

12. See P. A. Prishchepchik, "Nachal'nik PURa," in N. F. Brychev and I. L. Obertas, eds., *Poslantsy partii* (Moscow, Voenizdat, 1967), pp. 314-321.

13. See I. B. Berkhin, *Voennaia reforma v SSSR (1924-1925 gg.)* (Moscow, Voenizdat, 1958), pp. 326-328; *Krasnaia zvezda*, Aug. 14, 1940, p. 1.

14. See Popel', *V tiazhkuiu poru*, p. 106; S. S. Biriuzov, *Kogda gremeli pushki* (Moscow, Voenizdat, 1961), p. 29.

15. Kalashnik, *Ispytanie ognem*. p. 83.

16. A. I. Shebunin, *Skol'ko nami proideno* (Moscow, Voenizdat, 1971), p. 53.

17. S. I. Gusev, *Grazhdanskaia voina i Krasnaia Armiia* (Moscow, Voenizdat, 1960), p. 111.

18. A. S. Bubnov, *O Krasnoi Armii* (Moscow, Voenizdat, 1958), p. 153; A. Pigurnov, "Deiatel'nost' voennykh sovetov, politorganov i partiinykh organizatsii po ukrepleniiu edinonachaliia v period Velikoi Otechestvennoi voiny," *VIZh*, 1961, no. 4, p. 50.

19. *Krasnaia zvezda*, Oct. 24, 1972, p. 2.

20. Petrov, *Partiinoe stroitel'stvo*, p. 40.

21. A. A. Epishev, *Nekotorye voprosy partiino-politicheskoi raboty* (Moscow, Voenizdat, 1970), p. 98.

22. V. O. Vilenskii, *Dva goda Krasnoi Akademii General'nogo Shtaba (1918 g.-sentiabr' 1920 g.)* (Moscow, RVSR, 1921), p. 22.

23. M. V. Frunze, *Sobranie sochinenii*, 3 vols. (Moscow and Leningrad, Gosizdat, 1925-26), II, 59-60.

24. Petrov, *Partiinoe stroitel'stvo*, pp. 182, 191, 195.

25. Ibid., p. 290.

26. *Krasnaia zvezda*, Dec. 31, 1937, p. 1; Feb. 1, 1939, p. 2.

27. Statistics from S. Zakharov, "Povyshenie urovnia voennykh znanii politrabotnikov v gody minuvshei voiny," *VIZh*, 1966, no. 12, pp. 9-10;

Petrov, *Partiinoe stroitel'stvo*, p. 382; Iu. P. Petrov, *Stroitel'stvo politorga-nov, partiinykh i komsomol'skikh organizatsii Armii i Flota (1918-1968)* (Moscow, Voenizdat, 1968), p. 319.

28. *Krasnaia zvezda*, May 15, 1960, p. 2; April 18, 1961, p. 3.

29. Epishev, *Nekotorye voprosy*, pp. 98-99.

30. *TIS*, 1968, no. 3, p. 27.

31. This and subsequent notes on careers will cite only the best source for the information in the text (see Appendix A). Information on Frunze and Shchadenko is in *BSE*, 2nd. Alksnis, Baranov, Berzin, Bluikher, Kuibyshev, Muklevich, Smushkevich, Tukhachevskii, Voroshilov, and Zof are in *BSE*, 3rd. Iakir and Shtern are in *SIE*. For Appoga, Bulin, and Rybin, see *Krasnaia zvezda*, Dec. 1, 1963, p. 2; Feb. 1, 1964, p. 6; March 16, 1939, p. 4. Kireev and Slavin are covered in biographical notes in *VIZh*, 1965, no. 1, p. 123, and 1964, no. 3, pp. 117-122. For Kosich, Oshlei, and Sediakin, see M. M. Zomov et al., *Marshal Tukhachevskii* (Moscow, Voenizdat, 1965), pp. 241, 243, 245; for N. G. Kuznetsov, Petrov, *Partiinoe stroitel'stvo*, p. 199.

32. The former political officers do not include two men (G. K. Zhukov and A. Kh. Babadzhanian) known to have served as party secretaries while carrying out command duties.

33. See *BSE*, 3rd, for Aban'kin, Agal'tsov, Golikov, Konev, F. F. Kuznetsov, Meretskov, Nedelin, Peresypkin, and Rybalko; *SIE* for Falaleev; *SVE* for Beloborodov, Belokoskov, Kazakov, Korovnikov, Krasovskii, Kurkotkin, Leliushenko, Zheltov, and Zhuravlev. Information on Anisimov, Basistyi, Beliaev, Chukhnov, Khotenko, Khrulev, Oktiabr'skii, and Shev-chuk is in *Krasnaia zvezda*, Nov. 22, 1977, p. 4; Oct. 22, 1971, p. 4; Jan. 11, 1970, p. 3; April 1, 1965, p. 4; Oct. 27, 1976, p. 4; June 12, 1962, p. 3; July 9, 1969, p. 3; June 28, 1975, p. 2. For N. G. Kuznetsov and Vorozheikin, only Petrov, *Partiinoe stroitel'stvo*, pp. 198-199, mentions MPA experience. For Golovnin, see E. F. Ivanovskii et al., *Ordena Lenina Moskovskii voennyi okrug* (Moscow, Voenizdat, 1971), p. 446; for Malandin, A. I. Eremenko, *V nachale voiny* (Moscow, Nauka, 1964), p. 496. Information on Kabanov and Shebunin is taken from their memoirs.

34. *Tolmachevets*, 1925, no. 1, p. 26.

35. Petrov, *Partiinoe stroitel'stvo*, p. 290.

36. Popel', *V tiazhkuiu poru*, pp. 137-139.

37. A. A. Lobachev, *Trudnymi dorogami* (Moscow, Voenizdat, 1960), p. 88.

38. See *Krasnaia zvezda*, July 13, 1962, p. 4. Susaikov had served as member of the military council of the Belorussian Military District in the late 1930s, then returned to command work as director of a military school.

39. For another example, see the biography of N. I. Biriukov in *Krasnaia zvezda*, June 28, 1974, p. 4.

40. Ibid., May 15, 1960, p. 2.

41. Epishev, *Nekotorye voprosy*, p. 98. For biographies, see *Krasnaia zvezda*, Feb. 23, 1972, pp. 2-3; March 28, 1976, p. 2; Feb. 19, 1977, p. 2.

42. Petrov, *Stroitel'stvo politorganov*, p. 439.

43. *KVS*, 1962, no. 17, p. 16.

44. N. B. Ivushkin, *Za vse v otvete* (Moscow, Voenizdat, 1969), p. 51.

45. These terms are used in *Krasnaia zvezda*, Aug. 2, 1970, p. 2; Sept. 17, 1968, p. 2; *KVS*, 1968, no. 22, p. 19.

46. *Pravda*, Nov. 26, 1957, p. 1.

47. Morris Janowitz, *The Professional Soldier* (Glencoe, Ill., Free Press, 1960), p. 6.

48. Biographies of Antonov-Ovseenko, Bubnov, and Gusev are in *BSE*, 3rd. Iurenev's biography is in *SIE*, Smilga's in *Vos'moi s"ezd RKP (b): Protokoly* (Moscow, Gospolitizdat, 1959), p. 588.

49. For Gamarnik and Mekhlis, see *BSE*, 3rd; for Shcherbakov, *BSE*, 2nd; for Shikin, *Ezhegodnik*, 1971, p. 640, and *Krasnaia zvezda*, Aug. 1, 1973, p. 3.

50. Iurenev, Smilga, and Antonov-Ovseenko became diplomats, their careers blighted by their association with Trotsky. Antonov-Ovseenko was also procurator of the Russian Republic from 1934 to 1936, and Bubnov became People's Commissar of Education. All perished in the Great Purge. Gusev worked in the party Secretariat and Comintern after 1922 and died of natural causes in 1933. Mekhlis was Minister of State Control from 1946 to 1950 and between his two terms in the MPA; he died in 1953. After brief service as head of the Lenin Academy, Shikin moved into the Secretariat in 1950 (and was for several years first deputy head of the department supervising party appointments); he was ambassador to Albania in 1961-62, then until his death in 1973 first deputy head of the Committee of People's (Party-State) Control.

51. On Bulin and Smirnov, see *Krasnaia zvezda*, Feb. 1, 1964, p. 6, and Nov. 26, 1937, p. 2; on Zaporozhets, ibid., May 28, 1938, p. 2, and *SVE*; on Shaposhnikov, *Krasnyi flot*, June 24, 1938, p. 2; on Rogov, *Pravda*, Dec. 7, 1949, p. 3.

52. Petrov, *Partiinoe stroitel'stvo*, pp. 291-292. Prior to this there was some recruitment on an individual basis (for example, of the Armenian first secretary, G. A. Osepian, in 1928). Shortly after the 1931-32 mobilizations into the MPA came the only large-scale infusion of political officers into civilian party work (except for postwar demobilization), the sending of 300 political officers to work in beleaguered machine tractor stations and state farms in the North Caucasus and Ukraine in 1933. For biographies of Efimov and Kalashnik, see *SVE* and *Krasnaia zvezda*, May 8, 1974, p. 3.

53. Statistics in N. M. Kiriaev et al., *KPSS i stroitel'stvo Sovetskikh Vooruzhennykh Sil* (Moscow, Voenizdat, 1967), pp. 230-231. The description of Kuznetsov as a purger is in *Krasnaia zvezda*, June 1, 1938, p. 2.

54. Figures in Petrov, *Partiinoe stroitel'stvo*, pp. 310, 350; *Istoriia Kommunisticheskoi Partii Sovetskogo Soiuza*, 6 vols. (Moscow, Politizdat, 1964-), vol. V, bk. 1, p. 170; V. P. Bokarev, "Reshenie problemy podgotovki kadrov politsostava Sovetskoi Armii v gody Velikoi Otechestvennoi voiny," *Voprosy istorii KPSS*, 1972, no. 8, p. 97.

55. G. N. Kupriianov, *Ot Varentseva moria do Ladogi* (Leningrad, Lenizdat, 1972), p. 31.

56. N. K. Popel', *Tanki povernuli na zapad* (Moscow, Voenizdat, 1960), p. 39. Brezhnev is said to have told a colleague in 1943 that he could "hardly

wait to take off my military uniform" and resume civilian administration. K. V. Krainiukov, *Ot Dnepra do Visly* (Moscow, Voenizdat, 1971), p. 107.

57. A. V. Vorozheikin, *Istrebiteli* (Moscow, Voenizdat, 1961), pp. 5, 9.

58. N. A. Antipenko, *Na glavnom napravlenii* (Moscow, Nauka, 1971), p. 82. Shabalin returned to planning work in 1951; his biography is in *Krasnaia zvezda*, April 11, 1961, p. 4.

59. I. V. Stavitskii, "Rol' voennykh sovetov v organizatsii partiino-politicheskoi raboty na frontakh Velikoi Otechestvennoi voiny (1941-1945 gg.)," *Voprosy istorii KPSS*, 1968, no. 2, p. 30. Stavitskii gives no information on one of the military council members.

60. Petrov, *Stroitel'stvo politorganov*, p. 407. This experience of using civilians has made it not at all uncommon for Soviet politicians to have had prior MPA experience ranging anywhere from several months to five or more years. All three heads of the party since Lenin have had such experience— Stalin in the Civil War, Khrushchev in both major wars, and Brezhnev from 1941 to 1946 and again in 1953-54. Besides Khrushchev and Brezhnev, the post-Stalin Politburos have had nine (voting) members with MPA experience —three from the Civil War (Malenkov, Pel'she, Voroshilov), one from the 1939-40 war with Finland (Shelepin), and five from World War II (Bulganin, Kaganovich, Kirichenko, Kirilenko, and Suslov).

61. Biographies of all these men are in *SVE*, and of all but Krainiukov in *BSE*, 3rd.

62. Details of Epishev's biography are elusive. The best sketch is in *SVE*, but one also finds useful addenda in memoirs.

63. For biographies of the returnees (N. V. Egorov, I. F. Khalipov, and G. P. Gromov), see *Krasnaia zvezda*, May 5, 1970, p. 3; July 18, 1975, p. 3; Feb. 20, 1973, p. 3. Among the 1950 graduates who remained outside the army were Nikolai Savinkin, the current head of the administrative organs department, and A. P. Uskov, who worked in the Secretariat until becoming Deputy Minister of Civil Aviation in 1969. Biographies are in *Ezhegodnik*, 1977, p. 616, and *Krasnaia zvezda*, Oct. 9, 1977, p. 4.

64. See *Voennyi vestnik*, 1961, no. 11, p. 18.

65. On Mzhavanadze and Rudnev, see *Ezhegodnik*, 1971, p. 612, and *Krasnaia zvezda*, Nov. 27, 1975, p. 3. In 1961 there also occurred the transfer of a deputy district commander, Basan B. Gorodovikov, to the post of second secretary (later first secretary) of the Kalmyk oblast party committee. The chief reason for this unusual move, as for Mzhavanadze's transfer in 1953, was presumably Gorodovikov's ethnic background (he is a Kalmyk). His biography is in *Deputaty*, 1974, p. 119.

66. The obituaries seem to omit some information about pre-army experience, particularly nonadministrative work for which higher education is not required, but there is no reason to believe political officers acquire such unreported experience more frequently than commanders.

67. See K. F. Telegin, *Ne otdali Moskvy* (Moscow, Sovetskaia Rossiia, 1968), pp. 21-23; I. I. Petrov, "Zabota partii ob ukreplenii pogranichnykh voisk (1939-1941 gg.)," *Voprosy istorii KPSS*, 1968, no. 5, p. 95.

68. Biographies of these men (V. E. Makarov and D. S. Leonov) are in *Krasnaia zvezda*, Sept. 3, 1975, p. 3, and *SVE*.

69. A typical police official with brief MPA experience (but otherwise a diverse background) is G. K. Tsinev, deputy KGB chief since 1970. On the other hand, A. N. Ianauri, the head of the Georgian KGB since 1954, spent twenty-six years in the army command. For biographies, see *Ezhegodnik*, 1977, p. 624; *Deputaty*, 1974, p. 182. According to *Morskoi sbornik*, 1974, no. 4, p. 61, the KGB border guards recruit graduates of higher naval schools and send officers for retraining in naval academies. Such an arrangement is probably found for other service academies and schools as well.

70. Vasiagin's NKVD experience is mentioned in *SVE*, II, 29, but not in previous biographies.

71. The biography of the cadres official, I. A. Kuzovkov, is in *VIZh*, 1973, no. 5, p. 56. For the district commanders (A. M. Andreev, I. V. Tutarinov, and F. A. Oliforov), see *Deputaty*, 1958, p. 22; 1962, p. 428; 1970, p. 326.

72. *Krasnaia zvezda*, March 1, 1978, p. 2.

73. See ibid., June 2, 1972, p. 2; May 26, 1973, p. 2; July 23, 1969, p. 2.

74. *Sputnik politrabotnika*, 1926, no. 10, p. 20.

75. *Krasnyi voin*, Jan. 19, 1922, p. 2.

76. *Tolmachevets*, 1923, no. 11-12, p. 17.

77. Ibid., no. 7, p. 27; no. 11-12, p. 18.

78. See especially Petrov, *Partiinoe stroitel'stvo*, pp. 146-147, 290-294, 378-387; Voropaev and Iovlev, pp. 104-105, 174-177; Zakharov, pp. 3-10.

79. On student recruitment, see *KVS*, 1969, no. 4, p. 44, and 1976, no. 9, p. 16. The experiences of students on probation assignments in military units have not always been pleasant. Some have been "used as draftsmen, photographers, film mechanics, library clerks, and even typists" (*Krasnaia zvezda*, Jan. 5, 1977, p. 2).

80. *Nestareiushchee oruzhie* (Moscow, Molodaia gvardiia, 1977), pp. 179-180.

81. Quotation from Zheltov et al., *Imeni Lenina*, p. 6; this book is the source for the details on the academy except for the statistics on advanced degrees (in *SVE*, II, 247). The Lenin Academy did not formally exist between 1943 and 1947. From the late 1930s to the mid-1950s there were two other higher schools catering mainly to political officers, the Military Pedagogical Institute and the Military Juridicial Academy.

82. Seventy-six percent of the 1975 entrants to the Lenin Academy were graduates of higher military schools (*KVS*, 1976, no. 9, p. 16). There are no statistics available on the proportion of all political officers who have attended military academies or schools other than the Lenin Academy, but judging from biographies and scattered press references such attendance is quite common. Study at the Higher Party School and other senior civilian institutions seems to be rare. The only major MPA official in the last two decades for whom attendance at the Higher Party School can be verified is G. V. Sredin, first deputy MPA chief since 1974, who seems to have graduated before join-

ing the army in 1942. General Sredin, who was born in 1917, also graduated from the Lenin Academy after 1945. See *Deputaty*, 1974, p. 416.

83. Petrov, *Partiinoe stroitel'stvo*, pp. 214, 291; K. V. Krainiukov et al., *Partiino-politicheskaia rabota v Sovetskikh Vooruzhennykh Silakh v gody Velikoi Otechestvennoi voiny 1941-1945* (Moscow, Voenizdat, 1963), p. 498.

84. Petrov, *Stroitel'stvo politorganov*, p. 318.

85. Ibid., pp. 405, 513; *KVS*, 1962, no. 23, p. 23; Zheltov et al., *Imeni Lenina*, p. 240. Twenty-five percent of all military officers had a higher education in 1961, the same proportion as for the MPA in 1965.

86. *Krasnaia zvezda*, Jan. 15, 1976, p. 2; June 3, 1976, p. 2; Dec. 20, 1977, p. 2. As early as 1965, all zampolits of interceptor regiments in the air defense forces were certified pilots. *Voiska protivovozdushnoi oborony strany* (Moscow, Voenizdat, 1968), p. 378.

87. *Krasnaia zvezda*, June 18, 1976, p. 2; *KVS*, 1973, no. 9, p. 25.

88. V. N. Mazur et al., *Budni politrabotnika roty* (Moscow, Voenizdat, 1970), p. 84.

89. *Voprosy partiino-organizatsionnoi raboty* (Moscow, Voenizdat, 1967), p. 181; *Krasnaia zvezda*, March 17, 1973, p. 2.

90. *KVS*, 1965, no. 17, pp. 66-67.

91. Dmitrii Furmanov, *Chapaev* (Moscow, FLPH, 1955), p. 174.

92. K. S. Moskalenko, *Na Iugo-Zapadnom napravlenii*, 2 vols. (Moscow, Nauka, 1969-72), II, 34-35, 154.

93. N. S. Demin, *Voina i liudi* (Moscow, Voenizdat, 1972), pp. 148-149.

94. Zomov et al., pp. 164-167.

95. Demin, p. 152.

96. This phrase is used in an episode in *KVS*, 1961, no. 1, p. 58.

97. In 1964, 57 percent of primary party organization secretaries and 60 percent at the subunit level were elected for the first time, as compared to 35 percent of regiment-level secretaries and half at subunit levels in 1973. *KVS*, 1965, no. 3, p. 30; *Krasnaia zvezda*, March 13, 1974, p. 3.

98. See *KVS*, 1962, no. 23, p. 24; 1973, no. 9, p. 30.

99. Krainiukov, p. 38.

100. For use of *voenizatsiia* in this sense, see *Krasnaia zvezda*, March 7, 1926, p. 3; or Petrov, *Partiinoe stroitel'stvo*, p. 293.

101. See *Krasnaia zvezda*, Feb. 8, 1964, p. 1; Sept. 6, 1969, p. 3.

5. Routine Administrative Politics

1. See especially H. Gordon Skilling and Franklyn Griffiths, eds., *Interest Groups in Soviet Politics* (Princeton, Princeton University Press, 1971), in particular the essays by Skilling.

2. Ezra N. Suleiman, *Politics, Power, and Bureaucracy in France: The Administrative Elite* (Princeton, Princeton University Press, 1974), p. 235.

3. *Krasnaia zvezda*, Jan. 29, 1936, p. 3.

4. Ibid., Jan. 15, 1936, p. 3.

5. *Sovetskii flot*, Jan. 21, 1958, p. 3.

6. *KVS*, 1963, no. 24, pp. 23-24.

7. *Krasnyi flot*, July 4, 1946, p. 3.

8. *KVS*, 1966, no. 10, pp. 72-73.

9. The extreme was the division in 1939 where commissars had to submit reports every three hours; even in 1965, one politotdel was required to file fifty-nine different plans with superior agencies. *Krasnaia zvezda*, Sept. 12, 1939, p. 2; Aug. 23, 1966, p. 3.

10. This description, by the head of the political administration of the Transbaikal Military District, is said to apply to military staffs as well as political organs. Ibid., May 11, 1976, p. 2.

11. Ibid., Jan. 15, 1936, p. 3.

12. Ibid., April 3, 1969, p. 2.

13. *Pravda*, March 6, 1973, p. 2.

14. I have found one example of a senior political officer criticizing staff colleagues for giving insufficient help in transporting newspapers (*KVS*, 1964, no. 13, p. 21). The statement concerned only delivery of papers on ocean cruises; within the Soviet Union the MPA transports its own materials.

15. *Krasnaia zvezda*, April 9, 1972, p. 2. This is not to say there is agreement on the relative importance of every measure. It is sometimes said, for instance, that some staffs stand aside from socialist competition and that coordination between them and political organs in this area "is not universal" (ibid., Jan. 8, 1976, p. 2).

16. Ibid., April 2, 1959, p. 3.

17. This is in the words of a deputy MPA chief from 1954, and refers to a long-standing situation (ibid., Feb. 12, 1954, p. 4). For similar statements, see ibid., April 15, 1943, p. 3; *KVS*, 1969, no. 10, p. 33.

18. *Krasnyi flot*, June 22, 1946, p. 1.

19. *Krasnaia zvezda*, Aug. 26, 1943, p. 1.

20. Ibid., March 13, 1966, p. 3.

21. A. S. Bubnov, *O Krasnoi Armii* (Moscow, Voenizdat, 1958), p. 131.

22. *KVS*, 1977, no. 1, p. 65.

23. The restrictions are discussed in Iu. P. Petrov, *Stroitel'stvo politorganov, partiinykh i komsomol'skikh organizatsii Armii i Flota (1918-1968)* (Moscow, Voenizdat, 1968), pp. 424-425, 446-448. Earlier positions were fixed in 1938, 1943, 1951, and 1953. Under the 1951 arrangement, even very junior commanders could have their personal affairs examined only by party commissions two or three levels above them.

24. *Krasnaia zvezda*, April 8, 1965, p. 3.

25. Ibid., Oct. 10, 1970, p. 2.

26. Ibid., Jan. 11, 1962, p. 2.

27. Ibid., June 25, 1957, p. 3.

28. *Krasnyi flot*, Aug. 19, 1943, p. 1; *Krasnaia zvezda*, June 20, 1963, p. 3.

29. For a good example see *Sovetskii flot*, Aug. 23, 1958, p. 3.

30. *Krasnaia zvezda*, Dec. 17, 1974, p. 2. One division commander, asked why he appeared morose on beginning his interview during the exchange, replied that in the previous month his formation did not have a single *piaterka* (five, the best training mark) (*Pravda*, March 6, 1973, p. 2). He clearly felt

that his command's military performance would be crucial in determining his party standing. On the other hand, it is obvious that the documents exchange involved some interrogation concerning participation in ideological and propaganda work.

31. For a typical case, see *Krasnaia zvezda*, Sept. 10, 1972, p. 3.

32. For recent examples, see *TIS*, 1968, no. 5, pp. 28-32; *Krasnaia zvezda*, Dec. 4, 1971, p. 2 (for a case involving a political officer); *KVS*, 1975, no. 13, pp. 50-51.

33. *Krasnaia zvezda*, Aug. 11, 1940, p. 1.

34. *KVS*, 1975, no. 6, p 59.

35. Ibid., no. 13, p. 53.

36. Ibid., 1971, no. 19, p. 32.

37. For example in *Krasnaia zvezda*, Aug. 25, 1960, p. 2. Some early discussions distinguished between general self-accounts (*otchety*) and reports (*doklady*) on specific questions, disapproving of the first but endorsing the second. Others approved of accounts as well, deploring only the turning of them into occasions for self-justification.

38. This is carefully specified in ibid., June 13, 1972, p. 2.

39. *Vestnik PVO*, 1969, no. 2, p. 22.

40. *KVS*, 1977, no. 19, p. 22.

41. *Vestnik PVO*, 1973, no. 8, p. 28.

42. *Krasnaia zvezda*, Aug. 25, 1960, p. 2; April 27, 1972, p. 1.

43. Ibid., April 27, 1936, p. 3.

44. For example in *KVS*, 1963, no. 5, p. 83; 1977, no. 1, p. 47.

45. *Krasnaia zvezda*, Feb. 2, 1967, p. 2.

46. *Sovetskii flot*, April 12, 1957, p. 3; *KVS*, 1965, no. 20, p. 16.

47. *KVS*, 1968, no. 11, p. 60.

48. *Voprosy partiino-organizatsionnoi raboty* (Moscow, Voenizdat, 1967), p. 126. The opportunity to structure party meetings in this fashion is presumably the reason that a 1971 story could term inattendance by commanders as rare. As the story put it, failure to attend "is reflected in work" (*Morskoi sbornik*, 1971, no. 4, p. 15).

49. *KVS*, 1966, no. 17, p. 17.

50. Ibid., 1964, no. 20, pp. 47-48.

51. Ibid., 1968, no. 1, p. 55.

52. *Voprosy partiino-organizatsionnoi raboty*, p. 48.

53. *Krasnaia zvezda*, Feb. 2, 1967, p. 2.

54. *KVS*, 1963, no. 10, pp. 57-58.

55. *Krasnaia zvezda*, June 5, 1962, p. 2.

56. See, for example, the report of the 1938 appeal to Stalin by the member of the military council of the Moscow Military District (Zaporozhets) on behalf of the district's First Air Defense Corps; in E. F. Ivanovskii et al., *Ordena Lenina Moskovskii voennyi okrug* (Moscow, Voenizdat, 1971), p. 155.

57. Quotations from *Krasnaia zvezda*, July 6, 1976, p. 2; *TIS*, 1967, no. 8, p. 23.

58. *Krasnaia zvezda*, March 26, 1978, p. 4.

59. Ibid., Feb. 5, 1976, p. 2

60. Ibid., Aug. 19, 1959, p. 3.

61. Ibid., March 11, 1936, p. 3.

62. Ibid., Jan. 24, 1936, p. 3.

63. *KVS*, 1970, no. 20, pp. 57-58.

64. Ibid., no. 4, pp. 36-37.

65. See *Krasnaia zvezda*, May 23, 1938, p. 1; May 25, 1977, p. 2.

66. L. Trotsky, *Kak vooruzhalas' revoliutsiia*, 3 vols. (Moscow, Vysshii voennyi redaktsionnyi sovet, 1923-25), vol. II, bk. 1, p. 30.

67. *Krasnaia zvezda*, March 11, 1936, p. 3; Jan. 29, 1972, p. 2.

68. *KVS*, 1965, no. 13, p. 48.

69. For examples see *Krasnaia zvezda*, June 29, 1958, p. 2; *KVS*, 1970, no. 22, p. 53; 1972, no. 9, p. 61.

70. There are good examples in *Krasnaia zvezda*, Nov. 11, 1964, p. 1, and March 3, 1972, p. 2.

71. Ibid., May 11, 1938, p. 3; Nov. 15, 1947, p. 1; Jan. 17, 1956, p. 2; May 30, 1961, p. 1; Sept. 16, 1966, p. 1; Aug. 15, 1975, p. 2.

72. Ibid., April 12, 1947, p. 2; Jan. 19, 1972, p. 2.

73. Ibid., July 6, 1938, p. 2; Oct. 15, 1938, p. 2.

74. Ibid., March 1, 1978, p. 2. The examples given in the reports can be quite revealing. See, for instance, the case of the poor student at a military school, "not wholly dedicated" to his work, but given an enthusiastic recommendation "for having headed the football team for three uninterrupted years" (ibid., Aug. 23, 1967, p. 2).

75. *KVS*, 1975, no. 7, p. 58.

76. *Sovetskii flot*, Aug. 23, 1958, p. 3; *Krasnaia zvezda*, March 1, 1961, p. 3, and Nov. 11, 1970, p. 2.

77. *Krasnaia zvezda*, March 4, 1967, p. 3.

78. Ibid., Jan. 24, 1936, p. 3.

79. Ibid., May 30, 1973, p. 2.

80. Ibid., Jan. 12, 1965, p. 3.

6. The Great Purge

1. *Bol'shevik*, 1929, no. 20, p. 17; 1933, no. 7-8, p. 17; *XVII s"ezd Vsesoiuznoi Kommunisticheskoi Partii(b): Stenograficheskii otchet* (Moscow, Partizdat, 1934), p. 287.

2. See Robert Conquest, *The Great Terror: Stalin's Purge of the Thirties* (Harmondsworth, Penguin, 1971), pp. 287-293.

3. *Krasnaia zvezda*, July 12, 1935, p. 3; July 15, 1935, p. 1.

4. Iu. P. Petrov, *Partiinoe stroitel'stvo s Sovetskoi Armii i Flote (1918-1961)* (Moscow, Voenizdat, 1964), p. 300.

5. I. Rachkov, "Iz vospominanii o Ia. B. Gamarnike," *VIZh*, 1964, no. 5, pp. 69-70.

6. *Report of Court Proceedings in the Case of the Anti-Soviet "Bloc of*

Rights and Trotskyites" (Moscow, People's Commissariat of Justice, 1938), pp. 75-78, 86-87, 256-257; P. I. Yakir, "A Plea for a Criminal Investigation," *Survey*, no. 70-71, 1969, pp. 267-268; A. Iakovlev, *Tsel' zhizni (Zapiski aviakonstruktora)*, 3rd ed. (Moscow, Politizdat, 1970), pp. 260-262; A. T. Stuchenko, *Zavidnaia nasha sud'ba* (Moscow, Voenizdat, 1964), p. 64.

7. *Krasnaia zvezda*, Feb. 12, 1938, p. 3. One former intelligence officer claimed Gamarnik refused to denounce Tukhachevskii in exchange for reprieve. W. G. Krivitsky, *In Stalin's Secret Service* (New York, Harper, 1939), p. 231.

8. N. Zavalishin, "Vstrechi s marshalom A. I. Egorovym," *VIZh*, 1963, no. 11, p. 76.

9. *Krasnaia zvezda*, June 2, 1937, p. 1.

10. See especially Petrov, *Partiinoe stroitel'stvo*, pp. 299-301, which shows Stalin's receptivity to NKVD information and active encouragement of the military purge in mid-1937 and again in April 1938.

11. Lev Nikulin, *Marshal Tukhachevskii* (Moscow, Voenizdat, 1964), p. 190; D. V. Pankov, *Komkor Eideman* (Moscow, Voenizdat, 1965), p. 103; K. K. Mednis et al., *Komandarm krylatykh* (Riga, Liesma, 1967), pp. 39-40; P. I. Iakir et al., *Komandarm Iakir* (Moscow, Voenizdat, 1963), pp. 229-232; P. N. Aleksandrov et al., *Komandarm Uborevich* (Moscow, Voenizdat, 1964), pp. 205-206; M. Baklach et al., "Komandarm 2 ranga A. I. Sediakin," *VIZh*, 1963, no. 11, p. 126.

12. M. M. Zomov et al., *Marshal Tukhachevskii* (Moscow, Voenizdat, 1965), pp. 220-221; *XXII s"ezd Kommunisticheskoi Partii Sovetskogo Soiuza: Stenograficheskii otchet*, 3 vols. (Moscow, Gospolitizdat, 1962), II, 403; I. T. Starinov, *Miny zhdut svoego chasa* (Moscow, Voenizdat, 1964), 118-119.

13. Aleksandrov et al., p. 206. For early criticism of Smirnov, see *Krasnaia zvezda*, March 23, 1937, p. 3; May 11, 1937, p. 2.

14. A. G. Rytov, *Rytsari piatogo okeana*, 2nd ed. (Moscow, Voenizdat, 1970), pp. 8-10. The date of Smirnov's elevation is unclear. He is first mentioned as MPA chief in the press only on November 4, but a biography in *Krasnaia zvezda*, Nov. 26, 1937, p. 2, said he had been chief of the MPA since June and Deputy People's Commissar of Defense since October.

15. N. G. Kuznetsov, *Nakanune* (Moscow, Voenizdat, 1969), p. 224.

16. The only published reference to Smirnov's death (Aleksandrov et al., p. 258) gives the date as simply 1938. Notice of Frinovskii's appointment was published November 7, 1938, but a recent encyclopedia entry (*BSE*, 3rd, V, 230) puts his accession in August. The last press reference to Shaposhnikov is in *Krasnyi flot*, June 10, 1938.

17. A. V. Gorbatov, *Gody i voiny* (Moscow, Voenizdat, 1965), p. 123.

18. Stuchenko, pp. 67-68.

19. Gorbatov, p. 126. A more favorable impression of Shchadenko is in G. D. Plaskov, *Pod grokhot kanonady* (Moscow, Voenizdat, 1969), pp. 114-115.

20. P. I. Batov, *V pokhodakh i boiakh*, 2nd ed. (Moscow, Voenizdat, 1966), p. 23; Starinov, *Miny zhdut*, p. 221; I. T. Zamertsev, *Cherez gody i rasstoianiia* (Moscow, Voenizdat, 1965), p. 7.

21. *Krasnaia zvezda,* Sept. 26, 1938, p. 3.

22. I. V. Stavitskii, "O voennykh komissarakh perioda Velikoi Otechestvennoi voiny," *Voprosy istorii KPSS,* 1965, no. 3, p. 23.

23. *Krasnaia zvezda,* June 21, 1938, p. 2.

24. Petrov, *Partiinoe stroitel'stvo,* p. 307. Conquest (*The Great Terror,* p. 313) incorrectly reads Petrov as saying that by 1938 only a third of the political workers had survived.

25. *Krasnaia zvezda,* Oct. 11, 1938, p. 1.

26. Statistics from *Istoriia Velikoi Otechestvennoi voiny Sovetskogo Soiuza 1941-1945,* 6 vols. (Moscow, Voenizdat, 1960-65), VI, 124; Voroshilov statement from A. A. Lobachev, *Trudnymi dorogami* (Moscow, Voenizdat, 1960), p. 87. By early 1938 all but two of the thirty-nine original officials in the political administration of the Ural Military District had been arrested (*Krasnaia zvezda,* March 16, 1938, p. 3).

27. Rachkov, p. 70.

28. *Krasnaia zvezda,* Feb. 1, 1964, p. 6, is the only source to mention Bulin's tenure in the MPA. No source is specific as to date of arrest. Bulin was first publicly condemned in ibid., Jan. 22, 1938, p. 2.

29. *Propagandist i agitator RKKA,* 1939, no. 22, p. 17.

30. Lobachev, p. 83. See the story on the Engels Military-Political School in *Krasnaia zvezda,* Sept. 27, 1938, p. 3.

31. M. Frankel', "Armeiskii komissar 2 ranga M. P. Amelin," *VIZh,* 1964, no. 7, p. 119. Amelin is identified as "former" chief in *Krasnaia zvezda,* June 2, 1937, p. 1.

32. The criticism of Pismanik is in *Krasnaia zvezda,* May 30, 1937, p. 3. On Mezis, see S. Kotov, "Armeiskii komissar," *VIZh,* 1964, no. 6, pp. 126-128; he is last mentioned in *Krasnaia zvezda,* Oct. 26, 1937, p. 2. Statistics on the Fifth Brigade are in Petrov, *Partiinoe stroitel'stvo,* p. 300.

33. E. F. Ivanovskii et al., *Ordena Lenina Moskovskii voennyi okrug* (Moscow, Voenizdat, 1971), pp. 433-439.

34. A. Vostrov, "Armeiskii komissar 2 ranga S. N. Kozhevnikov," *VIZh,* 1966, no. 9, p. 128; *Ukrain'skii Radian'skii entsiklopedichnii slovnik,* II, 670.

35. A. Arnol'dov, "Armeiskii komissar 2 ranga G. S. Okunev," *VIZh,* 1965, no. 7, p. 127.

36. P. Klipp, "Flagman Severnogo flota," ibid., pp. 60-63.

37. G. Airepetian, "Komkor G. D. Khakhan'ian," ibid., no. 12, p. 122.

38. *Krasnaia zvezda,* April 21, 1938, p. 3; Oct. 17, 1938, p. 3.

39. Stuchenko, p. 64.

40. Starinov, *Miny zhdut,* pp. 150-152; D. A. Morozov, *O nikh ne upominalos' v svodkakh* (Moscow, Voenizdat, 1965), p. 168; Stuchenko, p. 64.

41. *Krasnaia zvezda,* Aug. 6, 1937, p. 1.

42. See ibid., Jan. 30, 1938, p. 2; Feb. 3, 1938, p. 3.

43. Ibid., Feb. 5, 1938, p. 3.

44. Ibid., July 23, 1937, p. 3.

45. *XVIII s"ezd Vsesoiuznoi Kommunisticheskoi Partii(b): Stenograficheskii otchet* (Moscow, Gospolitizdat, 1939), p. 275; *Krasnaia zvezda,* Aug.

10, 1938, p. 1.

46. I. Bagramian, "Zapiski nachal'nika operativnogo otdela," *VIZh*, 1967, no. 1, pp. 56-57.

47. *Krasnaia zvezda*, Jan. 22, 1938, pp. 1-2.

48. Ibid., p. 2.

49. Ibid., April 10, 1939, p. 2.

50. Ibid., May 10, 1939, p. 2.

51. Ibid., June 8, 1938, p. 2.

52. Iakir et al., p. 101.

53. *Krasnaia zvezda*, Aug. 1, 1964, p. 3.

54. *Krasnyi flot*, June 12, 1938, p. 2.

55. L. M. Sandalov, *Trudnye rubezhi* (Moscow, Voenizdat, 1965), p. 10; emphasis added.

56. A. Ia. Vedenin, *Gody i liudi* (Moscow, Voenizdat, 1964), p. 54.

57. *Krasnaia zvezda*, April 17, 1938, p. 3; June 20, 1938, p. 2.

58. Ibid., July 8, 1938, p. 3.

59. Ibid., March 15, 1938, p. 3.

60. Vedenin, pp. 54-59.

61. For examples, see *Krasnyi flot*, June 8, 1938, p. 2.

62. See *Krasnaia zvezda*, Feb. 12, 1938, p. 3; Feb. 28, 1938, p. 3; *Krasnyi flot*, Oct. 24, 1938, p. 3; Starinov, *Miny zhdut*, p. 166.

63. *Krasnaia zvezda*, Jan. 29, 1938, p. 1.

64. Ibid., Oct. 11, 1938, p. 1.

65. See ibid., May 1, 1937, p. 3; A. A. Novikov, *V nebe Leningrada* (Moscow, Nauka, 1970), p. 63. Rychagov was arrested in June 1941 and apparently perished soon thereafter.

66. K. K. Rokossovskii, *Soldatskii dolg* (Moscow, Voenizdat, 1972), p. 47.

67. Kuznetsov, *Nakanune*, p. 240.

68. I. Kh. Bagramian, *Tak nachinalas' voina* (Moscow, Voenizdat, 1971), p. 9.

69. Kuznetsov, *Nakanune*, p. 224.

7. World War II Decision Making

1. G. K. Zhukov, *Vospominaniia i razmyshleniia* (Moscow, Novosti, 1969), pp. 203, 217; A. M. Vasilevskii, *Delo vsei zhizni*, 2nd ed. (Moscow, Politizdat, 1975), pp. 111-115; V. A. Anfilov, *Bessmertnyi podvig* (Moscow, Nauka, 1971), pp. 182-183.

2. Zhukov (1969), pp. 240-241.

3. A. Grechko, "25 let tomu nazad," *VIZh*, 1966, no. 6, p. 8.

4. V. A. Anfilov, *Nachalo Velikoi Otechestvennoi voiny* (Moscow, Voenizdat, 1962), pp. 45-46; I. V. Boldin, *Stranitsy zhizni* (Moscow, Voenizdat, 1961), pp. 85-86.

5. Aleksandr Rozen, *Poslednie dve nedeli* (Moscow and Leningrad, Sovetskii pisatel', 1965), pp. 231-232.

6. *Bor'ba za Sovetskuiu Pribaltiku v Velikoi Otechestvennoi voine 1941-1945*, 3 vols. (Riga, Liesma, 1966-69), I, 46.

7. Iu. P. Petrov, *Partiinoe stroitel'stvo v Sovetskoi Armii i Flote (1918-1961)* (Moscow, Voenizdat, 1964), pp. 335-336.

8. Ibid., pp. 334-335; A. A. Novikov, *V nebe Leningrada* (Moscow, Nauka, 1970), p. 65.

9. N. G. Kuznetsov, *Nakanune* (Moscow, Voenizdat, 1969), p. 345; N. Kuznetsov, "Vidnyi politrabotnik armii i flota," *VIZh*, 1969, no. 8, p. 43.

10. I. I. Azarov, *Osazhdennaia Odessa* (Moscow, Voenizdat, 1962), pp. 9-11 (emphasis added); A. M. Gushchin, *Kurs, prolozhennyi ognem* (Moscow, Voenizdat, 1964), pp. 7-8.

11. I. Kh. Bagramian, *Tak nachinalas' voina* (Moscow, Voenizdat, 1971), p. 70.

12. *Bor'ba za Sovetskuiu Pribaltiku*, I, 45-46; K. N. Galitskii, *Gody surovykh ispytanii 1941-1944* (Moscow, Nauka, 1973), p. 25; A. I. Rodimtsev, *Tvoi, Rodina, synov'ia* (Kiev, Gospolitizdat, 1962), p. 20.

13. P. V. Sevast'ianov, *Neman-Volga-Dunai* (Moscow, Voenizdat, 1961), p. 6.

14. A. A. Lobachev, *Trudnymi dorogami* (Moscow, Voenizdat, 1960), p. 120.

15. See S. S. Aleksandrov, *Krylatye tanki* (Moscow, Voenizdat, 1970), p. 4; I. A. Khizenko, *Ozhivshie stranitsy* (Moscow, Voenizdat, 1963), p. 6.

16. See the case involving a Rumanian defector in A. A. Sviridov, *Batal'ony vstupaiut v boi* (Moscow, Voenizdat, 1967), pp. 7-9.

17. See S. I. Kabanov, *Na dal'nikh postupakh* (Moscow, Voenizdat, 1971), pp. 127-132; N. K. Smirnov, *Matrosy zashchishchaiut Rodinu* (Moscow, Politizdat, 1968), p. 16; B. Borisov, *Zapiski sekretaria gorkoma* (Moscow, Politizdat, 1964), p. 30.

18. V. P. Agafonov, *Neman! Neman! Ia—Dunai!* (Moscow, Voenizdat, 1967), pp. 20-24.

19. Sevast'ianov, p. 10. At the same time, Dibrov and the chief political officer of one of the district's armies raised with Moscow the possibility of rescinding the order. N. M. Khlebnikov, *Pod grokhot soten batarei* (Moscow, Voenizdat, 1974), p. 105.

20. V. A. Grekov et al., *Bug v ogne* (Minsk, Belarus', 1965), pp. 136-138, 168; L. M. Sandalov, *Perezhitoe* (Moscow, Voenizdat, 1961), pp. 57-60, 68-76.

21. A. G. Rytov, *Rytsari piatogo okeana* (Moscow, Voenizdat, 1967), pp. 109-113.

22. Stavka, whose membership changed several times, was more a collection of highly placed individuals than a collegium. It rarely met as a group and it "had no administrative apparatus other than the General Staff" (Zhukov [1969], p. 292).

23. *Pravda*, Jan. 4, 1967, p. 3.

24. See for example I. Bagramian, "Flangovyi udar 11-i gvardeiskoi armii," *VIZh*, 1963, no. 7, pp. 83-95, on a Stalin decision in 1943. Marshal

Bagramian later wrote (*Tak nachinalas' voina*, p. 404) that when he was a front commander in 1944-45, Stalin almost always gave in to him.

25. For a factional interpretation see the discussion of the "Stalingrad group" in Roman Kolkowicz, *The Soviet Military and the Communist Party* (Princeton, Princeton University Press, 1967), chap. 7.

26. S. S. Biriuzov, *Sovetskii soldat na Balkanakh* (Moscow, Voenizdat, 1963), p. 57; Zhukov (1969), p. 297.

27. Zhukov (1969), p. 295.

28. S. M. Shtemenko, *General'nyi shtab v gody voiny*, 2 vols. (Moscow, Voenizdat, 1968-73), I, 3.

29. Vasilevskii, p. 549.

30. Novikov, p. 290.

31. There seems little reason to doubt the statement in *Istoriia Velikoi Otechestvennoi voiny Sovetskogo Soiuza 1941-1945*, 6 vols. (Moscow, Voenizdat, 1960-65), VI, 131, that most of Stalin's directives were prepared by the General Staff or other military officials and "were the products of collective rather than individual creativity."

32. On the General Staff reports, see Shtemenko, I, 114-115, and II, 294. Stalin's only other daily report came from the Moscow air defense command. Khrushchev's jibe that Stalin plotted operations on a globe is conclusively refuted by Shtemenko (I, 117) and Vasilevskii (pp. 550-551).

33. Vasilevskii, p. 542.

34. K. A. Meretskov, *Na sluzhbe narodu* (Moscow, Politizdat, 1968), p. 380.

35. Shtemenko, I, 116.

36. Zhukov (1969), pp. 294, 298, 492.

37. See, for instance, A. Iakovlev, *Tsel'zhizni* (*Zapiski aviakonstruktora*), 3rd ed. (Moscow, Politizdat, 1970), pp. 337-338; N. G. Kuznetsov, *Na flotakh boevaia trevoga* (Moscow, Voenizdat, 1971), p. 81. There is considerable variation in warmth toward Stalin in the memoirs of the Moscow group. The most favorable is certainly Shtemenko. Vasilevskii gives the most balanced and sensitive portrayal, emphasizing (p. 548) that "it would be inaccurate to look upon Stalin from only one point of view."

38. M. A. Reiter, quoted in L. M. Sandalov, *Na Moskovskom napravlenii* (Moscow, Nauka, 1970), p. 220; Reiter was a logistics specialist.

39. S. S. Biriuzov, *Kogda gremeli pushki* (Moscow, Voenizdat, 1961), pp. 246-247.

40. Vasilevskii, p. 526. For the antics of Kulik, see Boldin, p. 98; P. I. Batov, *V pokhodakh i boiakh*, 2nd ed. (Moscow, Voenizdat, 1966), pp. 140-141; N. K. Popel', *Tanki povernuli na zapad* (Moscow, Voenizdat, 1960), pp. 184-186. Popel', a political officer, is the most devastating critic.

41. Biriuzov, *Kogda gremeli pushki*, p. 247.

42. Vasilevskii, p. 526.

43. See K. Telegin, "Na zakliuchitel'nom etape voiny," *VIZh*, 1965, no. 4, pp. 62-69; Vasilevskii, pp. 592-594; Shtemenko, I, 84-86; Novikov, p. 160; I. T. Peresypkin, *A v boiu eshche vazhnei* (Moscow, Sovetskaia Rossiia, 1970), pp. 122-123, 214-218.

44. F. I. Golikov, *V Moskovskoi bitve* (Moscow, Nauka, 1967), p. 6; K. S. Moskalenko, *Na Iugo-Zapadnom napravlenii*, 2 vols. (Moscow, Nauka, 1969-72), I, 450.

45. K. K. Rokossovskii, *Soldatskii dolg* (Moscow, Voenizdat, 1972), p. 92.

46. See especially ibid., pp. 69-70, 91, 143, 334; Bagramian, *Tak nachinalas' voina*, pp. 153-155, 171-172, 181-182; P. V. Batov, *V pokhodakh i boiakh*, 1st ed. (Moscow, Voenizdat, 1962), pp. 272-275; A. P. Beloborodov, *Ratnyi podvig* (Moscow, Politizdat, 1965), pp. 48-49; P. A. Belov, *Za nami Moskva* (Moscow, Voenizdat, 1963), pp. 48-49, 62, 168-169, 215-216; I. I. Fediuninskii, *Podniatye po trevoge* (Moscow, Voenizdat, 1961), p. 61; A. V. Gorbatov, *Gody i voiny* (Moscow, Voenizdat, 1965), pp. 282-285; V. I. Kazakov, *Na perelome* (Moscow, Voenizdat, 1962), pp. 34, 42; D. D. Leliushenko, *Zaria pobedy* (Moscow, Voenizdat, 1966), pp. 93-94; I. I. Liudnikov, *Doroga dlinoiu v zhizni* (Moscow, Voenizdat, 1969), p. 103; Moskalenko, II, 144, 163, 172, 224-226; A. I. Shebunin, *Skol'ko nami proideno* (Moscow, Voenizdat, 1971), p. 115; A. T. Stuchenko, *Zavidnaia nasha sud'ba* (Moscow, Voenizdat, 1964), p. 146.

47. Otto Preston Chaney, Jr., *Zhukov* (Norman, University of Oklahoma Press, 1971), p. 257.

48. Popel', *Tanki povernuli*, pp. 164-165, is the most hostile account.

49. B. V. Bychevskii, *Gorod-front* (Moscow, Voenizdat, 1963), p. 94; emphasis added.

50. Batov (1962), pp. 290-291.

51. Gorbatov, p. 236.

52. Moskalenko, II, 567-568; I. T. Starinov, *Miny zhdut svoego chasa* (Moscow, Voenizdat, 1964), pp. 220-221; A. P. Teremov, *Pylaiushchie berega* (Moscow, Voenizdat, 1965), pp. 5-8; Gorbatov, p. 185.

53. D. A. Zhuravlev, *Ognevoi shchit Moskvy* (Moscow, Voenizdat, 1972), pp. 26-27; Peresypkin, p. 73.

54. Meretskov, pp. 217-218.

55. Ibid., p. 256.

56. Shtemenko, I, 49; Kuznetsov, *Na flotakh*, pp. 162-163.

57. Kuznetsov, *Nakanune*, p. 269; F. I. Galkin, *Tanki vozvrashchaiutsia v boi* (Moscow, Voenizdat, 1964), p. 47.

58. A. Kovtun', "Sevastopol'skie dnevniki," *Novyi mir*, 1963, no. 8, p. 137.

59. Vasilevskii, pp. 210-211.

60. Galkin, pp. 44-45; N. N. Voronov, *Na sluzhbe voennoi* (Moscow, Voenizdat, 1963), pp. 234, 378.

61. Meretskov, p. 320.

62. Ibid., pp. 320-321.

63. F. P. Polynin, *Boevye marshruty* (Moscow, Voenizdat, 1972), p. 105; Rytov, pp. 80-82.

64. Galkin, pp. 67, 75; *Khrushchev Remembers*, ed. Strobe Talbott (New York, Bantam, 1971), p. 174.

65. K. F. Telegin, *Ne otdali Moskvy* (Moscow, Sovetskaia Rossiia, 1968),

p. 66; Rytov, pp. 99-101. Mekhlis's successor, Shcherbakov, did not tour the front, but he did have abrasive relations with a number of field-level political officers. See K. V. Krainiukov, *Ot Dnepra do Visly* (Moscow, Voenizdat, 1971), pp. 233-234, 262; Telegin, "Na zakliuchitel'nom etape," p. 56; *Khrushchev Remembers*, p. 183 (which describes him as contemptible).

66. Sandalov, *Perezhitoe*, pp. 142-143; Sandalov, *Na Moskovskom napravlenii*, p. 115.

67. Rytov, pp. 145-149.

68. Telegin, *Ne otdali Moskvy*, pp. 104, 115-117.

69. F. Blumental', *Politicheskaia rabota v voennoe vremia* (Moscow and Leningrad, Gosizdat, 1927), p. 41.

70. Sandalov, *Na Moskovskom napravlenii*, p. 91.

71. Rodimtsev, pp. 89-92.

72. N. K. Popel', *V tiazhkuiu poru* (Moscow, Voenizdat, 1959), pp. 137-141.

73. Bagramian, *Tak nachinalas' voina*, pp. 334-335; *Istoriia Velikoi Otechestvennoi voiny*, II, 104-111; Moskalenko, I, 77-92.

74. Khrushchev's secret speech (*Khrushchev Remembers*, pp. 647-648) recounted telephone calls to Vasilevskii and Stalin, subsequently dated May 18, in which he appealed for termination of the offensive. What he did not disclose was that on May 17 he had phoned Stavka and "expressed the same opinion as the command of the Southwestern Front—that . . . there was no reason to curtail the operation" (Zhukov [1969], pp. 386-387). Moskalenko (I, 189-190) shows Khrushchev to have been an ardent promoter of the operation from the start.

75. A. I. Eremenko, *Stalingrad* (Moscow, Voenizdat, 1961), pp. 411-414.

76. Zhukov (1969), p. 470.

77. Rokossovskii, p. 232.

78. Krainiukov, p. 209.

79. A. K. Blazhei, *V armeiskom shtabe* (Moscow, Voenizdat, 1967), p. 131.

80. N. A. Antipenko, *Na glavnom napravlenii* (Moscow, Nauka, 1971), p. 78.

81. Rytov, p. 94.

82. Telegin, *Ne otdali Moskvy*, p. 305.

83. Rytov, p. 166.

84. M. Popov, "Iuzhnee Stalingrada," *VIZh*, 1961, no. 2, p. 91.

85. G. Odintsov, "Sovetskaia artilleriia v boiakh za Leningrad," ibid., 1964, no. 12, p. 58.

86. A. Khrulev, "V bor'be za Leningrad," ibid., 1962, no. 11, pp. 31-32.

87. Voronov, p. 206.

88. Meretskov, p. 254; Smirnov, *Matrosy*, p. 91; G. N. Kupriianov, *Ot Varentseva moria do Ladogi* (Leningrad, Lenizdat, 1972), pp. 273-275.

89. V. G. Guliaev, *Chelovek v brone* (Moscow, Voenizdat, 1964), pp. 77-78.

90. M. Kh. Kalashnik, *Ispytanie ognem* (Moscow, Voenizdat, 1971), p. 105.

91. Quotation from Batov (1966), p. 182.

92. Kupriianov, p. 76.

93. Ibid., pp. 126-127.

94. Ibid., pp. 155-156, 276-279.

95. Rytov, p. 179.

96. Krainiukov, p. 265.

97. See the example of the Stalingrad Tractor Plant in K. S. Grushevoi, *Togda, v sorok pervom* (Moscow, Voenizdat, 1972), p. 174.

98. D. V. Pavlov, *Leningrad v blokade (1941 god)* (Moscow, Voenizdat, 1961), p. 177.

99. P. N. Pospelov et al., *Sovetskii tyl v Velikoi Otechestvennoi voine*, 2 vols. (Moscow, Mysl', 1974), I, 55.

100. Grushevoi, pp. 80-83.

101. N. Strakhov, "Na voenno-avtomobil'nykh dorogakh," *VIZh*, 1964, no. 3, pp. 68-70; A. M. Samsonov, *Stalingradskaia bitva* (Moscow, Nauka, 1960), pp. 182-183.

102. Kupriianov, pp. 33, 79.

103. I. Starinov, "Eto bylo tainoi," *VIZh*, 1964, no. 4, pp. 76-91.

104. Popel', *Tanki povernuli*, pp. 64-65. Shtykov, a civilian recruit from Zhdanov's Leningrad organization, was a candidate member of the Central Committee and was presumably far better connected in the Secretariat than most MPA officials. Some nonpolitical officers also turned occasionally to the Secretariat for assistance. For an example see A. L. Shepelev, *V nebe i na zemle* (Moscow, Voenizdat, 1974), p. 143.

8. The Zhukov Affair

1. Carl A. Linden, *Khrushchev and the Soviet Leadership, 1957-1964* (Baltimore, Johns Hopkins Press, 1966), p. 43; emphasis added.

2. Otto Preston Chaney, Jr., *Zhukov* (Norman, University of Oklahoma Press, 1971), p. 401; Merle Fainsod, *How Russia Is Ruled*, rev. ed. (Cambridge, Mass., Harvard University Press, 1967), p. 485. See also Roman Kolkowicz, *The Soviet Military and the Communist Party* (Princeton, Princeton University Press, 1967), pp. 130-136; Paul M. Cocks, "The Purge of Marshal Zhukov," *Slavic Review*, 22 (September 1963), 483-498.

3. On Budennyi's patronage, see S. M. Budennyi, *Proidennyi put'*, 3 vols. (Moscow, Voenizdat, 1958-73), III, 350-355. Although Zhukov fought in Budennyi's army, the two did not meet until 1927; G. K. Zhukov, *Vospominaniia i razmyshleniia* (Moscow, Novosti, 1969), p. 94.

4. S. M. Shtemenko, *General'nyi shtab v gody voiny*, 2 vols. (Moscow, Voenizdat, 1968-73), II, 18-21. Whatever Stalin's distemper in 1944, he telephoned Zhukov in the spring of 1946 to ask him what post he would prefer upon returning to Moscow and suggest that he work out the details with Bulganin and Vasilevskii. G. K. Zhukov, *Vospominaniia i razmyshleniia*, 2nd ed., 2 vols. (Moscow, Novosti, 1974), II, 440.

5. A. Iakovlev, *Tsel' zhizni (Zapiski aviakonstruktora)*, 3rd ed. (Moscow, Politizdat, 1970), p. 337; *Khrushchev Remembers*, ed. Strobe Talbott

(New York, Bantam, 1971), p. 649.

6. Milovan Djilas, *Conversations with Stalin* (New York, Harcourt, Brace and World, 1962), p. 170.

7. The best summary of the plenum and foregoing events is Iu. P. Petrov, *Partiinoe stroitel'stvo v Sovetskoi Armii i Flote (1918-1961)* (Moscow, Voenizdat, 1964), pp. 460-462. The indictment is in *Pravda*, Nov. 3, 1957, pp. 1-3.

8. *Khrushchev Remembers*, p. 366. It should be noted that Marshal Moskalenko, then commander of the Moscow Military District and the man in whose personal custody Beria was kept until trial, is at the time of this writing still in the army leadership (as a Deputy Defense Minister).

9. See *Politicheskii dnevnik, 1964-1970* (Amsterdam, Alexander Herzen Foundation, 1972), p. 107; also the recollections of the then Yugoslav ambassador to Moscow, Veljko Micunovic, in Radio Free Europe Research, *Background Report*, Jan. 20, 1978, pp. 11-13.

10. *Pravda*, June 20, 1974, p. 3.

11. Charles E. Bohlen, *Witness to History, 1929-1969* (New York, Norton, 1973), p. 497.

12. *Vneocherednoi XXI s"ezd Kommunisticheskoi Partii Sovetskogo Soiuza: Stenograficheskii otchet*, 2 vols. (Moscow, Gospolitizdat, 1959), II, 127.

13. *XXII s"ezd Kommunisticheskoi Partii Sovetskogo Soiuza: Stenograficheskii otchet*, 3 vols. (Moscow, Gospolitizdat, 1962), I, 107; II, 120. The "seizure of power" phrase was used in the indictment of Beria in 1953.

14. *Khrushchev Remembers: The Last Testament*, ed. Strobe Talbott (New York, Bantam, 1976), p. 14.

15. Only in 1956 the head of the navy, Nikolai Kuznetsov, had been dismissed and demoted three ranks to vice-admiral. In 1963 S. S. Varentsov was demoted four ranks, dismissed, and removed from the Central Committee because of his acquaintance with convicted spy Oleg Pen'kovskii.

16. *Vecherniaia Moskva*, Dec. 1, 1971, p. 3.

17. *Pravda*, June 22, 1974, p. 3.

18. Ibid., Oct. 4, 1974, p. 3.

19. *Khrushchev Remembers: The Last Testament*, p. 14.

20. Of the three retired district commanders, one (A. I. Eremenko) remained a Central Committee candidate until his death in 1970 and another (A. V. Gorbatov) until 1961. Appointment of the new deputy minister, Anton Gerasimov, is evident only from a recent biography (*SVE*, II, 525) and is not reflected in the table in an earlier version of this chapter (in *Soviet Studies*, 29 [April 1977], 193).

21. There is nothing to support Kolkowicz's claim (*The Soviet Military*, p. 135) that Rokossovskii (whom he terms a member of "the Zhukov camp") was transferred so he would be "away from Moscow during the fateful days" surrounding Zhukov's dismissal. Rokossovskii bore no special love for Zhukov (see the references to his memoirs in notes 45 and 46 to Chapter 7). Although his transfer was announced on October 23 (*Zaria vostoka*, p. 1), he was listed as among those denouncing Zhukov at the plenum and did not

appear at his new posting until November 6 (ibid., Nov. 7, 1957, p. 7). He returned unscathed to his duties as deputy minister in January 1958.

22. According to an authoritative history of the navy, Chekurov was replaced by V. A. Fokin on February 12 (*Boevoi put' Sovetskogo Voenno-Morskogo Flota*, 3rd ed. [Moscow, Voenizdat, 1974], p. 523). This work also mentions Chekurov's earlier service favorably three times.

23. There was no announcement of Luchinskii's removal from the committee, but a recent biography (*BSE*, 3rd, XV, 79) puts it in 1959; he was not a delegate to the Twenty-first Congress in mid-January 1959.

24. *Pravda*, Nov. 3, 1957, p. 2; *Pravda vostoka*, Nov. 5, 1957, p. 2.

25. The commander of the Transbaikal Military District was sent to the Ural district in June 1958 as part of the adjustment to Malinovskii's promotion; the commander of the Far Eastern district remained until mid-1961.

26. See especially his Navy Day speech in *Pravda*, July 15, 1957, p. 3.

27. One need only recall that Khrushchev's position on spending priorities during the debate of 1953-55 was considerably more promilitary than that of his chief adversary, Malenkov; or that a year after Zhukov's fall Khrushchev touched off a crisis over Berlin which required consolidation of Soviet military forces.

28. See, for example, Linden; or Michel Tatu, *Power in the Kremlin: From Khrushchev to Kosygin* (New York, Viking, 1970).

29. *Khrushchev Remembers: The Last Testament*, pp. 13-14.

30. Robert Conquest, *Power and Policy in the USSR* (New York, St. Martin's, 1961), p. 345.

31. For the bust, see *Pravda*, Jan. 1, 1954, p. 2. This practice was quite common under Stalin. See, for example, the report of a bust of Marshal S. I. Bogdanov in Leningrad in *Krasnaia zvezda*, Jan. 13, 1953, p. 1.

32. See especially A. Ryzhakov, "K voprosu o stroitel'stve bronetankovykh voisk Krasnoi Armii v 30-e gody," *VIZh*, 1968, no. 8, pp. 105-111; Zhukov (1969), p. 205; P. A. Rotmistrov, *Vremia i tanki* (Moscow, Voenizdat, 1972), pp. 85-89; I. Kh. Bagramian, *Tak nachinalas' voina* (Moscow, Voenizdat, 1971), pp. 16-17.

33. On wartime rivalries, see especially Shtemenko, I, 329-340; I. S. Konev, *Sorok piatyi* (Moscow, Voenizdat, 1966), pp. 87-93, 117, 146; Zhukov (1969), pp. 624-625. One of the least credible aspects of Khrushchev's account of Zhukov's ouster is his claim that Zhukov wanted Konev as his successor.

34. V. I. Chuikov, *Nachalo puti*, 2nd ed. (Moscow, Voenizdat, 1962), pp. 245-246.

35. Zhukov (1969), p. 420.

36. *Pravda*, June 21, 1974, p. 3.

37. *Khrushchev Remembers*, p. 207.

38. A. M. Vasilevskii, *Delo vsei zhizni*, 2nd ed. (Moscow, Politizdat, 1975), p. 269. Compare with *Khrushchev Remembers: The Last Testament*, p. 5. Zhukov's resentment of Khrushchev's rendering of wartime events is especially clear at several points in his memoirs. He describes an urgent conference with Stalin in June 1941 being interrupted by a telephone call to Stalin

from Khrushchev in Kiev in which Khrushchév (who while in power implied that he had tirelessly warned Stalin of the impending attack) spoke only of the Ukraine's prospects for a good harvest in 1941. Zhukov also belittles Khrushchev's claim to have warned against the Khar'kov disaster of May 1942, one of the casualties of which was Fedor Kostenko, a deputy front commander and a friend of Zhukov's since the 1920s. See Zhukov (1969), pp. 241-242, 387.

39. Zhukov (1969), p. 98.

40. A. Iakovlev, *Tsel' zhizni (Zapiski aviakonstruktora)*, 4th ed. (Moscow, Politizdat, 1974), pp. 444-445.

41. *Pravda*, Nov. 3, 1957, p. 2.

42. See the critics cited in note 46 to Chapter 7. Adding Marshals Biriuzov and Konev produces a list which included in October 1957 two deputy ministers, seven district commanders, and the head of the General Staff Academy. The others held senior appointments, and one of them was made a deputy minister in 1958.

43. *XXII s'ezd*, II, 67.

44. Petrov, *Partiinoe stroitel'stvo*, pp. 462-465.

45. Iu. P. Petrov, *Stroitel'stvo politorganov, partiinykh i komsomol'skikh organizatsii Armii i Flota (1918-1968)* (Moscow, Voenizdat, 1968), pp. 434-439. This work also takes pains to cite (p. 388) a report by Zhukov to the Central Committee in July 1941 pronouncing the reinstatement of commissars as extremely necessary.

46. *Krasnaia zvezda*, Oct. 5, 1957, p. 2.

47. The distinction between the two Presidium sessions emerges most clearly in Petrov, *Stroitel'stvo politorganov*, p. 434.

48. Zhukov (1969), pp. 106-107; this part of his biography was unknown until his memoirs were published. Zhukov's memoirs disclose that the commissar of the division in which he served in the Civil War advised him to become a cadre political officer, but he declined because he was "more inclined to command work"; they also describe his friendship with political officers at several points in his career. See ibid., pp. 54-55, 78, 169.

49. *Krasnaia zvezda*, April 26, 1956, p. 3.

50. Ibid., Oct. 10, 1954, p. 3.

51. *Sovetskii flot*, Nov. 14, 1956, pp. 2-3.

52. *Pravda Ukrainy*, Nov. 3, 1957, p. 1.

53. According to Petrov (*Partiinoe stroitel'stvo*, pp. 462-463), Zhukov "strove to limit the rights" of the councils, "managed to turn them into consultative organs attached to commanders," and personally insulted some military council members. Petrov claims that Zhukov "insisted (*nastaival*) on the liquidation of the post of member of the military council from among the cadre political workers"—yet it is clear from press accounts that council members with such backgrounds remained in place throughout Zhukov's term. Zhukov is also said to have insisted on the liquidation of the Supreme Military Council (*Vysshii voennyi sovet*), the highest collegium for discussing defense policy (and including civilian party leaders), but there is no way of telling whether Zhukov's insistence produced results. An article in the author-

itative new military encyclopedia by MPA chief Epishev (*SVE*, II, 274) states that military councils were advisory bodies from January 1947 until April 1958 and makes no reference to dissolution of the Supreme Military Council. In the revised edition of his book (*Stroitel'stvo politorganov*, p. 414) Petrov says councils were advisory only from 1947 until July 1950.

54. *Krasnaia zvezda*, March 20, 1957, p. 2.

55. At the Twentieth Congress it was announced that the military had lost 145,000 party members in 1955 "in connection with" demobilization (*XX s"ezd Kommunisticheskoi Partii Sovetskogo Soiuza: Stenograficheskii otchet*, 2 vols. [Moscow, Gospolitizdat, 1956], I, 236). There were occasional remarks about lagging party recruitment during Zhukov's tenure, but they tended to blame lax political workers and pointed out that slack recruitment was especially bad for party-minded commanders (*Krasnaia zvezda*, May 20, 1955, p. 3). On restriction of paid officials, see M. Kh. Kalashnik, *Politorgany i partiinye organizatsii Sovetskoi Armii i Voenno-Morskogo Flota* (Moscow, Voenizdat, 1963), p. 17.

56. Petrov, *Stroitel'stvo politorganov*, p. 439.

57. *Krasnaia zvezda*, March 12, 1959, p. 3; April 13, 1954, p. 3.

58. Ibid., Oct. 26, 1954, p. 3.

59. Ibid., Oct. 10, 1954, p. 3.

60. See Ellen Propper Mickiewicz, *Soviet Political Schools* (New Haven, Yale University Press, 1967), chap. 5.

61. *Krasnaia zvezda*, April 3, 1954, p. 4; Sept. 17, 1954, p. 3

62. Ibid., Oct. 2, 1958, p. 3.

63. The newspapers were *Leningradskaia pravda, Moskovskaia pravda, Pravda Ukrainy, Pravda vostoka*, and *Sovetskaia Belorussiia*. This average does not include pro forma articles on the army's anniversary in February.

64. *Zaria vostoka*, Jan. 21, 1958, p. 3; *Sovetskaia Belorussiia*, Dec. 7, 1957, p. 2. For a typical discussion of civilian laxity, see *Sovetskaia Latviia*, Jan. 24, 1958, p. 3. In 1959 twice as many servicemen were elected to local soviets in the Moscow Military District as had been elected in 1957 (Petrov, *Partiinoe stroitel'stvo*, p. 480); this could only have been at civilian initiative.

65. *Krasnaia zvezda*, Sept. 10, 1954, p. 2.

66. Ibid., Jan. 28, 1958, p. 1.

67. See *Khrushchev Remembers*, pp. 205-206. Zhukov's memories of Golikov were also unflattering, particularly concerning Golikov's failure as chief of intelligence in 1941 to give Stalin frank assessments of German preparations. See especially Zhukov (1974), I, 258.

68. Most of the changes were introduced in 1959-60, but were described as part of the reform of party work resulting from the October 1957 plenum.

69. The best example is the systematic exaggeration of the increase in commanders' participation in elected party organs. Also overblown was the campaign for party recruitment. In 1958 14 percent more party candidates were recruited in the army than in 1957, and in 1959 50 percent more; in the four years after October 1957 150 percent more were recruited than in the previous four years (Petrov, *Stroitel'stvo politorganov*, p. 449). Such figures acquire perspective when placed alongside those for overall party recruitment,

which increased in parallel periods by 13, 37, and 90 percent (calculated from figures in Merle Fainsod and Jerry F. Hough, *How Russia Is Ruled* [Cambridge, Mass., Harvard University Press, 1978], chap. 9). Thus party growth trends inside and outside the army were parallel. At the most it can be said that growth in the military was somewhat greater, particularly in 1960 and 1961, well after Zhukov's removal.

70. *Sovetskii flot*, Dec. 12, 1957, p. 1.

71. *Krasnaia zvezda*, Nov. 27, 1957, p. 3.

72. *Sovetskii flot*, Nov. 1, 1957, p. 3.

73. *Krasnaia zvezda*, Jan. 31, 1958, p. 3. *Krasnaia zvezda* also reported (Feb. 8, 1958, p. 3) criticism of Semen Vasiagin, member of the military council of the Odessa Military District, but with little apparent detriment to his career. Vasiagin was promoted to the Group of Soviet Forces in Germany later in 1958, was made chief political officer of the ground forces in 1967, and in 1976 became only the fourth political worker to attain the rank of general of the army. In the six months after the plenum 500 new political officer posts were established (an increase of about 1 percent), and in February 1958 69 political officers were awarded generals' and admirals' ranks (Petrov, *Stroitel'stvo politorganov*, p. 453). These moves may have been intended to offset criticism of the MPA at this time.

74. *Krasnaia zvezda*, May 25, 1958, p. 2; Nov. 18, 1960, p. 1; Sept. 15, 1961, p. 1.

75. Ibid., Feb. 14, 1958, p. 3.

76. Zhukov (1969), p. 53.

77. T. H. Rigby, "Crypto-Politics," in Frederic J. Fleron, Jr., ed., *Communist Studies and the Social Sciences* (Chicago, Rand McNally, 1969), p. 117.

78. Grey Hodnett, "Succession Contingencies in the Soviet Union," *Problems of Communism*, 24 (March-April 1975), 1-21.

79. It is characteristic that Admiral Gorshkov's eulogy to Grechko mentioned his great tact (*Krasnaia zvezda*, April 17, 1976, p. 2). This is not a virtue anyone ever imputed to Zhukov.

9. Public Demand Articulations

1. *Krasnaia zvezda*, July 8, 1976, p. 2.

2. On the range of Soviet images of the West, see Franklyn Griffiths, "Images, Politics, and Learning in Soviet Behaviour toward the United States," Ph.D. dissertation, Columbia University, 1972.

3. Biographies of Grishanov and Mal'tsev are in *BSE*, 3rd; Gorchakov's is in *Ezhegodnik*, 1977, p. 591.

4. A. Epishev, "50 let Sovetskogo gosudarstva," *VIZh*, 1967, no. 10, pp. 14-15.

5. *Krasnaia zvezda*, June 20, 1963, p. 3. The chief political officer in the Baku Air Defense District made a similar appeal to the Azerbaidzhani central committee two weeks later (*Bakinskii rabochii*, July 6, 1963, p. 3).

6. *KVS*, 1965, no. 20, p. 19.

7. *Pravda*, Feb. 23, 1954, p. 2.

8. Ibid., Jan. 16, 1960, p. 6.

9. *Izvestiia*, Feb. 23, 1971, pp. 1, 3; *Pravda*, March 25, 1971, p. 2.

10. Vice-Admiral A. M. Kosov, commander of the Baltic Fleet, to the 1976 Lithuanian party congress (*Sovetskaia Litva*, Jan. 23, 1976, p. 3).

11. A. Epishev, "Partiei rukovodimye," *VIZh*, 1972, no. 9, p. 4.

12. *KVS*, 1976, no. 11, p. 11; 1972, no. 22, p. 7; 1975, no. 16, p. 8; 1972, no. 16, pp. 9-16.

13. A. A. Epishev, "O vozrastaiushchei roli KPSS v rukovodstve Vooruzhennymi Silami," *Voprosy istorii KPSS*, 1963, no. 2, pp. 6-7.

14. A. Zheltov, "Rukovodstvo KPSS stroitel'stvom Sovetskikh Vooruzhennykh Sil v poslevoennyi period," *VIZh*, 1965, no. 2, pp. 5-6.

15. Roman Kolkowicz, *The Soviet Military and the Communist Party* (Princeton, Princeton University Press, 1967), pp. 301-302.

16. Zheltov, "Rukovodstvo KPSS," p. 11.

17. *KVS*, 1968, no. 16, pp. 9-13; 1969, no. 16, p. 12.

18. *Krasnaia zvezda*, Feb. 23, 1972, p. 2.

19. *KVS*, 1966, no. 17, p. 14.

20. See, for example, ibid., 1971, no. 20, pp. 16-17.

21. *Izvestiia*, Feb. 23, 1969, p. 3.

22. *TIS*, 1973, no. 7, p. 63.

23. *Izvestiia*, Nov. 16, 1965, p. 5.

24. *TIS*, 1969, no. 7, pp. 52-53.

25. See especially Shatilov's article in *Literaturnaia gazeta*, May 28, 1955, summarized in H. S. Dinerstein, *War and the Soviet Union*, rev. ed. (New York, Praeger, 1962), pp. 196-197. Dinerstein does not mention Shatilov's MPA affiliation which, as is common, is not given in the article.

26. *XXIII s"ezd Kommunisticheskoi Partii Sovetskogo Soiuza: Stenograficheskii otchet*, 2 vols. (Moscow, Politizdat, 1966), I, 553.

27. *KVS*, 1966, no. 21, pp. 11-12.

28. *Krasnaia zvezda*, Feb. 7, 1974, pp. 2-3. See also the views of Colonel E. I. Rybkin, a Lenin Academy lecturer, in *KVS*, 1965, no. 17, pp. 50-56, and 1973, no. 20, pp. 26-27. Rybkin and his colleague V. M. Bondarenko have figured prominently on Western lists of Soviet "hawks."

29. Ilya Zemtsov, *IKSI: The Moscow Institute of Applied Social Research*, Soviet Institutions Series, no. 6 (Jerusalem, Soviet and East European Research Centre, Hebrew University, n.d.), pp. 26-29. The main author, V. K. Konoplev, is referred to in the press as head of the MPA's sociological research department.

30. *KVS*, 1968, no. 1, p. 8; no. 24, p. 29.

31. *Krasnaia zvezda*, Feb. 23, 1972, p. 2; *KVS*, 1972, no. 16, p. 15.

32. I. Smilga, *Ocherednye voprosy stroitel'stva Krasnoi Armii* (Moscow, Gosizdat, 1921), pp. 3-18; I. B. Berkhin, *Voennaia reforma v SSSR (1924-1925 gg.)* (Moscow, Voenizdat, 1958), p. 33.

33. S. M. Kliatskin, *Na zashchite Oktiabria* (Moscow, Nauka, 1965), pp. 430-436; S. I. Gusev, *Grazhdanskaia voina i Krasnaia Armiia* (Moscow, Voenizdat, 1958), pp. 120-127.

34. Quotation from *Izvestiia*, July 25, 1971, pp. 1, 3.

35. S. S. Biriuzov, *Kogda gremeli pushki* (Moscow, Voenizdat, 1961), p. 215.

36. M. M. Zomov et al., *Marshal Tukhachevskii* (Moscow, Voenizdat, 1965), p. 172.

37. G. K. Zhukov, *Vospominaniia i razmyshleniia* (Moscow, Novosti, 1969), p. 133.

38. Epishev, "O vozrastaiushchei roli KPSS," p. 10.

39. M. Kh. Kalashnik, "Istoricheskii opyt KPSS v osushchestvlenie leninskikh idei o zashchite sotsialisticheskogo Otechestva," *Voprosy istorii KPSS*, 1969, no. 11, pp. 42-43.

40. *KVS*, 1971, no. 19, p. 17.

41. Kalashnik, "Istoricheskii opyt," p. 43.

42. *KVS*, 1971, no. 18, p. 17.

43. Kolkowicz, *The Soviet Military*, p. 202; "The Military," in H. Gordon Skilling and Franklyn Griffiths, eds., *Interest Groups in Soviet Politics* (Princeton, Princeton University Press, 1971), p. 139. The key Prochko article is in *VIZh*, 1961, no. 5; Makeev's essay is in *Izvestiia*, Feb. 12, 1963, p. 3.

44. Makeev began work on a rural newspaper and joined the army in 1941 (at the age of thirty); see the biography in *Zhurnalist*, 1970, no. 2, p. 8. For Prochko, see *Krasnaia zvezda*, April 11, 1971, p. 6.

45. Prochko criticized commanders who inflated their reputations, but his favorite target was N. K. Popel', a fellow political officer.

46. Some of the articles were used in writing Chapter 6. For a meeting of commemoration, see the one in Gamarnik's honor led by former MPA chief Krainiukov (*Pravda*, June 3, 1964, p. 4).

47. *Krasnaia zvezda*, July 21, 1956, p. 3.

48. A. Epishev, "Voennaia istoriia—vazhneishii uchastok ideologicheskoi raboty," *VIZh*, 1963, no. 1, pp. 4-5.

49. See, for example, Kalashnik in *KVS*, 1968, no. 1, pp. 4-5.

50. For recent reflections on the purge by a political officer, see N. B. Ivushkin, *Mesto tvoe vperedi* (Moscow, Voenizdat, 1976), pp. 90, 150.

51. *XXIV s"ezd Kommunisticheskoi Partii Sovetskogo Soiuza: Stenograficheskii otchet*, 2 vols. (Moscow, Politizdat, 1971), I, 434.

52. *Krasnaia zvezda*, Dec. 15, 1954, p. 3.

53. *Pravda*, June 15, 1957, p. 3; M. V. Popov, "Na kafedre istorii KPSS VPA imeni V. I. Lenina," *Voprosy istorii KPSS*, 1963, no. 1, pp. 155-156.

54. F. Golikov, "Za dal'neishee razvitie voenno-istoricheskoi raboty v Sovetskikh Vooruzhennykh Silakh," *VIZh*, 1960, no. 2, p. 11; *Krasnaia zvezda*, Nov. 14, 1959, p. 2.

55. *Krasnaia zvezda*, June 20, 1963, p. 3.

56. *Pravda*, June 21, 1963, p. 3; *Krasnaia zvezda*, Feb. 9, 1964, p. 2.

57. *Leningradskaia pravda*, Jan. 25, 1958, p. 5; *KVS*, 1961, no. 2, pp. 92-93; 1963, no. 14, pp. 26-27.

58. *Kommunist*, 1964, no. 5, 73.

59. *Krasnaia zvezda*, April 7, 1977, p. 2.

60. *Leningradskaia pravda*, Feb. 23, 1958, p. 2.

61. *Izvestiia*, Nov. 16, 1965, p. 5. Commanders often discuss education at republic party congresses. Recently it has been common to advise more attention to Russian-language training of future recruits. See, for example, *Turkmenskaia iskra*, Jan. 26, 1976, p. 3; *Pravda vostoka*, Feb. 5, 1976, p. 4.

62. *Krasnaia zvezda*, Nov. 23, 1958, p. 2.

63. Ibid., Aug. 2, 1960, p. 3.

64. *Izvestiia*, May 17, 1966, p. 6, and Aug. 3, 1969, p. 3; *Krasnaia zvezda*, May 21, 1970, pp. 1, 3, and June 10, 1972, p. 2.

65. *Krasnaia zvezda*, April 7, 1977, p. 2.

66. Ibid., Dec. 11, 1977, p. 2.

67. Ibid., Feb. 22, 1968, p. 4; June 12, 1974, p. 3; March 1, 1976, p. 4; Feb. 25, 1977, p. 3.

68. Ibid., Dec. 11, 1977, p. 2.

69. William E. Odom, "A Dissenting View on the Group Approach to Soviet Politics," *World Politics*, 28 (July 1976), p. 560.

70. Ibid., pp. 554-555.

71. H. Gordon Skilling, "Groups in Soviet Politics: Some Hypotheses," in Skilling and Griffiths, pp. 24-25; Philip D. Stewart, "Soviet Interest Groups and the Policy Process: The Repeal of Production Education," *World Politics*, 22 (October 1969), 29-50. It should be noted that Roman Kolkowicz, with whose views on military politics I have taken frequent issue, discusses military subgroups quite extensively in an essay published several years after his major volume ("The Military," pp. 146-153).

72. Franklyn Griffiths, "A Tendency Analysis of Soviet Policy-Making," in Skilling and Griffiths, p. 341.

73. Jerry F. Hough, *The Soviet Prefects: The Local Party Organs in Industrial Decision-Making* (Cambridge, Mass., Harvard University Press, 1969), p. 265; "The Party *Apparatchiki*," in Skilling and Griffiths, pp. 81-83.

10. The Army in Soviet Politics

1. See the discussion in Eric A. Nordlinger, *Soldiers in Politics: Military Coups and Governments* (Englewood Cliffs, N.J., Prentice-Hall, 1977), pp. 99-107.

2. Ernest W. Lefever, *Spear and Scepter: Army, Police, and Politics in Tropical Africa* (Washington, Brookings Institution, 1970), p. 173.

3. Gaetano Mosca, *The Ruling Class*, ed. Arthur Livingston (New York, McGraw-Hill, 1939), p. 228. David C. Rapoport has criticized Mosca for comparing domestic military usurpation to international warfare, but he may in turn overstate the obstacles to a seizure of power. See Rapoport, "The Political Dimensions of Military Usurpation," *Political Science Quarterly*, 83 (December 1968), 551-572. For more sanguine discussion of the technical aspects of coups, see Katharine Chorley, *Armies and the Art of Revolution* (London, Faber and Faber, 1943), and Edward Luttwak, *Coup d'Etat: A Practical Handbook* (New York, Knopf, 1969).

4. For example, there are cases of unsuccessful rebels who were pardoned and succeeded in bringing down the government on a second try. See the

case of General Eduardo Lonardi, leader of the 1955 coup in Argentina, in Marvin Goldwert, *Democracy, Militarism, and Nationalism in Argentina, 1930-1966* (Austin, University of Texas Press, 1971), pp. 156-157.

5. Eliezer Be'eri, *Army Officers in Arab Politics and Society* (New York, Praeger, 1970) p. 260.

6. John Steward Ambler, *Soldiers against the State: The French Army in Politics* (Garden City, N.Y., Doubleday, 1968), pp. 366-387; Thomas S. Cox, *Civil-Military Relations in Sierra Leone: A Case Study of African Soldiers in Politics* (Cambridge, Mass., Harvard University Press, 1976), chap. 10.

7. William H. Brill, *Military Intervention in Bolivia*, Political Studies Series, no. 3 (Washington, Institute for the Comparative Study of Political Systems, 1967); Be'eri, pp. 218-221; John Patrick Bell, *Crisis in Costa Rica: The 1948 Revolution* (Austin, University of Texas Press, 1971).

8. Nordlinger, p. 5.

9. In John W. Wheeler-Bennett, *The Nemesis of Power: The German Army in Politics, 1918-1945* (London, Macmillan, 1954), p. 108.

10. Roman Kolkowicz, "The Military," in H. Gordon Skilling and Franklyn Griffiths, eds., *Interest Groups in Soviet Politics* (Princeton, Princeton University Press, 1971), p. 137.

11. Aleksandr I. Solzhenitsyn, *The Gulag Archipelago* (New York, Harper and Row, 1974), p. 143.

12. Ironically, it was the PLA's general political department that first tried to curb military involvement in the Cultural Revolution. Its deputy director, Liang Pi-yeh, was the first major military victim, and its director, Hsiao Hua, dropped from sight in 1967, after which the department was inoperative for two years. Hsiao's successors, Li Teh-sheng (a former commander) and Chang Ch'un-ch'iao (a civilian), were also embroiled in factional struggles. See Harvey W. Nelsen, *The Chinese Military System* (Boulder, Colorado, Westview, 1977), pp. 102-107. On Bulgaria, see J. F. Brown, *Bulgaria under Communist Rule* (New York, Praeger, 1970), pp. 173-187.

13. J. T. Reitz, "Soviet Defense-Associated Activities outside the Ministry of Defense," in U.S. Congress, Joint Economic Committee, *Economic Performance and the Military Burden in the Soviet Union* (Washington, 1970), pp. 133-165. One memoir, S. A. Bannykh, *Boevye budni granitsy* (Minsk, Belarus', 1974), pp. 248-249, describes the border troops' "first-class weaponry," including armored personnel carriers, aircraft, helicopters, and patrol boats.

14. I. F. Pobezhimov et al., *Osnovy Sovetskogo voennogo zakonodatel'stva* (Moscow, Voenizdat, 1966), pp. 387-388; *Krasnaia zvezda*, Dec. 20, 1967, p. 2. There is no comprehensive Soviet history of the special departments. There is one excellent Civil War memoir: F. T. Fomin, *Zapiski starogo Chekista* (Moscow, Politizdat, 1964), but only several pallid books focusing on counterintelligence for World War II. Solzhenitsyn's *Gulag Archipelago* gives telling details from World War II, some from his own experience.

15. John Barron, *KGB: The Secret Work of Soviet Secret Agents* (New York, Reader's Digest, 1974), pp. 19-21.

16. The biography, in obituary form, of Rear-Admiral Mikhail N. Lepikhin is in *Krasnaia zvezda*, Dec. 24, 1964, p. 4. The only other biography I have found in comparable detail is in ibid., April 21, 1949, p. 4.

17. Eugene Victor Walter, *Terror and Resistance: A Study of Political Violence* (New York, Oxford University Press, 1969), p. 29.

18. Frederick C. Barghoorn, "The Security Police," in Skilling and Griffiths, p. 96.

19. Robert Conquest, *Power and Policy in the USSR* (New York, St. Martin's, 1961), p. 330.

20. Be'eri, p. 218.

21. Quotation from Edgar S. Furniss, *De Gaulle and the French Army* (New York, Twentieth Century Fund, 1964), p. 62.

22. [Hans] von Seeckt, *Thoughts of a Soldier*, trans. Gilbert Waterhouse (London, Benn, 1930), p. 77.

23. Gordon A. Craig, *The Politics of the Prussian Army, 1640-1945* (New York, Oxford University Press, 1964), p. 433.

24. F. L. Carsten, *The Reichswehr and Politics, 1918 to 1933* (Oxford, Oxford University Press, 1966), p. 400.

25. Orville D. Menard, *The Army and the Fifth Republic* (Lincoln, University of Nebraska Press, 1967), p. 83.

26. Ambler, pp. 121-122.

27. *Krasnaia zvezda*, June 9, 1963, p. 2.

28. *Pravda*, July 14, 1964, p. 2.

29. Loren R. Graham, "Cybernetics," in George Fischer, ed., *Science and Ideology in Soviet Society* (New York, Atherton, 1967), p. 101.

30. David Joravsky, *The Lysenko Affair* (Cambridge, Mass., Harvard University Press, 1970), p. 9.

31. *KVS*, 1965, no. 22, p. 5.

32. *XVIII s"ezd Vsesoiuznoi Kommunisticheskoi Partii(b): Stenograficheskii otchet* (Moscow, Gospolitizdat, 1939), p. 35.

33. Robert Conquest's phrase, from *The Great Terror: Stalin's Purge of the Thirties* (Harmondsworth, Penguin, 1971), p. 112.

34. I. V. Stalin, *Sochineniia*, 13 vols. (Moscow, Gospolitizdat, 1946-52), VI, 8.

35. Nordlinger, p. 26.

36. *Pravda*, June 22, 1968, p. 1; *Krasnaia zvezda*, Feb. 22, 1952, p. 1.

37. Kiwon Chung, "The North Korean People's Army and the Party," *China Quarterly*, 14 (April-June 1963), 122; Robert A. Scalapino and Chong-Sik Lee, *Communism in Korea* (Berkeley, University of California Press, 1972), p. 1010.

38. *New York Times*, Sept. 1, 1973, p. 6.

39. Kolkowicz, "The Military," p. 137.

40. These attributes of professionalism are outlined in Samuel P. Huntington, *The Soldier and the State: The Theory and Politics of Civil-Military Relations* (Cambridge, Mass., Harvard University Press, 1957).

41. Ambler, p. 157.

42. David A. Wilson, *Politics in Thailand* (Ithaca, N.Y., Cornell Uni-

344 Notes to Pages 236-241

versity Press, 1962), pp. 192-193.

43. Liisa North, *Civil-Military Relations in Argentina, Chile, and Peru,* Politics of Modernization Series, no. 2 (Berkeley, Institute of International Studies, University of California, 1966), p. 53. Nordlinger, chap. 5, points out that for many armies reformist rhetoric far outstrips actual reform.

44. P. J. Vatikiotis, *The Egyptian Army in Politics: Pattern for New Nations?* (Bloomington, Indiana University Press, 1961), p. 59.

45. Anwar El Sadat, *Revolt on the Nile* (New York, Day, 1957), p. 60.

46. Ernest E. Ramsaur, Jr., *The Young Turks: Prelude to the Revolution of 1908* (Princeton, Princeton University Press, 1957), p. 132.

47. Stanley G. Payne, *Politics and the Military in Modern Spain* (Stanford, Stanford University Press, 1967), p. 134.

48. John Kie-chiang Oh, *Korea: Democracy on Trial* (Ithaca, N.Y., Cornell University Press, 1968), pp. 103-104.

49. Martin C. Needler, *Political Development in Latin America* (New York, Random House, 1968), p. 73.

50. Alfred Stepan, *The Military in Politics: Changing Patterns in Brazil* (Princeton, Princeton University Press, 1971), pp. 67, 94. The point about civilian pressure has been made of other Latin American armies as well. See, for example, Winfield J. Burggraaff, *The Venezuelan Armed Forces in Politics, 1935-1959* (Columbia, University of Missouri Press, 1972), pp. 194-195.

51. Robin Luckham, *The Nigerian Military: A Sociological Analysis of Authority and Revolt 1960-67* (Cambridge, Cambridge University Press, 1971), pp. 248, 202. The army in Niger had actually been used to collect taxes for the civilian regime it deposed in 1974. Richard Higgott and Finn Fuglestad, "The 1974 Coup in Niger: Towards an Explanation," *Journal of Modern African Studies,* 13, (September 1975), 394-395.

52. The best study is Robert L. Gilmore, *Caudillism and Militarism in Venezuela, 1810-1910* (Athens, Ohio University Press, 1964).

53. Luckham, p. 60.

54. See Robert W. Dean, "Civil-Military Relations in Yugoslavia, 1971-1975," *Armed Forces and Society,* 3 (Fall 1976), 17-58.

55. Trevor N. Dupuy, "Burma and Its Army: A Contrast in Motivations and Characteristics," *Antioch Review,* 20 (Winter 1960-61), 430-431; Wayne Ayres Wilcox, "The Pakistan Coup d'Etat of 1958," *Pacific Affairs,* 38 (Summer 1965), 142-163.

56. Gerald D. Feldman, *Army, Industry, and Labor in Germany, 1914-1918* (Princeton, Princeton University Press, 1966), pp. 478, 31-33.

57. George Armstrong Kelly, *Lost Soldiers: The French Army and Empire in Crisis, 1947-1962* (Cambridge, Mass., MIT Press, 1965); Alan Rouquie, "Military Revolutions and National Independence in Latin America, 1968-1971," in Philippe C. Schmitter, ed., *Military Rule in Latin America: Function, Consequences, and Perspectives* (Beverly Hills, Sage, 1973), pp. 23-31.

58. Ellis Joffe, "The Chinese Army after the Cultural Revolution: The Effects of Intervention," *China Quarterly,* 55 (July-September 1973), 452.

59. Nordlinger, pp. 63-64.

60. Stepan, p. 98.

61. Luckham, pp. 48-49. See Nordlinger, pp. 37-43.

62. Dupuy, pp. 430-431.

63. See especially Furniss.

64. Luigi R. Eiunaudi and Alfred C. Stepan, *Latin American Institutional Development: Changing Military Perspectives in Peru and Brazil* (Santa Monica, RAND, 1971), p. 123.

65. *Partiino-politicheskaia rabota v Sovetskikh Vooruzhennykh Silakh* (Moscow, Voenizdat, 1974), p. 103.

66. Memoirs make it clear that wartime decisions were often discussed by informal groups including military and party officials, and recent sources refer occasionally to ad hoc consultations involving military officers, party leaders, and industrial officials. See for example A. Iakovlev, *Tsel' zhizni* (*Zapiski aviakonstruktora*), 4th ed. (Moscow, Politizdat, 1974), pp. 492-494. Marshal Grechko is said to have attended Politburo discussions on military matters even before becoming a member in 1973; Raymond L. Garthoff, "SALT and the Soviet Military," *Problems of Communism*, 24 (January-February 1975), 29.

67. *Khrushchev Remembers*, ed. Strobe Talbott (New York, Bantam, 1971), p. 572.

68. *Piatnadtsatyi s"ezd VKP(b): Stenograficheskii otchet*, 2 vols. (Moscow, Gospolitizdat, 1961-62), I, 785.

69. See especially Karl F. Spielmann, "Defense Industrialists in the USSR," *Problems of Communism*, 25 (September-October 1976), 52-69, which also points to possible tensions between the defense production ministries and the military.

70. K. A. Meretskov, *Na sluzhbe narodu* (Moscow, Politizdat, 1968), pp. 168-169; the quotation refers to meetings of the national military council in the several years prior to the war. Stalin several times castigated senior officers for being insufficiently vigorous in taking up their needs with him. See especially N. G. Kuznetsov, *Nakanune* (Moscow, Voenizdat, 1969), pp. 40, 282.

71. *Khrushchev Remembers: The Last Testament*, ed. Strobe Talbott (New York, Bantam, 1976), p. 540.

72. Vernon V. Aspaturian, "The Soviet Military-Industrial Complex—Does It Exist?" *Journal of International Affairs*, 26 (January 1972), 1-28. The military purchases equipment from a number of ministries other than the eight specializing in defense production, including the Ministries of Chemical Industry, Automobile Industry, and Instrument Building. See Michael Agursky, *The Research Institute of Machine-Building Technology*, Soviet Institutions Series, no. 8 (Jerusalem, Soviet and East European Research Centre, Hebrew University, 1976), p. 5.

73. Details for these contacts are best found in the military logistics journal, *TIS*. See, for example, 1973, no. 7, pp. 62-63, on the annual contracts.

74. See A. D. Tsirlin et al., *Inzhinernye voiska v boiakh za Sovetskuiu Rodinu* (Moscow, Voenizdat, 1970); A. I. Romashko, *Voennye stroiteli na stroikakh Moskvy* (Moscow, Voenizdat, 1972); A. N. Komarovskii, *Zapiski*

stroitelia (Moscow, Voenizdat, 1972); *SVE*, II, 251-252.

75. Statistics on railway construction are in *SVE*, III, 322. The best description is in P. A. Kabanov, *Stal'nye peregony* (Moscow, Voenizdat, 1973). The railroad troops work closely with the Ministry of Transport Construction. On peacetime coordination, see the description in *TIS*, 1969, no. 11, pp. 67-70.

76. Useful overviews are in William E. Odom, "The 'Militarization' of Soviet Society," *Problems of Communism*, 25 (September-October 1976), 34-51; Herbert Goldhamer, *The Soviet Soldier* (New York, Crane, Russak, 1975), chaps. 2-3.

77. A. A. Grechko, *Vooruzhennye Sily Sovetskogo gosudarstva* (Moscow, Voenizdat, 1974), p. 94; emphasis added.

11, Explaining the Army's Political Quiescence

1. Reported in A. Solzhenitsyn, *Arkhipelag Gulag, 1918-1956*, III (Paris, YMCA Press, 1975), 556-564.

2. A. A. Epishev, *Moguchee oruzhie partii* (Moscow, Voenizdat, 1973), p. 15.

3. Quotation from Stephen P. Cohen, *The Indian Army* (Berkeley, University of California Press, 1971), p. 180.

4. William E. Odom, *The Soviet Volunteers: Modernization and Bureaucracy in a Public Mass Organization* (Princeton, Princeton University Press, 1973), p. 308.

5. The post-1967 changes have been described as constituting a trend toward militarization (William E. Odom, "The 'Militarization' of Soviet Society," *Problems of Communism*, 25 [September-October 1976], 34-51). While this may be a useful characterization of the regime's commitment to increasing Soviet military capacity and social acceptance of certain military-related values, it should not be taken to imply that society is coming under increasing control of the army. It is important to appreciate the complexity of the post-1967 programs and not to overstate their innovativeness, exaggerate their impact, or equate them with broader military influence. See Timothy J. Colton, "The Impact of the Military on Soviet Society," forthcoming in a book on domestic determinants of foreign policy edited by Seweryn Bialer.

6. *Khrushchev Remembers: The Last Testament*, ed. Strobe Talbott (New York, Bantam, 1976), pp. 21, 46.

7. John Newhouse, *Cold Dawn: The Story of SALT* (New York, Holt, Rinehart, and Winston, 1973), pp. 55-56.

8. *Krasnaia zvezda*, Sept. 11, 1975, pp. 2-3; July 12, 1974, pp. 2-3.

9. Quotation from *Serp i molot* (organ of the First Labor Army), Dec. 1, 1920, p. 10. For Trotsky's plans see James Bunyan, *The Origin of Forced Labor in the Soviet State, 1917-1921* (Baltimore, Johns Hopkins Press, 1967), chaps. 3-4.

10. *Sputnik politrabotnika*, 1926, no. 10, p. 20.

11. P. I. Iakir et al., *Komandarm Iakir* (Moscow, Voenizdat, 1963), pp. 111-112; emphasis added. Another source reports a 1932 letter on the agri-

culture crisis by Iakir, commander of the district, and his chief of staff. Stalin is said to have exclaimed to Voroshilov, "Horrible! What do you have here, Kliment Efremovich, an army or a cooperative society? Why are your people sticking their noses where they don't belong?" I. Dubinskii, *Naperekor vetram* (Moscow, Voenizdat, 1964), p. 220.

12. *Krasnaia zvezda*, Aug. 10, 1977, p. 2.

13. *TIS*, 1973, no. 7, p. 62.

14. Military state farms (*voennye sovkhozy*) "began to develop strongly" in the mid-1950s, initially in the Far East, Central Asia, and north, but eventually in European regions as well. Operated by civilian laborers, they "occupy many thousands of hectares of land, contain tens of thousands of cattle and sheep and hundreds of thousands of hogs and fowl, and produce tens of thousands of tons of grain, potatoes, and vegetables." Most garrisons also contain smaller garden plots. Ibid., 1973, no. 4, pp. 52-53.

15. Ibid., 1966, no. 5, p. 48.

16. Ibid., 1974, no. 7, p. 53. There are no aggregate statistics, but in 1975 troops harvested 2 million tons of agricultural products in the small Moldavian republic (*Sovetskaia Moldaviia*, Jan. 31, 1976, p. 5).

17. *TIS*, 1973, no. 7, p. 62.

18. Ibid., 1967, no. 8, p. 68. Military and civilian users of the railroads abide by predetermined schedules, presumably negotiated at the ministry level. Coordinating organs (*organy koordinatsii*) exist at the local level, but these "do not have the right to issue orders equally binding on the subunits of all transporting ministries and agencies." Compartmentalized planning, the lack of interchangeable containers, and the prevalence of "departmental interests" further impede integration (ibid., 1965, no. 1, p. 70).

19. See especially I. T. Peresypkin, *A v boiu eshche vazhnei* (Moscow, Sovetskaia Rossiia, 1970); also N. A. Antipenko, *Na glavnom napravlenii* (Moscow, Nauka, 1971), pp. 310-367.

20. Isaac Deutscher, *The Prophet Unarmed: Trotsky, 1921-1929* (New York, Vintage, 1959), p. 161. Deutscher argues that Trotsky's chances of winning the leadership with active army support "might have been high."

21. I. V. Stalin, *Sochineniia*, 13 vols. (Moscow, Gospolitizdat, 1946-52), XI, 23.

22. *Pravda*, Feb. 24, 1958, p. 1.

23. Charles de Gaulle, *The Edge of the Sword*, trans. Gerard Hopkins (New York, Criterion Books, 1960), pp. 40-41.

24. John Stuart Mill, *Considerations on Representative Government* (New York, Holt, 1875), p. 311.

25. Quoted in S. Ivanovich, *Krasnaia Armiia* (Paris, Sovremennye zapiski, 1931), p. 27.

26. Konstantin Simonov, *Zhivye i mertvye* (Moscow, Izvestiia, 1966), pp. 103-104.

27. *Krasnaia zvezda*, Dec. 28, 1969, p. 2.

28. The national composition of the senior command between the wars was probably rather different. I have identified the national origin of fifty-seven officers ranked *komdiv* (division commander) or higher between 1935

and 1939 (and who did not attain marshal's rank then or later). Russians dominated with 63.2 percent, but other groups were as follows: Latvians 14.0 percent, Ukrainians 8.8, Poles 5.3, Jews 3.5, and Estonians, Serbs, and Germans each 1.8.

29. A. A. Grechko, *Vooruzhennye Sily Sovetskogo gosudarstva* (Moscow, Voenizdat, 1974), p. 133.

30. G. K. Zhukov, *Vospominaniia i razmyshleniia* (Moscow, Novosti, 1969), p. 103.

31. John Hughes, *Indonesian Upheaval* (New York, McKay, 1967), p. 189.

32. [Hans] von Seeckt, *Thoughts of a Soldier*, trans. Gilbert Waterhouse (London, Benn, 1930), p. 79.

33. Gerald Brenan, *The Spanish Labyrinth* (Cambridge, Cambridge University Press, 1950), p. 62.

34. John Steward Ambler, *Soldiers against the State: The French Army in Politics* (Garden City, N.Y., Doubleday, 1968), p. 105.

35. Gregory Henderson, *Korea: The Politics of the Vortex* (Cambridge, Mass., Harvard University Press, 1968), p. 346; George S. Harris, "The Causes of the 1960 Revolution in Turkey," *Middle East Journal*, 24 (Autumn 1970), 441.

36. Stanley G. Payne, *Politics and the Military in Modern Spain* (Stanford, Stanford University Press, 1967), p. 11.

37. John Kie-chiang Oh, *Korea: Democracy on Trial* (Ithaca, N.Y., Cornell University Press, 1968), p. 102.

38. The only adequate discussion of the postwar arrests is in Solzhenitsyn's *Gulag Archipelago*. The Central Committee members who perished in the Great Purge were V. K. Bliukher, A. S. Bubnov, A. S. Bulin, A. I. Egorov, Ia. B. Gamarnik, I. E. Iakir, M. N. Tukhachevskii, I. P. Uborevich, and I. S. Unshlikht. P. I. Baranov died in an air crash in 1933, leaving only two men (K. E. Voroshilov and S. M. Budennyi) who survived the purge. One military member of the 1939 Central Committee (G. M. Shtern) and two candidates (A. D. Loktionov and Ia. V. Smushkevich) were also shot. The five marshals who died were Bliukher, Egorov, S. A. Khudiakov, D. G. Pavlov, and Tukhachevskii. The nine who were mistreated but escaped death were A. V. Gorbatov, A. V. Khrulev, G. I. Kulik, N. G. Kuznetsov, K. A. Meretskov, A. A. Novikov, S. G. Poplavskii, K. K. Rokossovskii, and A. T. Stuchenko, Kulik and Pavlov were punished for military incompetence, Pavlov by the firing squad but Kulik by demotion and early retirement (he died in unrevealed circumstances in 1950, according to *SVE*). To this list could perhaps be added Zhukov, for his demotions in 1946 and 1957; A. I. Pokryshkin, the current head of DOSAAF, who was briefly expelled from the party during the war after offending his commander; A. Kh. Babadzhanian, arrested by the NKVD for several hours after a similar dispute; and V. D. Ivanov, temporarily demoted after a misunderstanding with Stalin in 1939. Details of these men's experiences can be found only in memoirs.

39. *Krasnyi voin*, Dec. 29, 1921, p. 2.

40. K. E. Voroshilov, *Stat'i i rechi* (Moscow, Partizdat, 1937), p. 27; M.

V. Frunze, *Sobranie sochinenii*, 3 vols. (Moscow and Leningrad, Gosizdat, 1925-26), III, 226.

41. See especially I. B. Berkhin, *Voennaia reforma v SSSR (1924-1925 gg.)* (Moscow, Voenizdat, 1958), pp. 326-328; Voroshilov, pp. 182, 615.

42. *Krasnaia zvezda*, Sept. 15, 1945, p. 1.

43. Quotation in *TIS*, 1972, no. 3, p. 5. This journal has been my main source for information on military living conditions.

44. *Krasnaia zvezda*, Jan. 17, 1970, p. 3.

45. Ibid., Dec. 15, 1962, p. 3.

46. See M. Martens, "Providing for the Soviet Officer," *Bulletin*, Institute for the Study of the USSR (Munich), 3 (February 1956), 30; L. Predtechevskii, *Sovetskii morskoi ofitser* (Munich, TsOPE, 1959), pp. 32-33; Mervyn Matthews, "Top Incomes in the USSR: Towards a Redefinition of the Soviet Elite," *Survey*, 21 (Summer 1975), 11, 26. Matthews estimates that a full marshal earns up to 2,000 rubles a month (the highest sum for any position listed), a major-general 600 rubles, and a colonel 500,

47. Calculated from diagram opposite p. 48 in V. V. Vodzinskaia, "O sotsial'noi obuslovlennosti vybora professii," in G. V. Osipov and Ia. Shchepan'skii, eds., *Sotsial'nye problemy truda i proizvodstva* (Moscow and Warsaw, Mysl', 1969).

48. For housing, consumer goods, and transportation, see M. A. Parshin and G. F. Krivtsov, *L'goty, pensii i posobiia voennosluzhashchim srochnoi sluzhby i ikh sem'iam: Spravochnik* (Moscow, Voenizdat, 1971); also Martens, pp. 26-32, and Predtechevskii, pp. 44-45. Garden plots are discussed in *TIS*, 1967, no. 4, p. 56, tourism for 1976 in *Krasnaia zvezda*, March 20, 1977, p. 4.

49. See I. F. Pobezhimov et al., *Osnovy Sovetskogo voennogo zakonodatel'stva* (Moscow, Voenizdat, 1966), pp. 198-211; *Sovetskoe pensionnoe obespechenie* (Moscow, Iuridicheskaia literatura, 1966), pp. 307-322.

50. Otto Preston Chaney, Jr., *Zhukov* (Norman, University of Oklahoma Press, 1971), p. 420; no source for this information is given.

51. See, for example, the complaints of reserve officers in Frunze, in *Krasnaia zvezda*, March 5, 1974, p. 4. Local military commissariats are frequently involved in pressing for civilian compliance.

52. Figures from P. Zhilin, "The Armed Forces of the Soviet State," in Jacques van Doorn, ed., *Military Profession and Military Regimes* (The Hague, Mouton, 1969), p. 165; D. A. Voropaev and A. M. Iovlev, *Bor'ba KPSS za sozdanie voennykh kadrov* (Moscow, Voenizdat, 1960), p. 227.

53. *Pravda*, Jan. 26, 1960, p. 1.

54. *Krasnaia zvezda*, Jan. 20, 1960, p. 2. Malinovskii accounted for about 92 percent of the officers; employment of another 4 percent as civilian administrators in the Moscow Military District can be inferred from his data.

55. *Voennyi vestnik*, 1974, no. 1, p. 9.

56. *Krasnaia zvezda*, Jan. 5, 1957, p. 3.

57. On this point, see Cohen, *The Indian Army*, p. 182.

58. This was probably the case in Egypt before 1952; Eliezer Be'eri, *Army Officers in Arab Politics and Society* (New York, Praeger, 1970), p. 321.

59. Alexis de Tocqueville, *Democracy in America*, 2 vols. (New York,

Knopf, 1945), II, 280, 287-288.

60. I. A. Kamkov and V. M. Konoplianik, *Voennye akademii i uchilish-cha* (Moscow, Voenizdat, 1972), pp. 39-40; F. R. Filippov, "Sotsial'naia orientatsiia shkol'nikov i obshchestvennoe mnenie uchitelei," in L. M. Arkhangel'skii, ed., *Sotsial'naia sreda i lichnost'* (Sverdlovsk, Sverdlovskii gosudarstvennyi pedagogicheskii institut, 1969), pp. 77-78.

61. Vodzinskaia, pp. 48-49, and diagram opposite p. 48.

62. Raymond L. Garthoff, "The Military in Russia, 1861-1965," in Jacques van Doorn, ed., *Armed Forces and Society* (The Hague, Mouton, 1968), pp. 255-256.

63. *Pravda*, Feb. 24, 1958, p. 1.

64. The situation was most extreme in the navy, where in mid-1924 26.2 percent of all commanders were former nobles, including 49.3 percent at levels of assistant division commander and above (Berkhin, p. 300).

65. In 1929 the army established preparatory courses for prospective officers of worker or peasant origin. As a general policy preference in admission was given to men whose social position (*sotsial'noe polozhenie*), meaning their most recent employment, was as an industrial worker or agricultural laborer. By 1933, 70.4 percent of all students at military schools had been industrial workers and 27.2 percent peasants. As of July 1940, 37.9 percent of all officers were former workers (that is, their last civilian employment had been as industrial workers), 19.1 percent were former peasants, 38.2 percent were former employees, and 4.1 percent were former students. Clearly many men of peasant origin were recruited after intermediate employment in urban industry. Voropaev and Iovlev, pp. 130-133; *Istoriia Velikoi Otechestvennoi voiny Sovetskogo Soiuza 1941-1945*, 6 vols. (Moscow, Voenizdat, 1960-65), I, 464.

66. N. G. Kuznetsov, *Nakanune* (Moscow, Voenizdat, 1969), pp. 7-8; Zhukov (1969), pp. 7-29; *Pravda*, April 1, 1967, p. 2.

67. See *Krasnaia zvezda*, Feb. 12, 1972, p. 2; April 3, 1977, p. 2; *Pravda*, Sept. 8, 1965, p. 6; *Izvestiia*, April 15, 1973, p. 4. The importance of the Suvorov schools should not be overstated. Of 1,000 lieutenants surveyed in 1969 only 3 percent were from the schools (*Krasnaia zvezda*, April 5, 1969, p. 3).

68. Ambler, chap. 5.

69. The survey of 1,000 lieutenants found that 17.5 percent were sons of collective farmers and 82.5 percent of "working class and other" origin. A story in 1972 reported that in a number of military schools 40 to 48 percent of the students were from working class families, including (by definition) peasant families on state farms. Thus 30 percent seems a good estimate for total peasant representation, and about the same for industrial workers. *Krasnaia zvezda*, April 5, 1969, p. 3, and Feb. 12, 1972, p. 2.

70. George M. Haddad, *Revolutions and Military Rule in the Middle East: The Northern Tier* (New York, Speller, 1965), pp. 65-79; P. J. Vatikiotis, *Politics and the Military in Jordan* (New York, Praeger, 1967), chap. 6; Payne, p. 53; Walter F. Weiker, *The Turkish Revolution, 1960-1961* (Washington, Brookings Institution, 1963), p. 129; Henderson, p. 356.

71. The group immediately around Stalin in 1920, when he was member of the military council of the Southwestern Front, later contributed five full marshals (Budennyi, Egorov, Kulik, Timoshenko, Voroshilov), two People's Commissars of Defense (Voroshilov and Timoshenko), and four deputy people's commissars (Budennyi, Egorov, Kulik, Shchadenko). Even with the purge of Egorov in 1938, this group virtually monopolized the high command in the late 1930s. In its lower ranks the First Cavalry Army, the heart of the Southwestern Front, contained dozens of future members of the military elite, most of them men of unquestioned talent. Among them were two future Defense Ministers (Zhukov and Grechko), twelve other future marshals, and nine generals of the army. These are my calculations, from biographical data.

72. Force figures from *The Military Balance, 1976-1977* (London, International Institute for Strategic Studies, 1976), p. 83.

73. A. V. Gorbatov, *Gody i voiny* (Moscow, Voenizdat, 1965), p. 59.

74. *XVIII s"ezd Vsesoiuznoi Kommunisticheskoi Partii(b): Stenografischeskii otchet* (Moscow, Gospolitizdat, 1939), p. 197.

75. A. S. Bubnov et al., *Grazhdanskaia voina 1918-1921*, 3 vols. (Moscow, Voennyi vestnik, 1928-30), II, 99-104.

76. *Krasnaia zvezda*, Aug. 5, 1971, p. 2.

77. For the adoption of the system, see especially Berkhin, pp. 313-320. Details of the current age limits are in *Izvestiia*, Oct. 13, 1967, pp. 3-4. Although sixty is set as the maximum age of active duty for colonel-generals, there are a number of older men of this rank in major positions. An extreme example is K. S. Grushevoi, head of the political administration of the Moscow Military District since 1965; he turned seventy in November 1976 and is now probably the oldest active official in MPA history.

78. *KVS*, 1963, no. 24, p. 5.

79. For example, the 1971 appointment of fifty-year-old V. G. Kulikov as Chief of General Staff is likely evidence of "the powerful hand of the Party Secretariat reaching deep into the ranks to make a selection" (William E. Odom, "The Party Connection," *Problems of Communism*, 22 [September-October 1973], 21). But it is also true that Kulikov had impeccable military credentials and did an apparently excellent job in his six years in the General Staff.

80. *Krasnaia zvezda*, May 6, 1961, p. 3.

81. Ibid., Nov. 1, 1963, p. 2.

82. De Gaulle, p. 110.

83. J. C. Hurewitz, *Middle East Politics: The Military Dimension* (New York, Praeger, 1969), p. 255; David A. Wilson, *Politics in Thailand* (Ithaca, N.Y., Cornell University Press, 1962), p. 12; Thomas E. Skidmore, *Politics in Brazil, 1930-1964* (New York, Oxford University Press, 1967), pp. 264-266; Robert M. Price, "Military Officers and Political Leadership: The Ghanaian Case," *Comparative Politics*, 3 (April 1971), 361-379.

84. See Gordon H. Torrey, *Syrian Politics and the Military, 1945-1958* (Columbus, Ohio State University Press, 1964), p. 137.

85. Reported in Aleksandr I. Solzhenitsyn, *The Gulag Archipelago* (New York, Harper and Row, 1974), p. 80.

86. A. Iakovlev, *Tsel' zhizni (Zapiski aviakonstruktora)*, 3rd ed. (Moscow, Politizdat, 1970), pp. 499-500.
87. Malcolm Mackintosh, "Influence on Foreign Policy," *Problems of Communism*, 22 (September-October 1973), 12.
88. V. I. Lenin, *Polnoe sobranie sochinenii*, 55 vols. (Moscow, Politizdat, 1967-70), LII, 327.
89. Stanley H. Cohn, "The Economic Burden of Soviet Defense Outlays," in U.S. Congress, Joint Economic Committee, *Economic Performance and the Military Burden in the Soviet Union* (Washington, 1970), p. 178.
90. See especially Michael Agursky, *The Research Institute of Machine-Building Technology*, Soviet Institutions Series, no. 8 (Jerusalem, Soviet and East European Research Centre, Hebrew University, 1976), pp. 8-13.
91. Statistics from Abram Bergson, *The Real National Income of Soviet Russia since 1928* (Cambridge, Mass., Harvard University Press, 1961), p. 366; Stanley H. Cohn, "Economic Burden of Defense Expenditures," in U.S. Congress, Joint Economic Committee, *Soviet Economic Prospects for the Seventies* (Washington, 1973), p. 158; U.S. Arms Control and Disarmament Agency, *World Military Expenditures and Arms Transfers, 1965-1974* (Washington, 1976).
92. *Pravda*, May 2, 1969, p. 1.
93. All quotations from "M. V. Frunze i reorganizatsiia Krasnoi Armii v 1924 godu," pt. 1, *VIZh*, 1966, no. 6, pp. 69-70.
94. D. Petrovskii, *Voennaia shkola v gody revoliutsii (1917-1924 gg.)* (Moscow, Vysshii voennyi redaktsionnyi sovet, 1924), pp. 107-109.
95. Lenin, XLIII, 16-17.
96. I. T. Starinov, *Miny zhdut svoego chasa* (Moscow, Voenizdat, 1964), p. 161.
97. Solzhenitsyn, *Gulag Archipelago*, p. 11.
98. I. Erenburg, "Liudi, gody, zhizn'," *Novyi mir*, 1962, no. 5, pp. 152-153; G. Vorozheikin et al., "Revoliutsii prizvannyi," *VIZh*, 1963, no. 6, p. 76.
99. Stalin, X, 85; *XXIII s"ezd Kommunisticheskoi Partii Sovetskogo Soiuza: Stenograficheskii otchet*, 2 vols. (Moscow, Politizdat, 1966), I, 92.
100. Aleksandr I. Solzhenitsyn, *The Gulag Archipelago Two* (New York, Harper and Row, 1975), p. 272.

12. Civil-Military Relations and Soviet Development

1. Roman Kolkowicz, *The Soviet Military and the Communist Party* (Princeton, Princeton University Press, 1967), pp. 104-105.
2. Robert Michels, *Political Parties*, trans. Eden and Cedar Paul (New York, Collier, 1962), p. 80.
3. See for example I. V. Stalin, *Sochineniia*, 13 vols. (Moscow, Gospolitizdat, 1946-52), V, 160-180, 205; VI, 172; VIII, 138; XII, 300.
4. V. I. Lenin, *Polnoe sobranie sochinenii*, 55 vols. (Moscow, Politizdat, 1967-70), XXXVIII, 140.
5. M. V. Frunze, *Sobranie sochinenii*, 3 vols. (Moscow and Leningrad, Gosizdat, 1925-26), I, 365.

6. A typical study which focuses on military organizations is Morris Janowitz, *The Military in the Political Development of New Nations* (Chicago, University of Chicago Press, 1964). A good discussion pitched at the societal level is Samuel P. Huntington, *Political Order in Changing Societies* (New Haven, Yale University Press, 1968), chap. 4.

7. Huntington, *Political Order*, p. 194.

8. Alfred Vagts, *A History of Militarism: Civilian and Military* (New York, Meridian Books, 1959), p. 30.

9. Dankwart A. Rustow, *A World of Nations: Problems of Political Modernization* (Washington, Brookings Institution, 1967), p. 106.

10. *XVIII s'ezd Vsesoiuznoi Kommunisticheskoi Partii(b): Stenograficheskii otchet* (Moscow, Gospolitizdat, 1939), p. 512.

11. *Pravda*, July 9, 1968, p. 2.

12. Stephen F. Cohen, "Bolshevism and Stalinism," in Robert C. Tucker, ed., *Stalinism: Essays in Historical Interpretation* (New York, Norton, 1977), p. 28.

13. Jerry F. Hough, *The Soviet Union and Social Science Theory* (Cambridge, Mass., Harvard University Press, 1977), p. 180.

14. William Taubman, "The Change to Change in Communist Systems: Modernization, Postmodernization, and Soviet Politics," in Henry W. Morton and Rudolf L. Tökés, eds., *Soviet Politics and Society in the 1970's* (New York, Free Press, 1974), p. 385.

15. Kolkowicz, *The Soviet Military*, p. 11.

16. Bruce M. Russett, *What Price Vigilance? The Burdens of National Defense* (New Haven, Yale University Press, 1970), p. 181.

17. At current rates of conscription, the military would have to draft 85 percent of all eighteen-year-olds in 1987 to maintain current manpower levels (*New York Times*, April 17, 1977, p. 8).

18. Philippe G. Schmitter, "Liberation by *Golpe*: Retrospective Thoughts on the Demise of Authoritarian Rule in Portugal," *Armed Forces and Society*, 2 (Fall 1975), 5-33.

19. Lenin, XII, 113.

20. Andrei Amalrik, *Will the Soviet Union Survive Until 1984?* (New York, Harper and Row, 1970), p. 66.

Index

Russian Research Center Studies

*Out of print.
†Publications of the Harvard Project on the Soviet Social System.